Thank you for picking up volume 37!
I really admire people who keep marching
forward when times are tough!

KOHEI HORIKOSHI

37

SHONEN JUMP Edition

STORY & ART **KOHEI HORIKOSHI**

TRANSLATION & ENGLISH ADAPTATION **Caleb Cook**
TOUCH-UP ART & LETTERING **John Hunt**
DESIGNER **Julian [JR] Robinson**
SHONEN JUMP SERIES EDITOR **Rae First**
GRAPHIC NOVEL EDITOR **Mike Montesa**

BOKU NO HERO ACADEMIA © 2014 by Kohei Horikoshi
All rights reserved.
First published in Japan in 2014 by SHUEISHA Inc., Tokyo.
English translation rights arranged by SHUEISHA Inc.

The stories, characters, and incidents mentioned in this publication are entirely fictional.

Printed in the U.S.A.

Published by VIZ Media, LLC
P.O. Box 77010
San Francisco, CA 94107

10 9 8 7 6 5 4 3 2 1
First printing, March 2024

MY HERO ACADEMIA vol.37

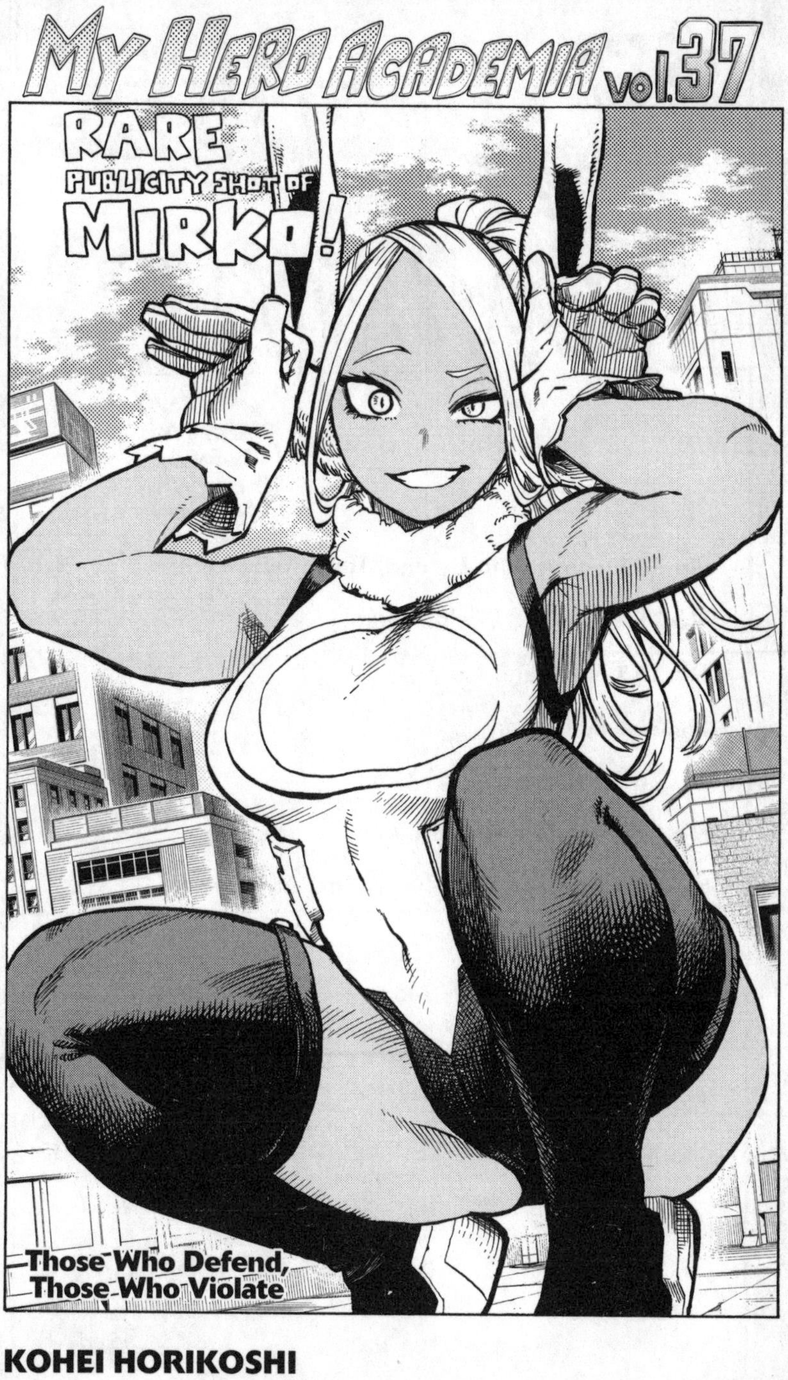
RARE PUBLICITY SHOT OF MIRKO!
Those Who Defend, Those Who Violate

KOHEI HORIKOSHI

Vol.37 MY HERO ACADEMIA

CONTENTS

Those Who Defend, Those Who Violate

No. 363 - Those Who Defend, Those Who Violate

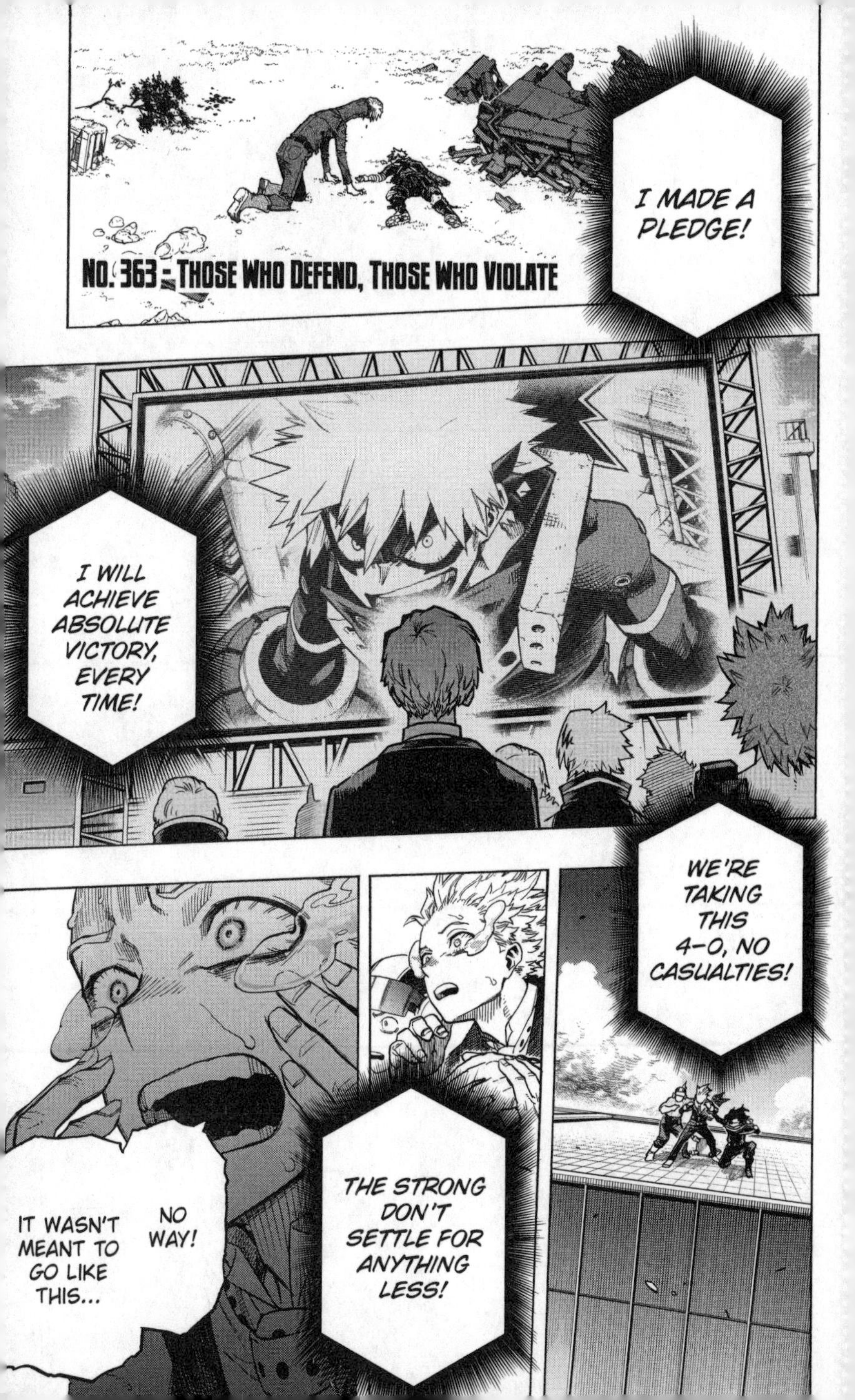

I MADE A PLEDGE!
I WILL ACHIEVE ABSOLUTE VICTORY, EVERY TIME!
WE'RE TAKING THIS 4-0, NO CASUALTIES!
THE STRONG DON'T SETTLE FOR ANYTHING LESS!
NO WAY!
IT WASN'T MEANT TO GO LIKE THIS...

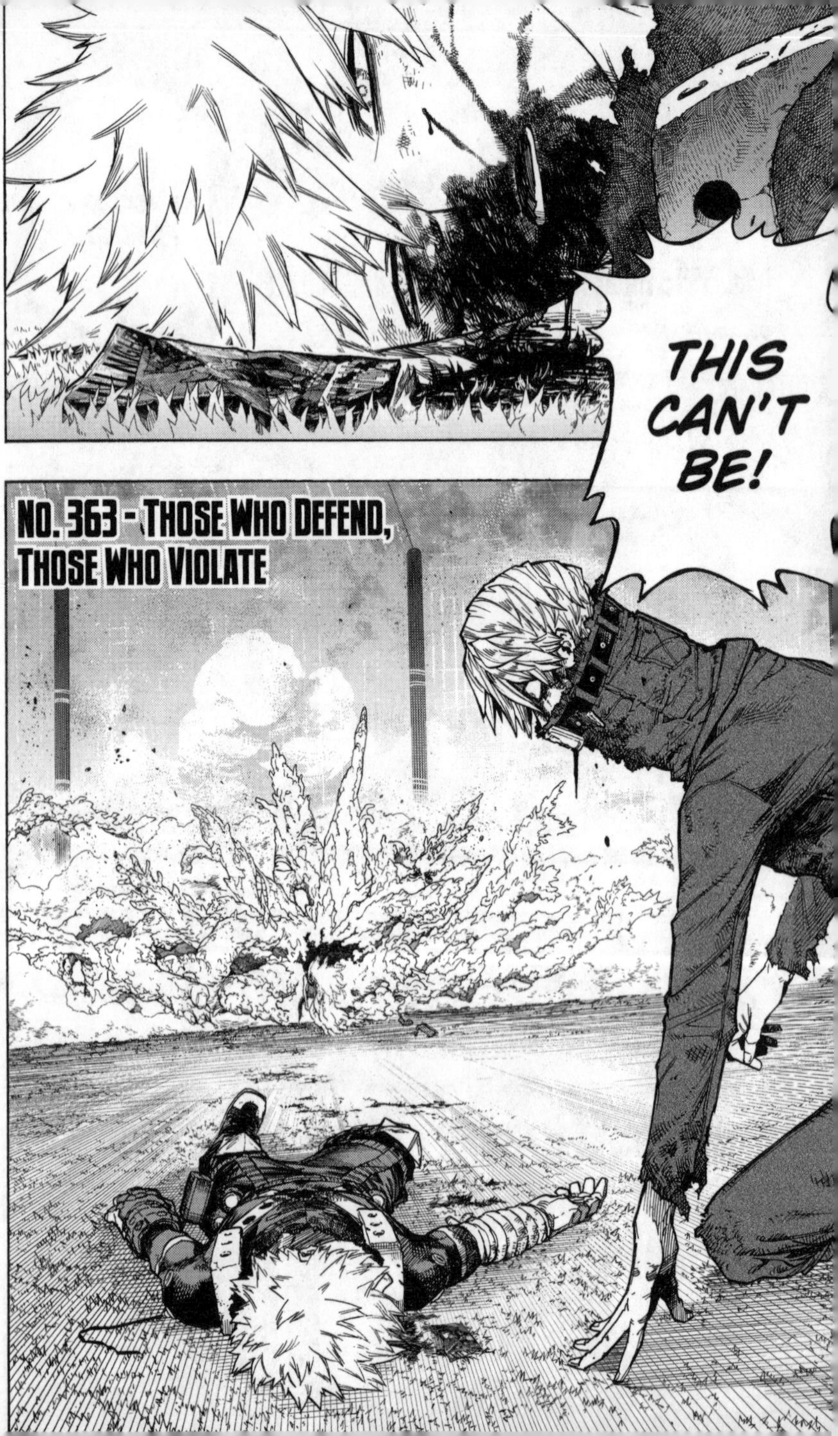
THIS CAN'T BE!
No. 363 - Those Who Defend, Those Who Violate

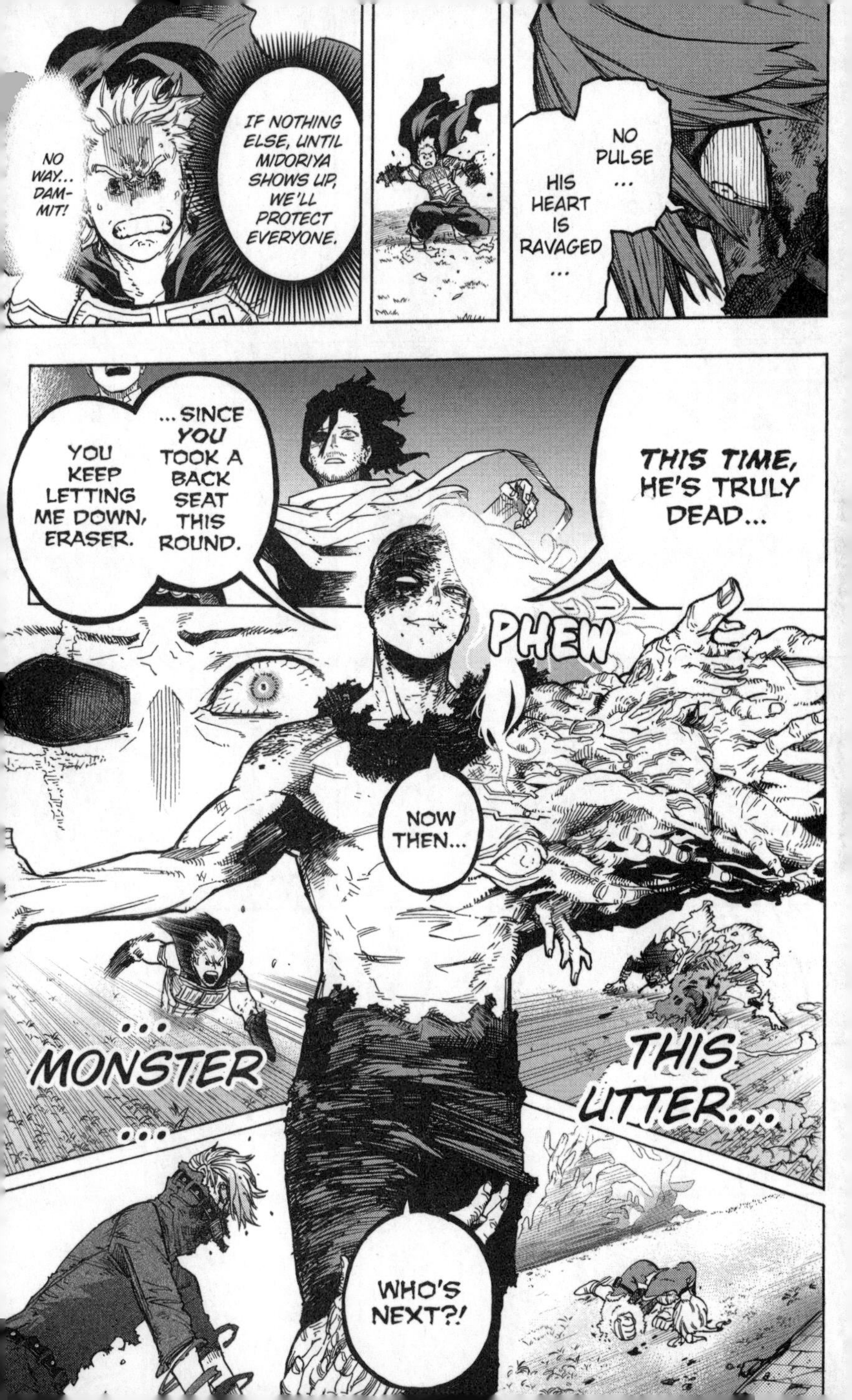
NO PULSE...
HIS HEART IS RAVAGED...
IF NOTHING ELSE, UNTIL MIDORIYA SHOWS UP, WE'LL PROTECT EVERYONE.
NO WAY... DAM-MIT!
THIS TIME, HE'S TRULY DEAD...
...SINCE YOU TOOK A BACK SEAT THIS ROUND.
YOU KEEP LETTING ME DOWN, ERASER.
PHEW
NOW THEN...
THIS UTTER...
...MONSTER...
WHO'S NEXT?!

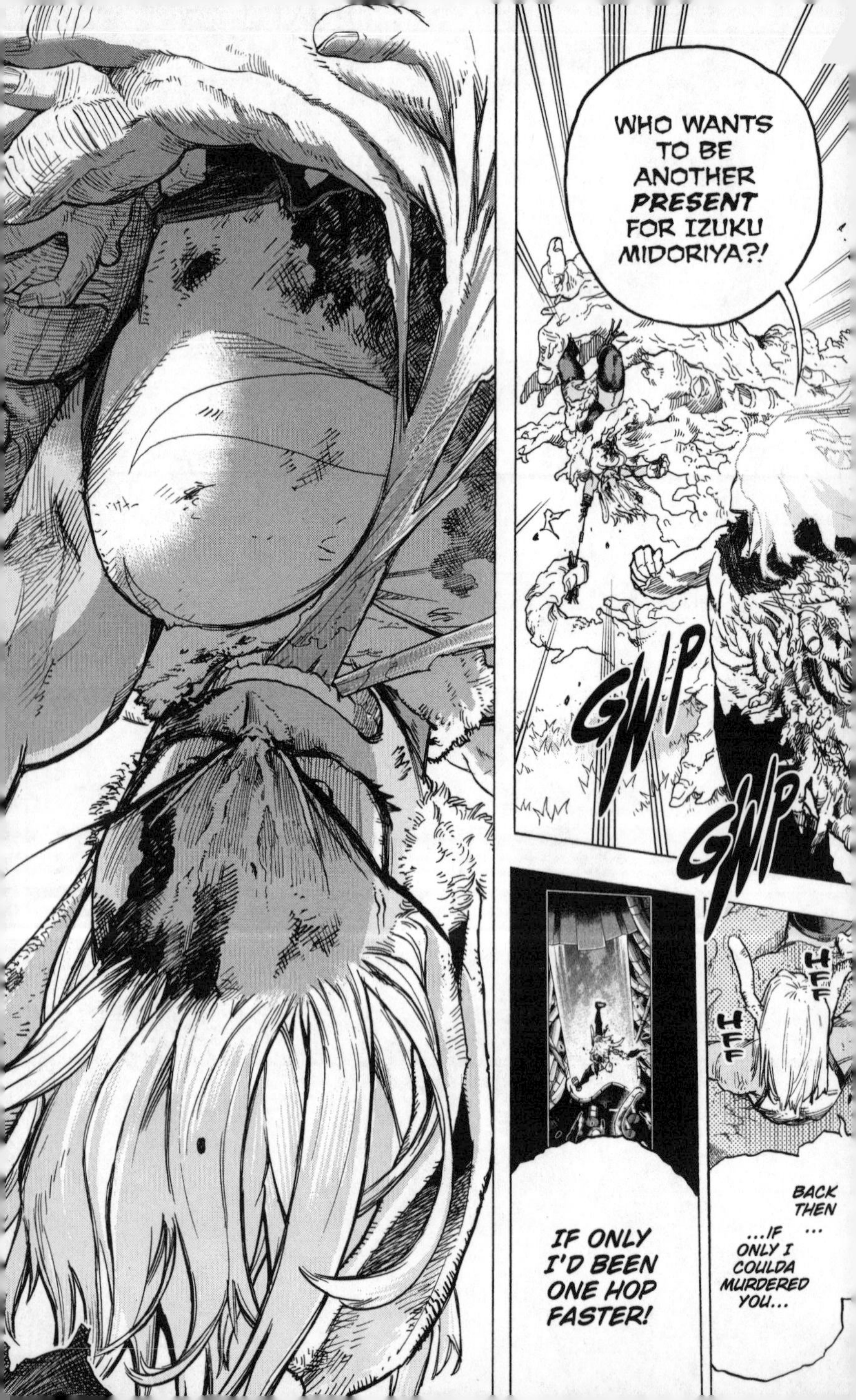

WHO WANTS TO BE ANOTHER **PRESENT** FOR IZUKU MIDORIYA?!
GWIP
GWIP
HFF
HFF
BACK THEN …
…IF ONLY I COULDA MURDERED YOU…
IF ONLY I'D BEEN ONE HOP FASTER!

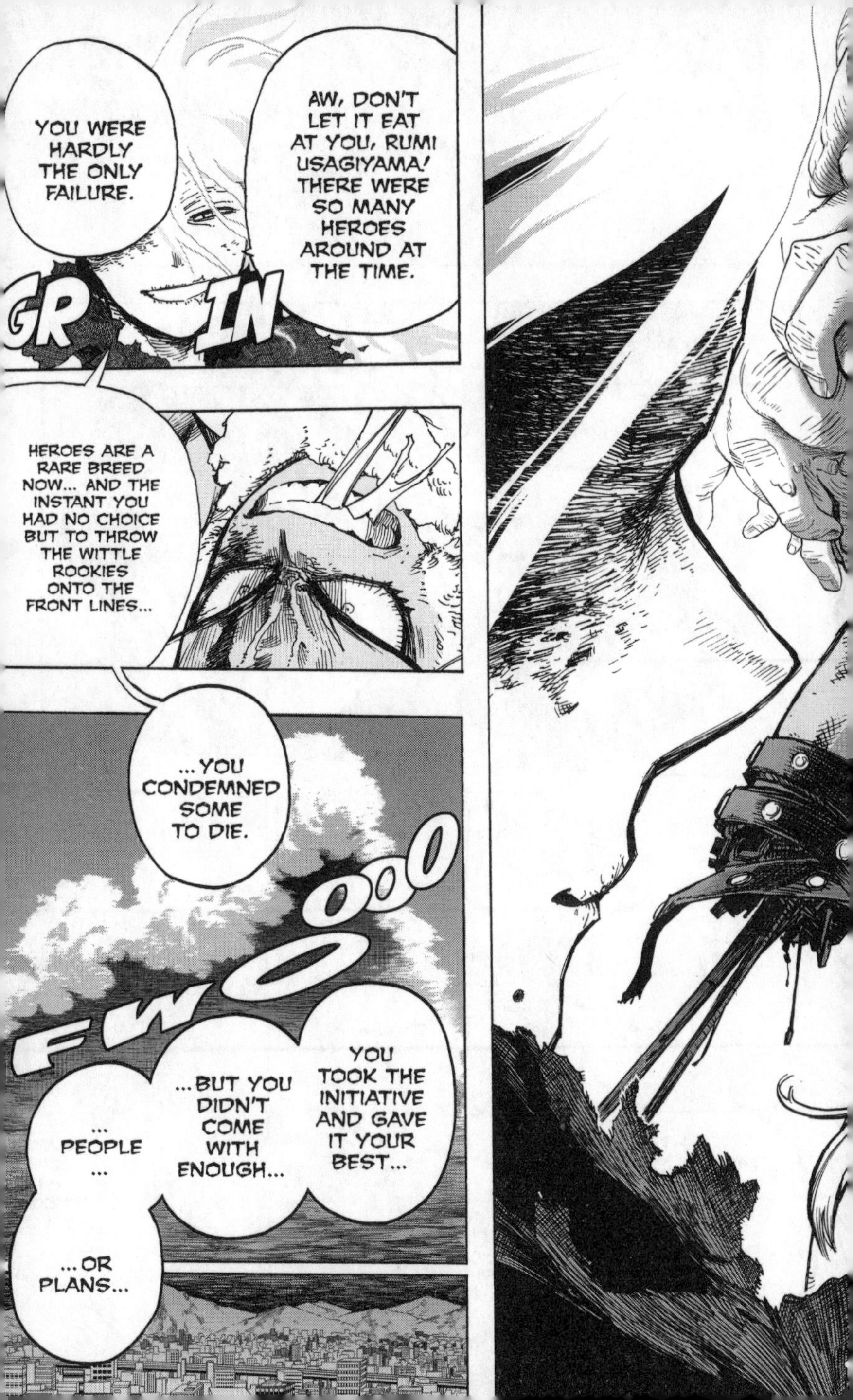
AW, DON'T LET IT EAT AT YOU, RUMI USAGIYAMA! THERE WERE SO MANY HEROES AROUND AT THE TIME.
YOU WERE HARDLY THE ONLY FAILURE.
GRIN
HEROES ARE A RARE BREED NOW... AND THE INSTANT YOU HAD NO CHOICE BUT TO THROW THE WITTLE ROOKIES ONTO THE FRONT LINES...
...YOU CONDEMNED SOME TO DIE.
FWOOOO
YOU TOOK THE INITIATIVE AND GAVE IT YOUR BEST...
...BUT YOU DIDN'T COME WITH ENOUGH...
...PEOPLE...
...OR PLANS...

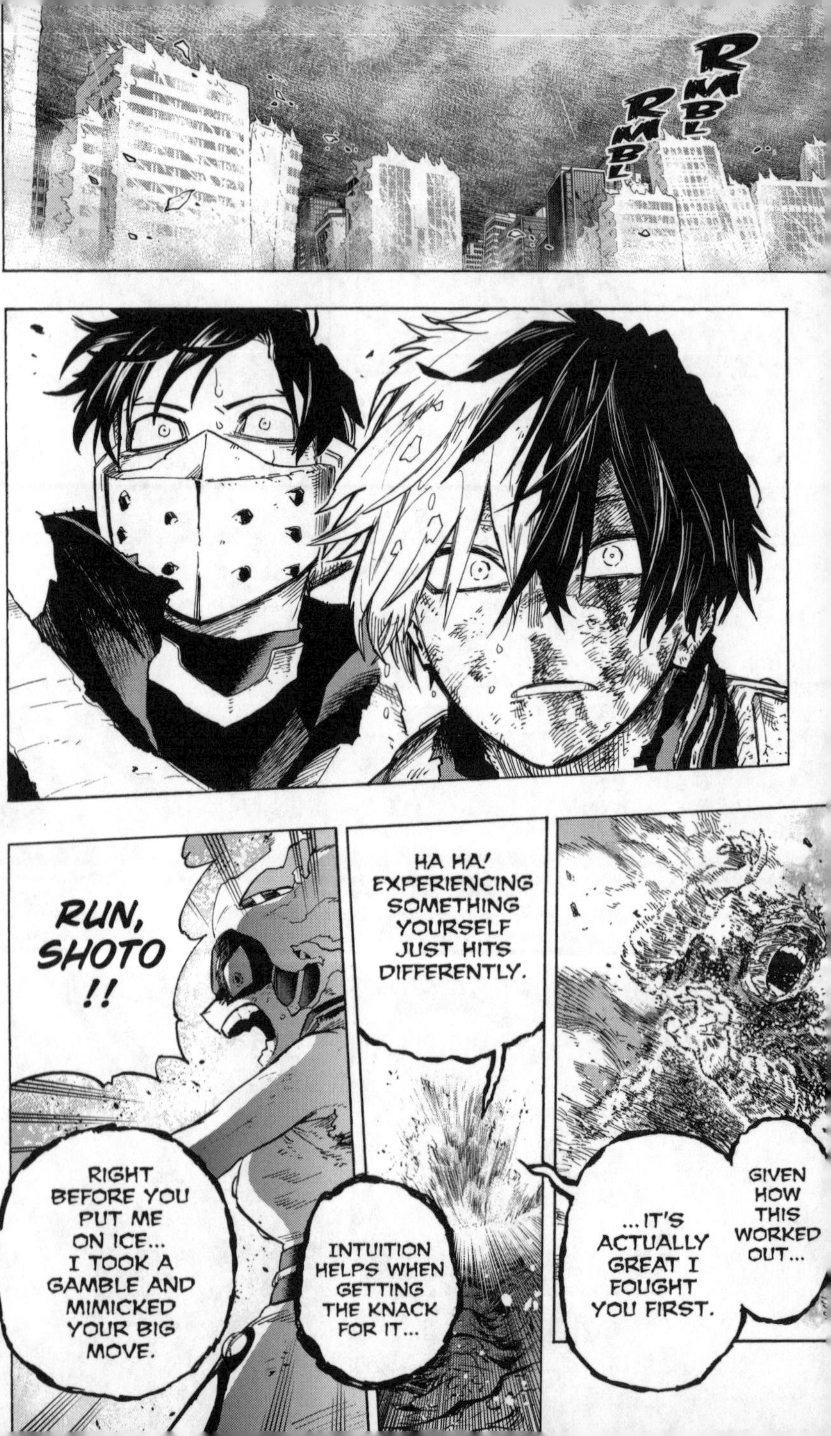
RMBL
RMBL
GIVEN HOW THIS WORKED OUT...
...IT'S ACTUALLY GREAT I FOUGHT YOU FIRST.
HA HA! EXPERIENCING SOMETHING YOURSELF JUST HITS DIFFERENTLY.
INTUITION HELPS WHEN GETTING THE KNACK FOR IT...
RUN, SHOTO!!
RIGHT BEFORE YOU PUT ME ON ICE... I TOOK A GAMBLE AND MIMICKED YOUR BIG MOVE.

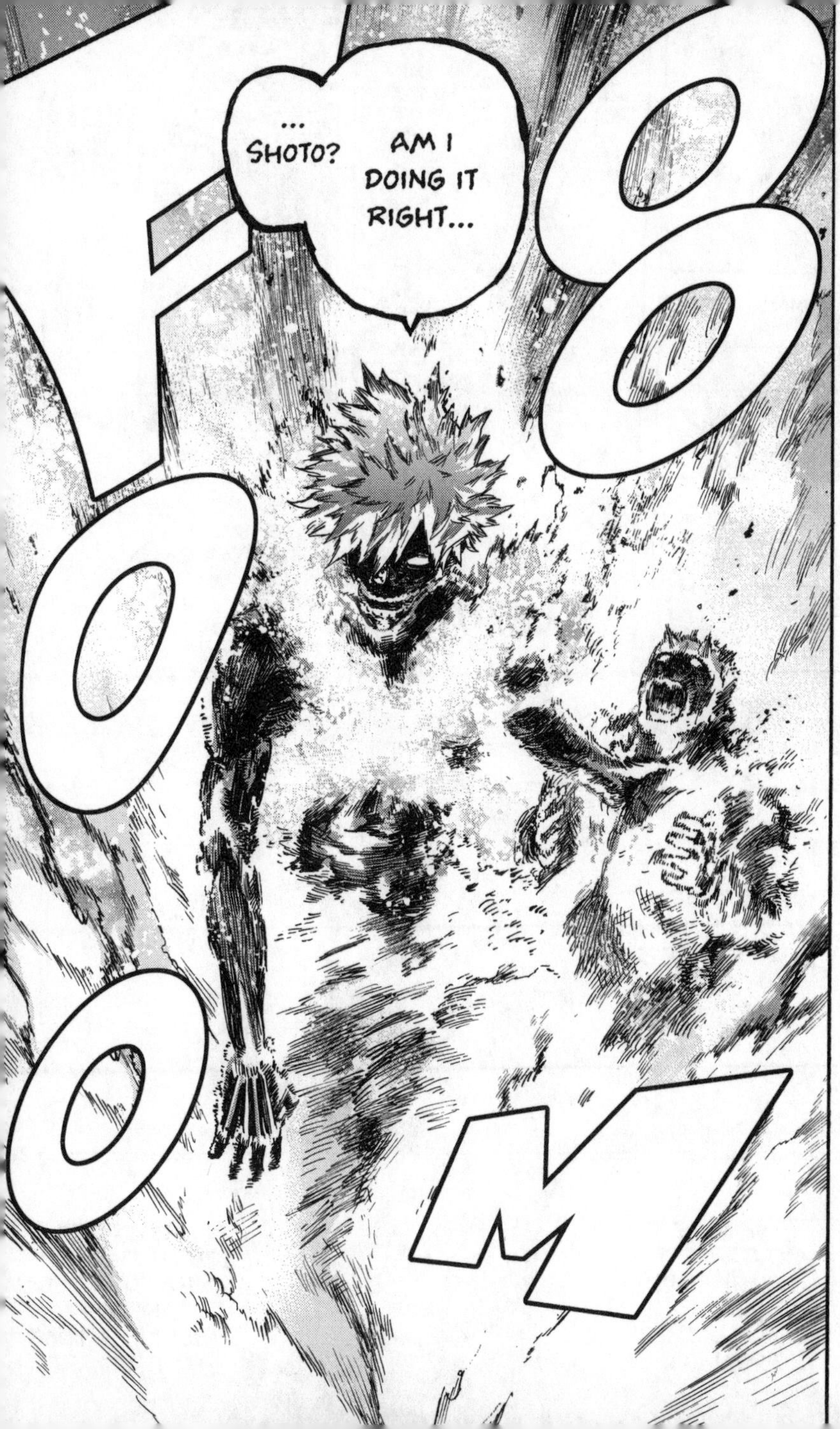
AM I DOING IT RIGHT...
... SHOTO?
FOOOOM

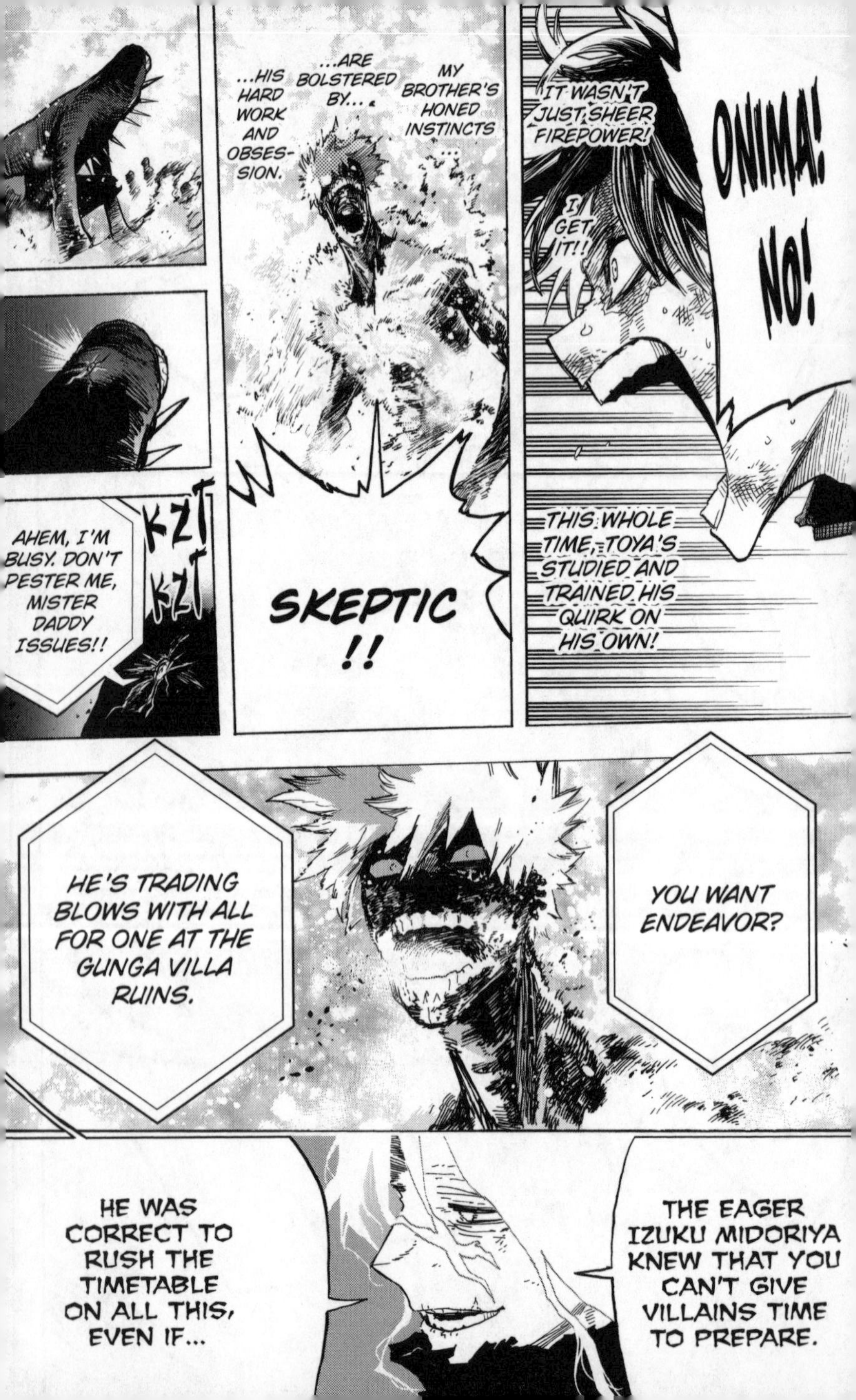
ONIMA! NO!
IT WASN'T JUST SHEER FIREPOWER!
I GET IT!!
THIS WHOLE TIME, TOYA'S STUDIED AND TRAINED HIS QUIRK ON HIS OWN!
MY BROTHER'S HONED INSTINCTS
...ARE BOLSTERED BY...
...HIS HARD WORK AND OBSESSION.
SKEPTIC!!
KZT KZT
AHEM, I'M BUSY. DON'T PESTER ME, MISTER DADDY ISSUES!!
YOU WANT ENDEAVOR?
HE'S TRADING BLOWS WITH ALL FOR ONE AT THE GUNGA VILLA RUINS.
THE EAGER IZUKU MIDORIYA KNEW THAT YOU CAN'T GIVE VILLAINS TIME TO PREPARE.
HE WAS CORRECT TO RUSH THE TIMETABLE ON ALL THIS, EVEN IF...

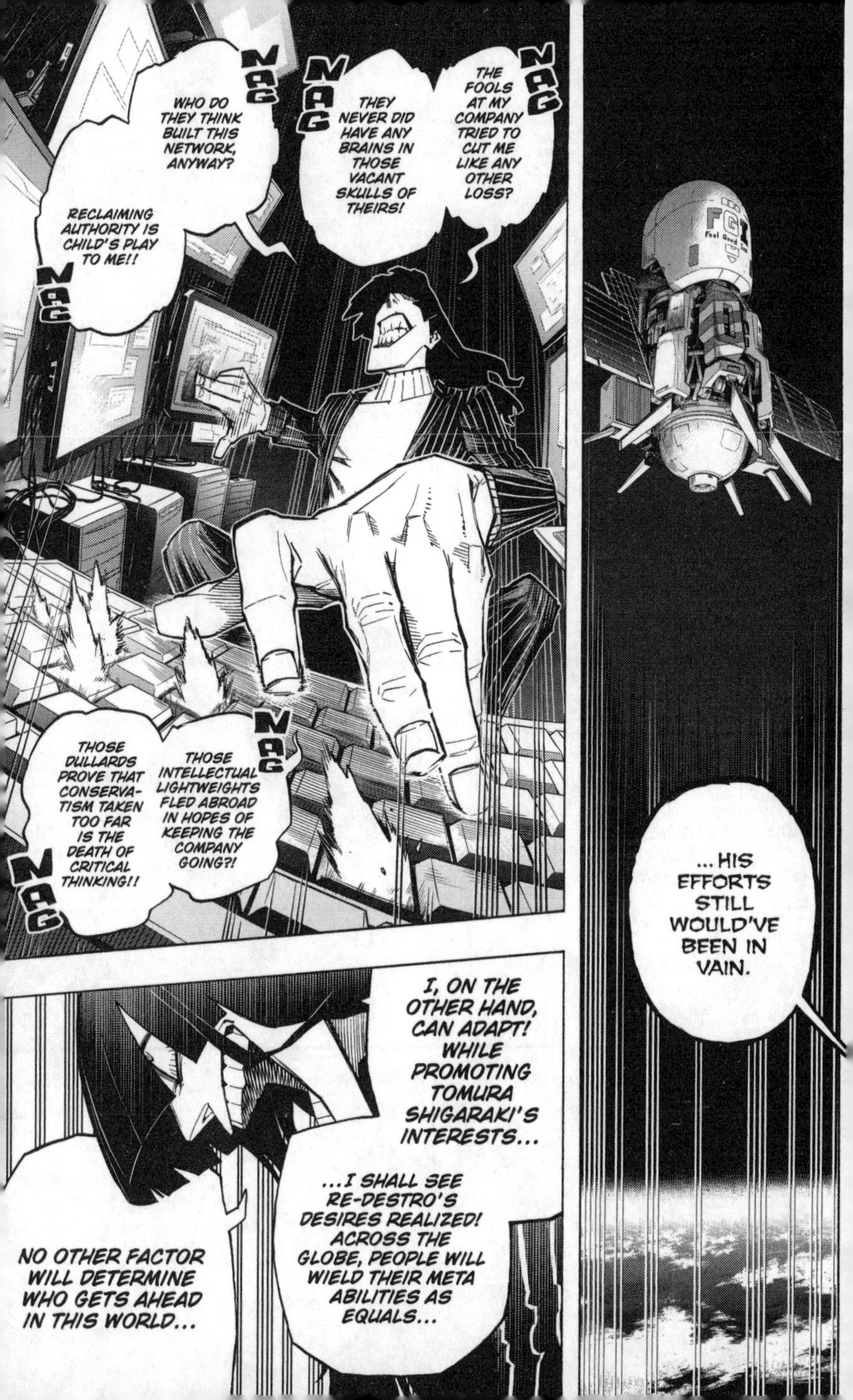
...HIS EFFORTS STILL WOULD'VE BEEN IN VAIN.
MAG
THE FOOLS AT MY COMPANY TRIED TO CUT ME LIKE ANY OTHER LOSS?
MAG
THEY NEVER DID HAVE ANY BRAINS IN THOSE VACANT SKULLS OF THEIRS!
MAG
WHO DO THEY THINK BUILT THIS NETWORK, ANYWAY?
RECLAIMING AUTHORITY IS CHILD'S PLAY TO ME!!
MAG
MAG
THOSE INTELLECTUAL LIGHTWEIGHTS FLED ABROAD IN HOPES OF KEEPING THE COMPANY GOING?!
THOSE DULLARDS PROVE THAT CONSERVA-TISM TAKEN TOO FAR IS THE DEATH OF CRITICAL THINKING!!
MAG
I, ON THE OTHER HAND, CAN ADAPT! WHILE PROMOTING TOMURA SHIGARAKI'S INTERESTS...
...I SHALL SEE RE-DESTRO'S DESIRES REALIZED! ACROSS THE GLOBE, PEOPLE WILL WIELD THEIR META ABILITIES AS EQUALS...
NO OTHER FACTOR WILL DETERMINE WHO GETS AHEAD IN THIS WORLD...

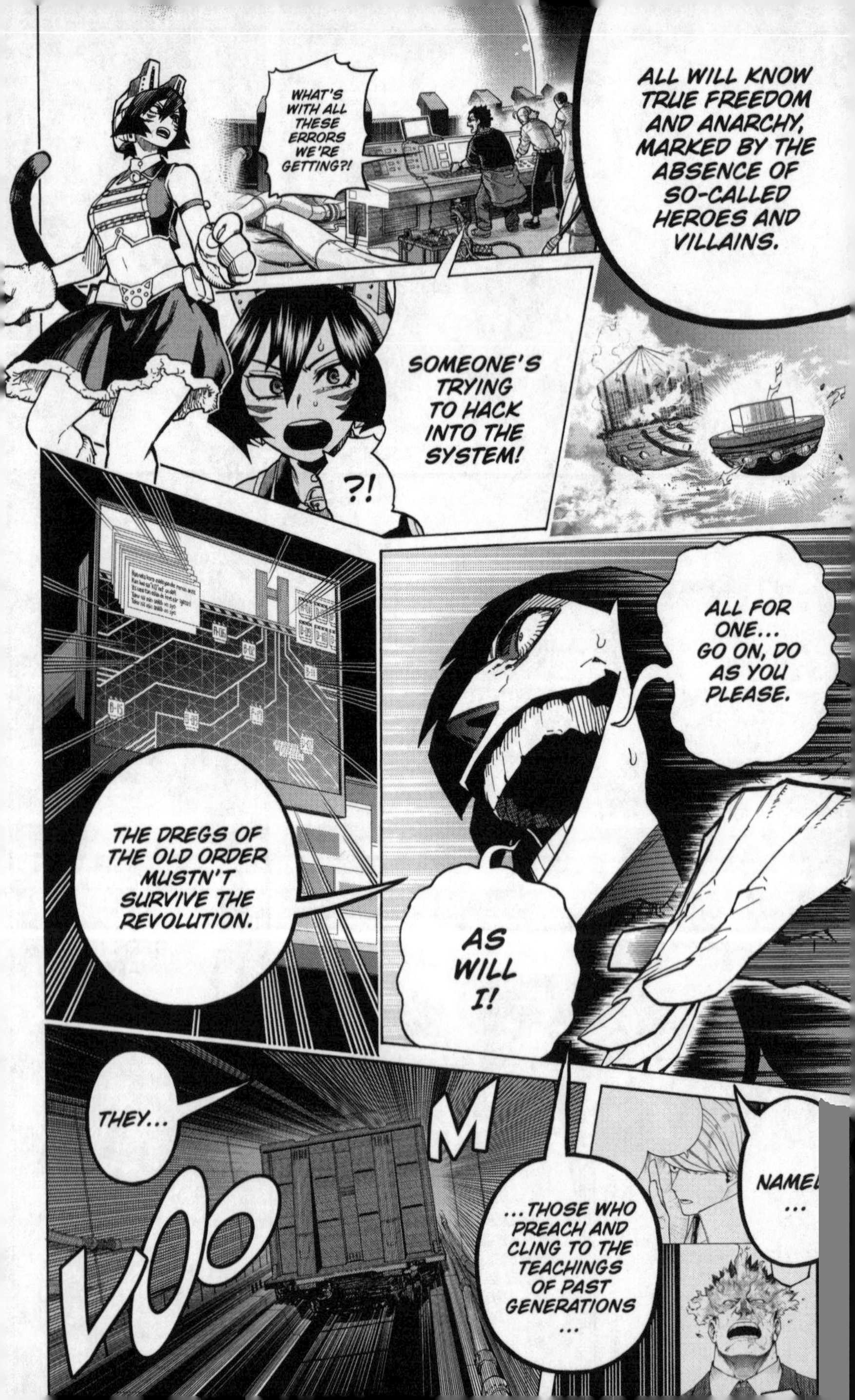

ALL WILL KNOW TRUE FREEDOM AND ANARCHY, MARKED BY THE ABSENCE OF SO-CALLED HEROES AND VILLAINS.
WHAT'S WITH ALL THESE ERRORS WE'RE GETTING?!
SOMEONE'S TRYING TO HACK INTO THE SYSTEM!
?!
ALL FOR ONE... GO ON, DO AS YOU PLEASE.
AS WILL I!
THE DREGS OF THE OLD ORDER MUSTN'T SURVIVE THE REVOLUTION.
NAMEL ...
...THOSE WHO PREACH AND CLING TO THE TEACHINGS OF PAST GENERATIONS ...
THEY...
VOOM

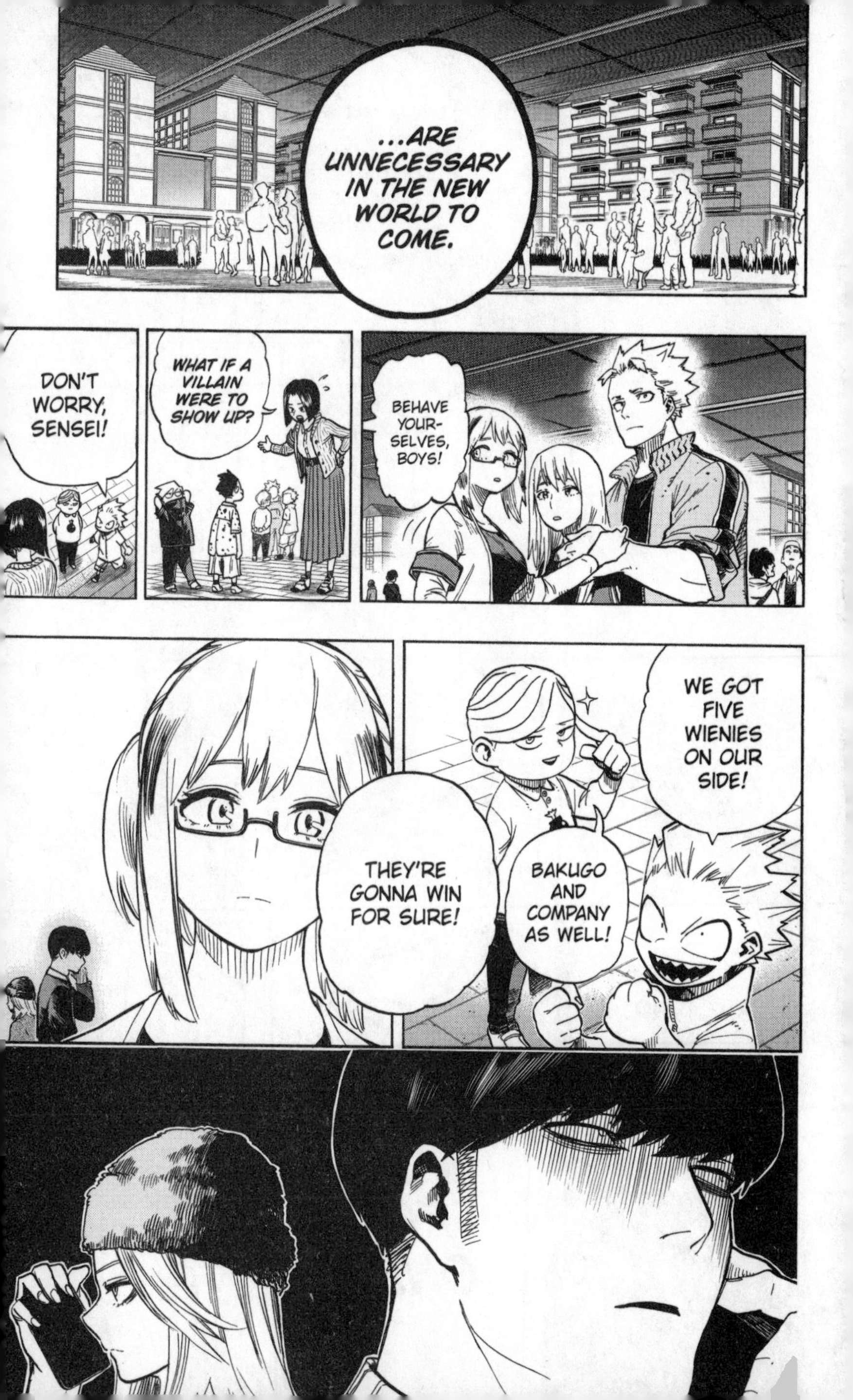
...ARE UNNECESSARY IN THE NEW WORLD TO COME.
BEHAVE YOUR-SELVES, BOYS!
WHAT IF A VILLAIN WERE TO SHOW UP?
DON'T WORRY, SENSEI!
WE GOT FIVE WIENIES ON OUR SIDE!
BAKUGO AND COMPANY AS WELL!
THEY'RE GONNA WIN FOR SURE!

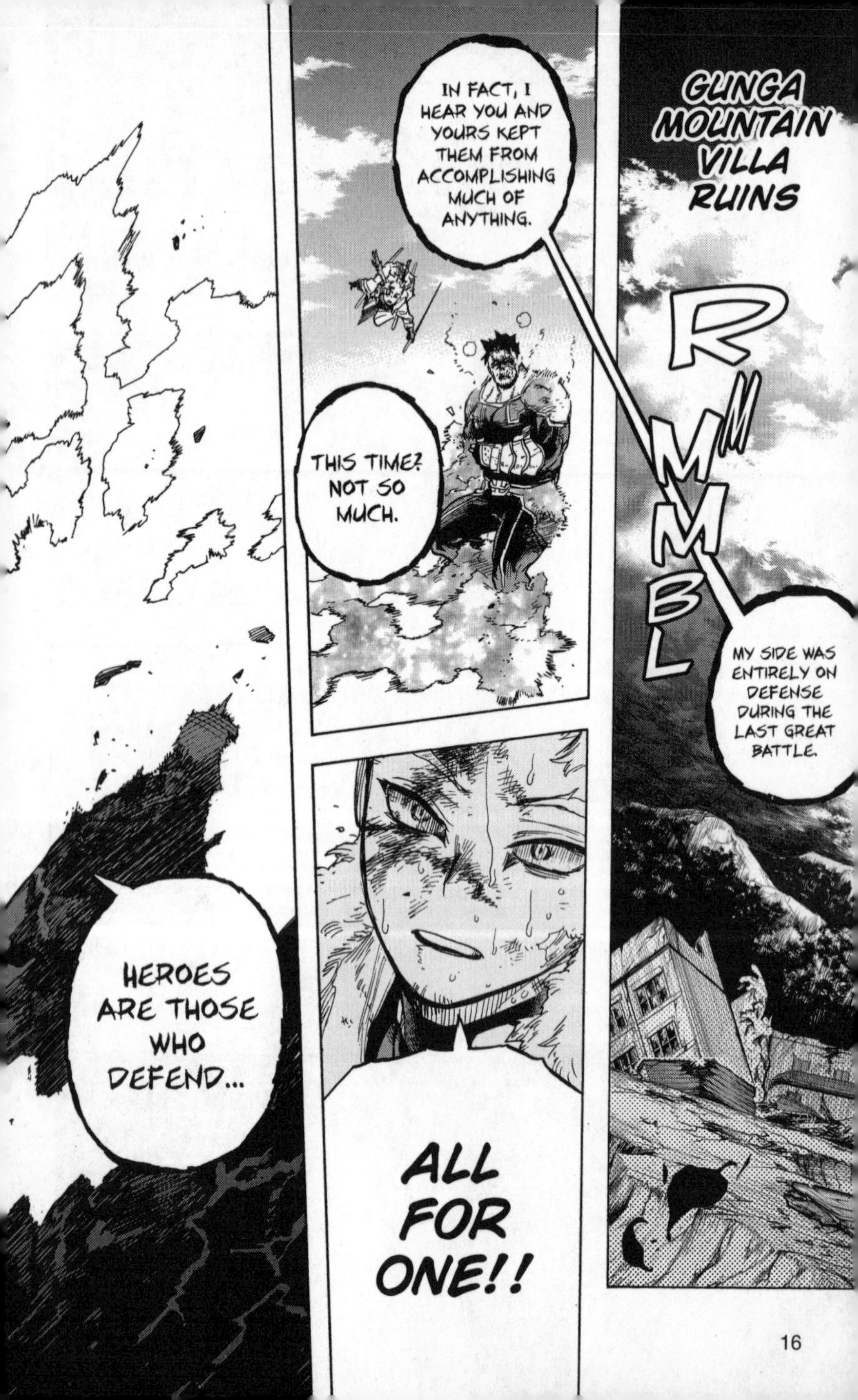
GUNGA MOUNTAIN VILLA RUINS
RMMMBL
MY SIDE WAS ENTIRELY ON DEFENSE DURING THE LAST GREAT BATTLE.
IN FACT, I HEAR YOU AND YOURS KEPT THEM FROM ACCOMPLISHING MUCH OF ANYTHING.
THIS TIME? NOT SO MUCH.
ALL FOR ONE!!
HEROES ARE THOSE WHO DEFEND...

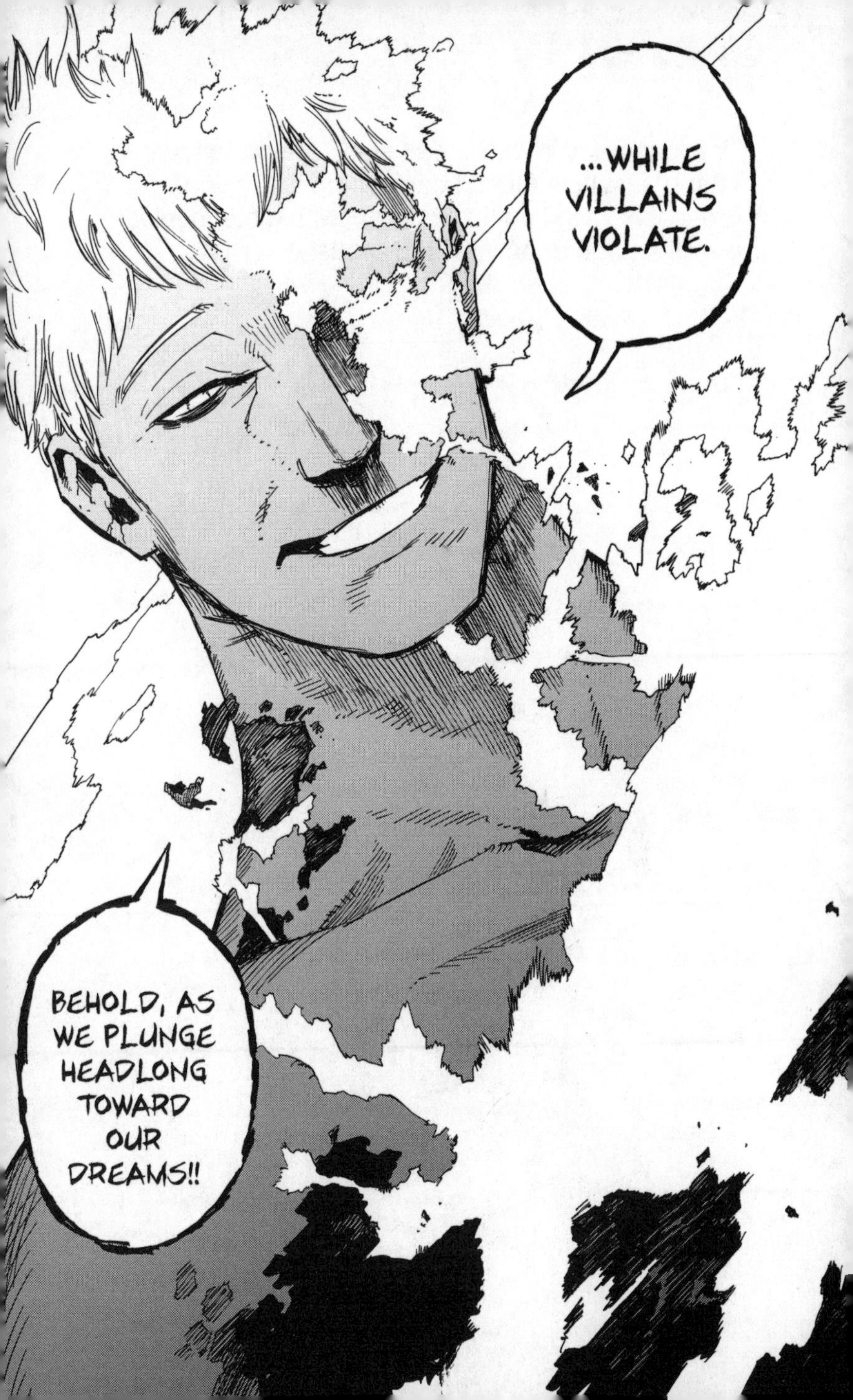
...WHILE VILLAINS VIOLATE.
BEHOLD, AS WE PLUNGE HEADLONG TOWARD OUR DREAMS!!

The longer I'm in this line of work, the more aware I am of just how much I can't stand the inking process. I wish I could just draw with a mechanical pencil and be done with it! Seriously!

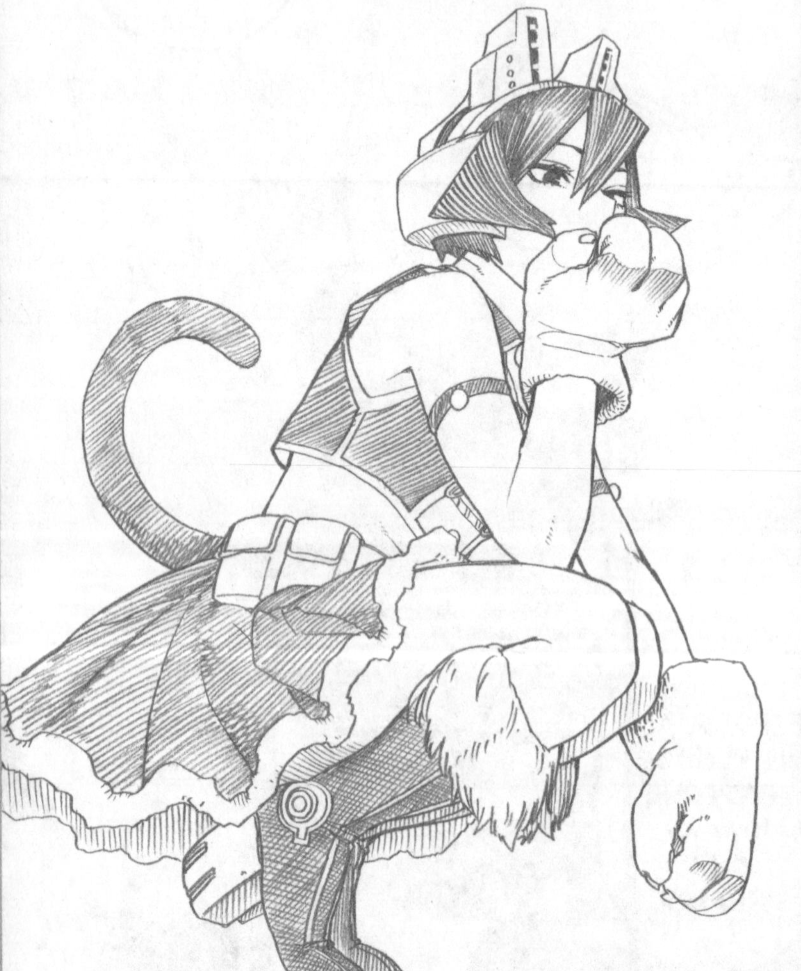

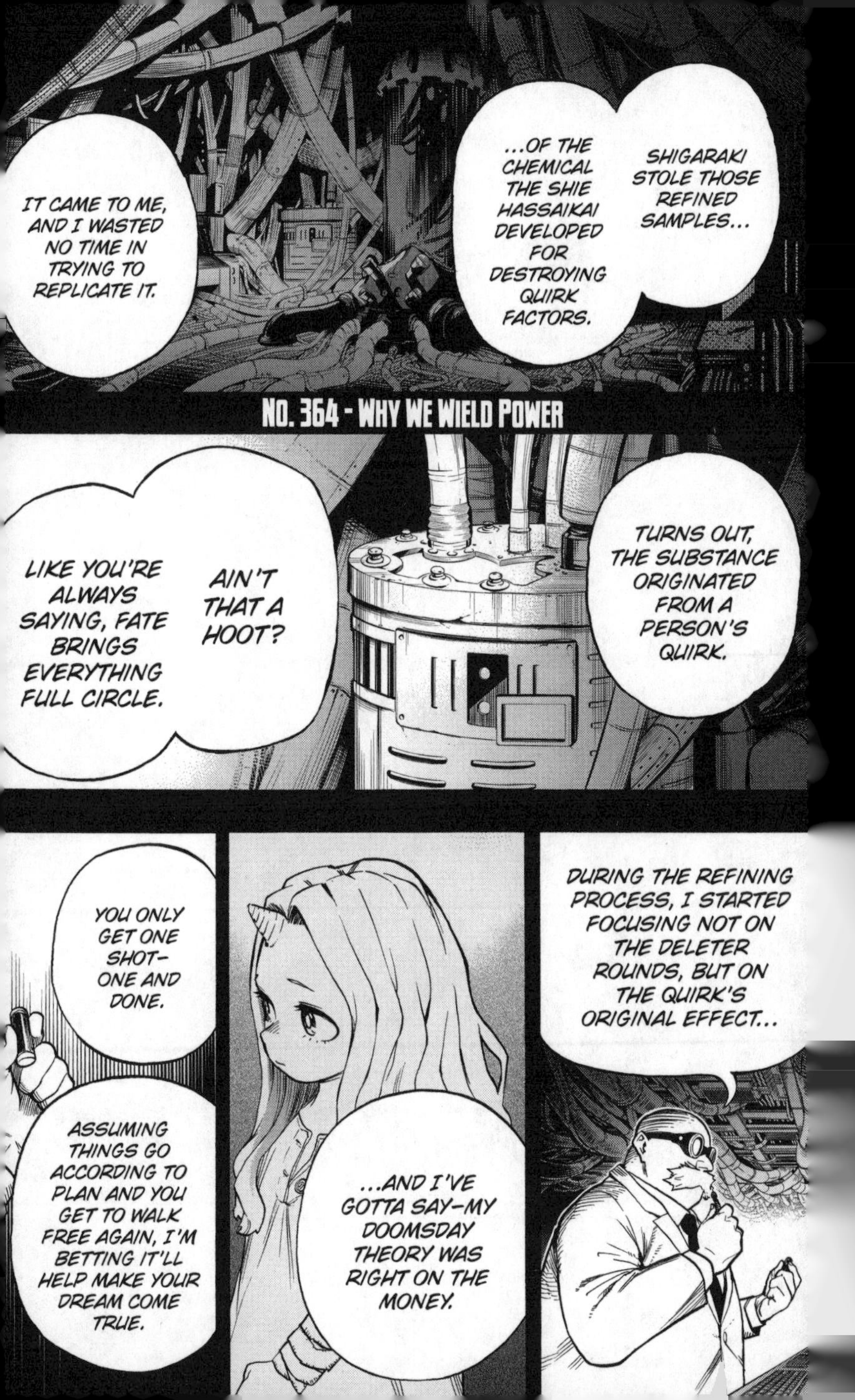
SHIGARAKI STOLE THOSE REFINED SAMPLES...
...OF THE CHEMICAL THE SHIE HASSAIKAI DEVELOPED FOR DESTROYING QUIRK FACTORS.
IT CAME TO ME, AND I WASTED NO TIME IN TRYING TO REPLICATE IT.
NO. 364 - WHY WE WIELD POWER
TURNS OUT, THE SUBSTANCE ORIGINATED FROM A PERSON'S QUIRK.
AIN'T THAT A HOOT?
LIKE YOU'RE ALWAYS SAYING, FATE BRINGS EVERYTHING FULL CIRCLE.
DURING THE REFINING PROCESS, I STARTED FOCUSING NOT ON THE DELETER ROUNDS, BUT ON THE QUIRK'S ORIGINAL EFFECT...
...AND I'VE GOTTA SAY—MY DOOMSDAY THEORY WAS RIGHT ON THE MONEY.
YOU ONLY GET ONE SHOT—ONE AND DONE.
ASSUMING THINGS GO ACCORDING TO PLAN AND YOU GET TO WALK FREE AGAIN, I'M BETTING IT'LL HELP MAKE YOUR DREAM COME TRUE.

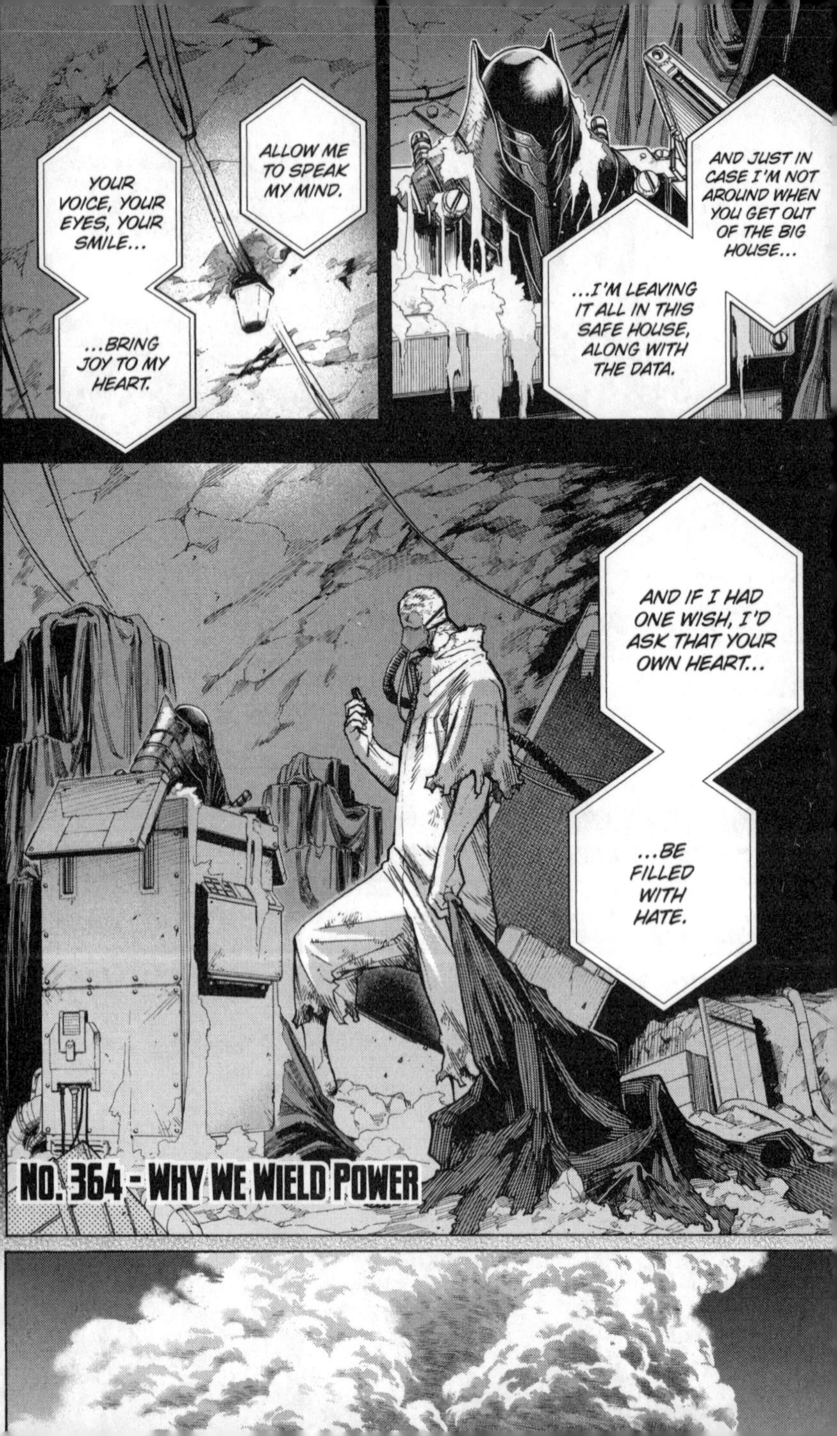
AND JUST IN CASE I'M NOT AROUND WHEN YOU GET OUT OF THE BIG HOUSE...
...I'M LEAVING IT ALL IN THIS SAFE HOUSE, ALONG WITH THE DATA.
ALLOW ME TO SPEAK MY MIND.
YOUR VOICE, YOUR EYES, YOUR SMILE...
...BRING JOY TO MY HEART.
AND IF I HAD ONE WISH, I'D ASK THAT YOUR OWN HEART...
...BE FILLED WITH HATE.
NO. 364 - WHY WE WIELD POWER

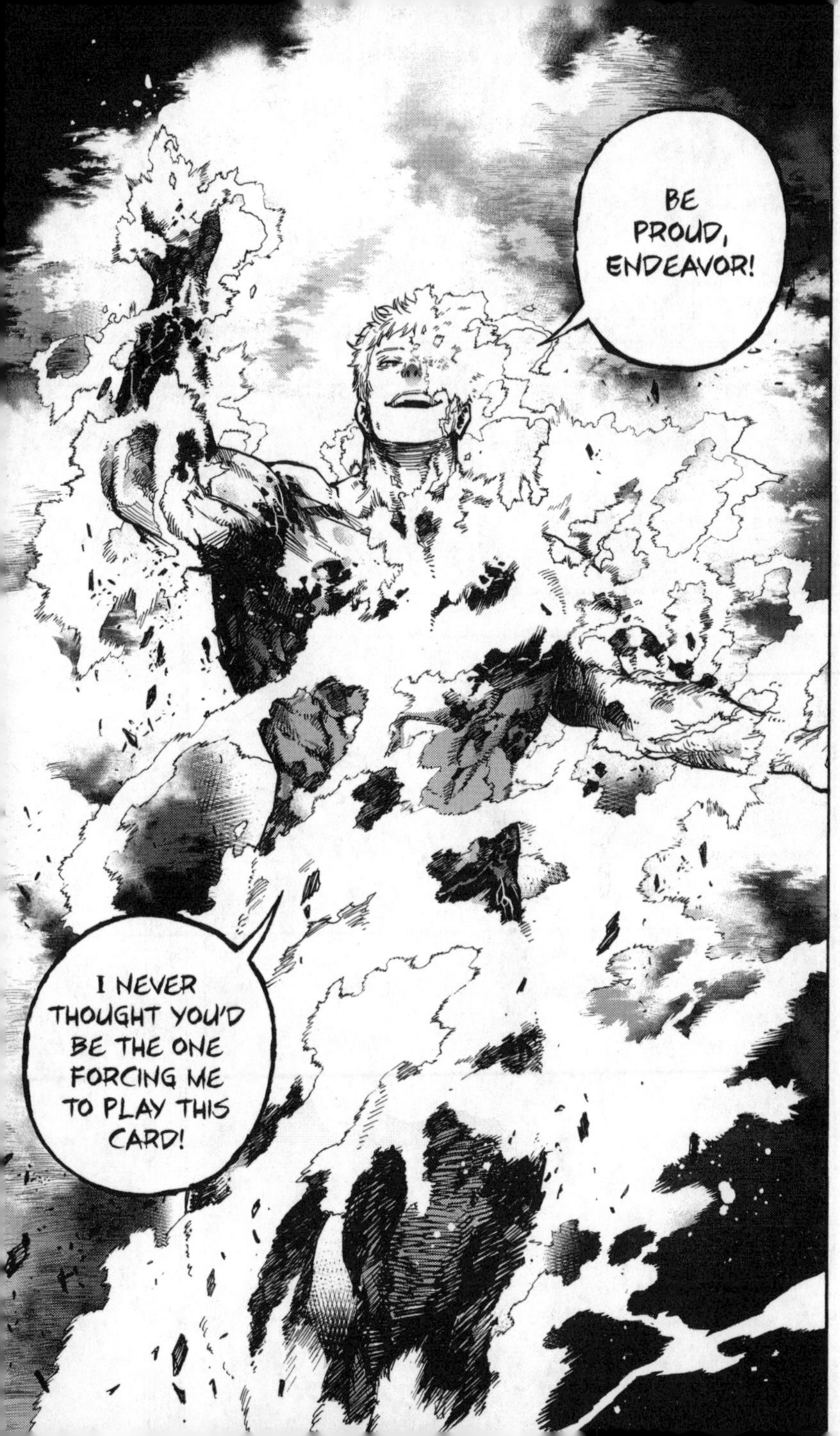
BE PROUD, ENDEAVOR!
I NEVER THOUGHT YOU'D BE THE ONE FORCING ME TO PLAY THIS CARD!

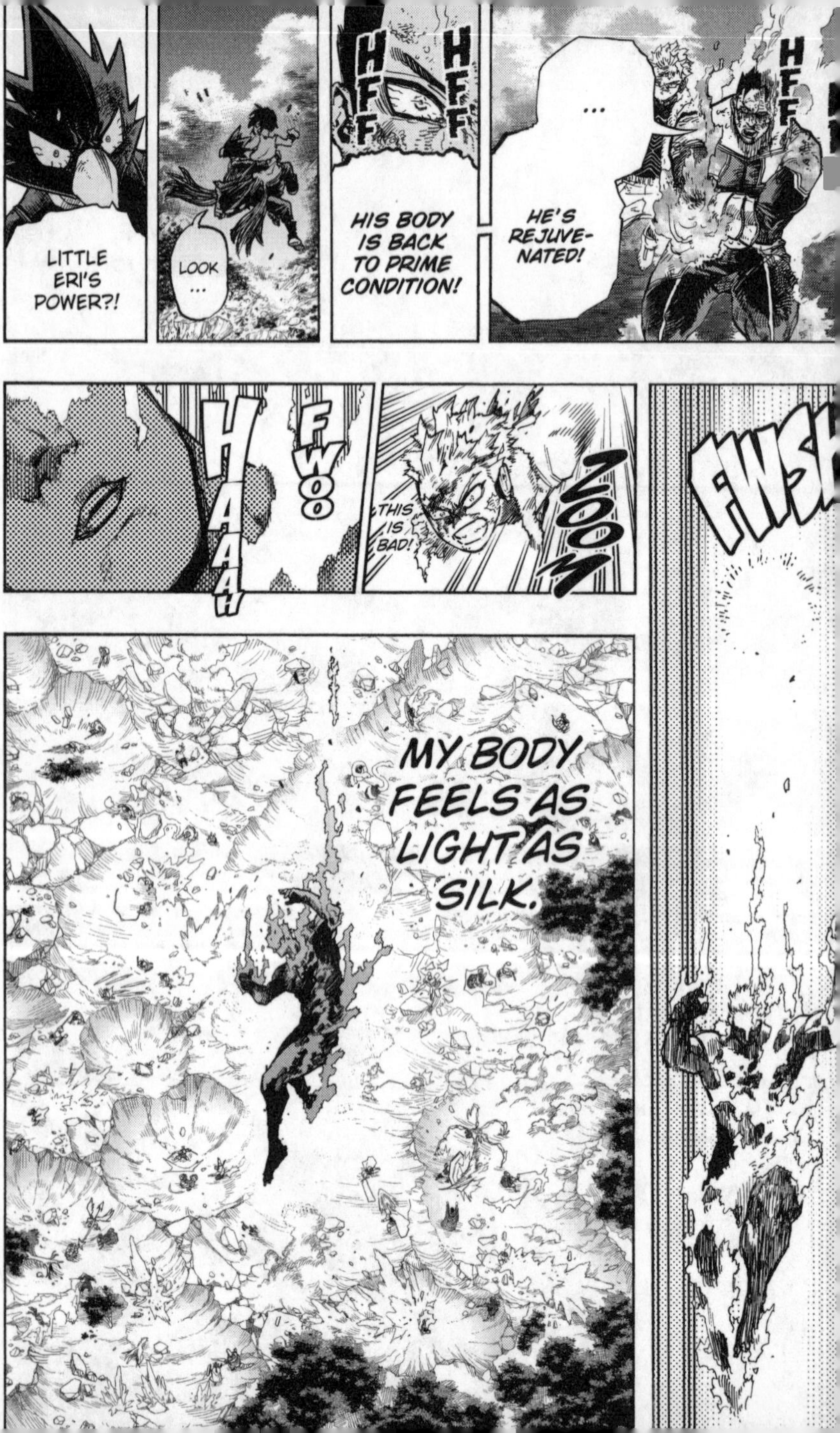
HFF HFF
...
HE'S REJUVE-NATED!
HFF HFF
HIS BODY IS BACK TO PRIME CONDITION!
LOOK ...
LITTLE ERI'S POWER?!
FWSH
ZOOM
THIS IS BAD!
FWOO
HAAAAH
MY BODY FEELS AS LIGHT AS SILK.

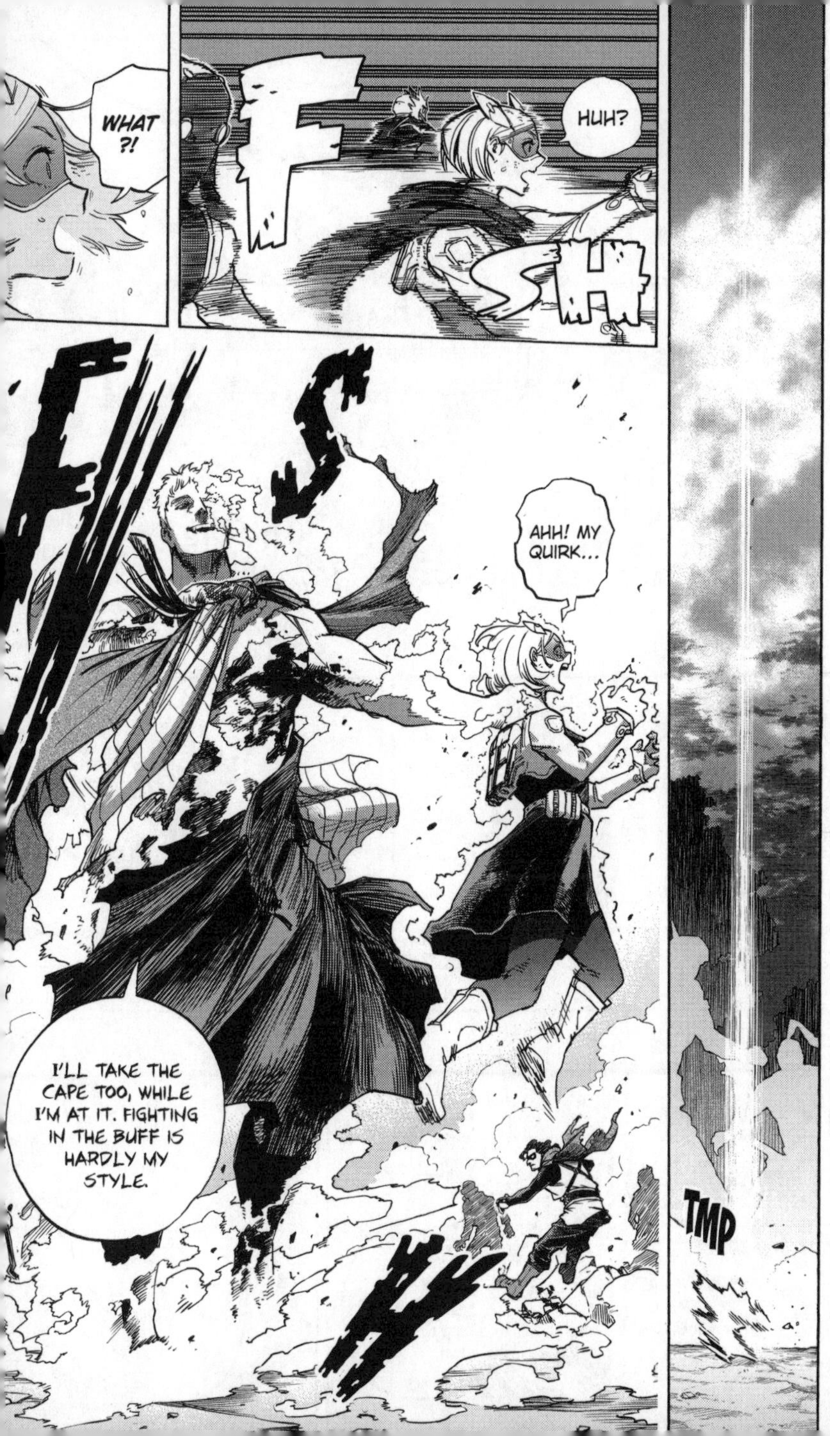
TMP
HUH?
FSH
WHAT ?!
AHH! MY QUIRK...
I'LL TAKE THE CAPE TOO, WHILE I'M AT IT. FIGHTING IN THE BUFF IS HARDLY MY STYLE.

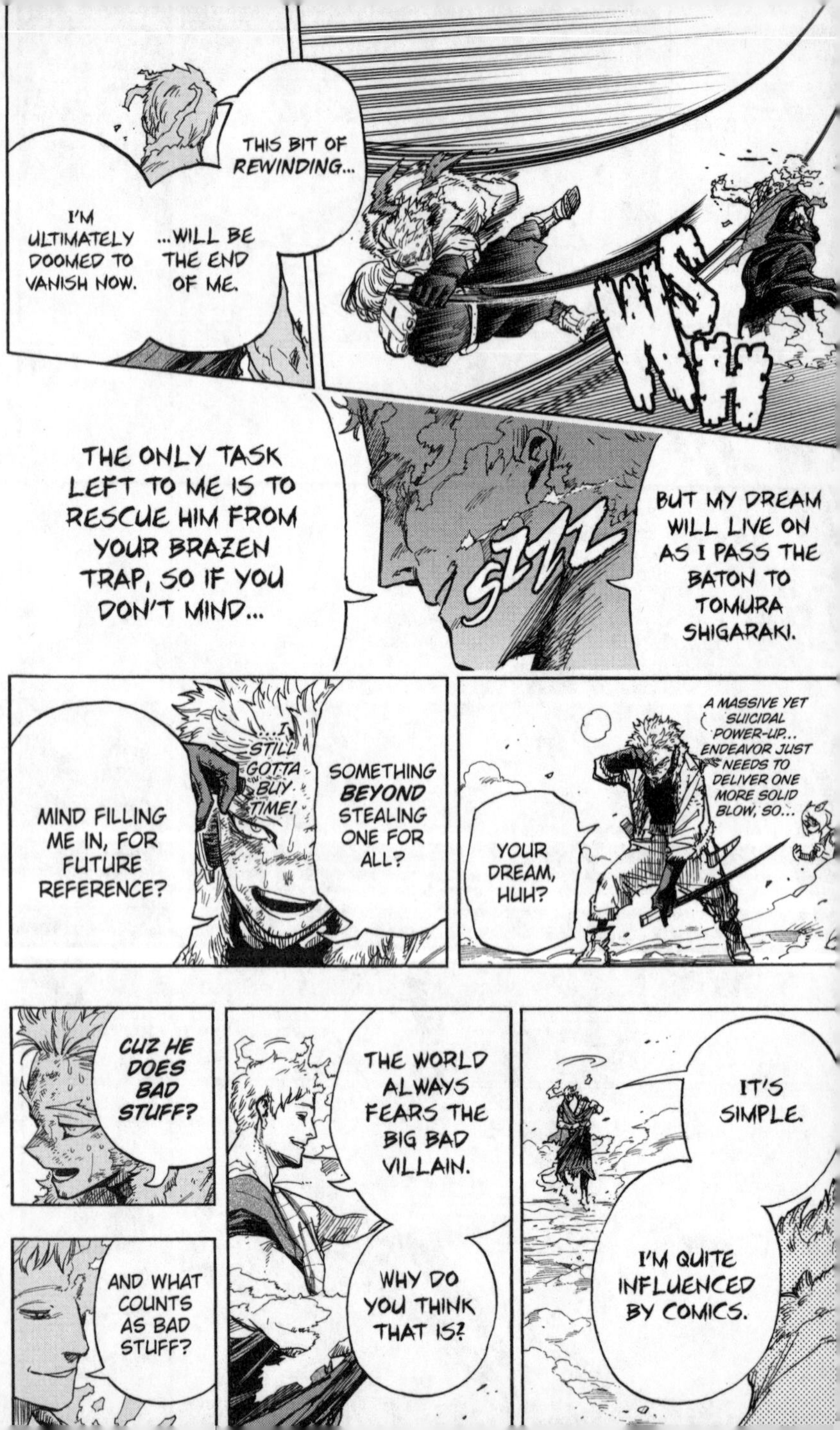
WSSH
THIS BIT OF REWINDING...
...WILL BE THE END OF ME.
I'M ULTIMATELY DOOMED TO VANISH NOW.
BUT MY DREAM WILL LIVE ON AS I PASS THE BATON TO TOMURA SHIGARAKI.
SZZZ
THE ONLY TASK LEFT TO ME IS TO RESCUE HIM FROM YOUR BRAZEN TRAP, SO IF YOU DON'T MIND...
A MASSIVE YET SUICIDAL POWER-UP... ENDEAVOR JUST NEEDS TO DELIVER ONE MORE SOLID BLOW, SO...
YOUR DREAM, HUH?
SOMETHING BEYOND STEALING ONE FOR ALL?
...I STILL GOTTA BUY TIME!
MIND FILLING ME IN, FOR FUTURE REFERENCE?
IT'S SIMPLE.
I'M QUITE INFLUENCED BY COMICS.
THE WORLD ALWAYS FEARS THE BIG BAD VILLAIN.
WHY DO YOU THINK THAT IS?
CUZ HE DOES BAD STUFF?
AND WHAT COUNTS AS BAD STUFF?

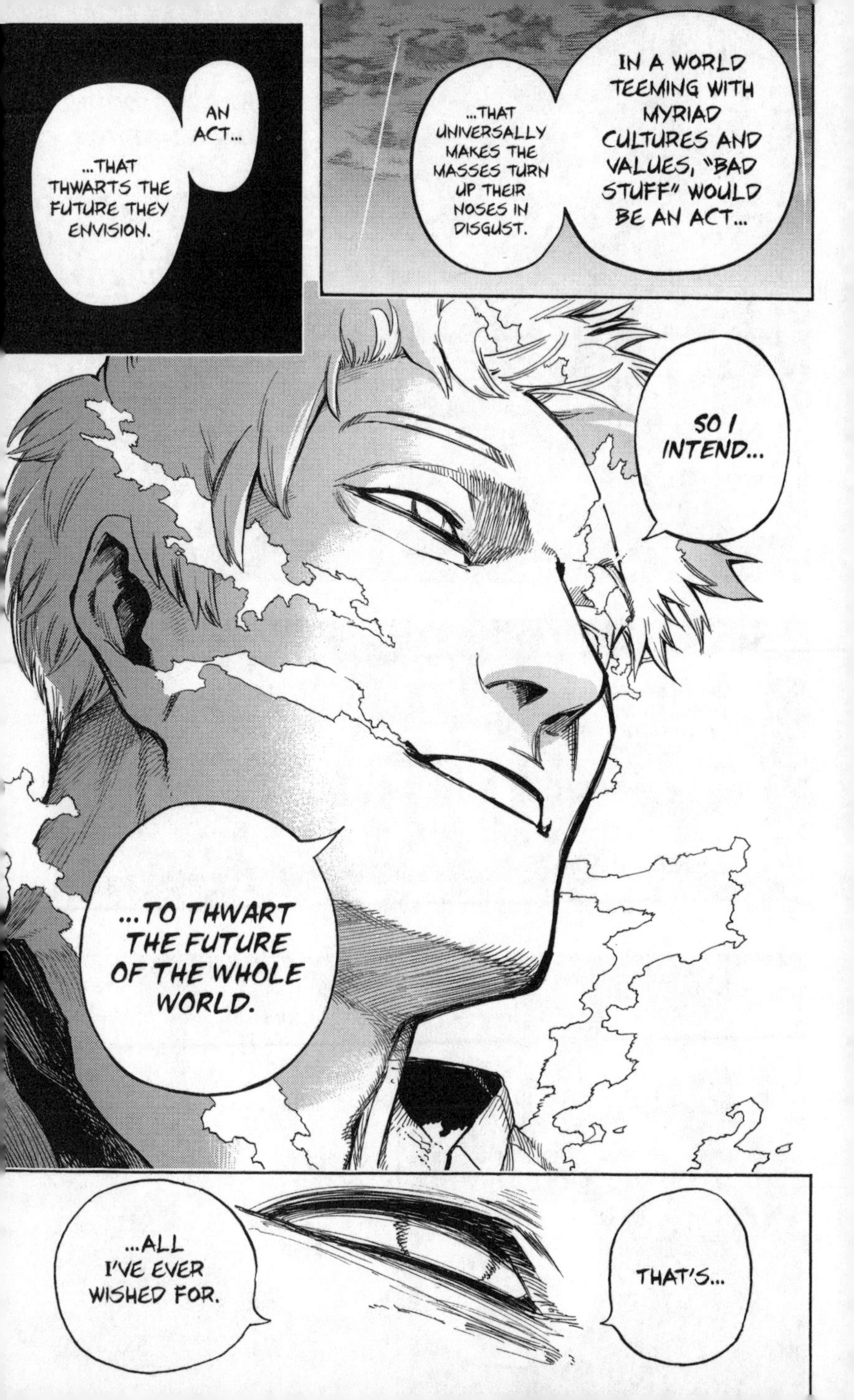
IN A WORLD TEEMING WITH MYRIAD CULTURES AND VALUES, "BAD STUFF" WOULD BE AN ACT...
...THAT UNIVERSALLY MAKES THE MASSES TURN UP THEIR NOSES IN DISGUST.
AN ACT...
...THAT THWARTS THE FUTURE THEY ENVISION.
SO I INTEND...
...TO THWART THE FUTURE OF THE WHOLE WORLD.
THAT'S...
...ALL I'VE EVER WISHED FOR.

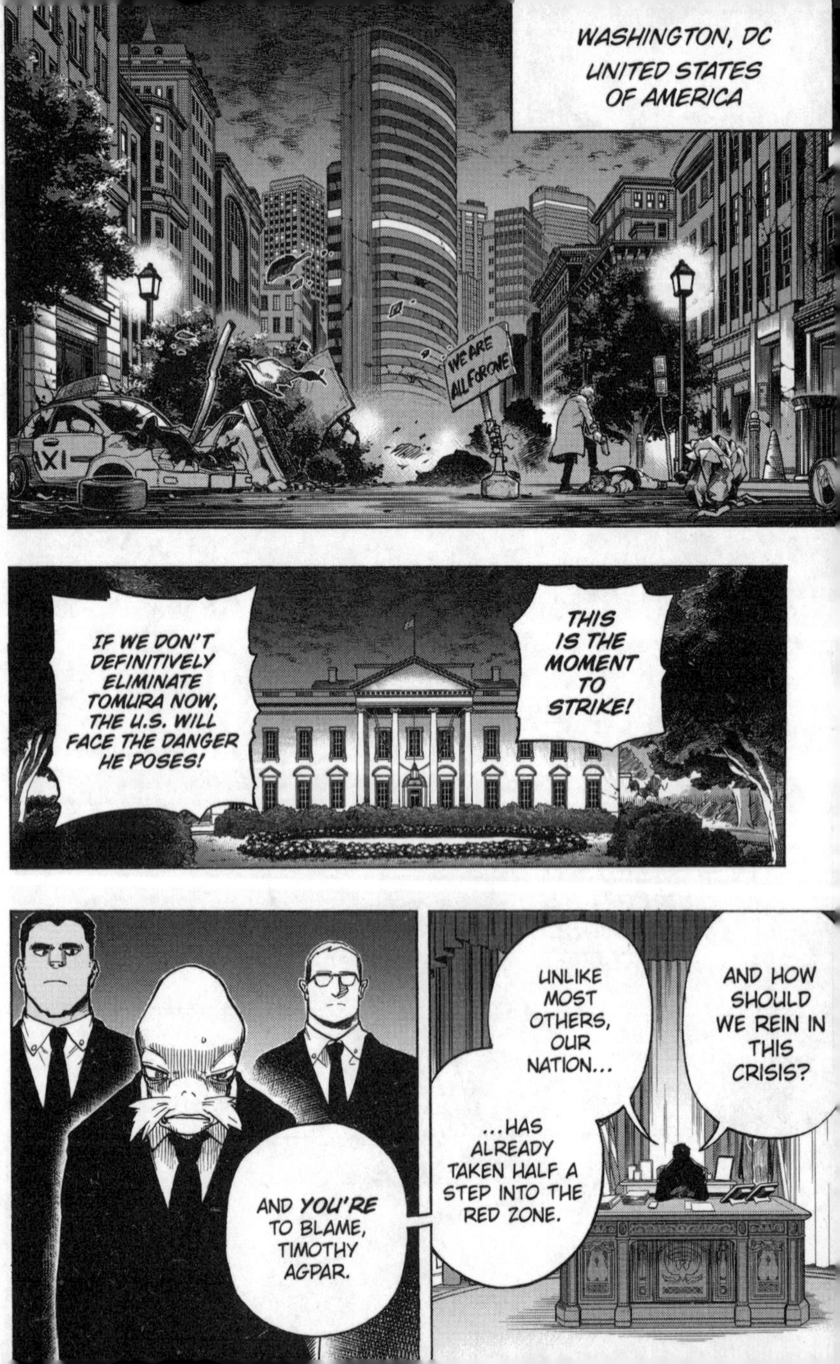
WASHINGTON, DC
UNITED STATES OF AMERICA
WE ARE ALL FOR ONE
THIS IS THE MOMENT TO STRIKE!
IF WE DON'T DEFINITIVELY ELIMINATE TOMURA NOW, THE U.S. WILL FACE THE DANGER HE POSES!
AND HOW SHOULD WE REIN IN THIS CRISIS?
UNLIKE MOST OTHERS, OUR NATION...
...HAS ALREADY TAKEN HALF A STEP INTO THE RED ZONE.
AND YOU'RE TO BLAME, TIMOTHY AGPAR.

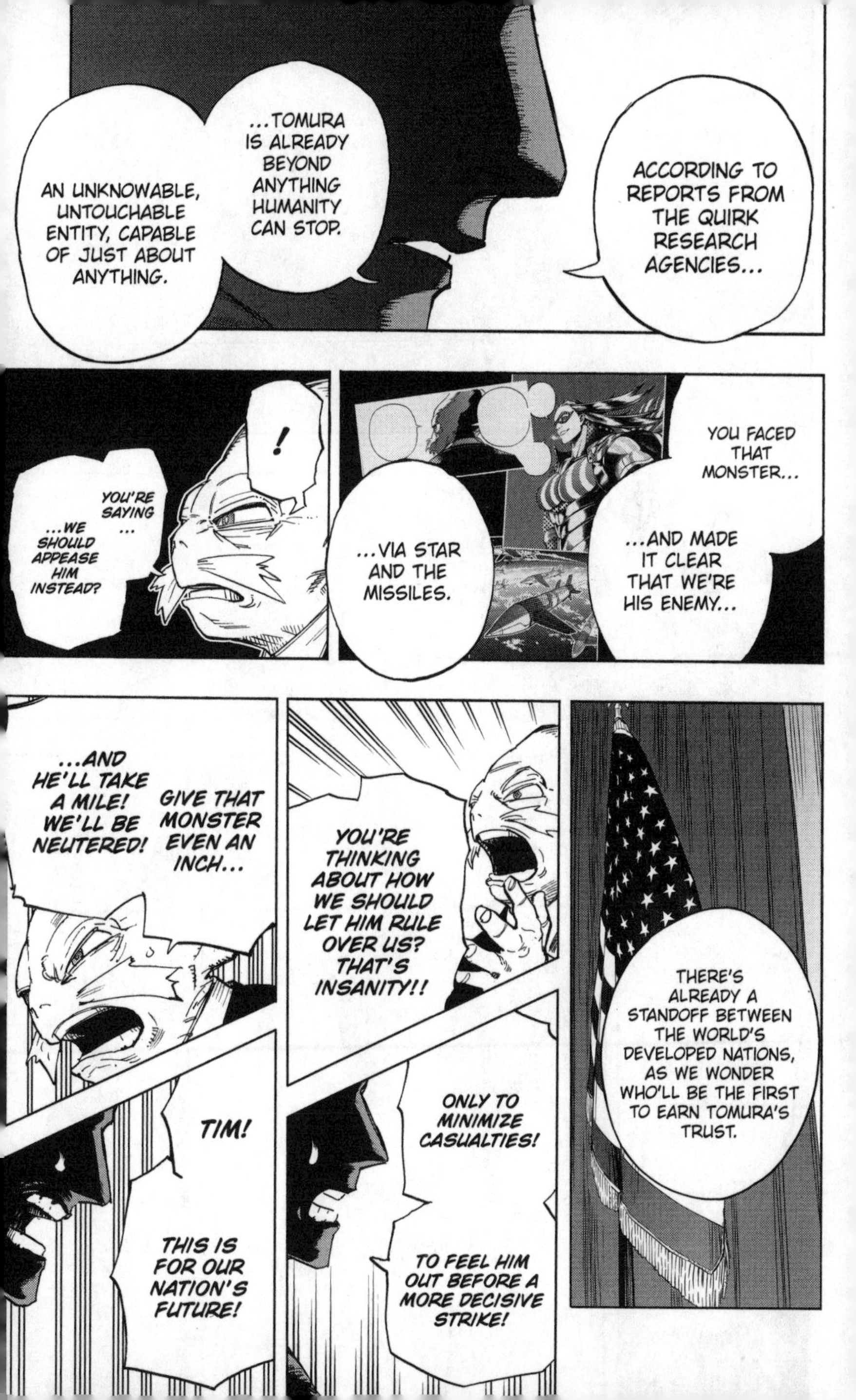
ACCORDING TO REPORTS FROM THE QUIRK RESEARCH AGENCIES...
...TOMURA IS ALREADY BEYOND ANYTHING HUMANITY CAN STOP.
AN UNKNOWABLE, UNTOUCHABLE ENTITY, CAPABLE OF JUST ABOUT ANYTHING.
YOU FACED THAT MONSTER...
...AND MADE IT CLEAR THAT WE'RE HIS ENEMY...
...VIA STAR AND THE MISSILES.
!
YOU'RE SAYING...
...WE SHOULD APPEASE HIM INSTEAD?
THERE'S ALREADY A STANDOFF BETWEEN THE WORLD'S DEVELOPED NATIONS, AS WE WONDER WHO'LL BE THE FIRST TO EARN TOMURA'S TRUST.
YOU'RE THINKING ABOUT HOW WE SHOULD LET HIM RULE OVER US? THAT'S INSANITY!!
GIVE THAT MONSTER EVEN AN INCH...
...AND HE'LL TAKE A MILE! WE'LL BE NEUTERED!
ONLY TO MINIMIZE CASUALTIES!
TO FEEL HIM OUT BEFORE A MORE DECISIVE STRIKE!
TIM!
THIS IS FOR OUR NATION'S FUTURE!

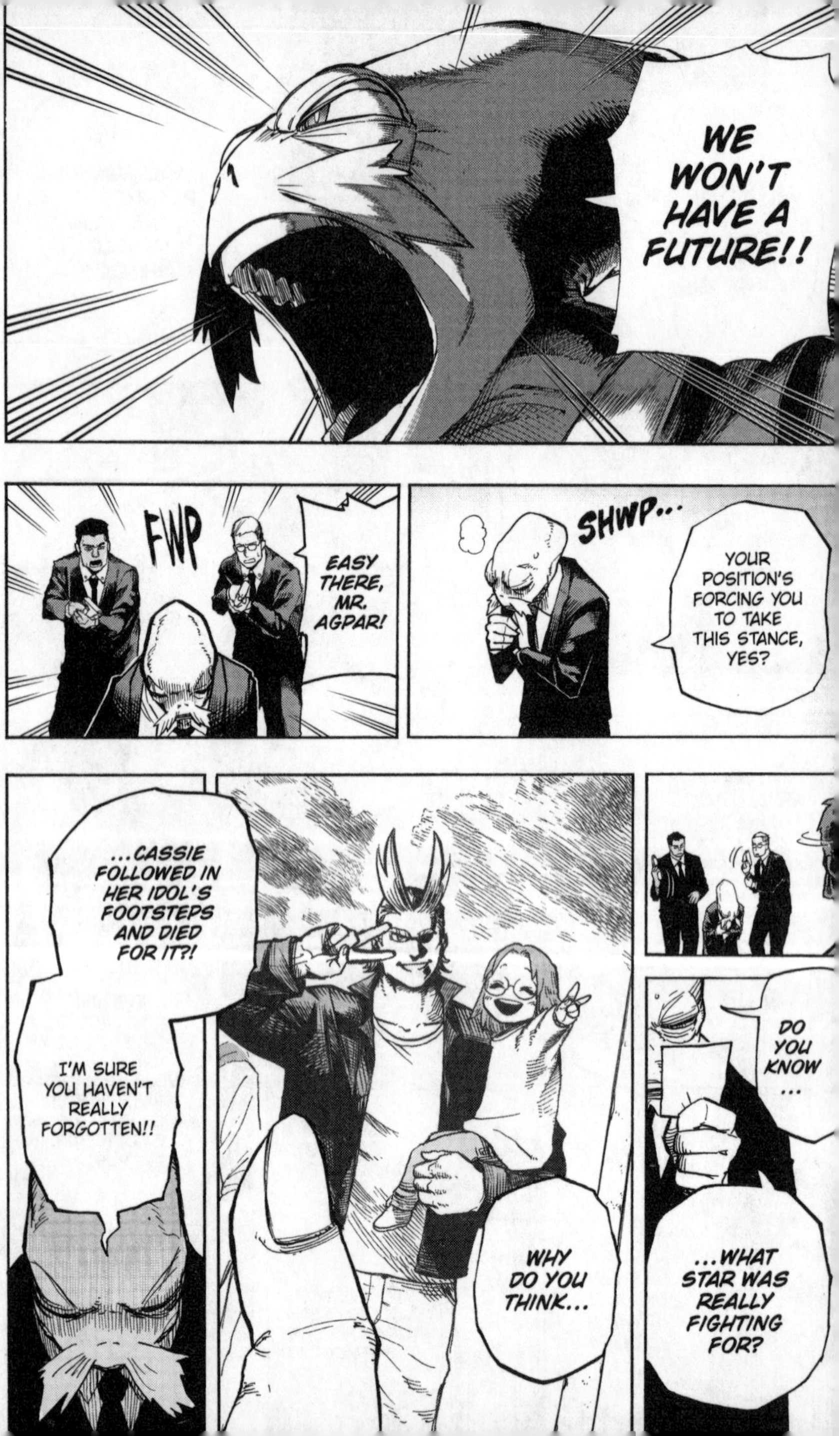
WE WON'T HAVE A FUTURE!!
SHWP...
YOUR POSITION'S FORCING YOU TO TAKE THIS STANCE, YES?
FWP
EASY THERE, MR. AGPAR!
DO YOU KNOW...
...WHAT STAR WAS REALLY FIGHTING FOR?
WHY DO YOU THINK...
...CASSIE FOLLOWED IN HER IDOL'S FOOTSTEPS AND DIED FOR IT?!
I'M SURE YOU HAVEN'T REALLY FORGOTTEN!!

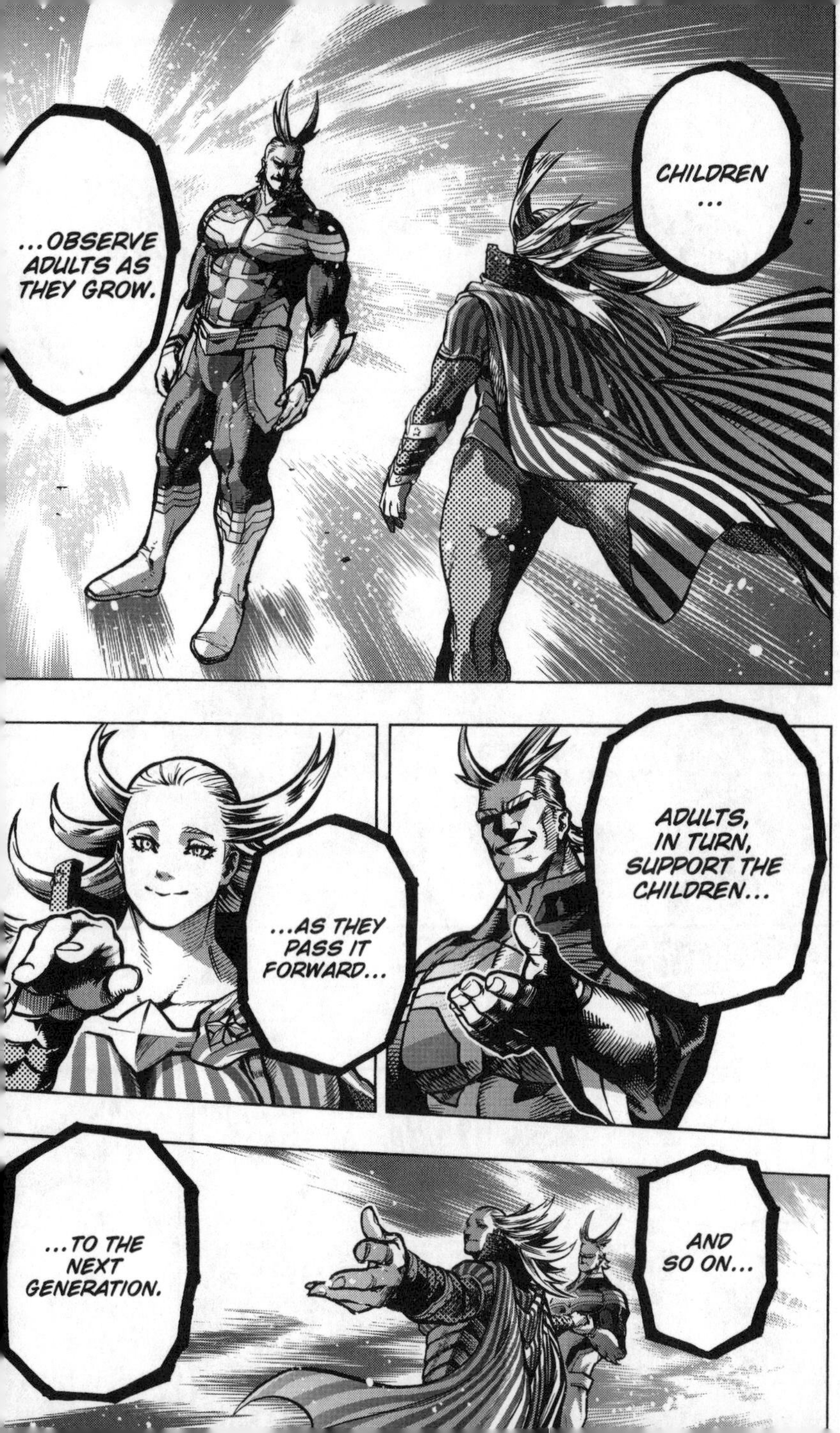
CHILDREN ...
...OBSERVE ADULTS AS THEY GROW.
ADULTS, IN TURN, SUPPORT THE CHILDREN...
...AS THEY PASS IT FORWARD...
AND SO ON...
...TO THE NEXT GENERATION.

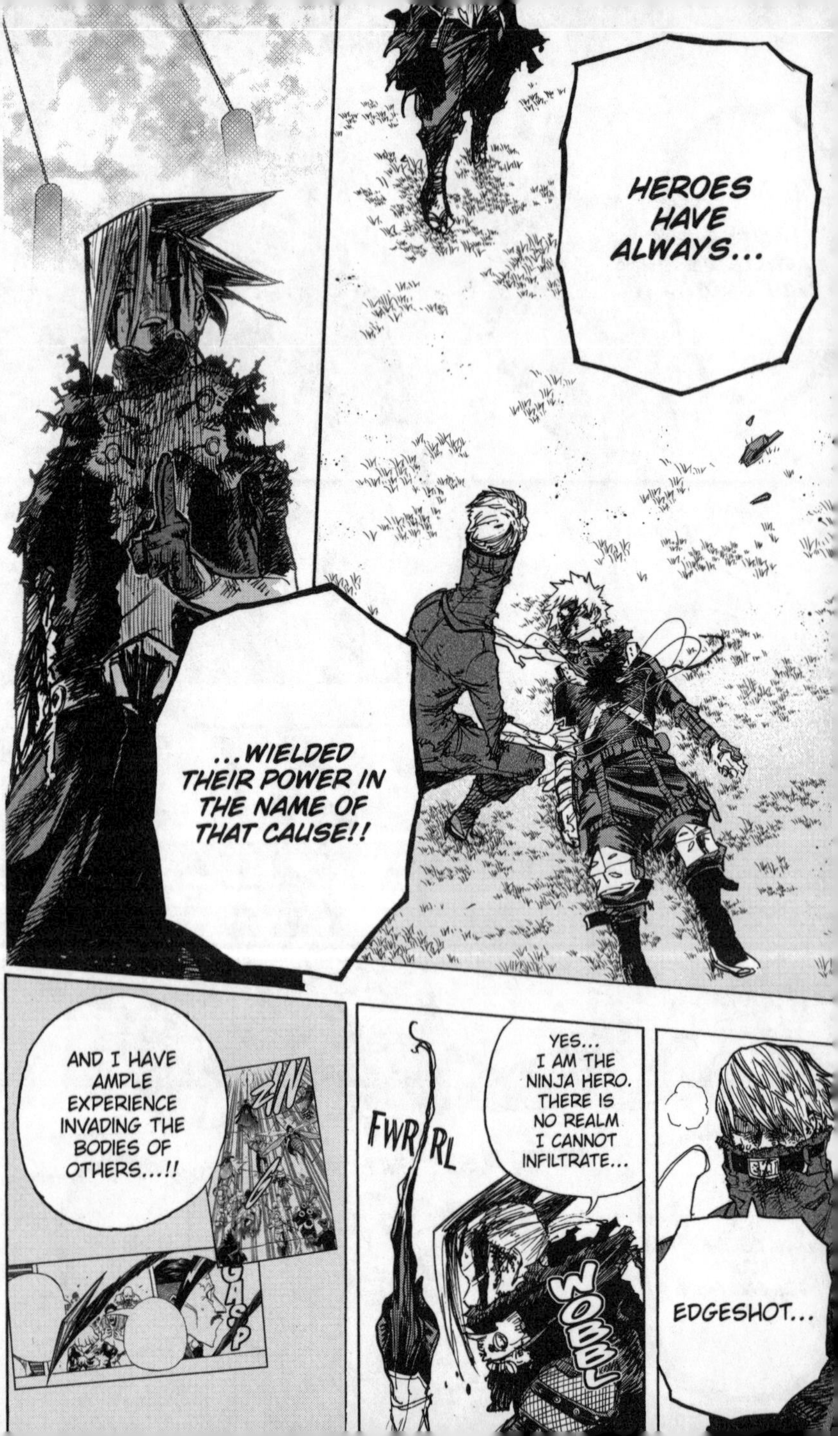
HEROES HAVE ALWAYS...
...WIELDED THEIR POWER IN THE NAME OF THAT CAUSE!!
EDGESHOT...
YES... I AM THE NINJA HERO. THERE IS NO REALM I CANNOT INFILTRATE...
FWRRL
WOBBL
AND I HAVE AMPLE EXPERIENCE INVADING THE BODIES OF OTHERS...!!
ZIN
GASP

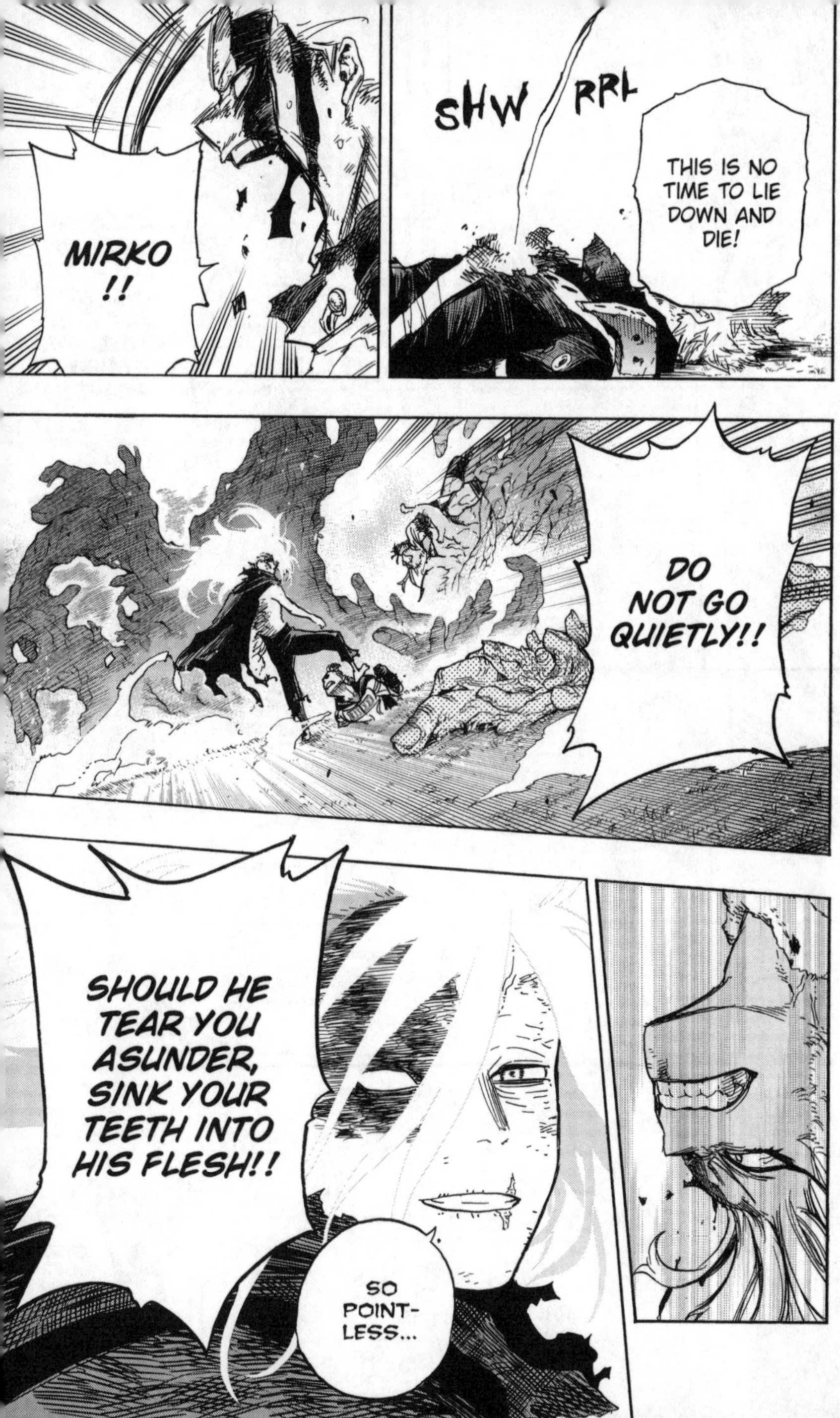
SHW RRL
THIS IS NO TIME TO LIE DOWN AND DIE!
MIRKO!!
DO NOT GO QUIETLY!!
SHOULD HE TEAR YOU ASUNDER, SINK YOUR TEETH INTO HIS FLESH!!
SO POINTLESS...

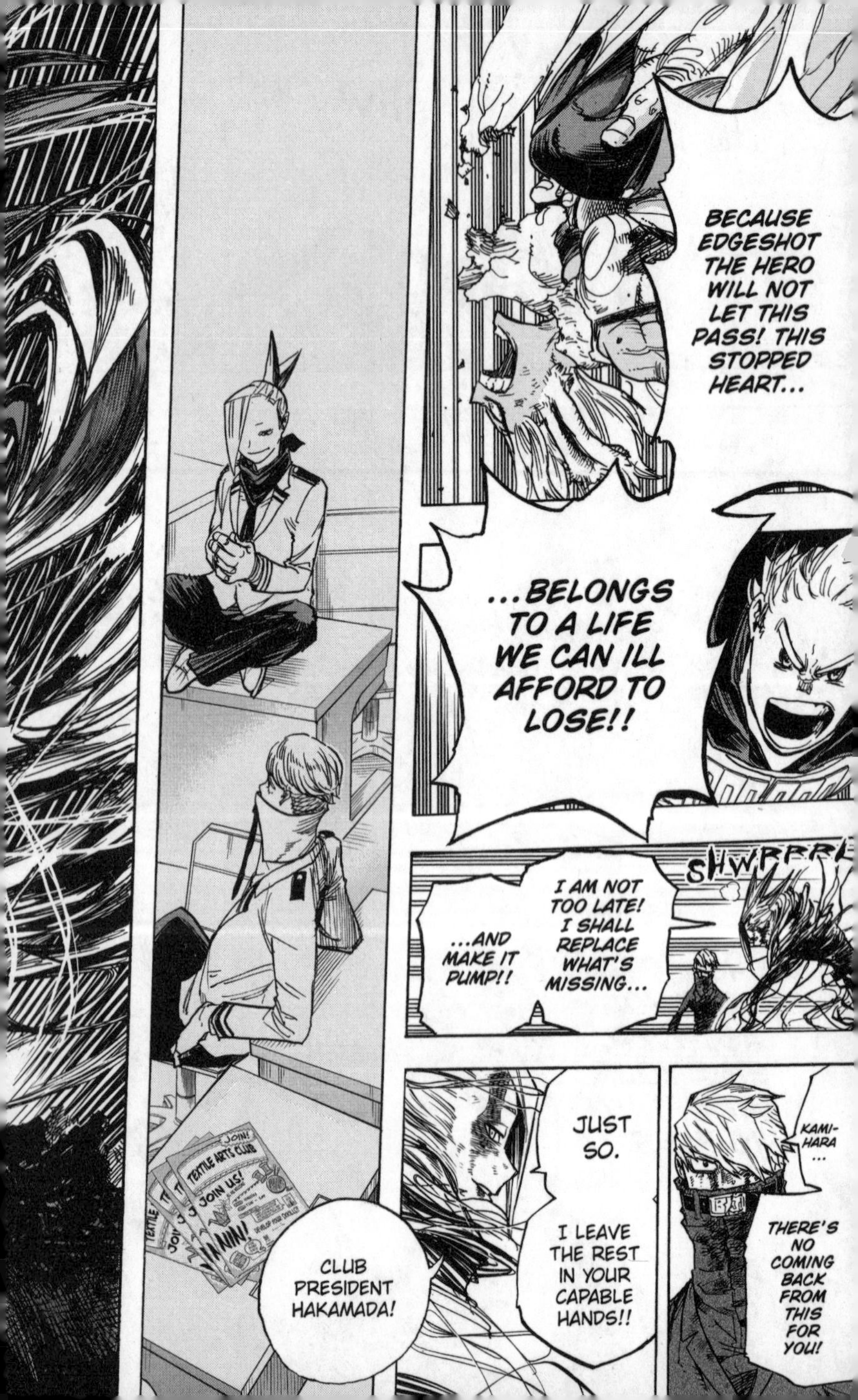
BECAUSE EDGESHOT THE HERO WILL NOT LET THIS PASS! THIS STOPPED HEART...
...BELONGS TO A LIFE WE CAN ILL AFFORD TO LOSE!!
SHWRRR
I AM NOT TOO LATE! I SHALL REPLACE WHAT'S MISSING...
...AND MAKE IT PUMP!!
KAMI-HARA...
THERE'S NO COMING BACK FROM THIS FOR YOU!
JUST SO.
I LEAVE THE REST IN YOUR CAPABLE HANDS!!
JOIN!
TEXTILE ARTS CLUB
JOIN US!
TEXTILE
CLUB PRESIDENT HAKAMADA!

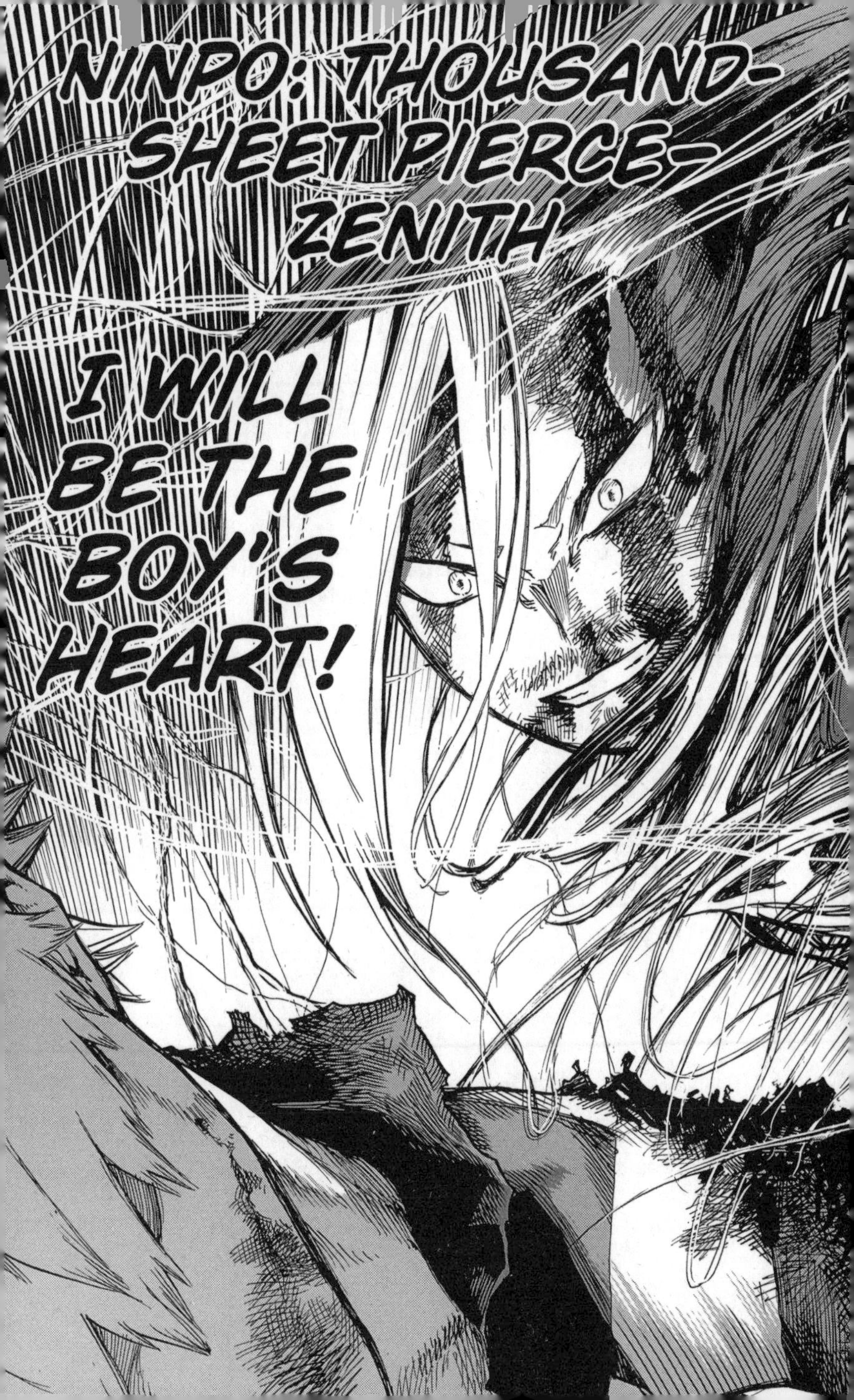
NINPO: THOUSAND-SHEET PIERCE-ZENITH
I WILL BE THE BOY'S HEART!

Hard to see through the wounds and blood, but he's got a mustache.

Edgeshot (Shinya Kamihara) is two years younger than Best Jeanist (Tsunagu Hakamada). They've got nostalgia for those youthful days when they were in their first and third years of high school, respectively.

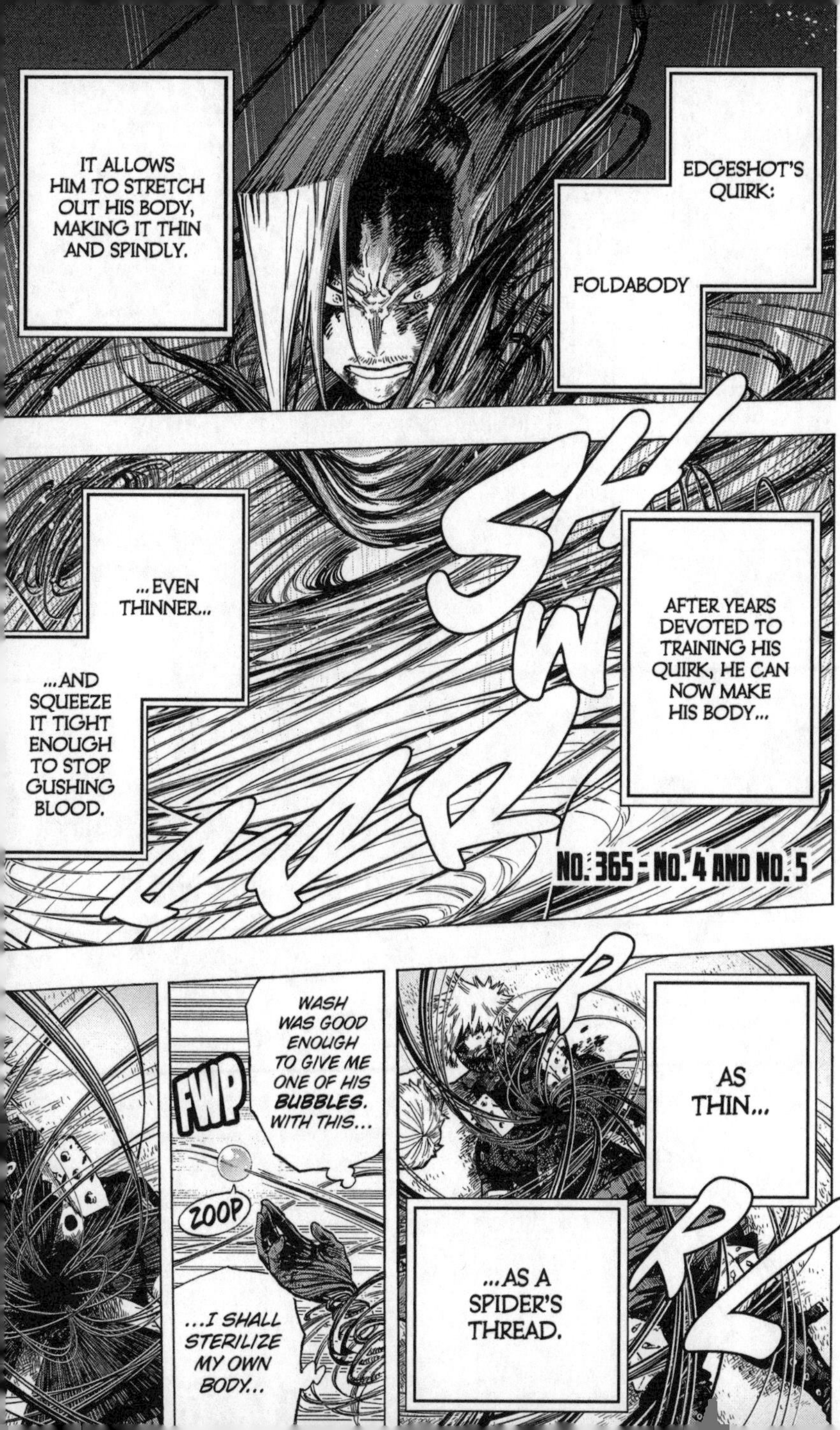
EDGESHOT'S QUIRK:
FOLDABODY
IT ALLOWS HIM TO STRETCH OUT HIS BODY, MAKING IT THIN AND SPINDLY.
AFTER YEARS DEVOTED TO TRAINING HIS QUIRK, HE CAN NOW MAKE HIS BODY...
...EVEN THINNER...
...AND SQUEEZE IT TIGHT ENOUGH TO STOP GUSHING BLOOD.
NO. 365 - NO. 4 AND NO. 5
AS THIN...
...AS A SPIDER'S THREAD.
WASH WAS GOOD ENOUGH TO GIVE ME ONE OF HIS BUBBLES. WITH THIS...
FWP
ZOOP
...I SHALL STERILIZE MY OWN BODY...

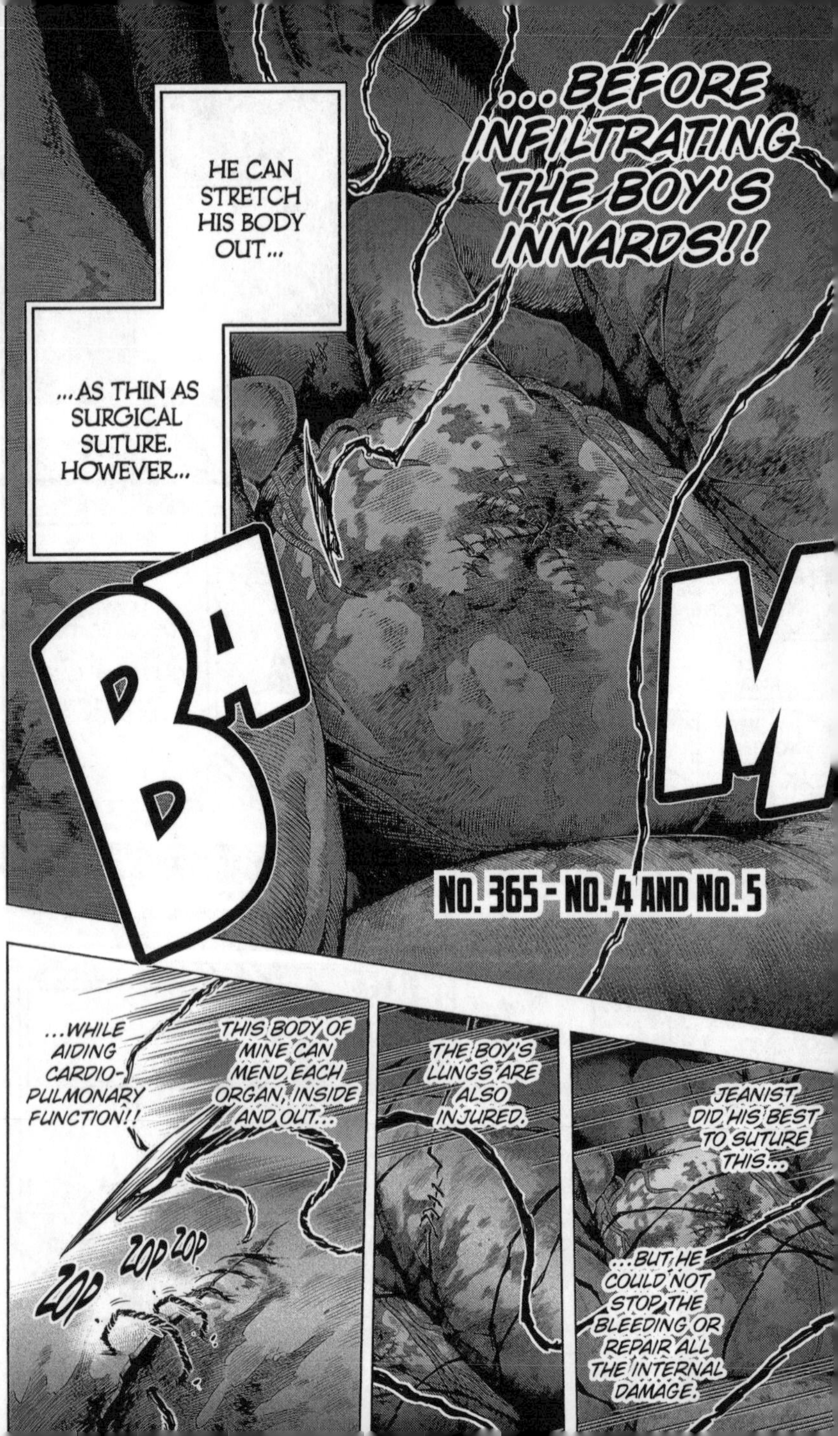
...BEFORE INFILTRATING THE BOY'S INNARDS!!
HE CAN STRETCH HIS BODY OUT...
...AS THIN AS SURGICAL SUTURE. HOWEVER...
BAM
NO. 365 - NO. 4 AND NO. 5
JEANIST DID HIS BEST TO SUTURE THIS...
...BUT HE COULD NOT STOP THE BLEEDING OR REPAIR ALL THE INTERNAL DAMAGE.
THE BOY'S LUNGS ARE ALSO INJURED.
THIS BODY OF MINE CAN MEND EACH ORGAN, INSIDE AND OUT...
...WHILE AIDING CARDIO-PULMONARY FUNCTION!!
ZOP ZOP ZOP

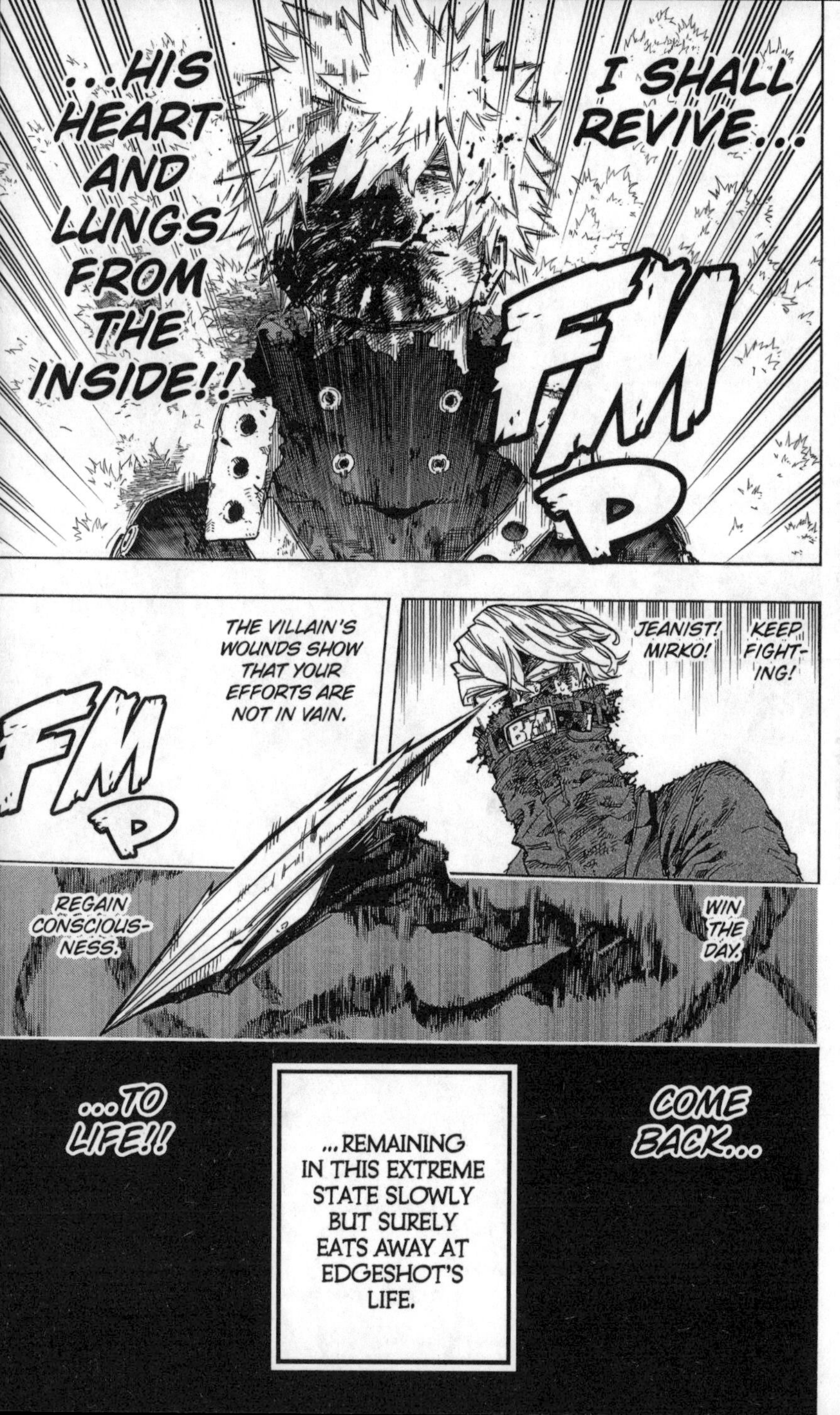

I SHALL REVIVE...
...HIS HEART AND LUNGS FROM THE INSIDE!!
FMP
KEEP FIGHTING!
JEANIST! MIRKO!
THE VILLAIN'S WOUNDS SHOW THAT YOUR EFFORTS ARE NOT IN VAIN.
FMP
WIN THE DAY.
REGAIN CONSCIOUSNESS.
COME BACK...
...TO LIFE!!
...REMAINING IN THIS EXTREME STATE SLOWLY BUT SURELY EATS AWAY AT EDGESHOT'S LIFE.

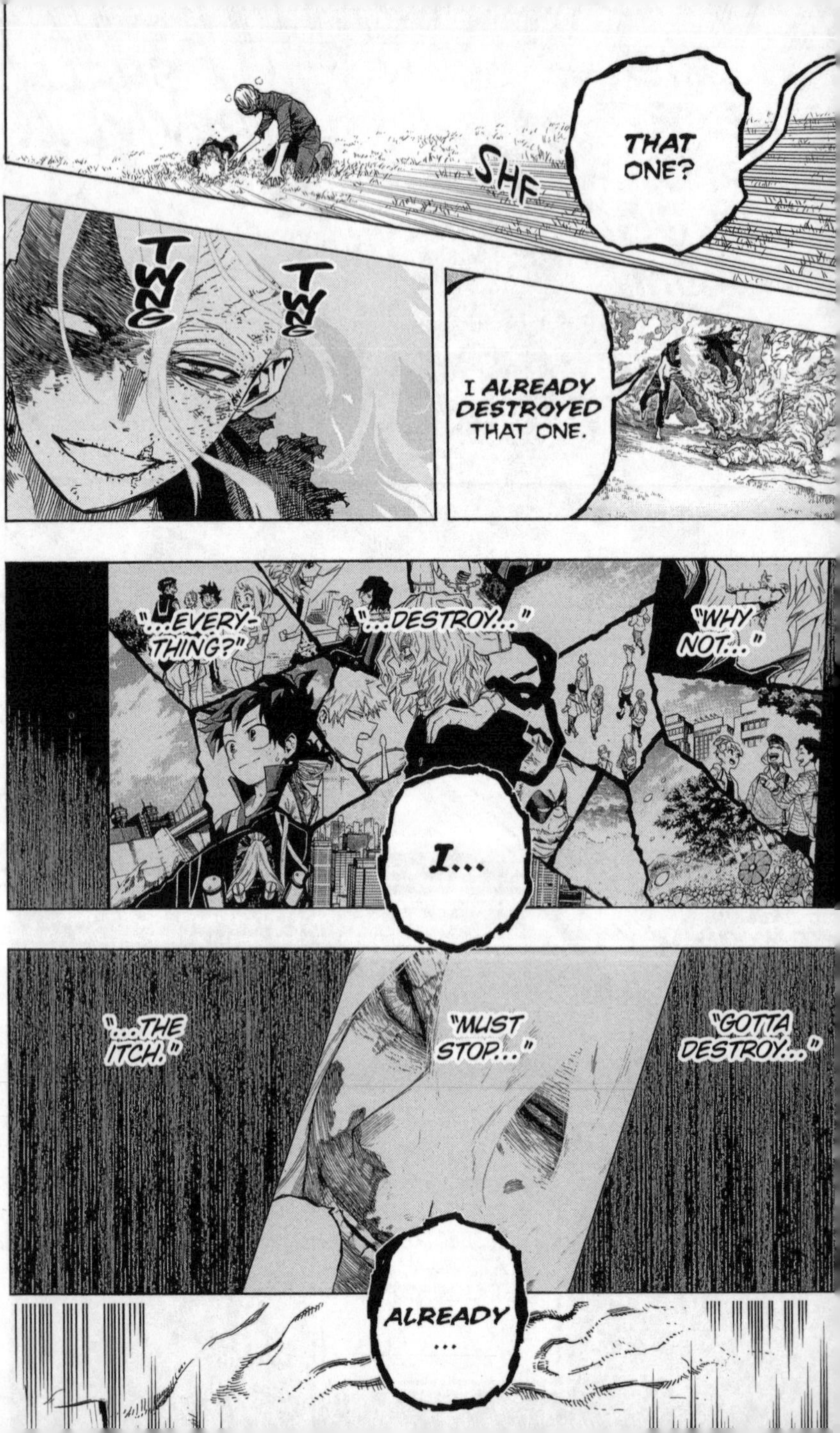
THAT ONE?
SHF
I ALREADY DESTROYED THAT ONE.
TWNG TWNG
"WHY NOT..."
"...DESTROY..."
"...EVERY-THING?"
I...
"GOTTA DESTROY..."
"MUST STOP..."
"...THE ITCH."
ALREADY ...

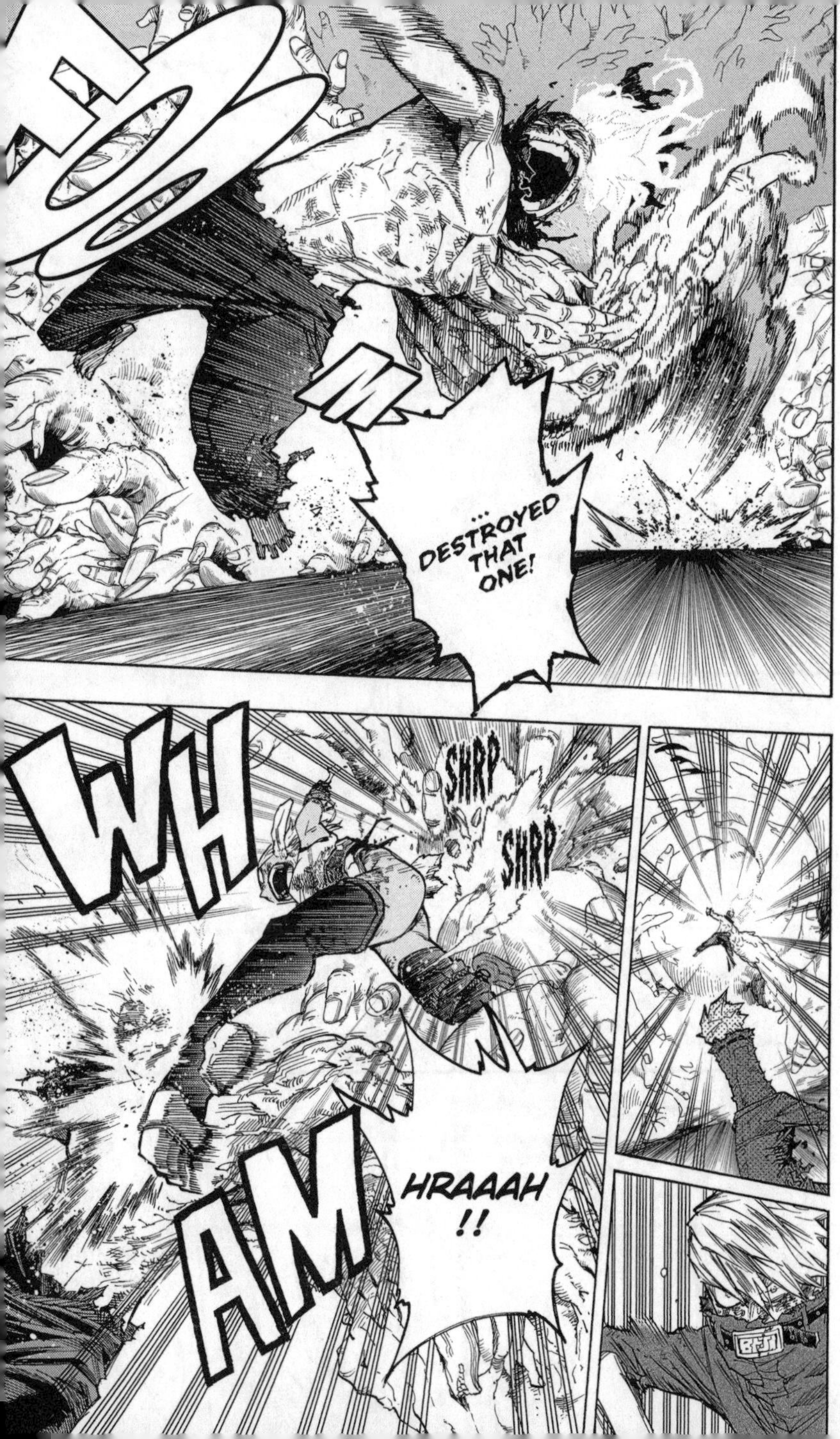

M
... DESTROYED THAT ONE!
SHRP
SHRP
WH
HRAAAH !!
AM

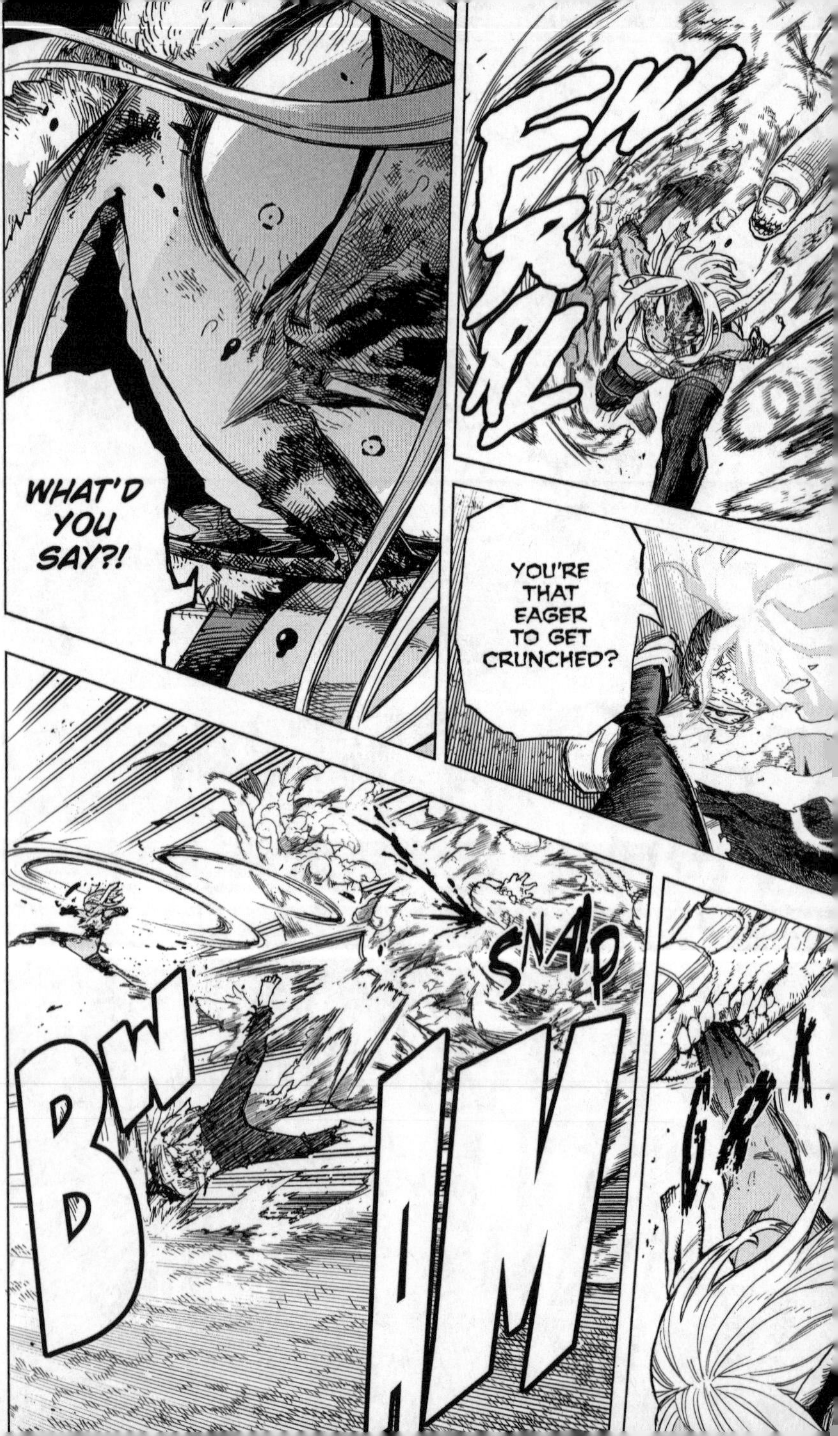
YOU'RE THAT EAGER TO GET CRUNCHED?
WHAT'D YOU SAY?!
SNAP
BWAM

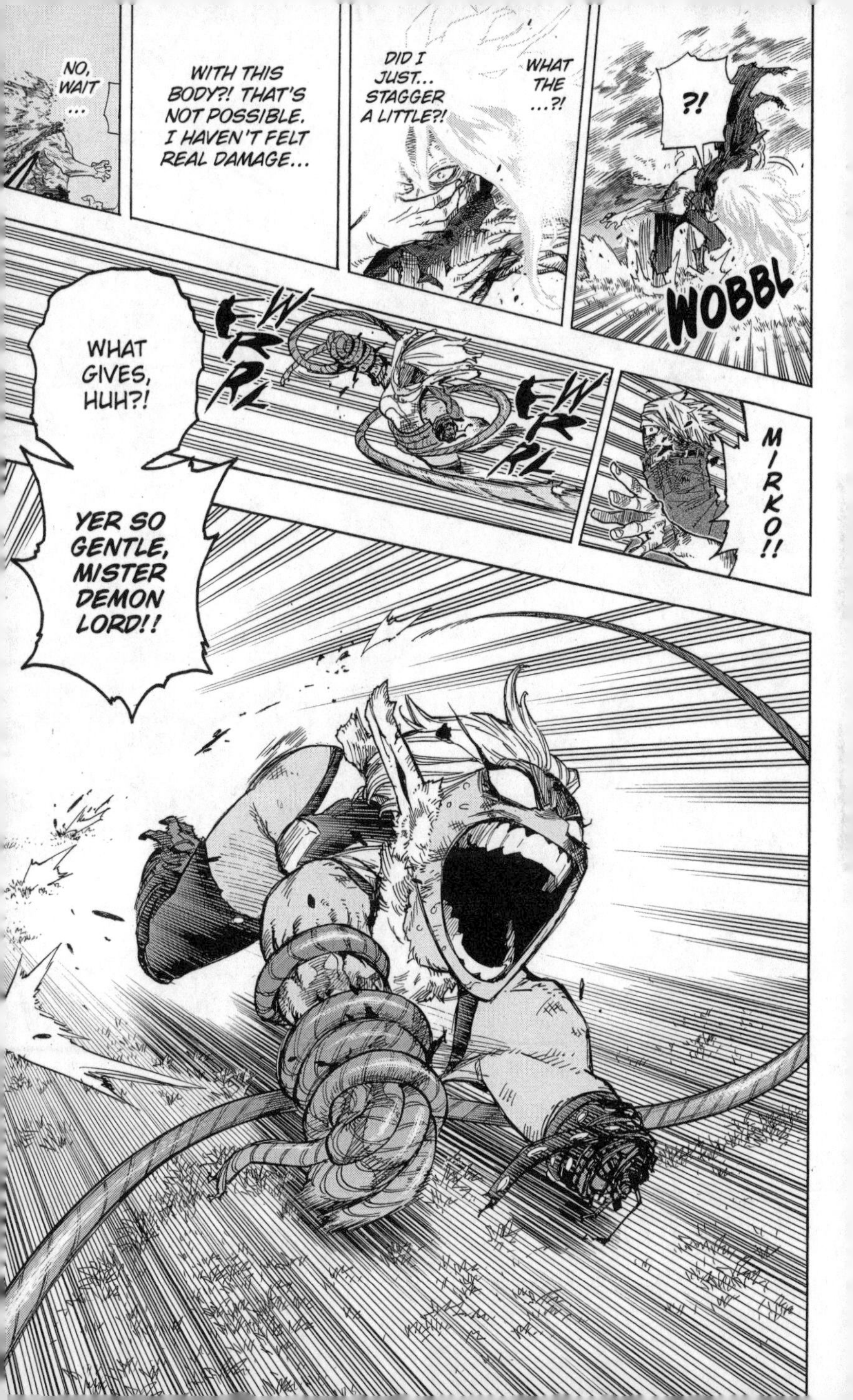
?!
WOBBL
WHAT THE ...?!
DID I JUST... STAGGER A LITTLE?!
WITH THIS BODY?! THAT'S NOT POSSIBLE. I HAVEN'T FELT REAL DAMAGE...
NO, WAIT ...
MIRKO!!
WRRL
WRRL
WHAT GIVES, HUH?!
YER SO GENTLE, MISTER DEMON LORD!!

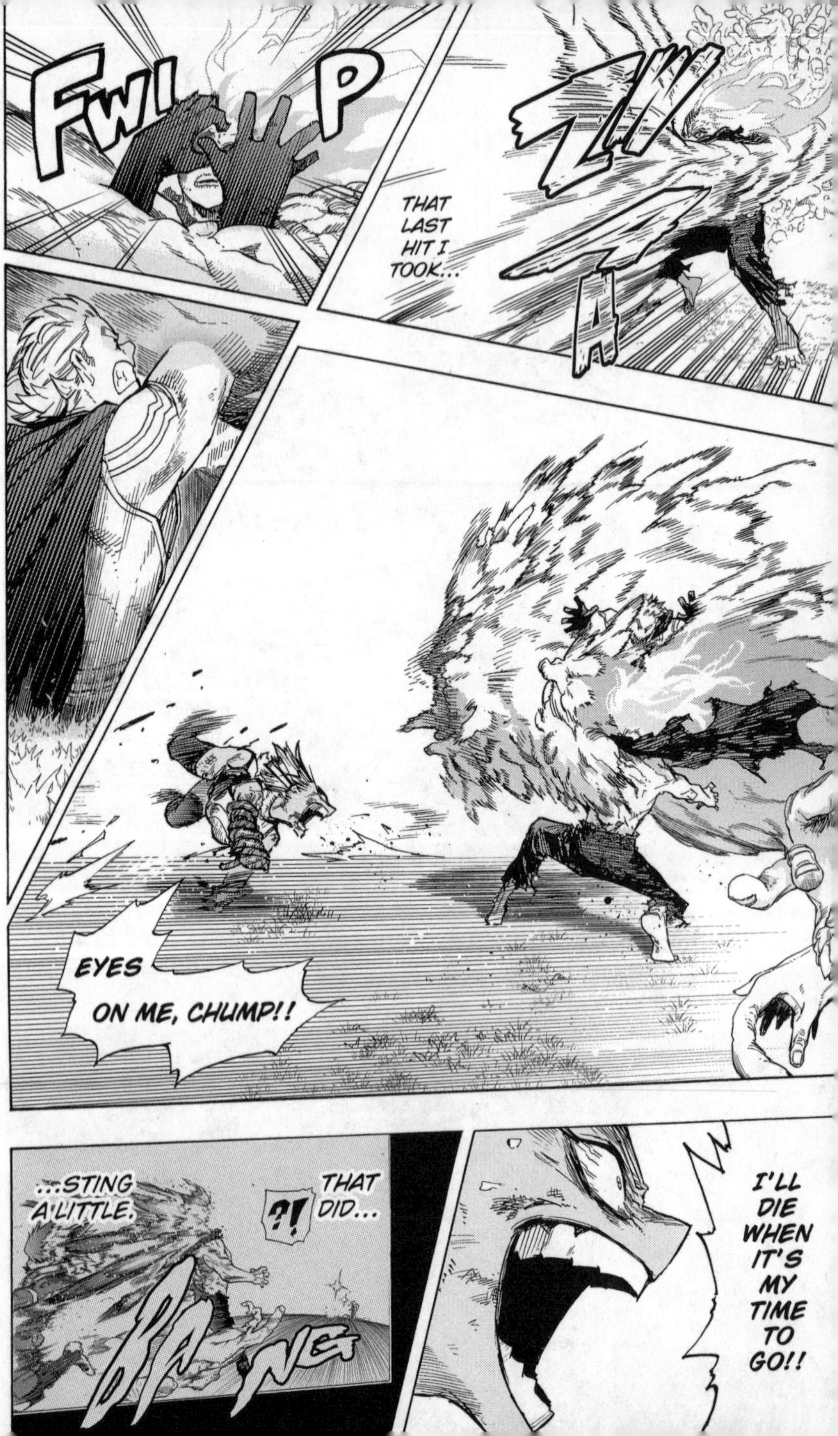
THAT LAST HIT I TOOK...
EYES ON ME, CHUMP!!
I'LL DIE WHEN IT'S MY TIME TO GO!!
THAT DID...
?!
...STING A LITTLE.

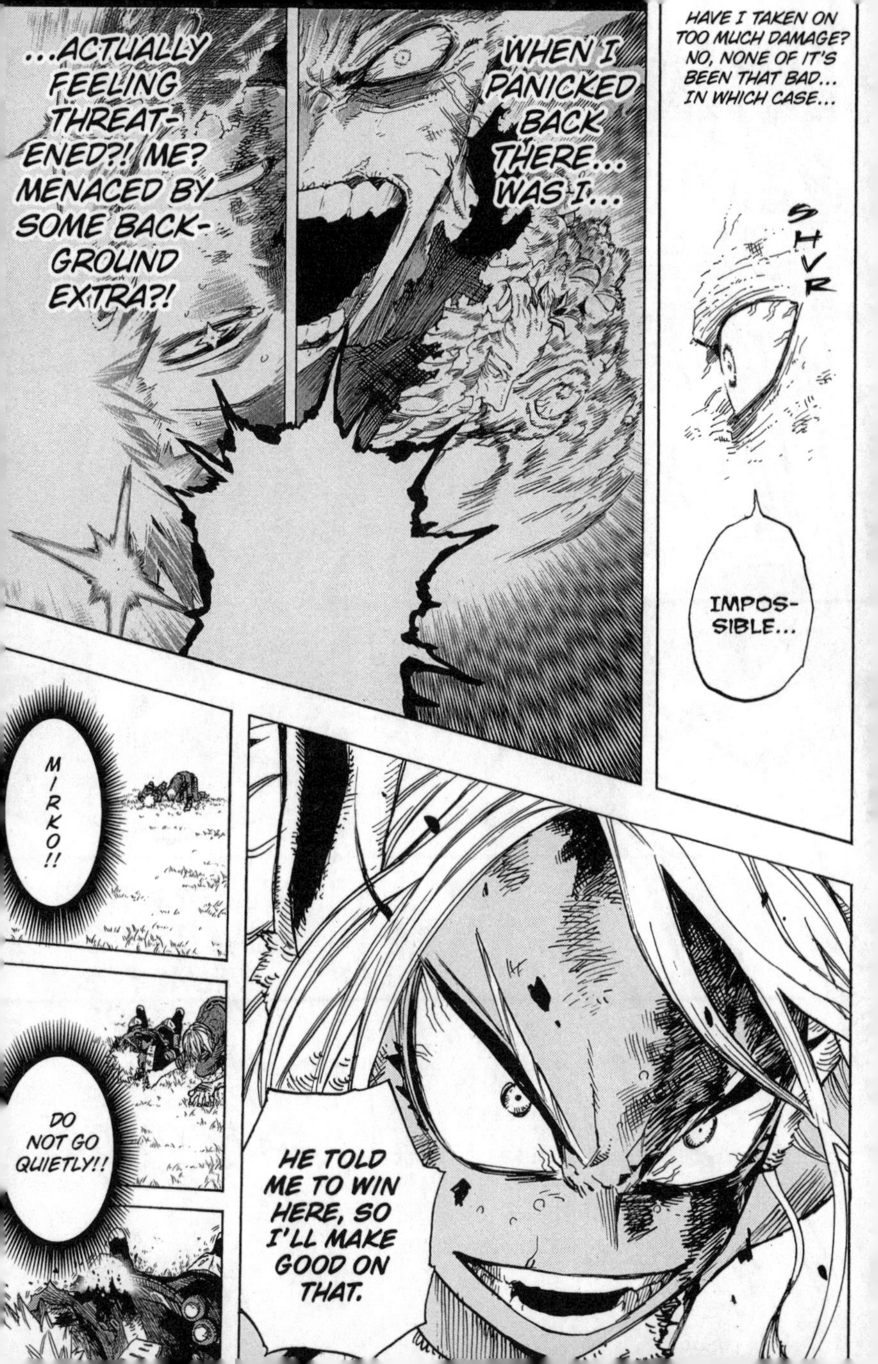
HAVE I TAKEN ON TOO MUCH DAMAGE? NO, NONE OF IT'S BEEN THAT BAD... IN WHICH CASE...
SHVR
IMPOSSIBLE...
WHEN I PANICKED BACK THERE... WAS I...
...ACTUALLY FEELING THREATENED?! ME? MENACED BY SOME BACKGROUND EXTRA?!
HE TOLD ME TO WIN HERE, SO I'LL MAKE GOOD ON THAT.
MIRKO!!
DO NOT GO QUIETLY!!

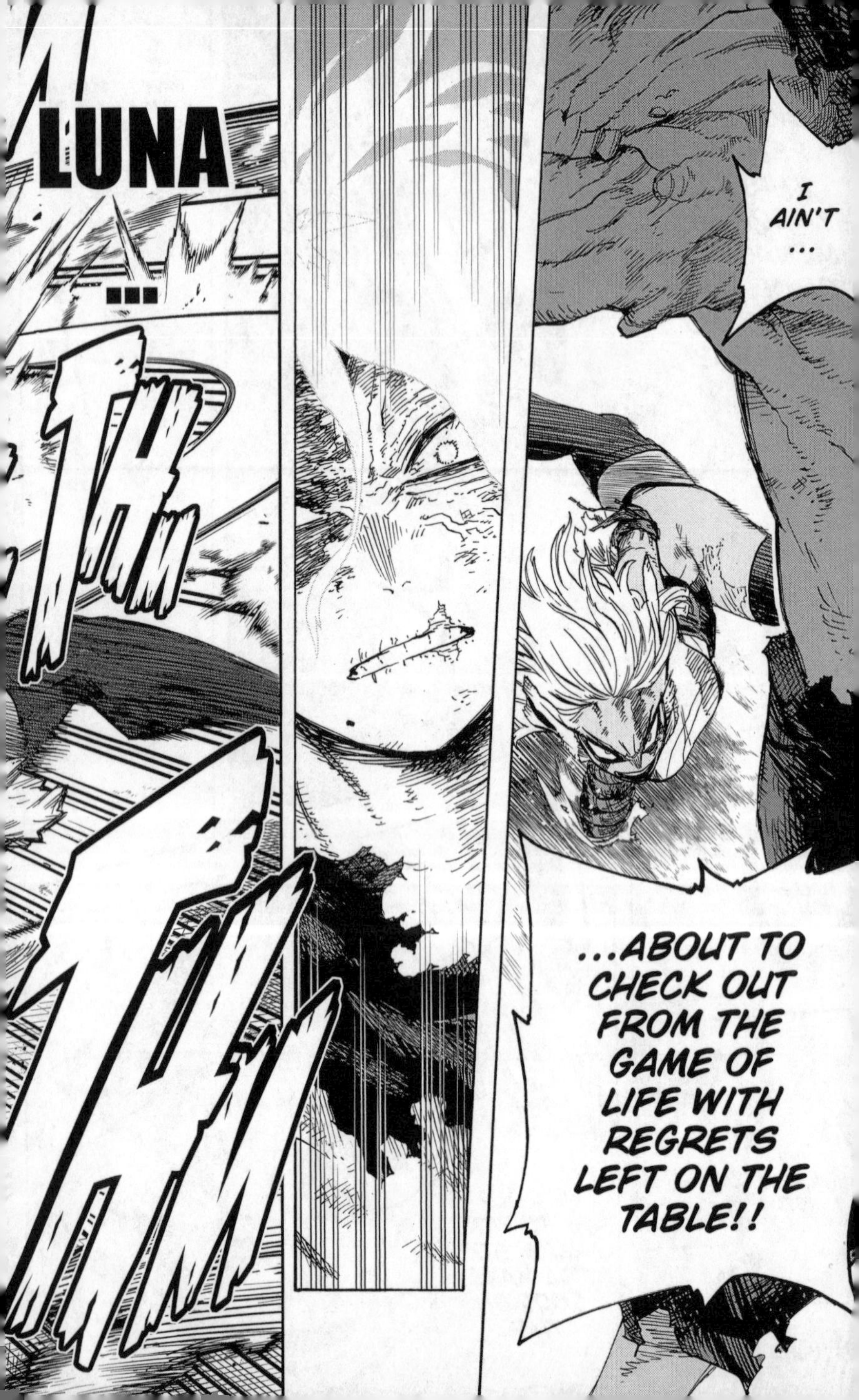
I AIN'T ...
...ABOUT TO CHECK OUT FROM THE GAME OF LIFE WITH REGRETS LEFT ON THE TABLE!!
LUNA ...

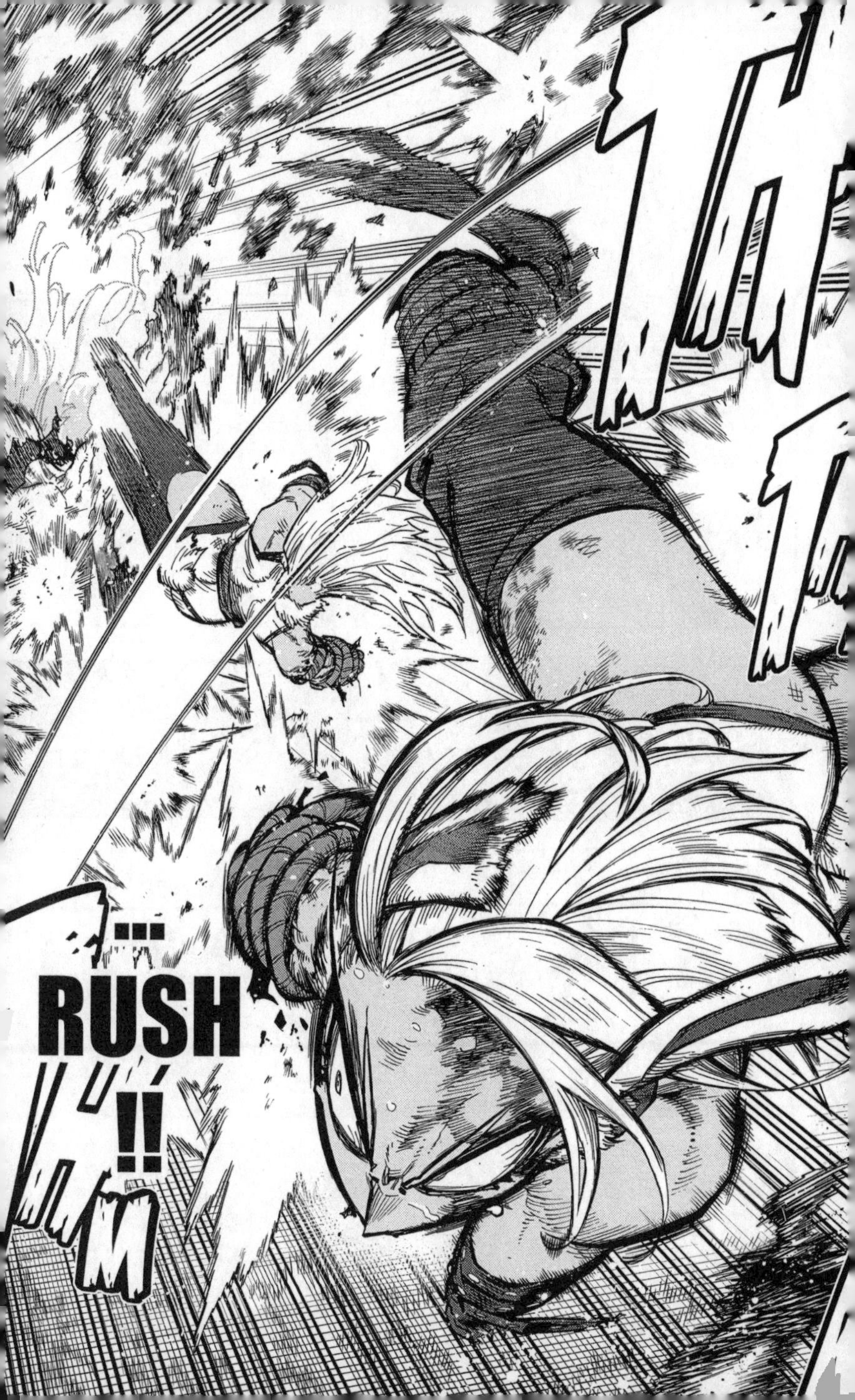
...RUSH!!

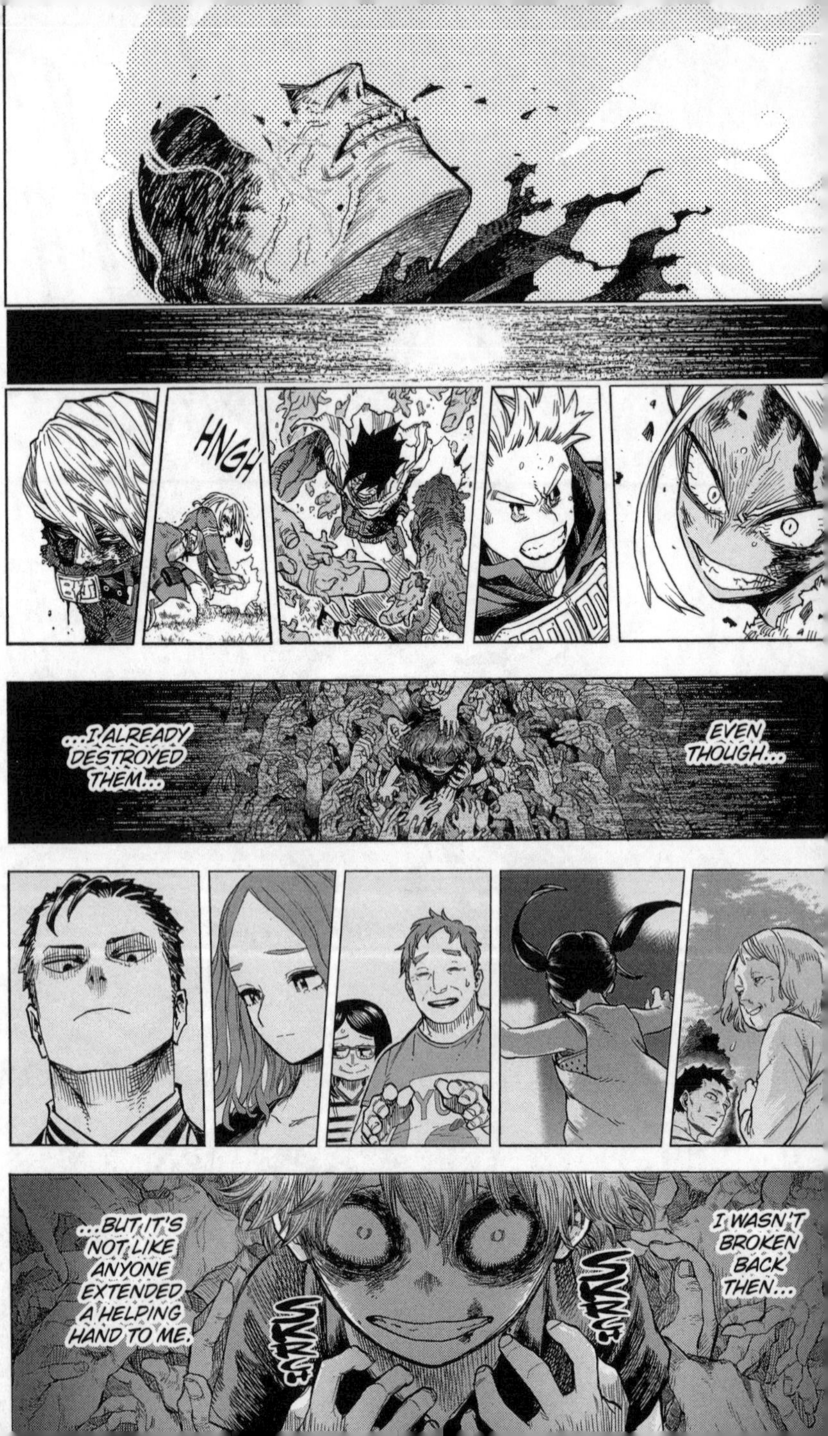
HNGH
EVEN THOUGH...
...I ALREADY DESTROYED THEM...
I WASN'T BROKEN BACK THEN...
...BUT IT'S NOT LIKE ANYONE EXTENDED A HELPING HAND TO ME.

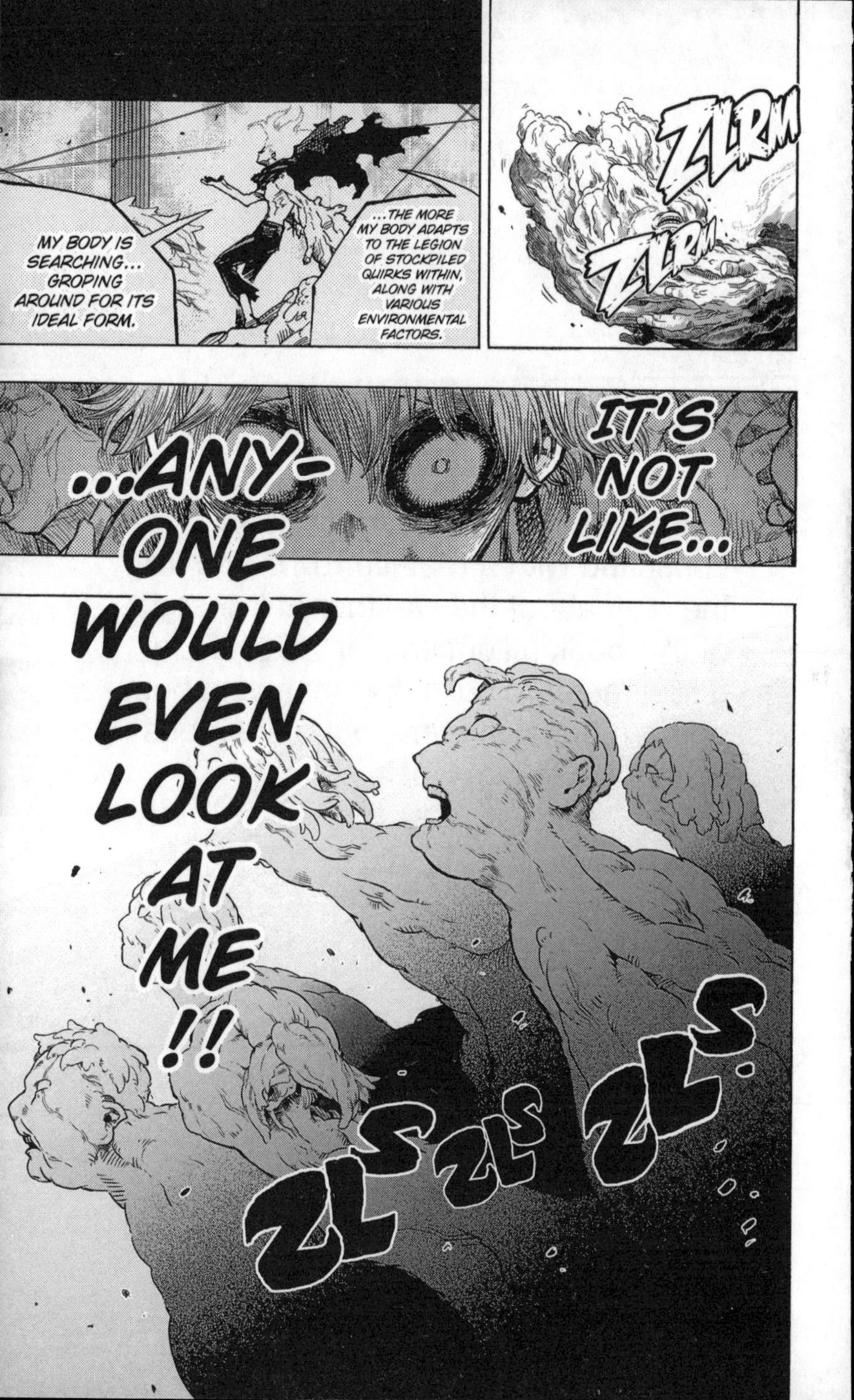
ZLRM
ZLRM
...THE MORE MY BODY ADAPTS TO THE LEGION OF STOCKPILED QUIRKS WITHIN, ALONG WITH VARIOUS ENVIRONMENTAL FACTORS.
MY BODY IS SEARCHING... GROPING AROUND FOR ITS IDEAL FORM.
IT'S NOT LIKE...
...ANY-ONE WOULD EVEN LOOK AT ME!!
ZLS
ZLS
ZLS

For the stuff about heart anatomy, I consulted with a real-life EMT. And for the stuff about the weather at the end of this book (slight spoiler), I talked to a real meteorologist. Big thanks to both of them for taking time out of their busy schedules to pitch in!

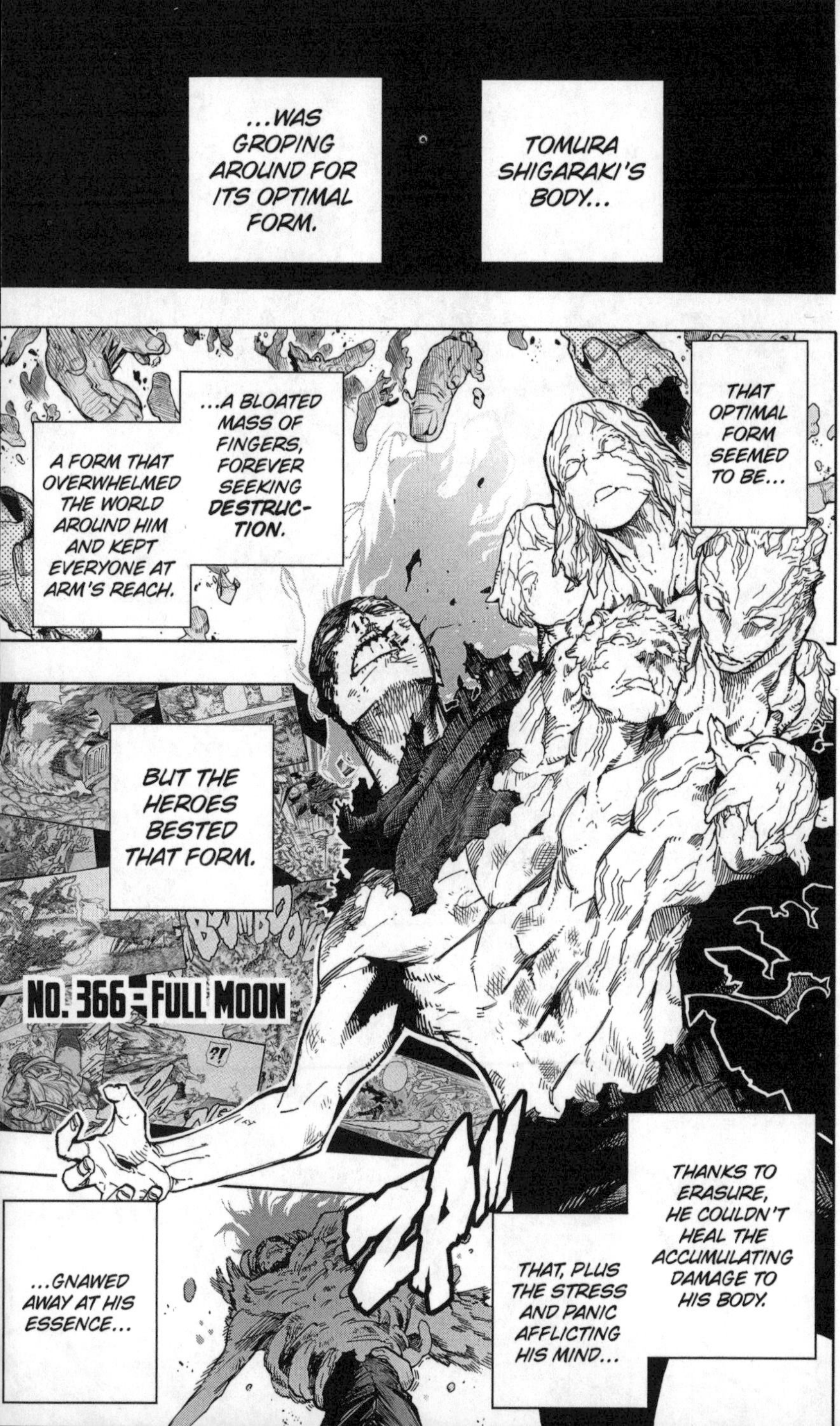
TOMURA SHIGARAKI'S BODY...
...WAS GROPING AROUND FOR ITS OPTIMAL FORM.
THAT OPTIMAL FORM SEEMED TO BE...
...A BLOATED MASS OF FINGERS, FOREVER SEEKING DESTRUCTION.
A FORM THAT OVERWHELMED THE WORLD AROUND HIM AND KEPT EVERYONE AT ARM'S REACH.
BUT THE HEROES BESTED THAT FORM.
NO. 366 = FULL MOON
THANKS TO ERASURE, HE COULDN'T HEAL THE ACCUMULATING DAMAGE TO HIS BODY.
THAT, PLUS THE STRESS AND PANIC AFFLICTING HIS MIND...
...GNAWED AWAY AT HIS ESSENCE...

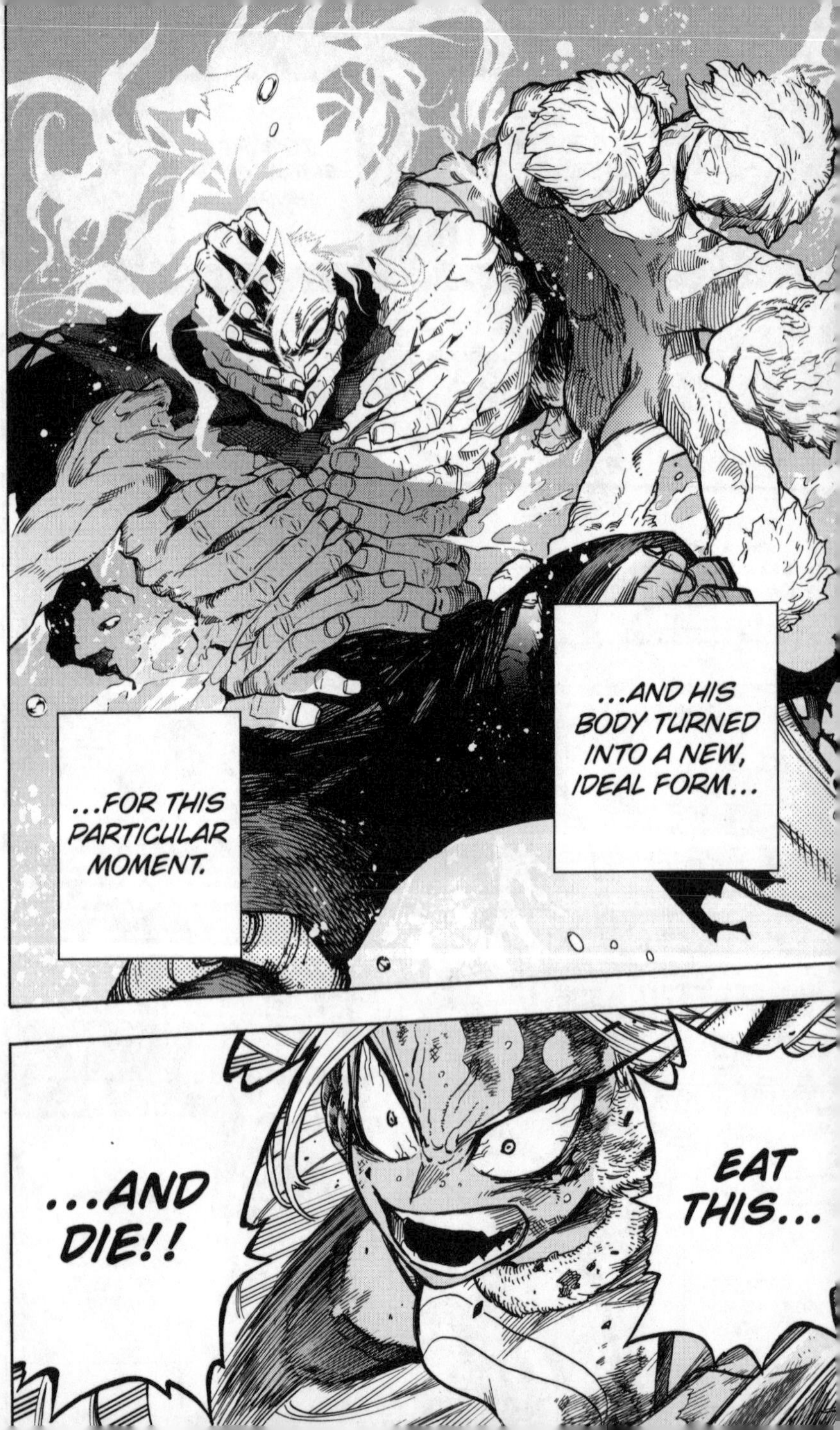
...AND HIS BODY TURNED INTO A NEW, IDEAL FORM...
...FOR THIS PARTICULAR MOMENT.
EAT THIS...
...AND DIE!!

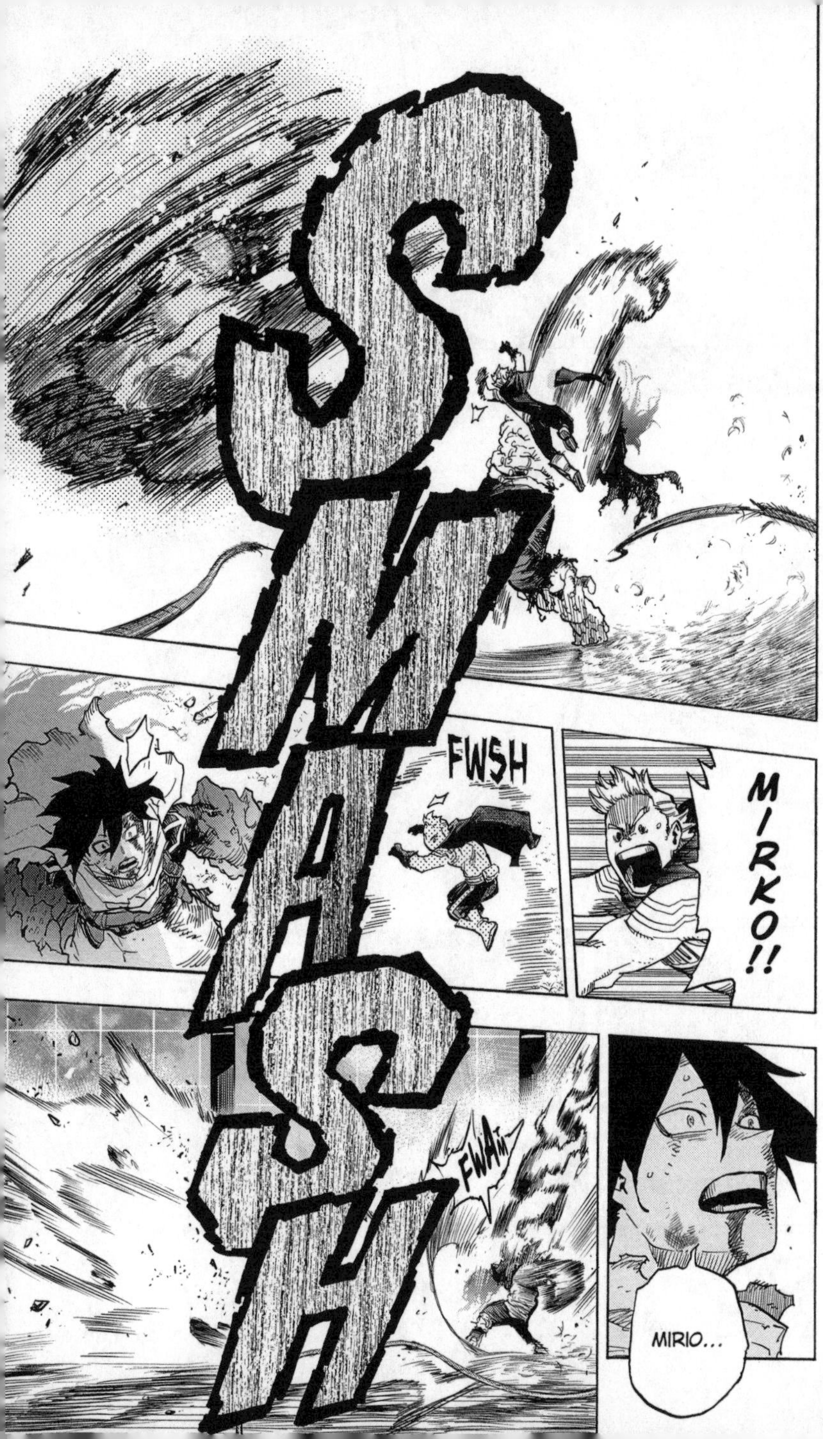
SMASH
MIRKO!!
FWSH
MIRIO...
FWAM

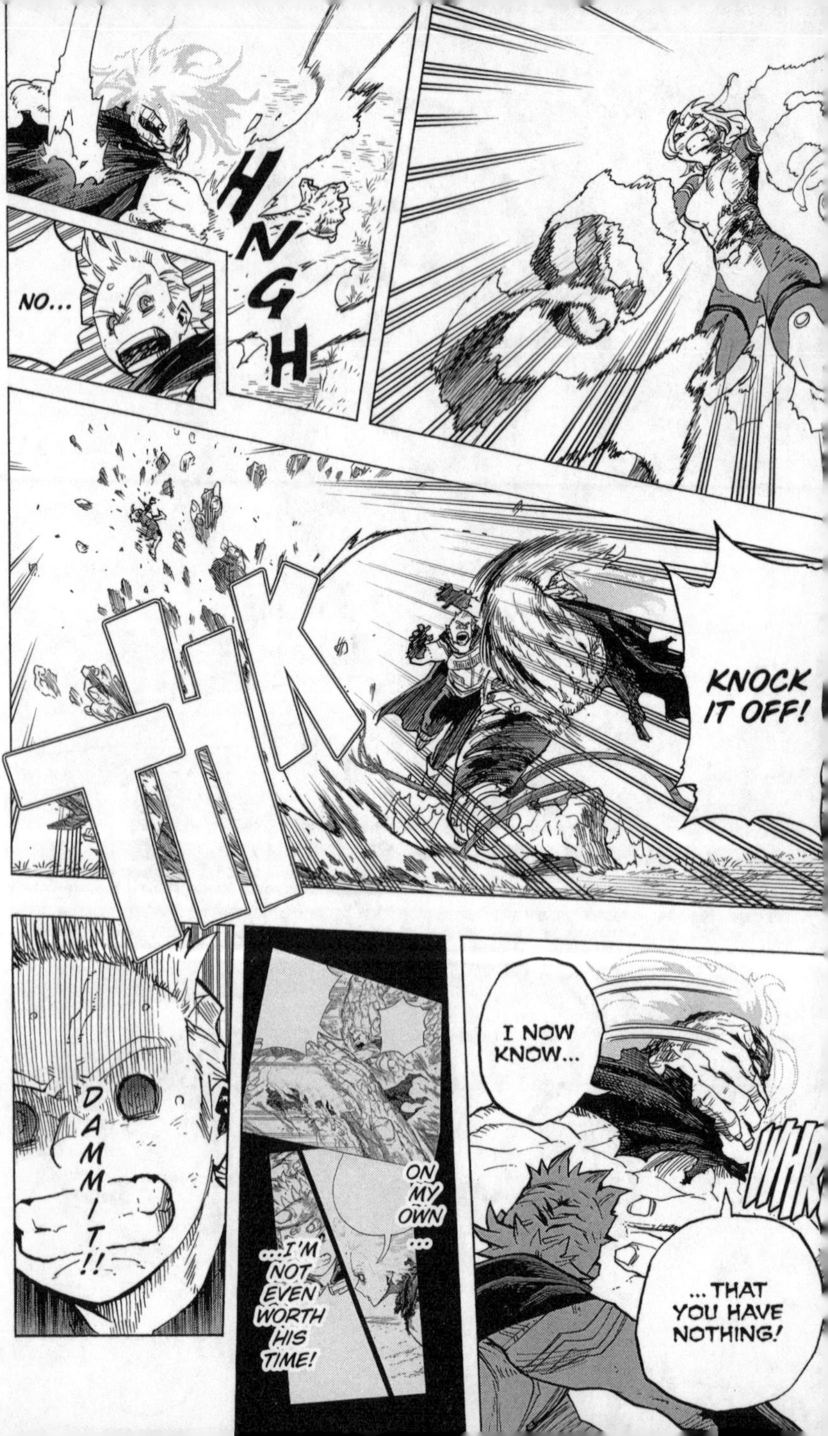
HNGH
NO...
KNOCK IT OFF!
THK
I NOW KNOW...
WHK
...THAT YOU HAVE NOTHING!
ON MY OWN...
...I'M NOT EVEN WORTH HIS TIME!
DAMMIT!!

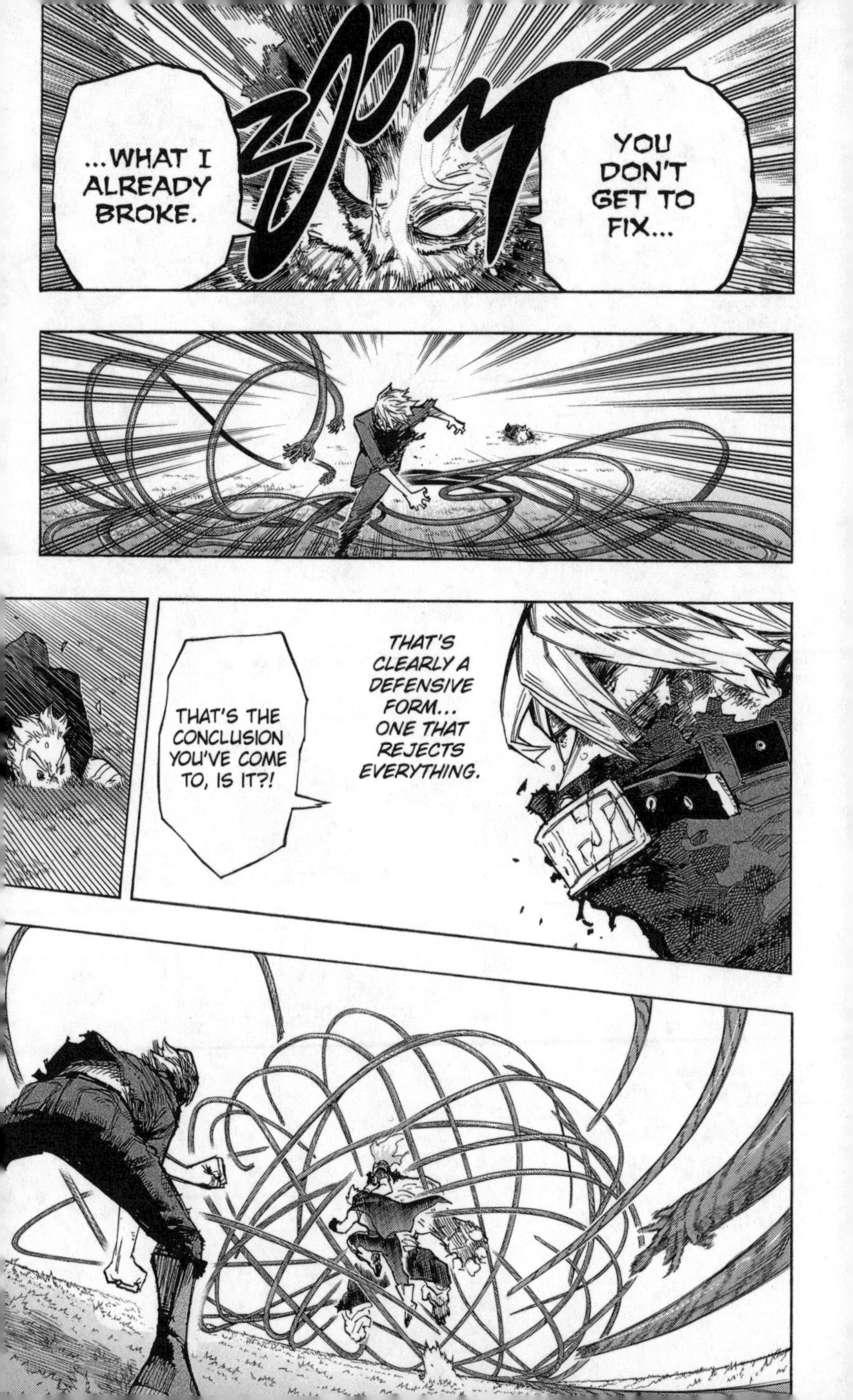
YOU DON'T GET TO FIX...
ZOOM
...WHAT I ALREADY BROKE.
THAT'S CLEARLY A DEFENSIVE FORM... ONE THAT REJECTS EVERYTHING.
THAT'S THE CONCLUSION YOU'VE COME TO, IS IT?!

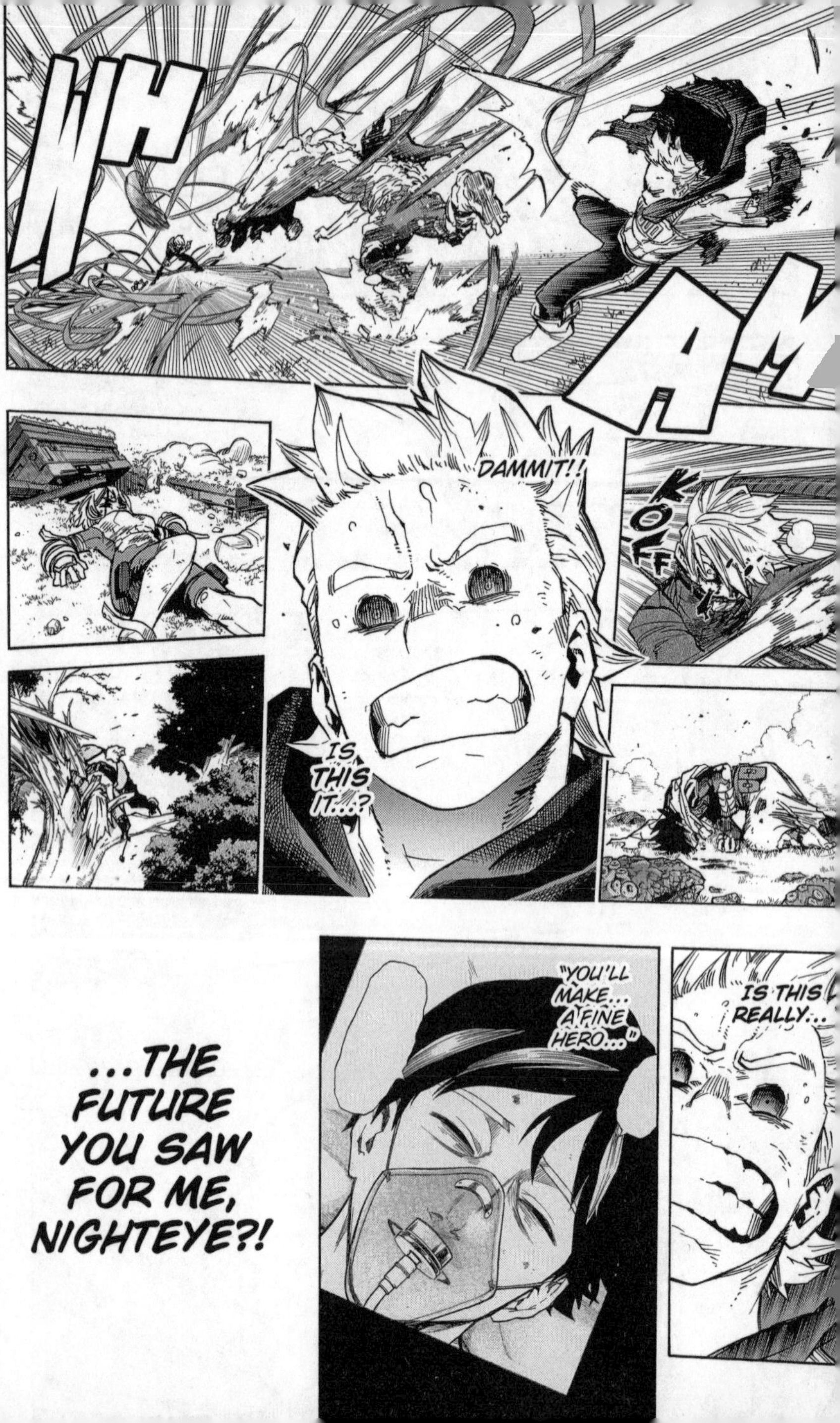
WHAM
KOFF
DAMMIT!!
IS THIS IT...?
IS THIS REALLY...
"YOU'LL MAKE... A FINE HERO..."
...THE FUTURE YOU SAW FOR ME, NIGHTEYE?!

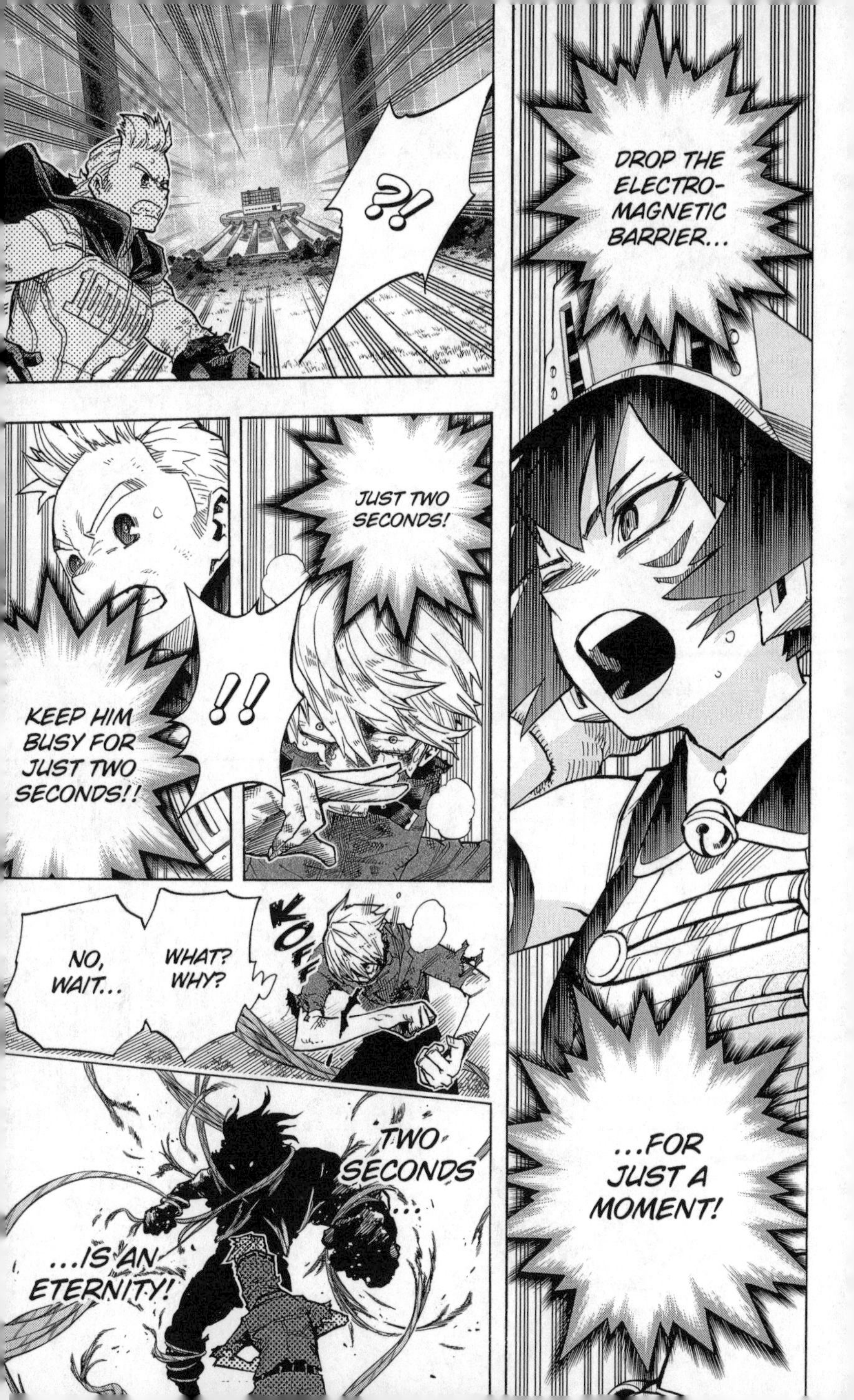
DROP THE ELECTRO-MAGNETIC BARRIER...
...FOR JUST A MOMENT!
?!
JUST TWO SECONDS!
!!
KEEP HIM BUSY FOR JUST TWO SECONDS!!
WHAT? WHY?
NO, WAIT...
TWO SECONDS...
...IS AN ETERNITY!

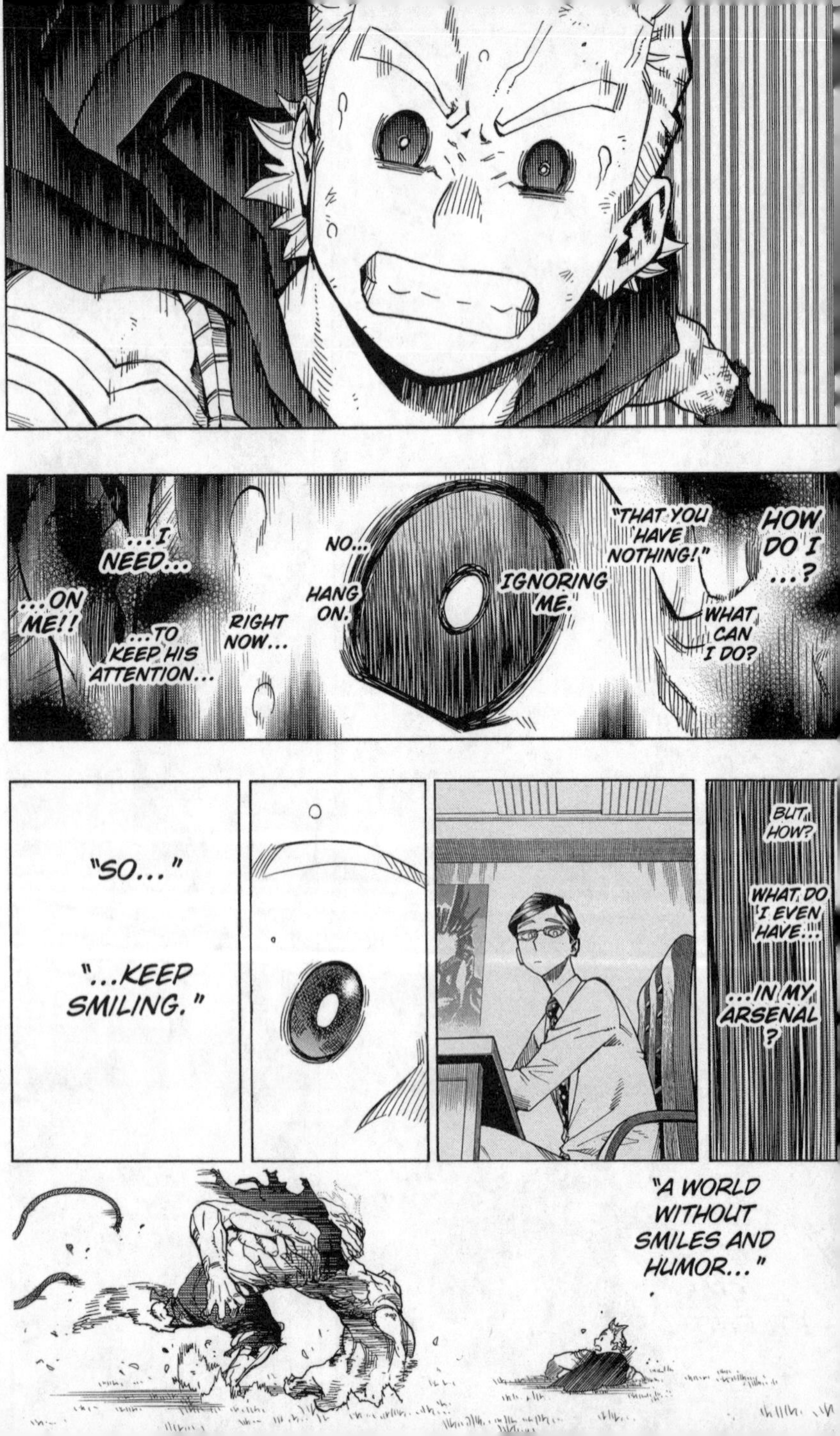
HOW DO I ...?
WHAT CAN I DO?
"THAT YOU HAVE NOTHING!"
IGNORING ME.
NO...
HANG ON.
RIGHT NOW...
...I NEED...
...TO KEEP HIS ATTENTION...
...ON ME!!
BUT HOW?
WHAT DO I EVEN HAVE...
...IN MY ARSENAL?
"SO..."
"...KEEP SMILING."
"A WORLD WITHOUT SMILES AND HUMOR..."

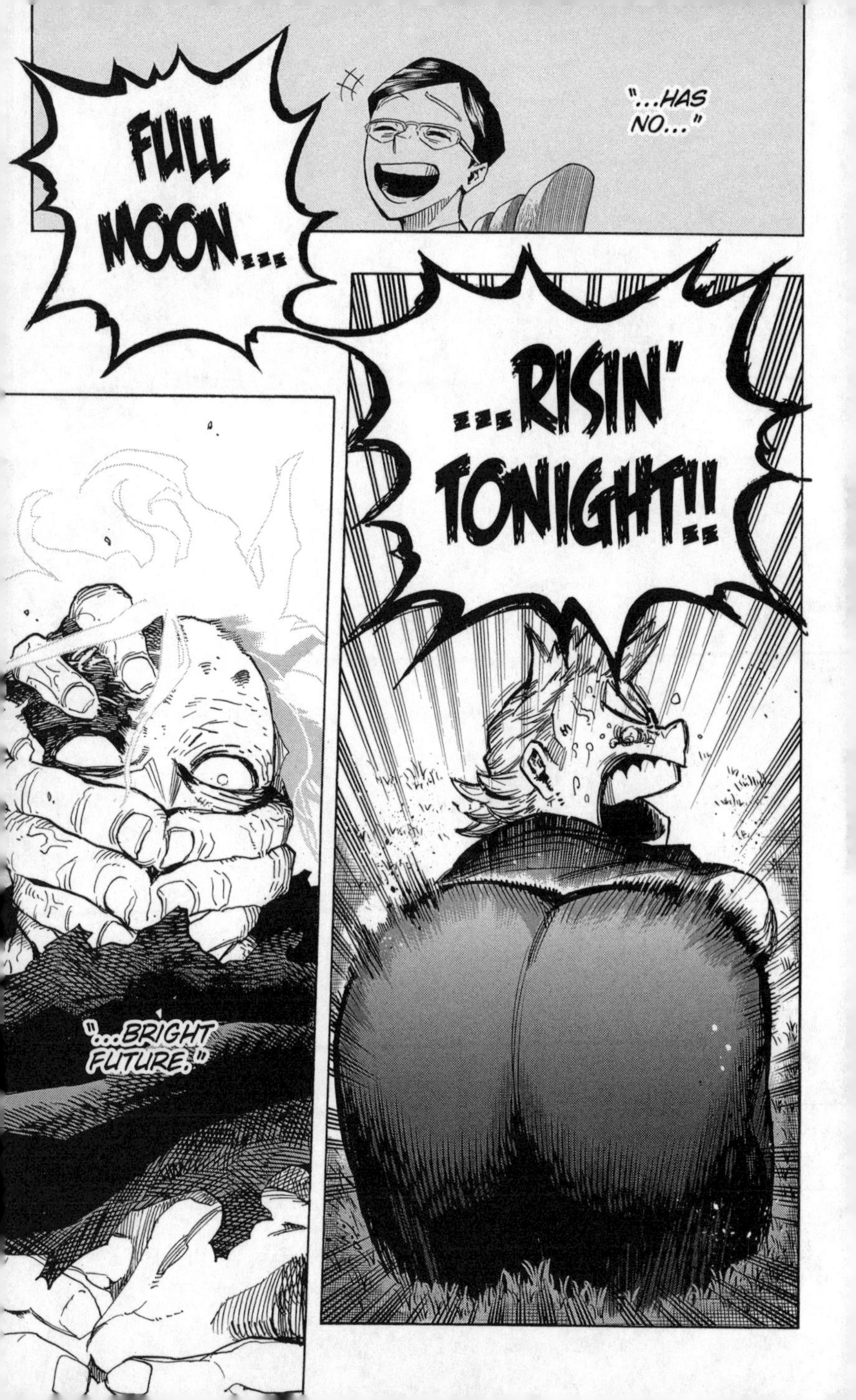
"...HAS NO..."
FULL MOON...
...RISIN' TONIGHT!!
"...BRIGHT FUTURE."

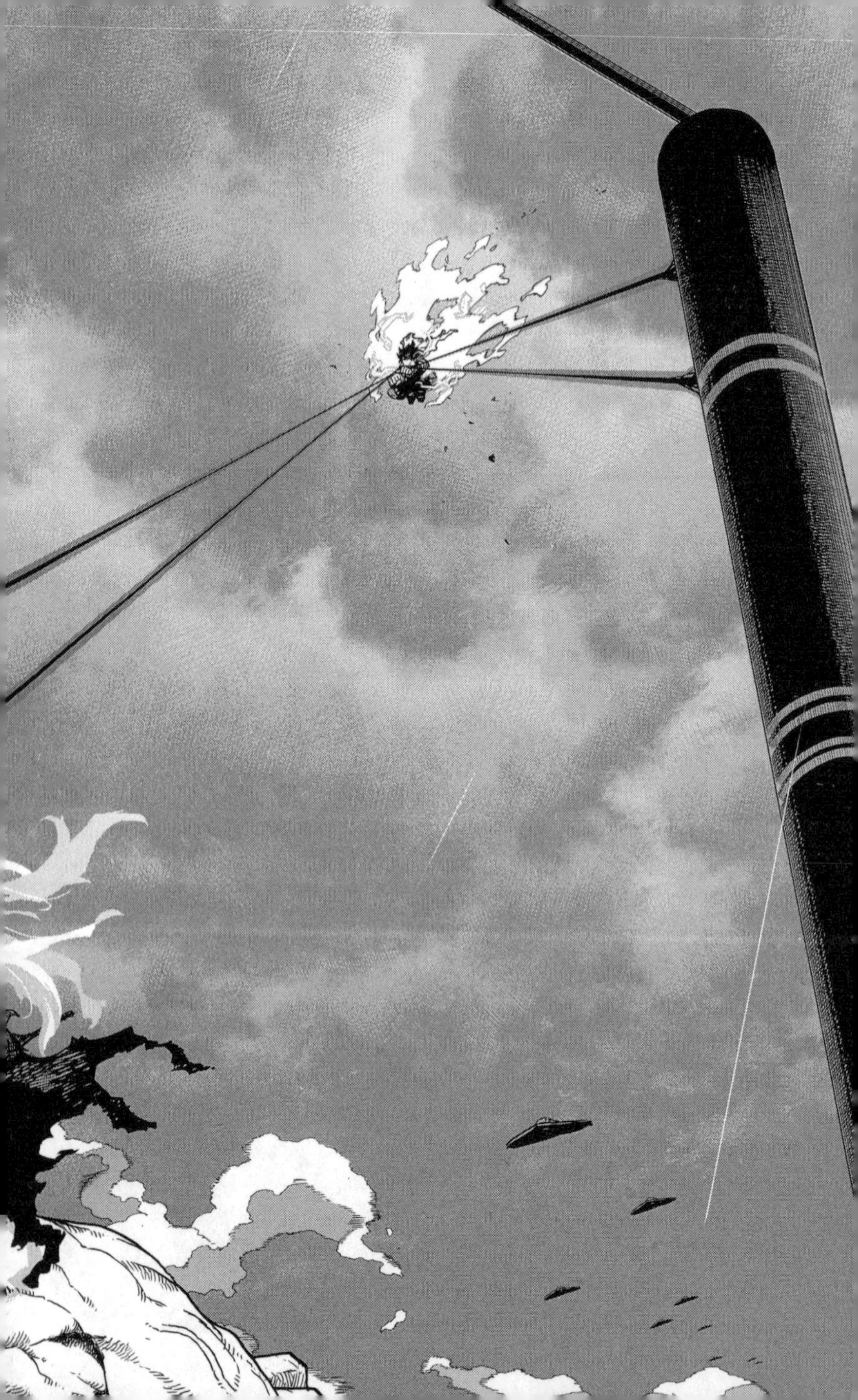

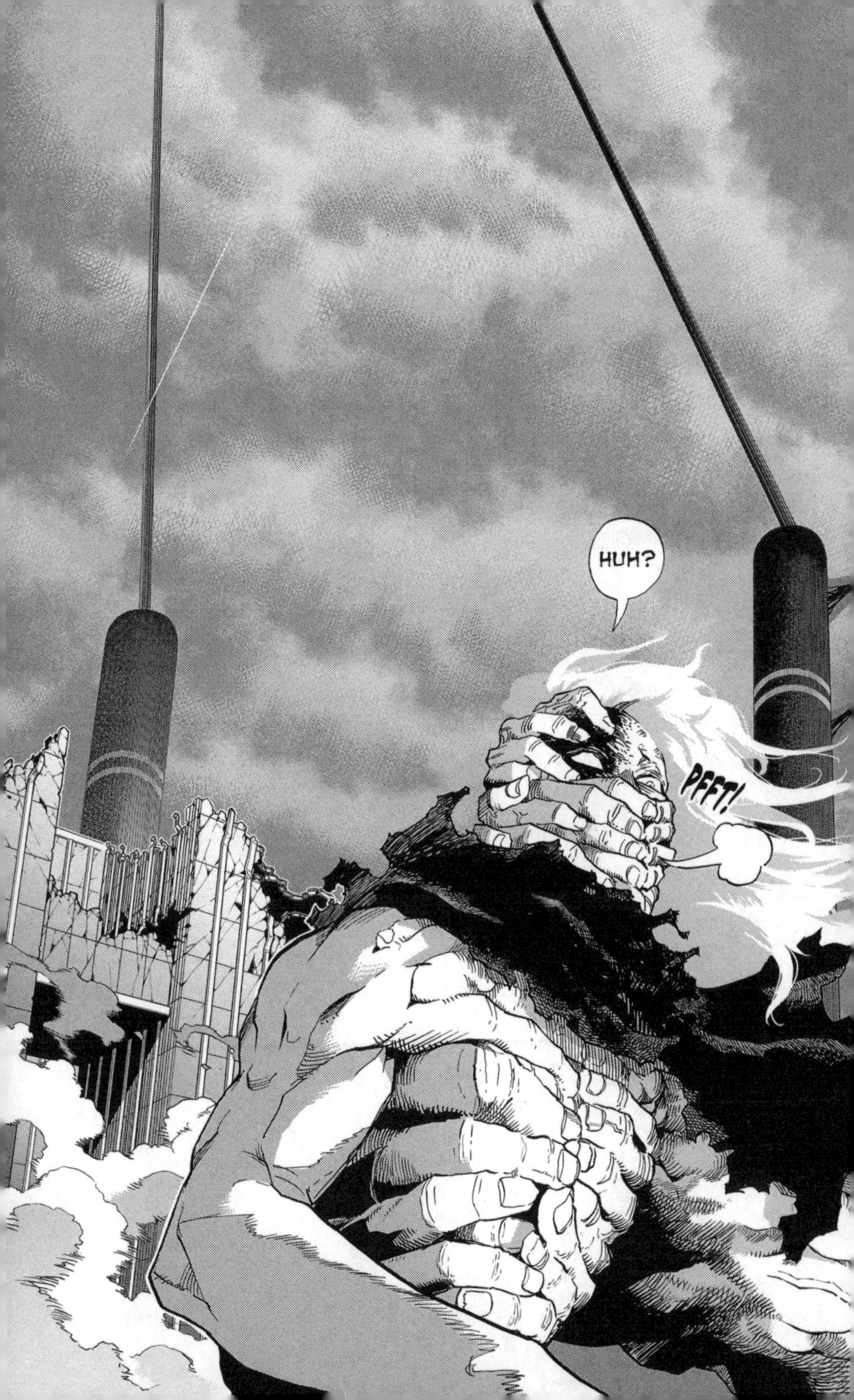
HUH?
PFFT!

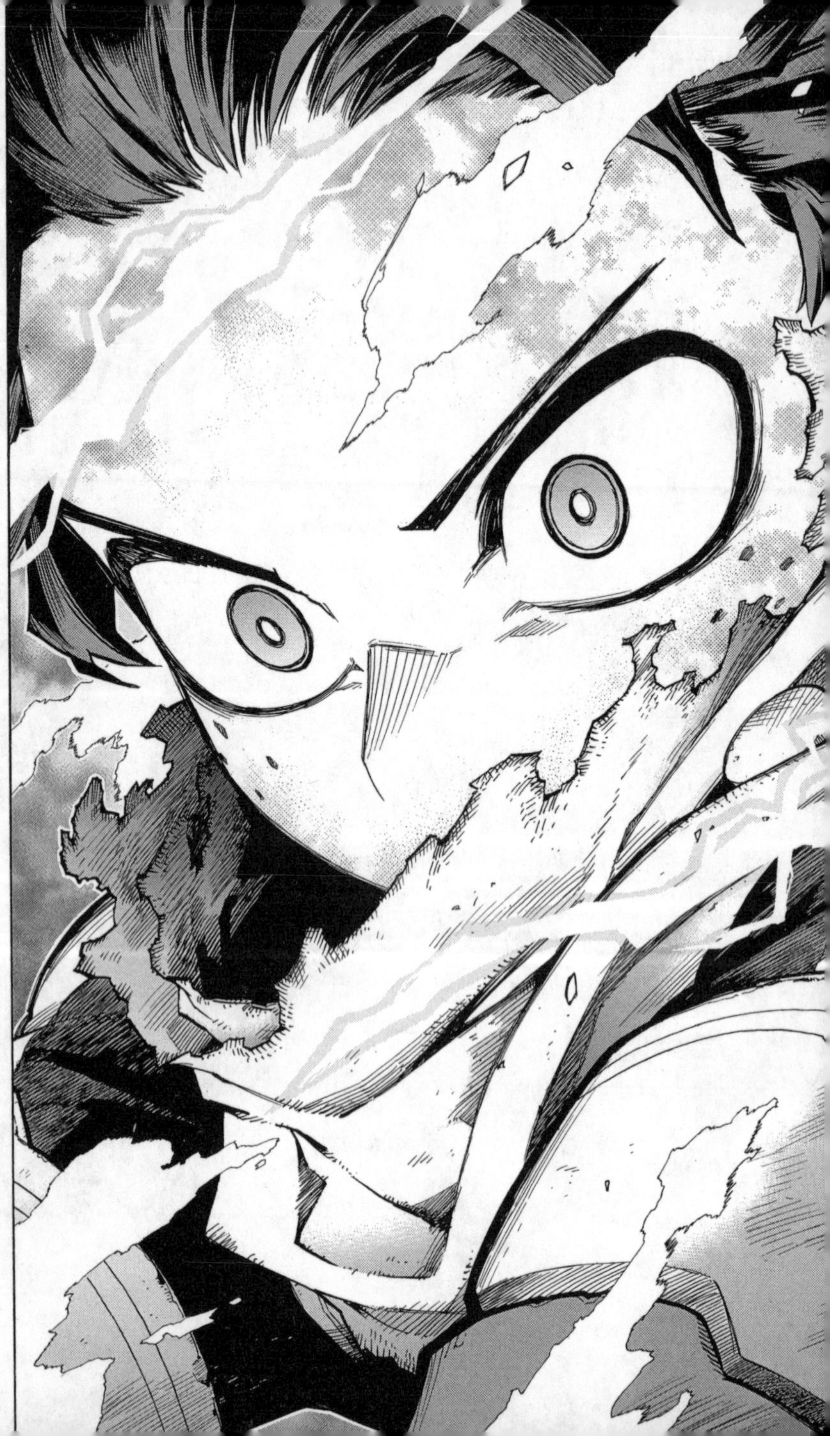

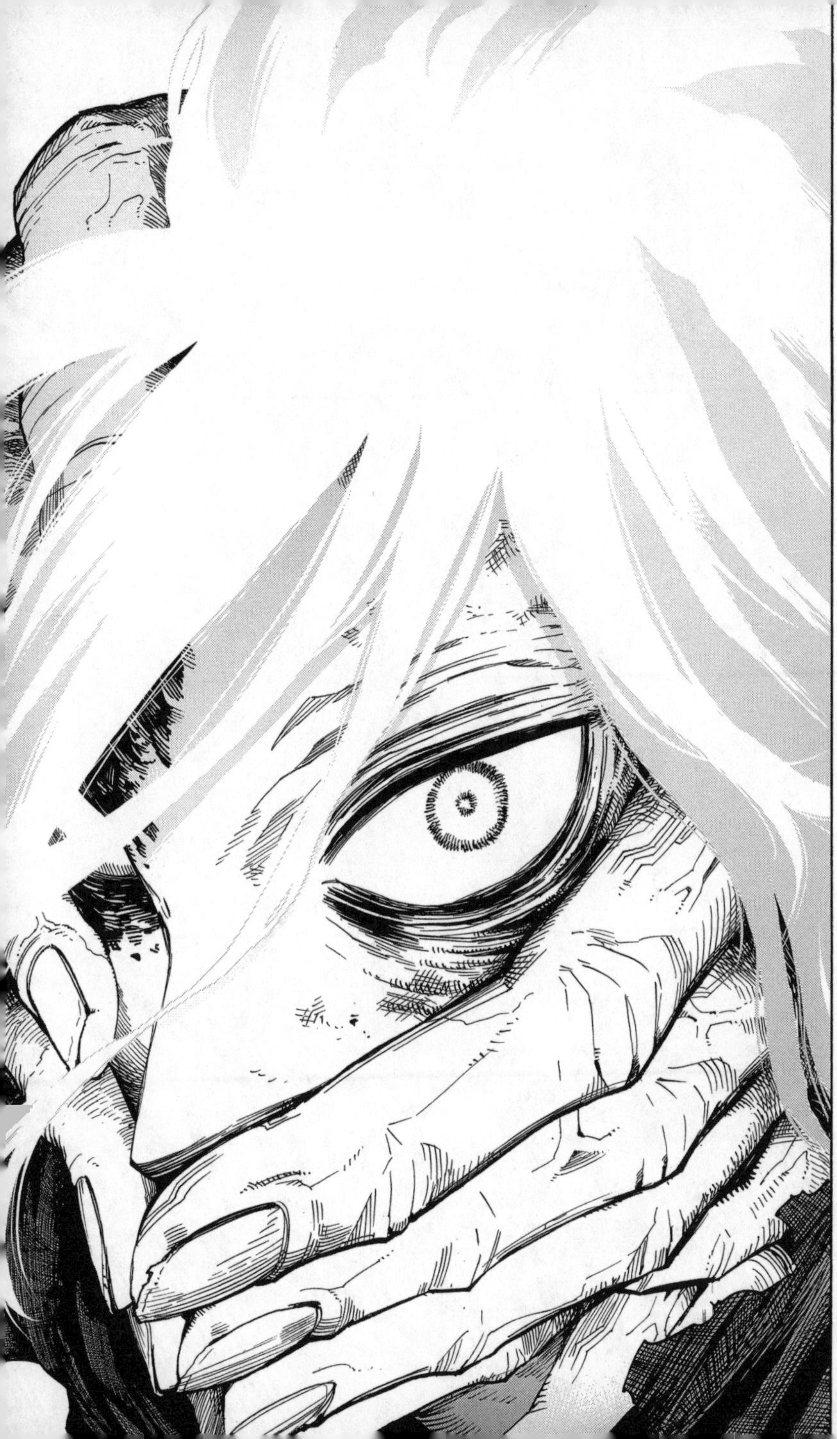

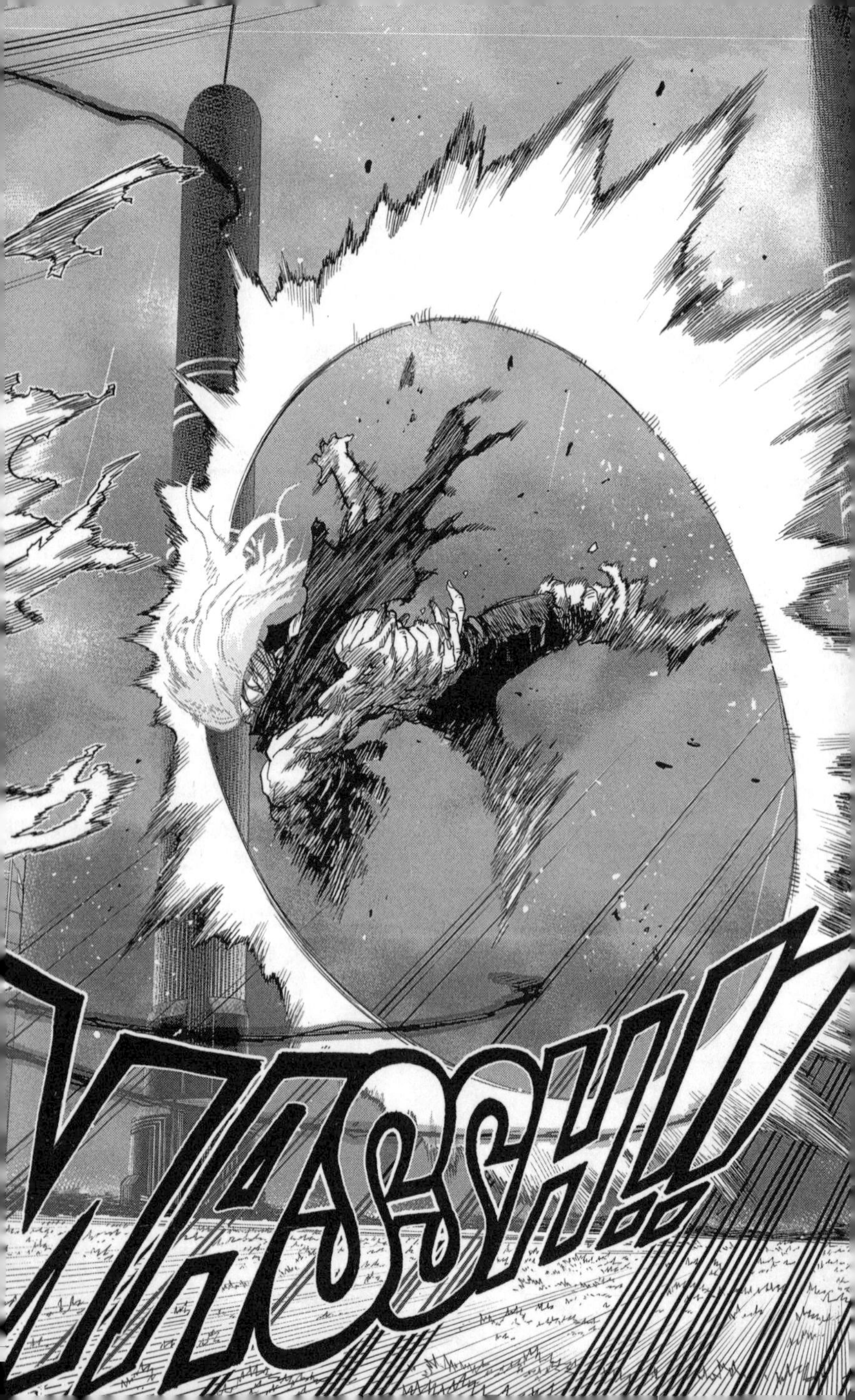

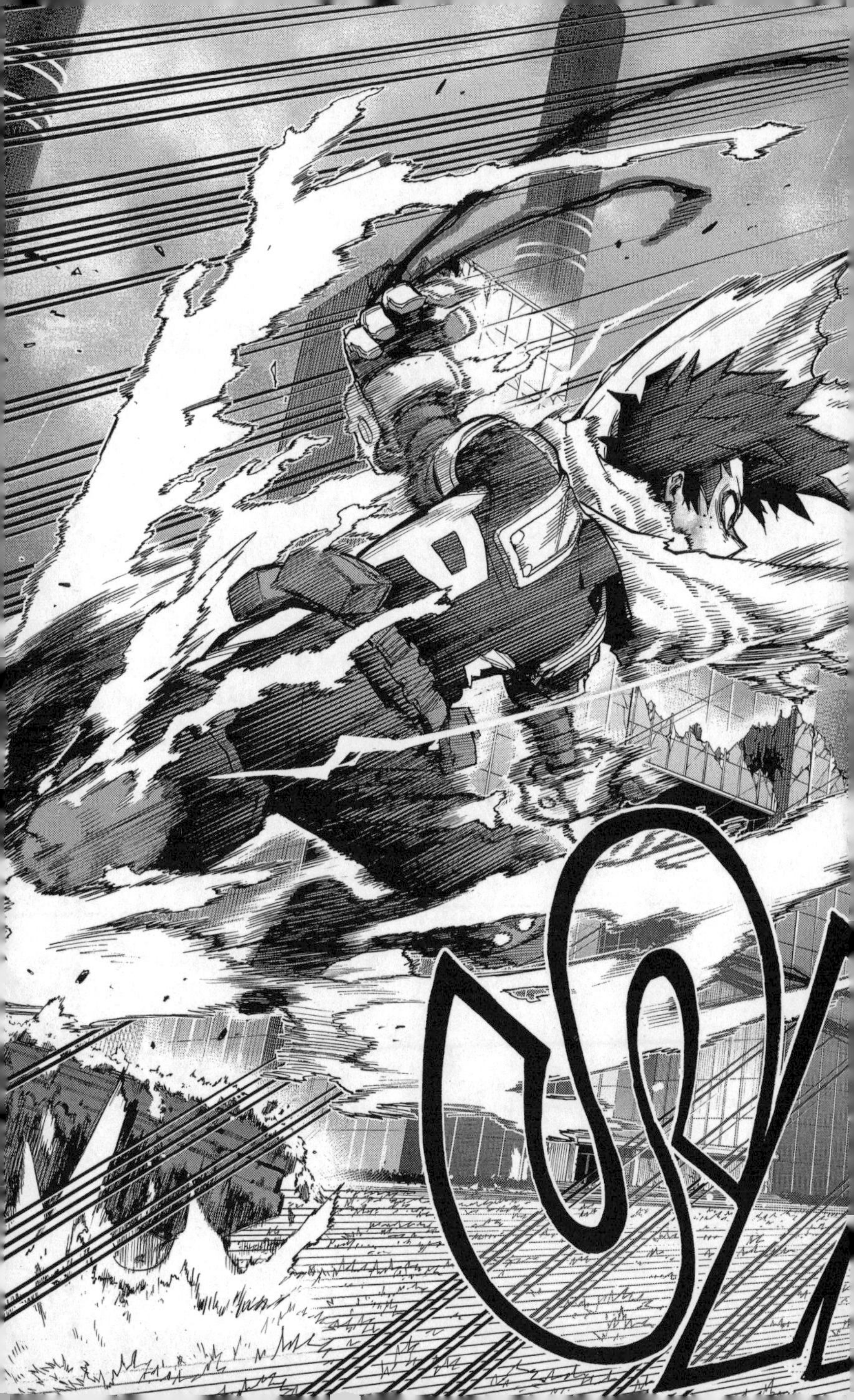

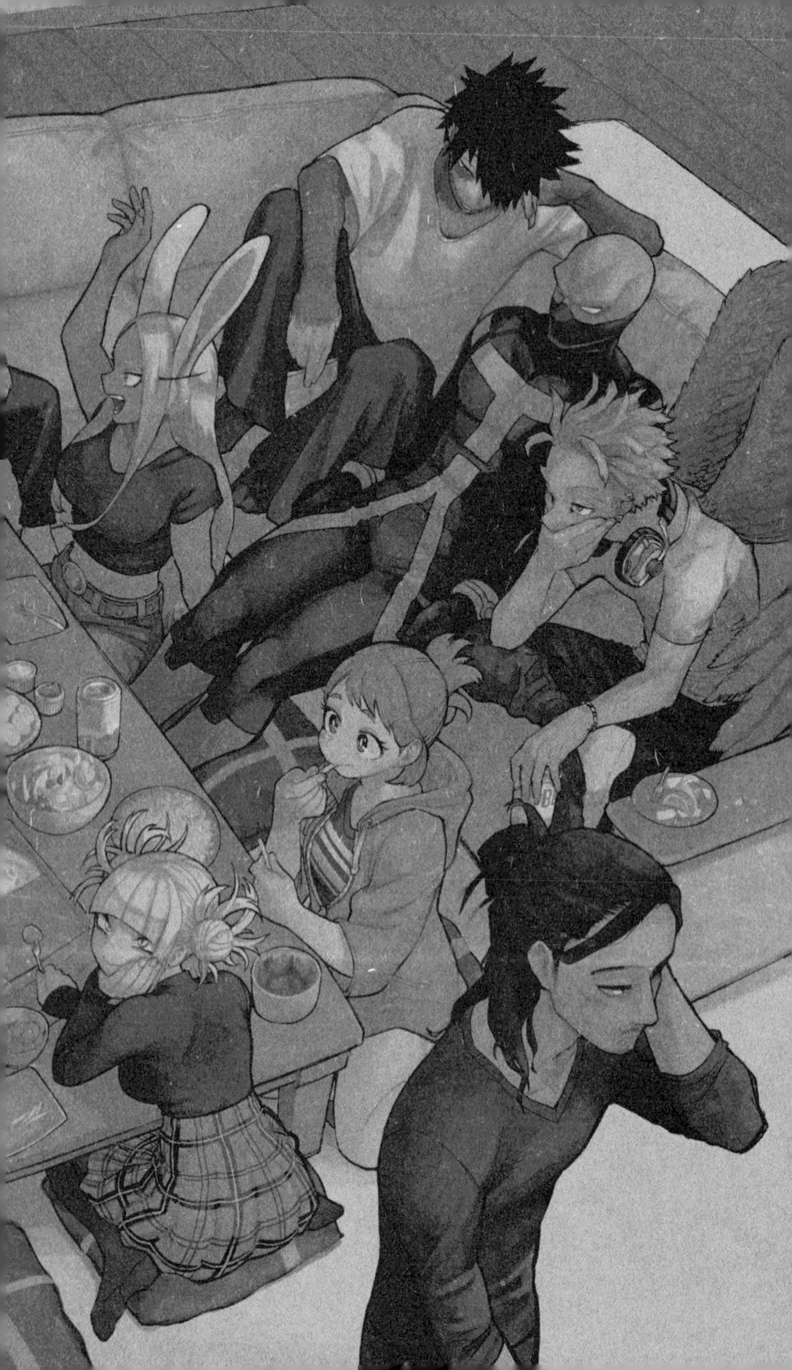

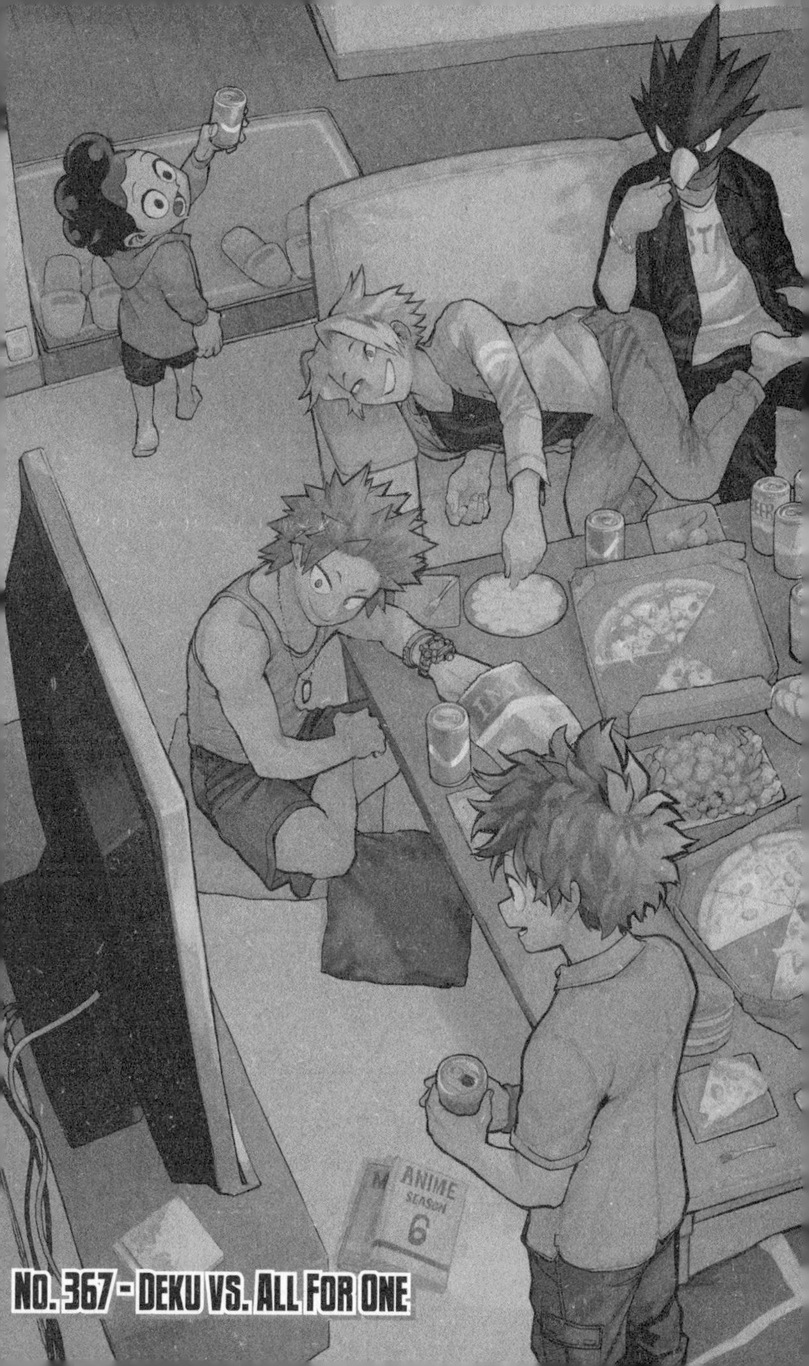
ANIME
SEASON
6

NO. 367 - DEKU VS. ALL FOR ONE

MY HERO ACADEMIA

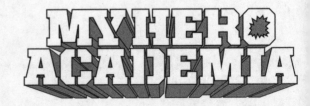

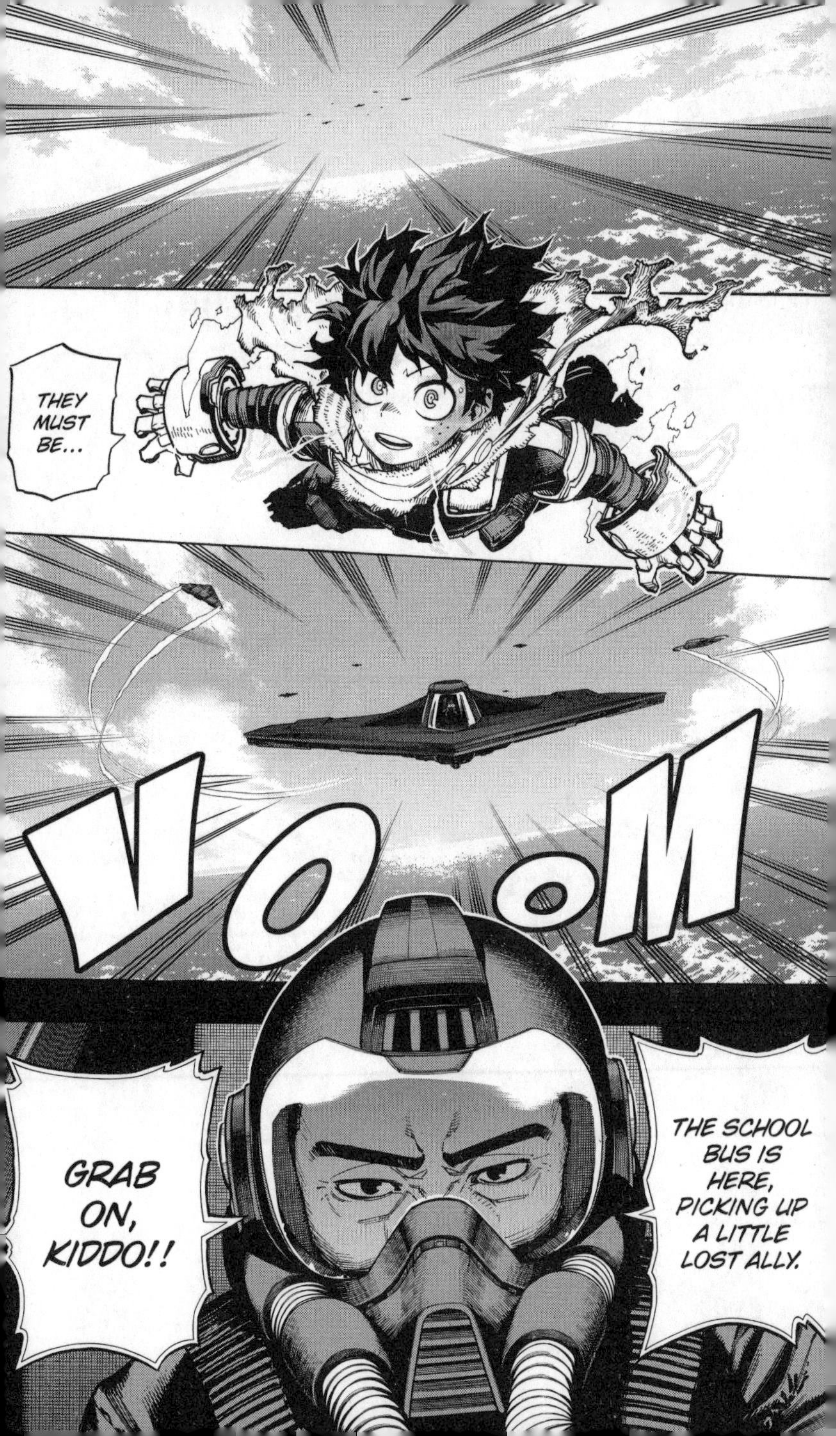
THEY MUST BE...
VOOM
THE SCHOOL BUS IS HERE, PICKING UP A LITTLE LOST ALLY.
GRAB ON, KIDDO!!

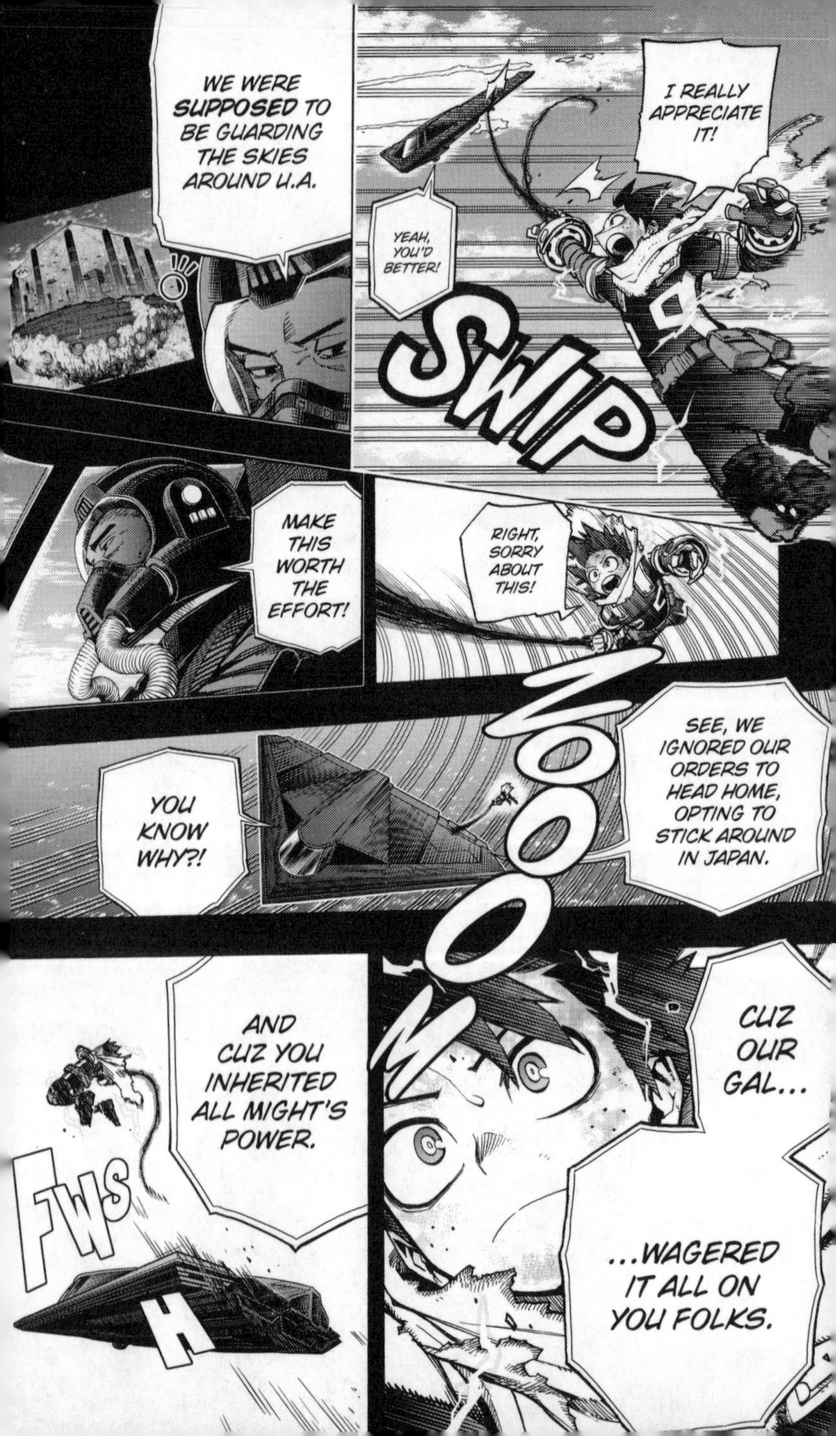
I REALLY APPRECIATE IT!
YEAH, YOU'D BETTER!
SWIP
WE WERE SUPPOSED TO BE GUARDING THE SKIES AROUND U.A.
RIGHT, SORRY ABOUT THIS!
MAKE THIS WORTH THE EFFORT!
NOOOM
SEE, WE IGNORED OUR ORDERS TO HEAD HOME, OPTING TO STICK AROUND IN JAPAN.
YOU KNOW WHY?!
CUZ OUR GAL...
...WAGERED IT ALL ON YOU FOLKS.
AND CUZ YOU INHERITED ALL MIGHT'S POWER.
FWSH

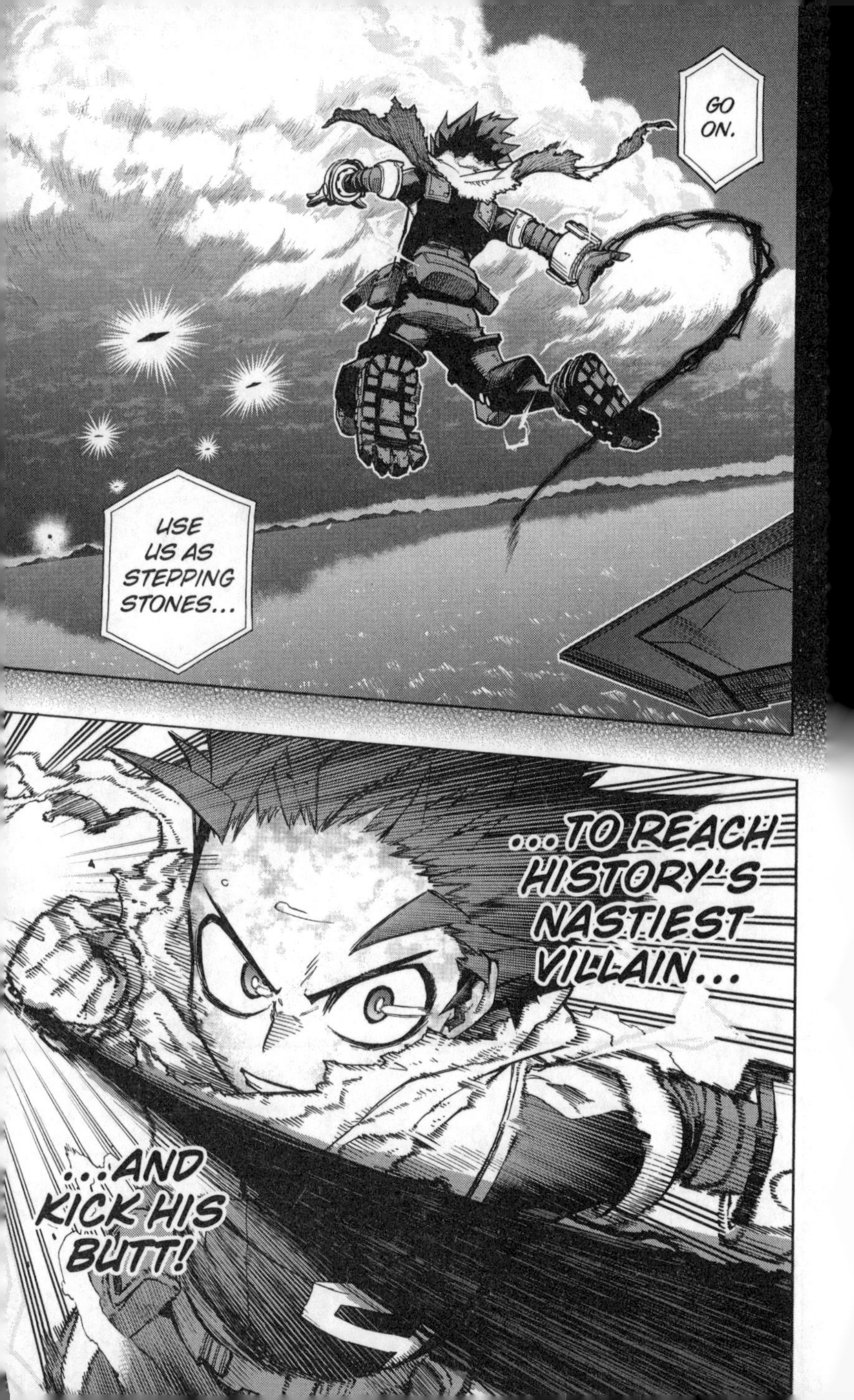
GO ON.
USE US AS STEPPING STONES...
...TO REACH HISTORY'S NASTIEST VILLAIN...
...AND KICK HIS BUTT!

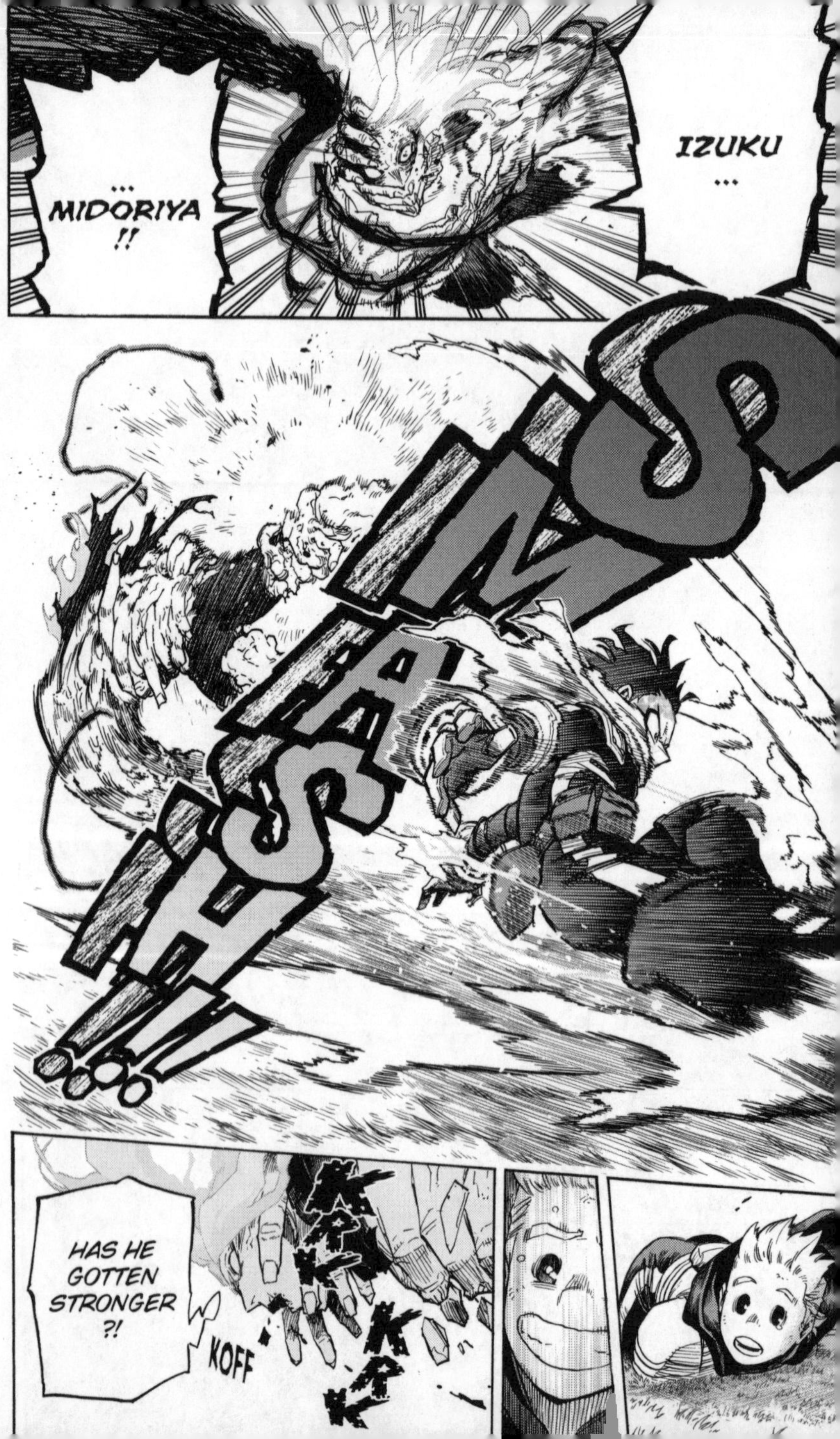
IZUKU ...
... MIDORIYA !!
SHASH!!
KAK
KAK
HAS HE GOTTEN STRONGER ?!
KOFF

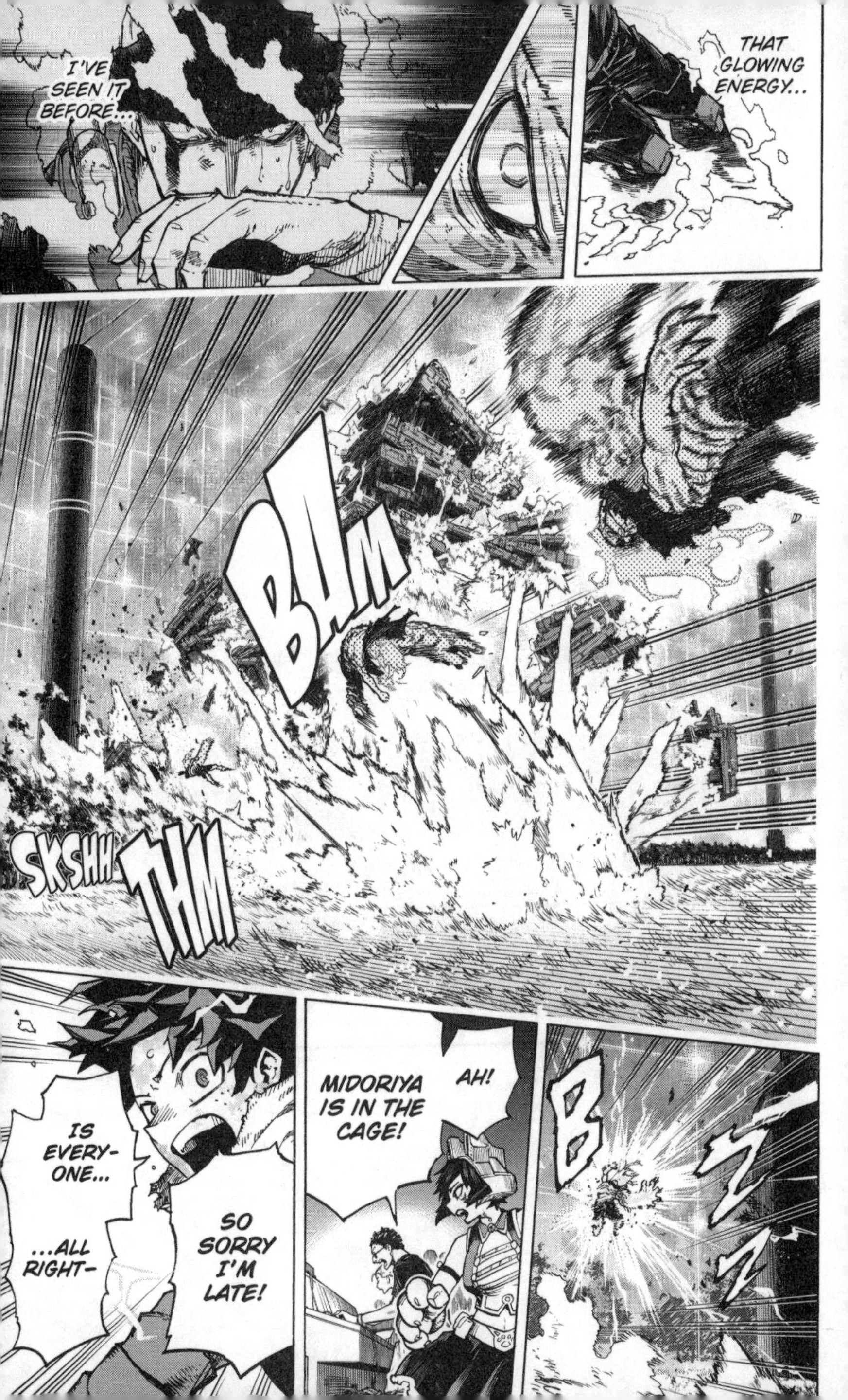
THAT GLOWING ENERGY...
I'VE SEEN IT BEFORE...
BAM
THM
SKSHH
BZZ
AH!
MIDORIYA IS IN THE CAGE!
IS EVERY-ONE...
...ALL RIGHT-
SO SORRY I'M LATE!

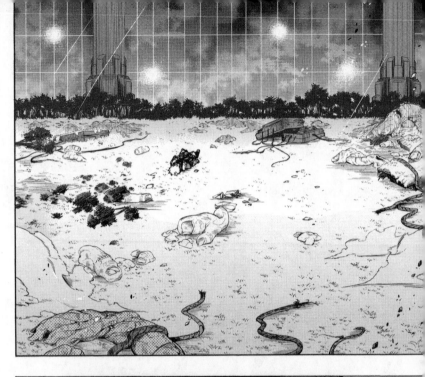

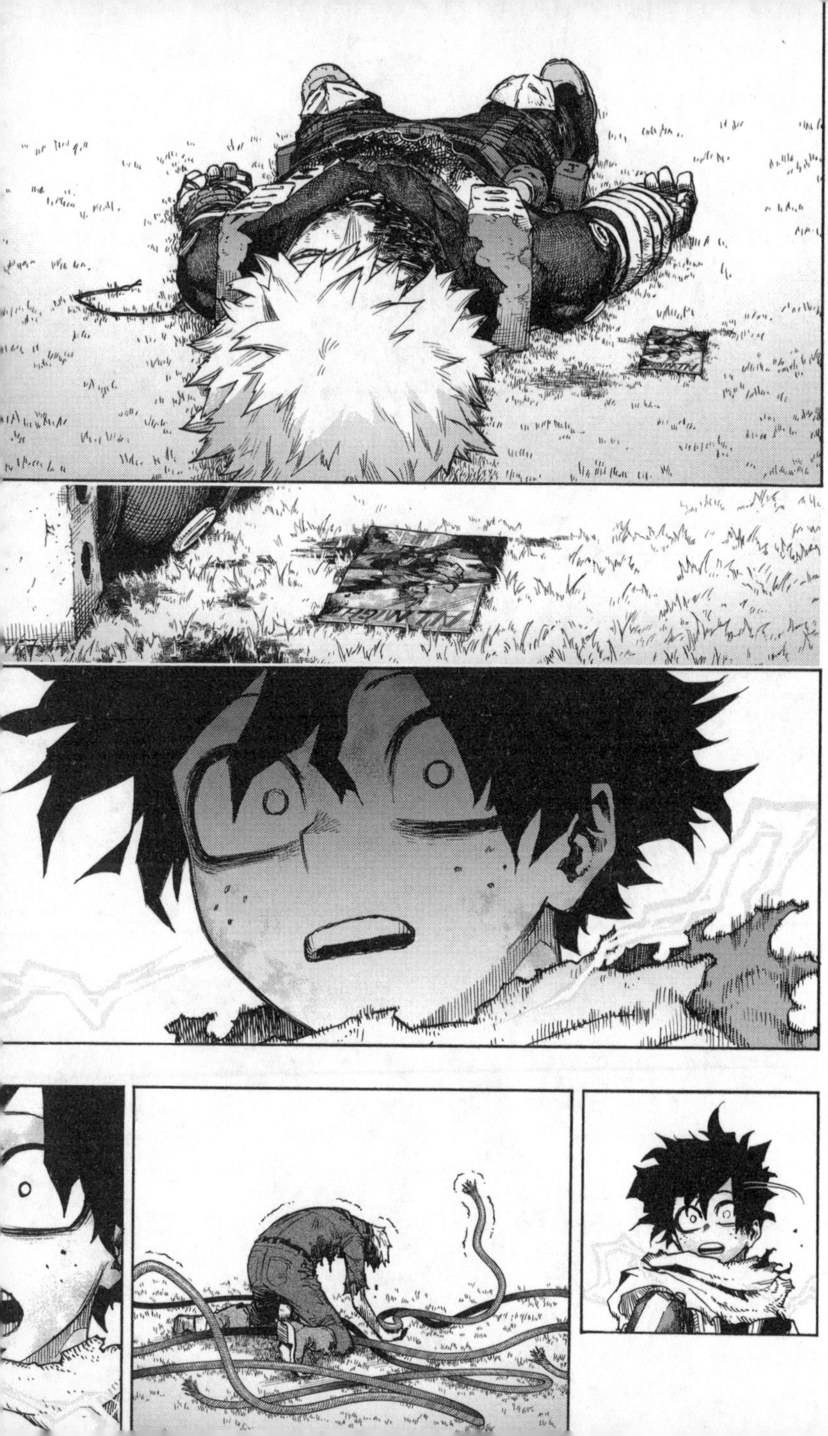

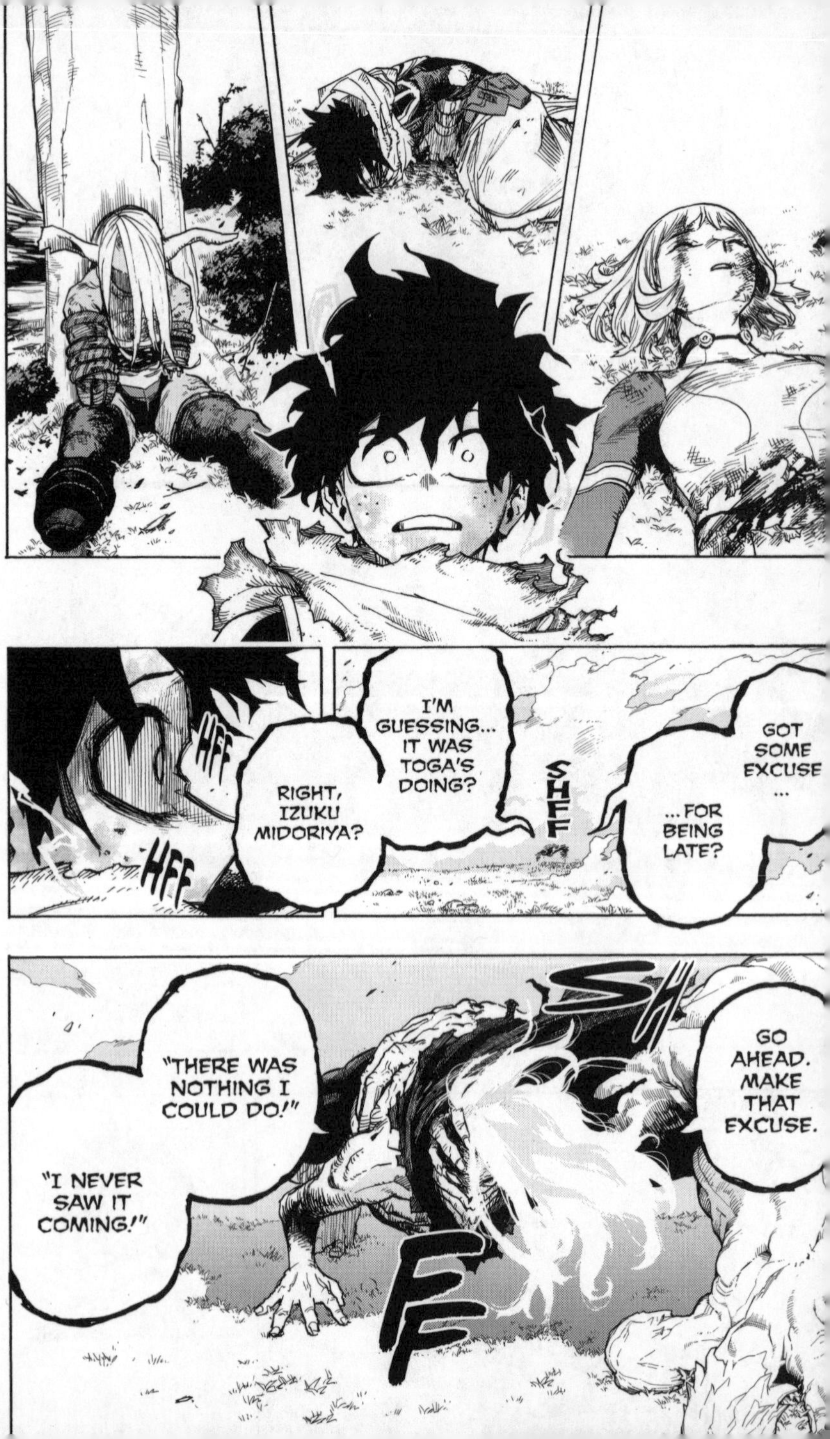
GOT SOME EXCUSE ...
...FOR BEING LATE?
SHFF
I'M GUESSING... IT WAS TOGA'S DOING?
RIGHT, IZUKU MIDORIYA?
HFF
HFF
GO AHEAD. MAKE THAT EXCUSE.
SH
"THERE WAS NOTHING I COULD DO!"
"I NEVER SAW IT COMING!"
FF

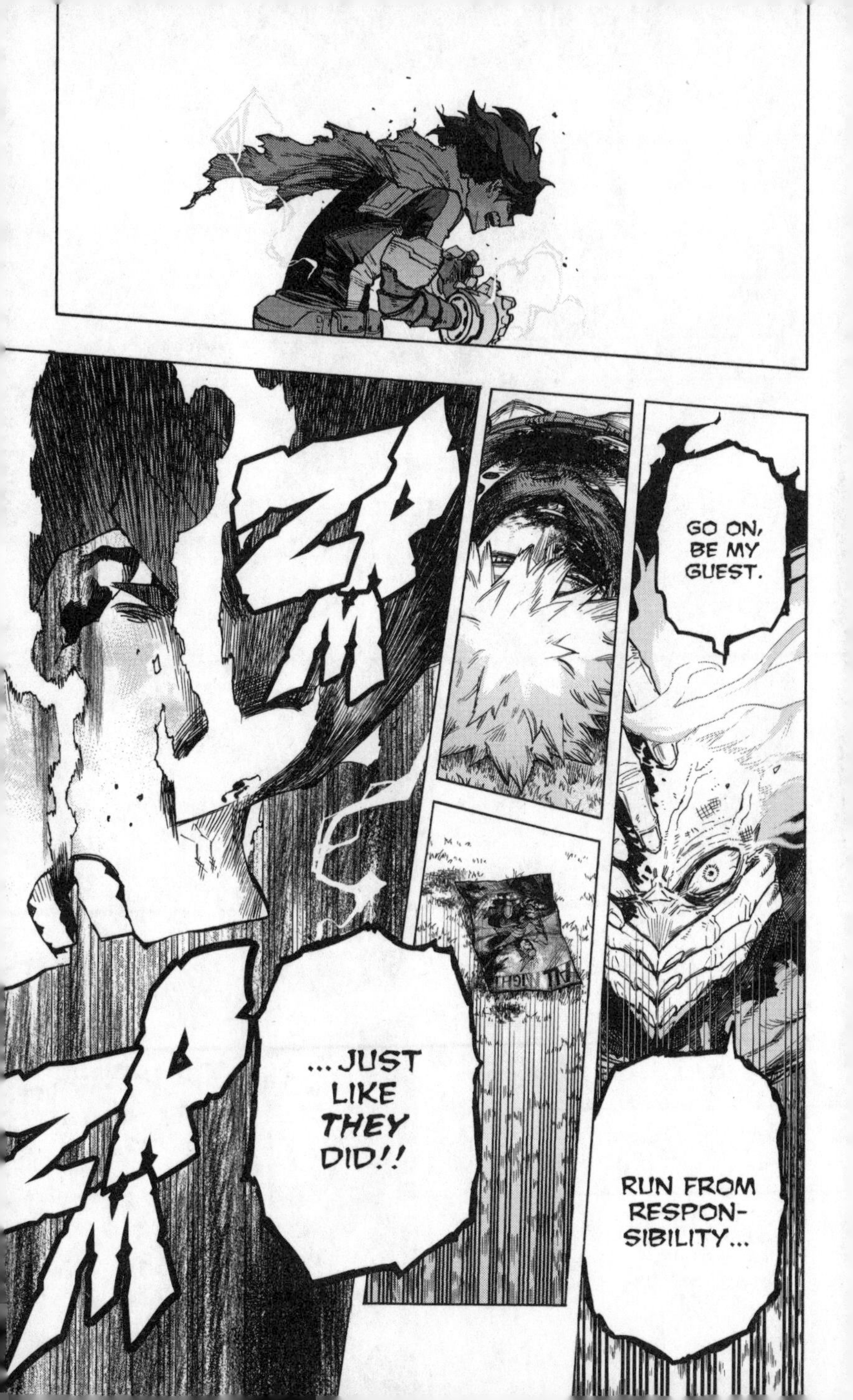
GO ON, BE MY GUEST.
RUN FROM RESPON-SIBILITY...
...JUST LIKE *THEY* DID!!
ZAM
ZAM

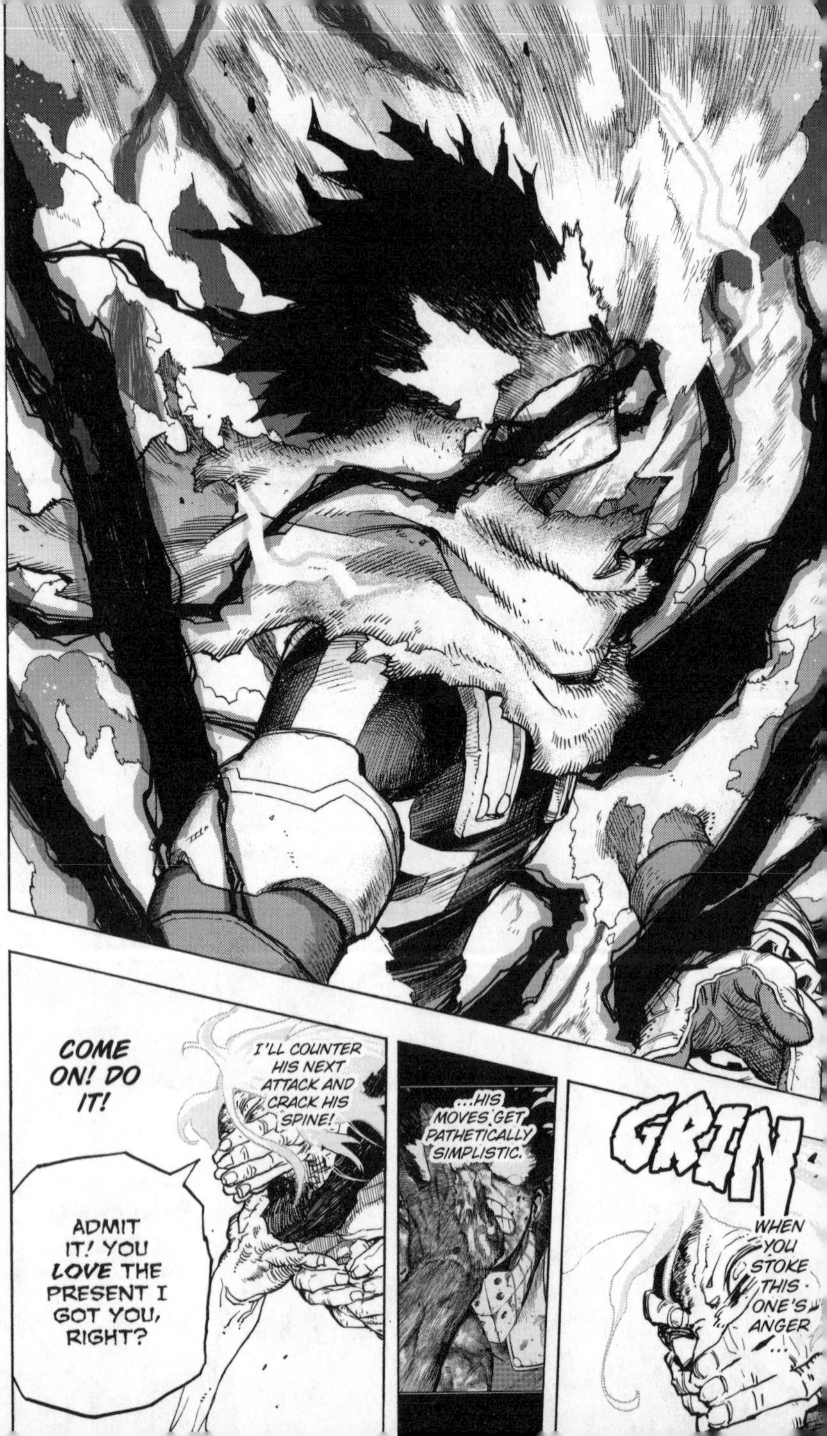
GRIN
WHEN YOU STOKE THIS ONE'S ANGER...
...HIS MOVES GET PATHETICALLY SIMPLISTIC.
I'LL COUNTER HIS NEXT ATTACK AND CRACK HIS SPINE!
COME ON! DO IT!
ADMIT IT! YOU LOVE THE PRESENT I GOT YOU, RIGHT?

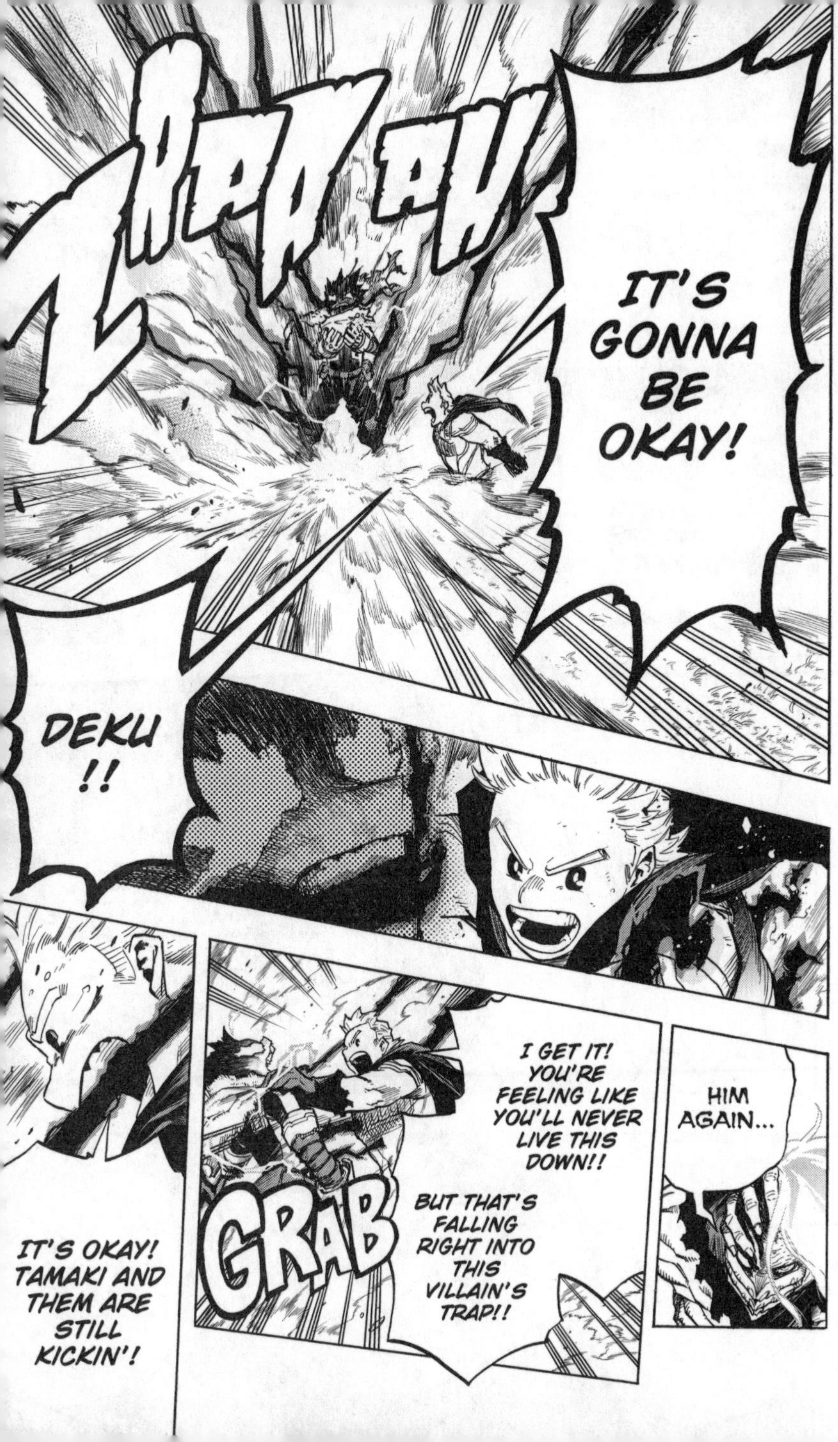
IT'S GONNA BE OKAY!
DEKU!!
HIM AGAIN...
I GET IT! YOU'RE FEELING LIKE YOU'LL NEVER LIVE THIS DOWN!!
GRAB
BUT THAT'S FALLING RIGHT INTO THIS VILLAIN'S TRAP!!
IT'S OKAY! TAMAKI AND THEM ARE STILL KICKIN'!

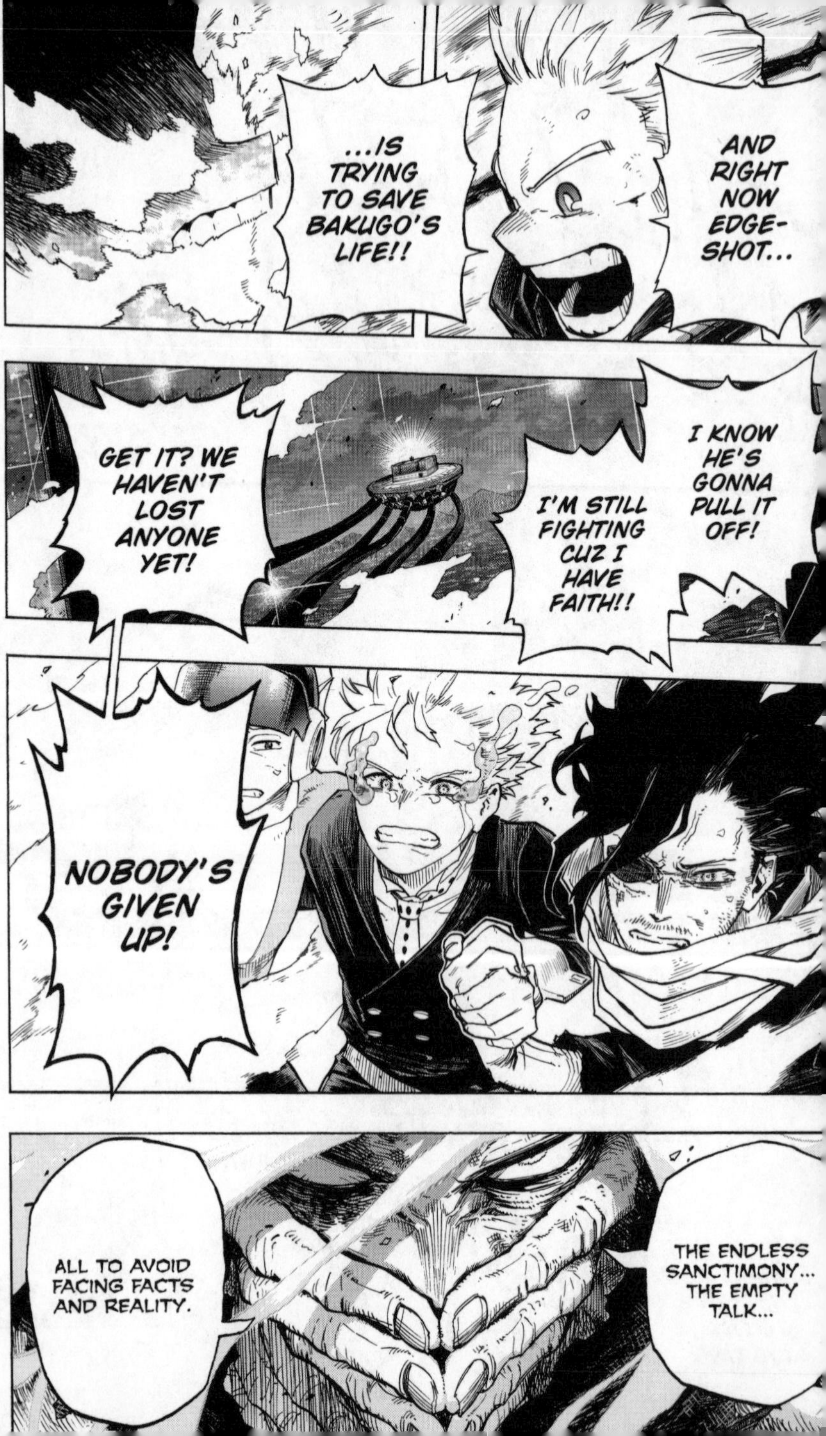
AND RIGHT NOW EDGE-SHOT...
...IS TRYING TO SAVE BAKUGO'S LIFE!!
I KNOW HE'S GONNA PULL IT OFF!
I'M STILL FIGHTING CUZ I HAVE FAITH!!
GET IT? WE HAVEN'T LOST ANYONE YET!
NOBODY'S GIVEN UP!
THE ENDLESS SANCTIMONY... THE EMPTY TALK...
ALL TO AVOID FACING FACTS AND REALITY.

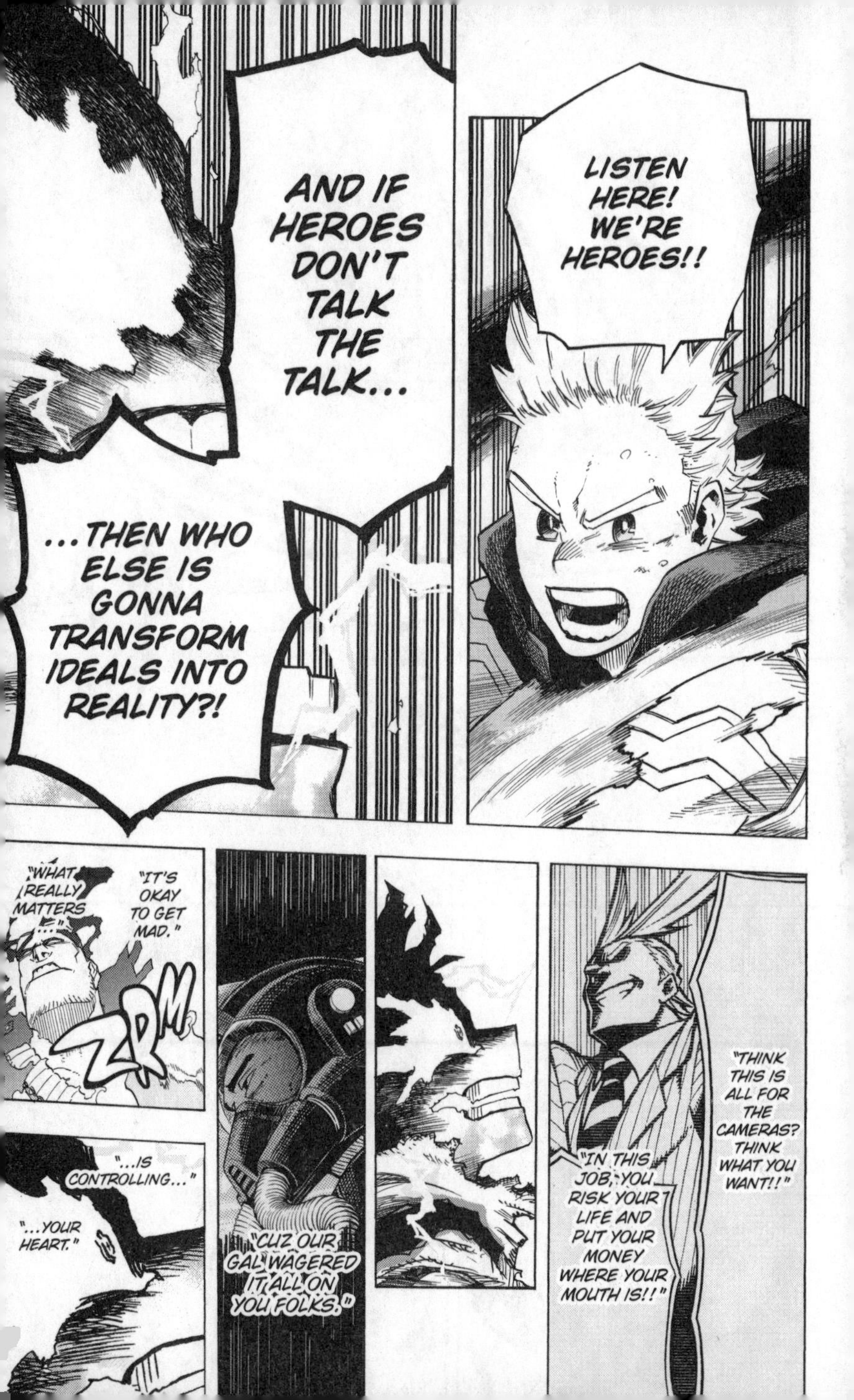
LISTEN HERE! WE'RE HEROES!!
AND IF HEROES DON'T TALK THE TALK...
...THEN WHO ELSE IS GONNA TRANSFORM IDEALS INTO REALITY?!
"THINK THIS IS ALL FOR THE CAMERAS? THINK WHAT YOU WANT!!"
"IN THIS JOB, YOU RISK YOUR LIFE AND PUT YOUR MONEY WHERE YOUR MOUTH IS!!"
"CUZ OUR GAL WAGERED IT ALL ON YOU FOLKS."
"IT'S OKAY TO GET MAD."
"WHAT REALLY MATTERS
ZDM
"...IS CONTROLLING..."
"...YOUR HEART."

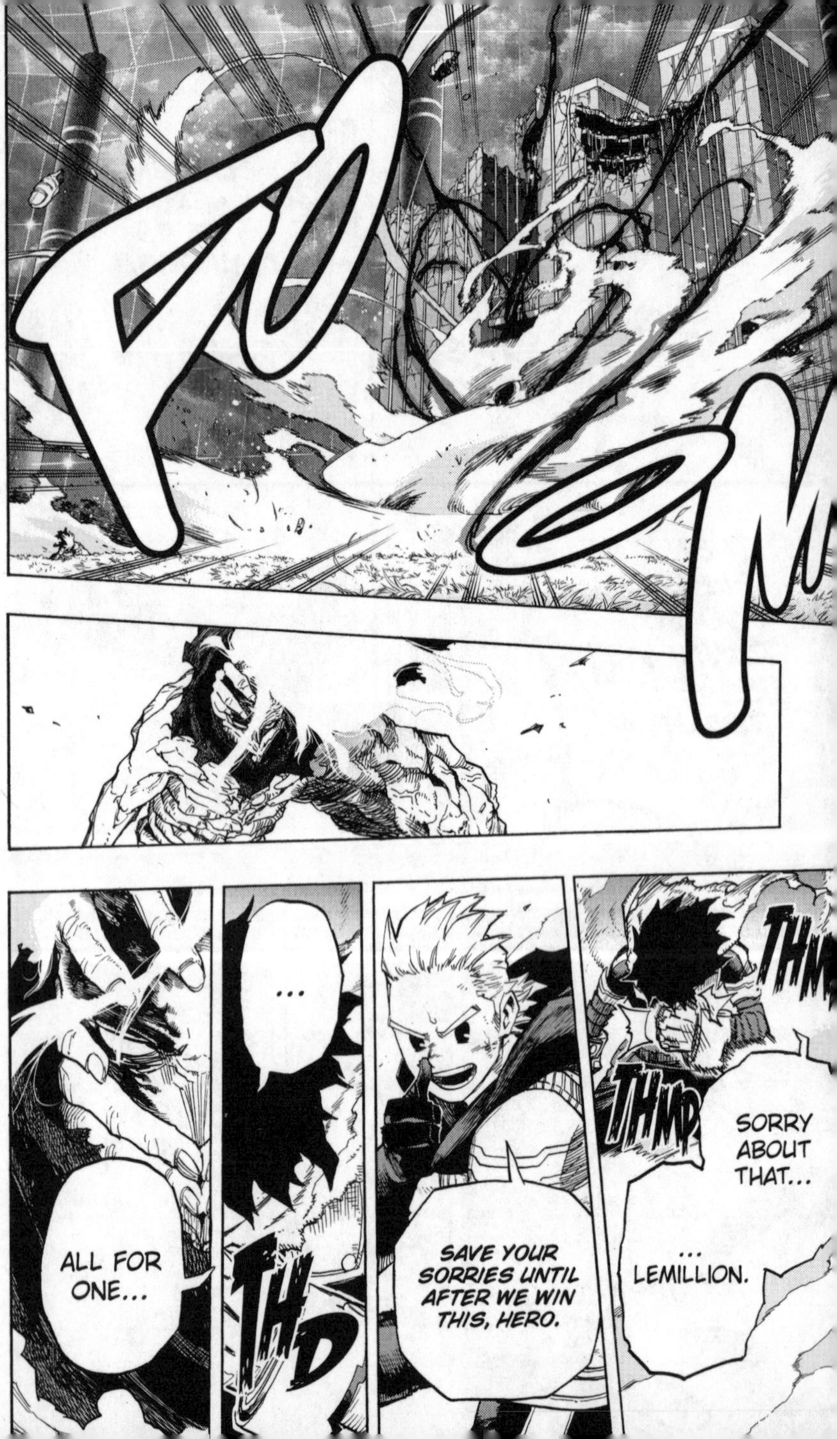
FOOM
THMP
THMP
SORRY ABOUT THAT...
... LEMILLION.
SAVE YOUR SORRIES UNTIL AFTER WE WIN THIS, HERO.
...
THD
ALL FOR ONE...

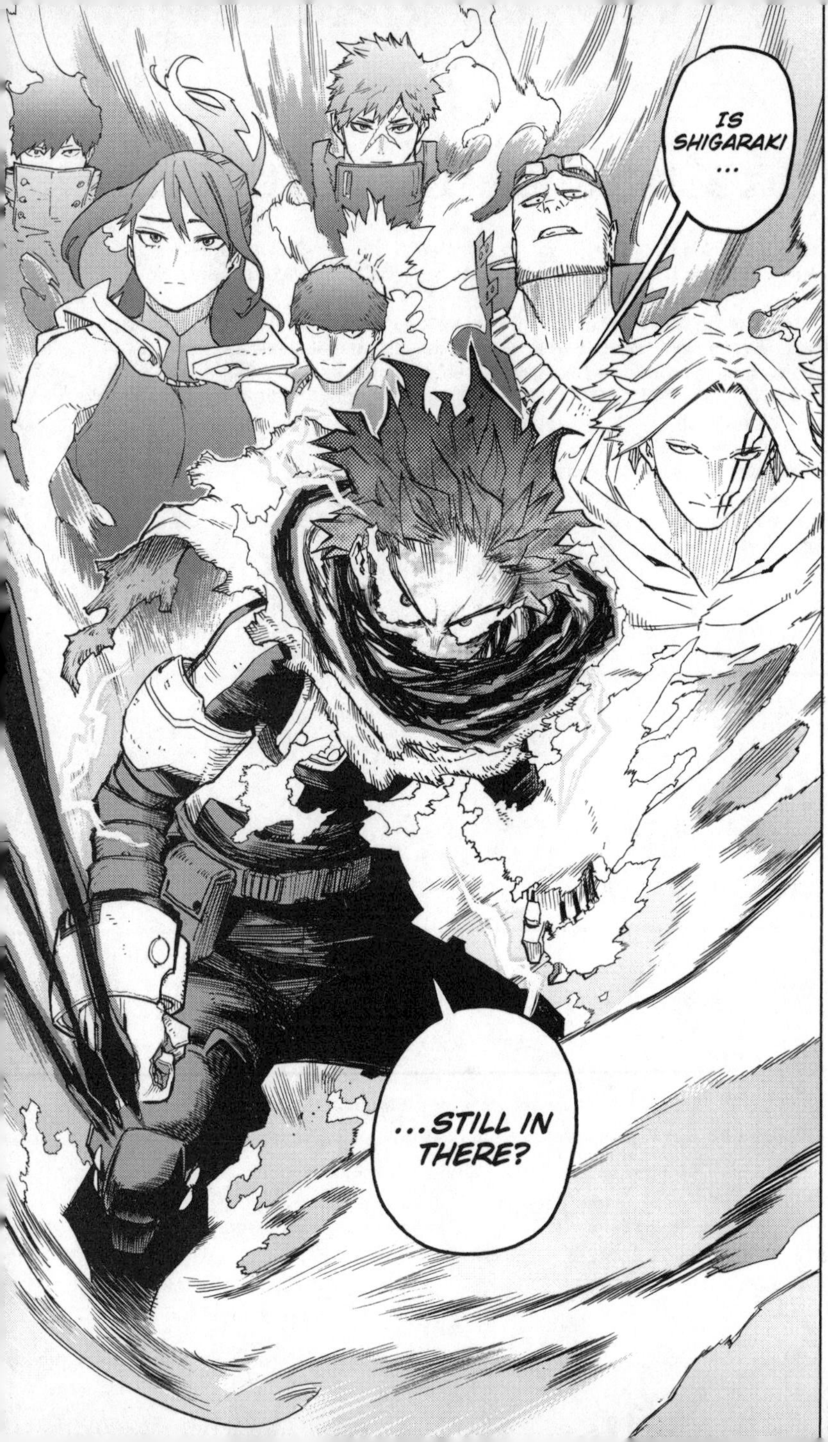
IS SHIGARAKI ...
...STILL IN THERE?

THE COLOR PAGE: BEHIND THE SCENES

The upcoming title page (which was printed in color for the weekly release) has nothing to do with the current storyline, yeah? Obviously, I'm aware.

This drawing was one I did years ago, as a sort of color test for my reference image collection. I never had any clear plans to make it public, but when it came time to produce a color page for this chapter, I was up against the clock. I needed something, anything with color, on the double, so I grabbed this one out of the vault.

I'm never really too concerned about the color pages having a connection to what's going on in the chapter, so all the hubbub came as a shock.

There was only a JPEG file, which caused a bit of a panic.

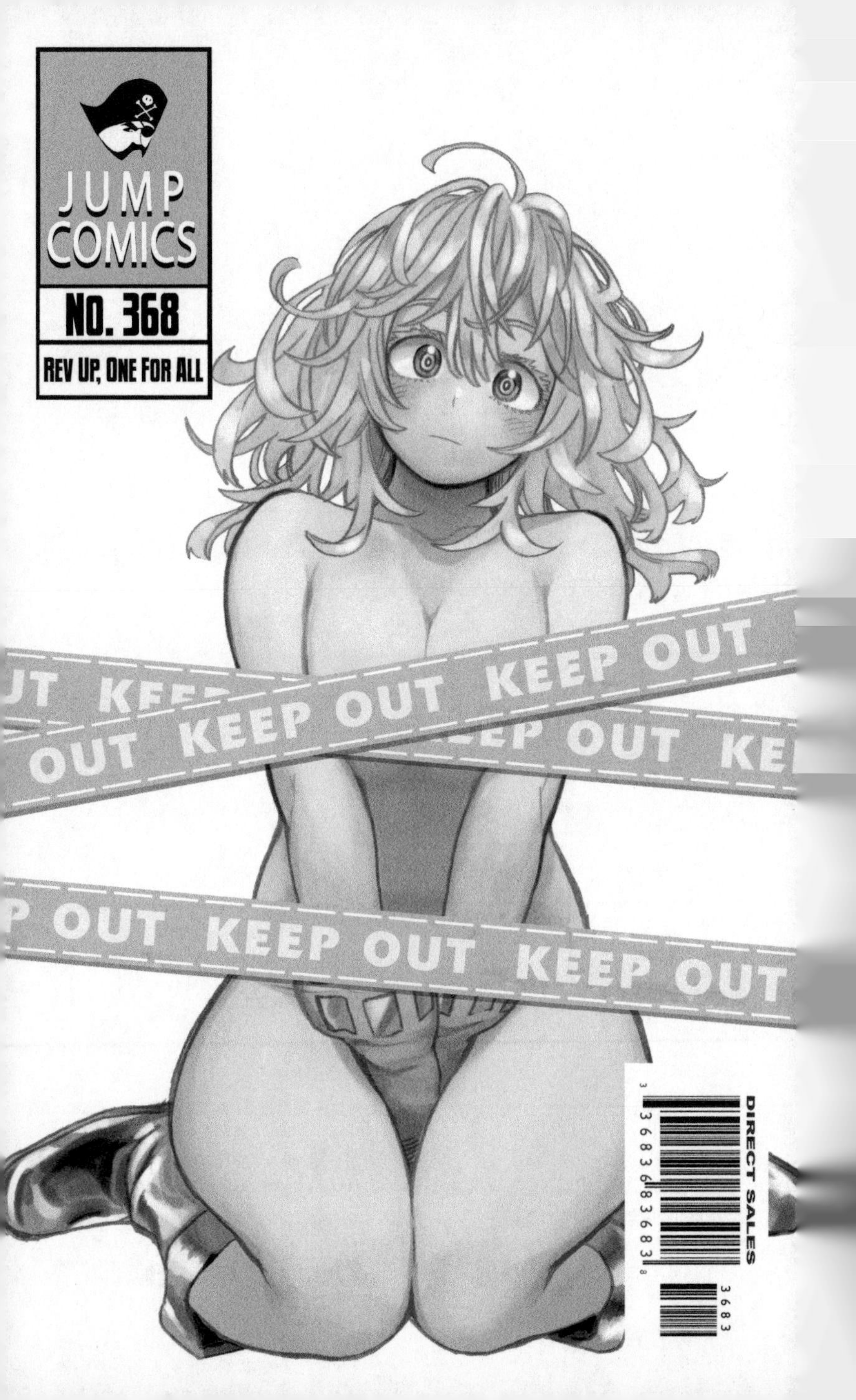
JUMP COMICS
No. 368
REV UP, ONE FOR ALL
KEEP OUT KEEP OUT KEEP OUT
DIRECT SALES

MY HERO
ACADEMIA

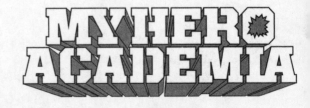

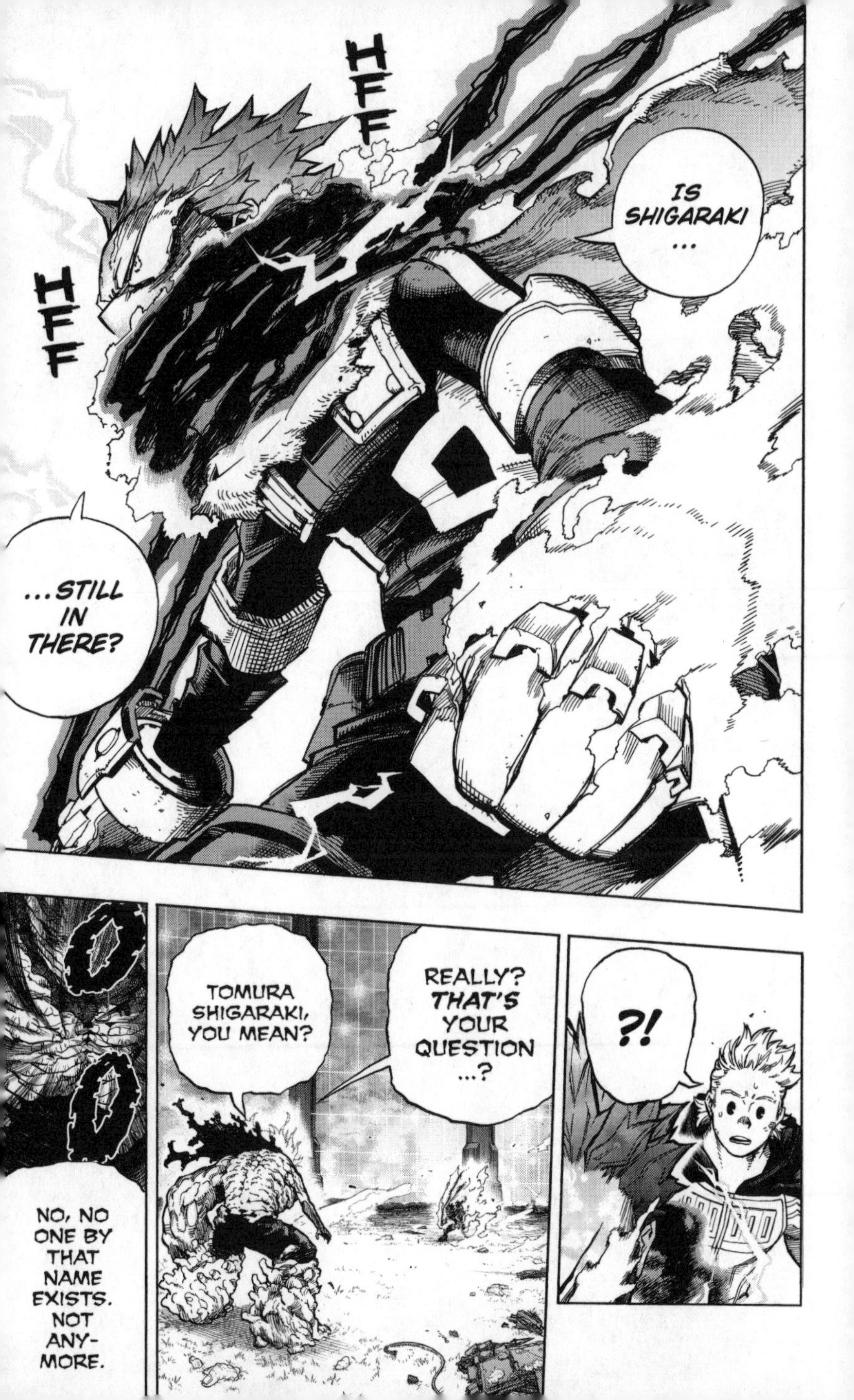
HFF
HFF
IS SHIGARAKI ...
HFF
HFF
...STILL IN THERE?
?!
REALLY? THAT'S YOUR QUESTION ...?
TOMURA SHIGARAKI, YOU MEAN?
NO, NO ONE BY THAT NAME EXISTS. NOT ANY-MORE.

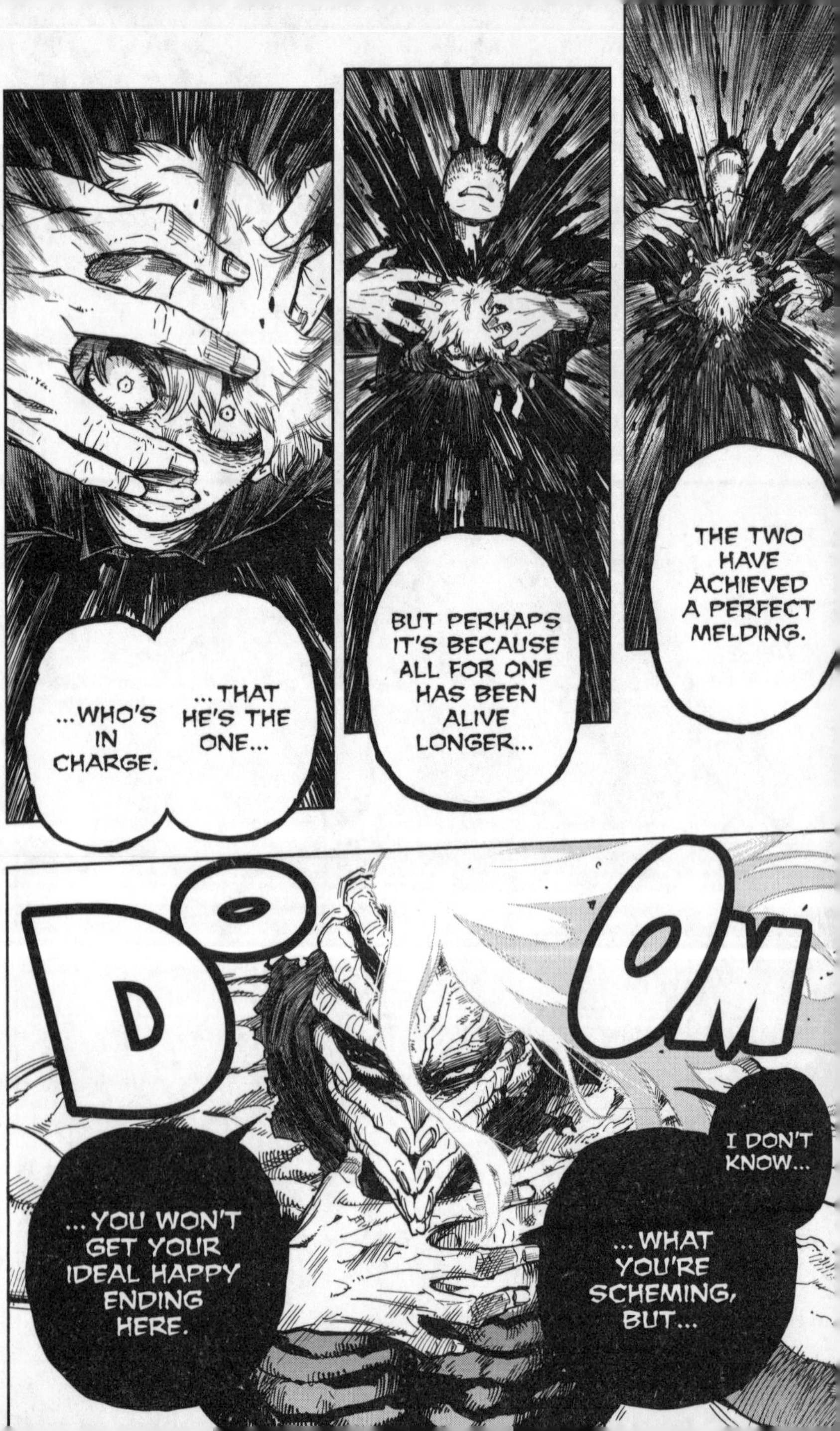
THE TWO HAVE ACHIEVED A PERFECT MELDING.
BUT PERHAPS IT'S BECAUSE ALL FOR ONE HAS BEEN ALIVE LONGER...
...THAT HE'S THE ONE...
...WHO'S IN CHARGE.
DOOM
I DON'T KNOW...
...WHAT YOU'RE SCHEMING, BUT...
...YOU WON'T GET YOUR IDEAL HAPPY ENDING HERE.

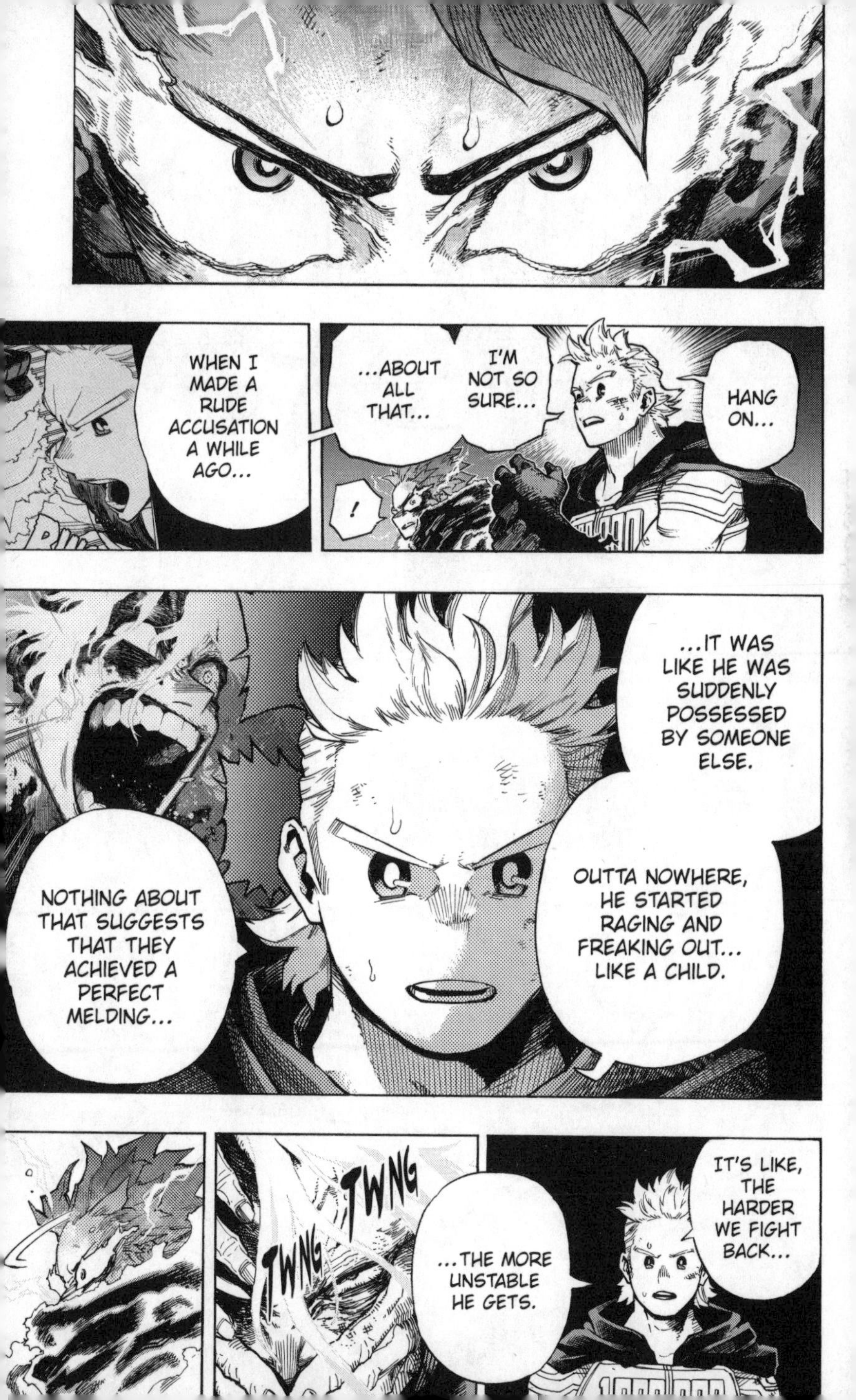
HANG ON...
I'M NOT SO SURE...
...ABOUT ALL THAT...
!
WHEN I MADE A RUDE ACCUSATION A WHILE AGO...
...IT WAS LIKE HE WAS SUDDENLY POSSESSED BY SOMEONE ELSE.
OUTTA NOWHERE, HE STARTED RAGING AND FREAKING OUT... LIKE A CHILD.
NOTHING ABOUT THAT SUGGESTS THAT THEY ACHIEVED A PERFECT MELDING...
IT'S LIKE, THE HARDER WE FIGHT BACK...
...THE MORE UNSTABLE HE GETS.
TWNG
TWNG

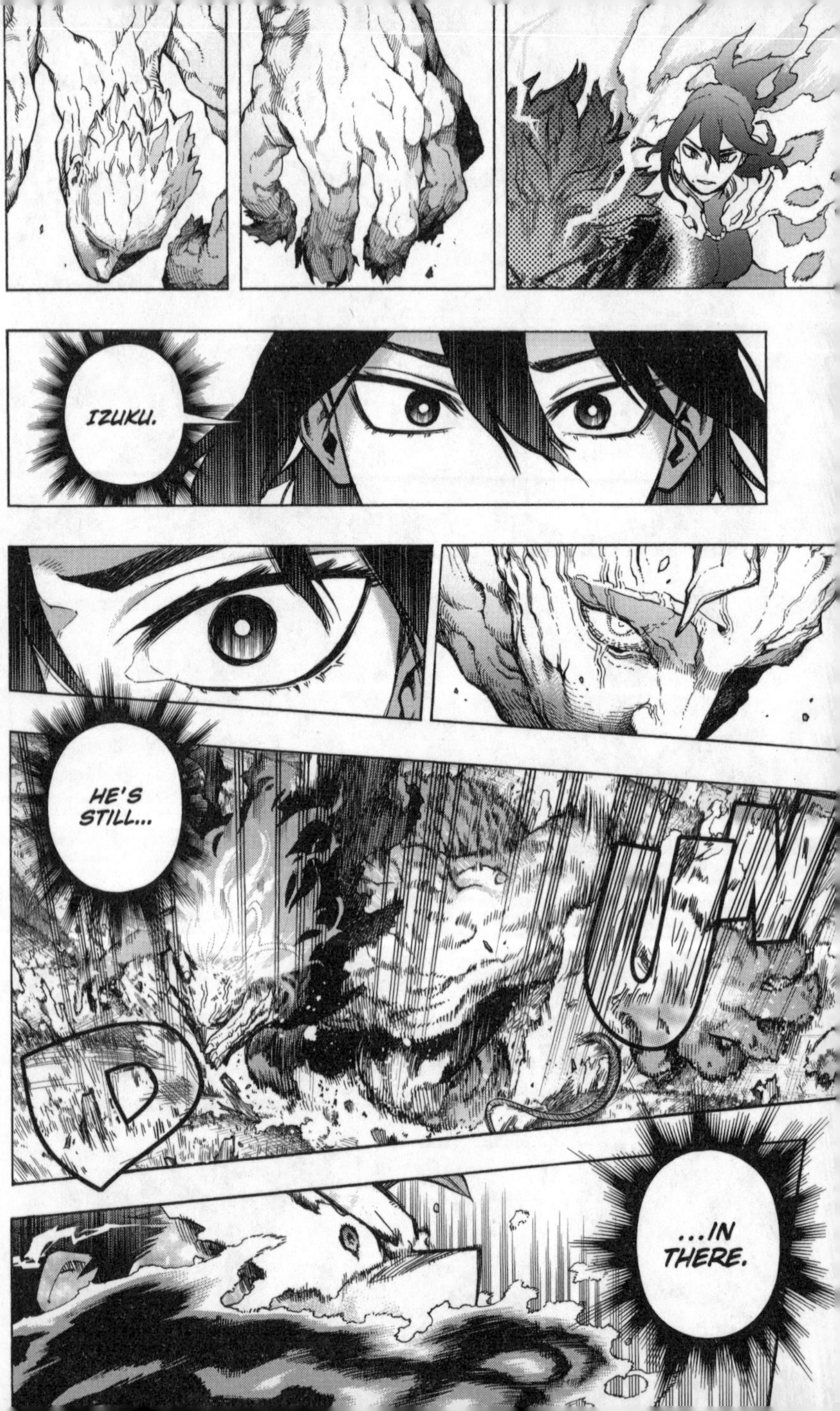
IZUKU.
HE'S STILL...
DUN
...IN THERE.

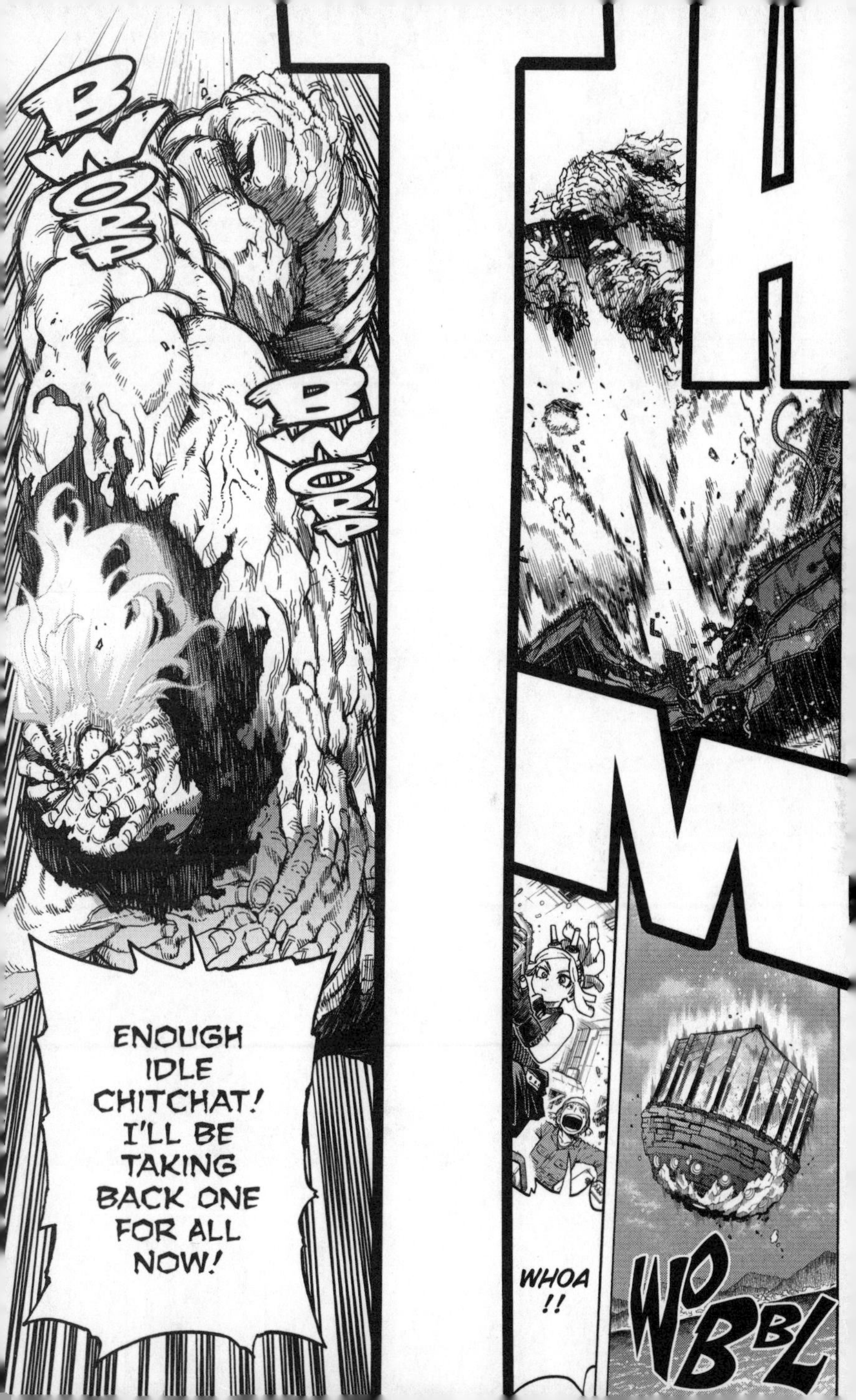
WHOA !!
WOBBL
BWORP
BWORP
ENOUGH IDLE CHITCHAT! I'LL BE TAKING BACK ONE FOR ALL NOW!

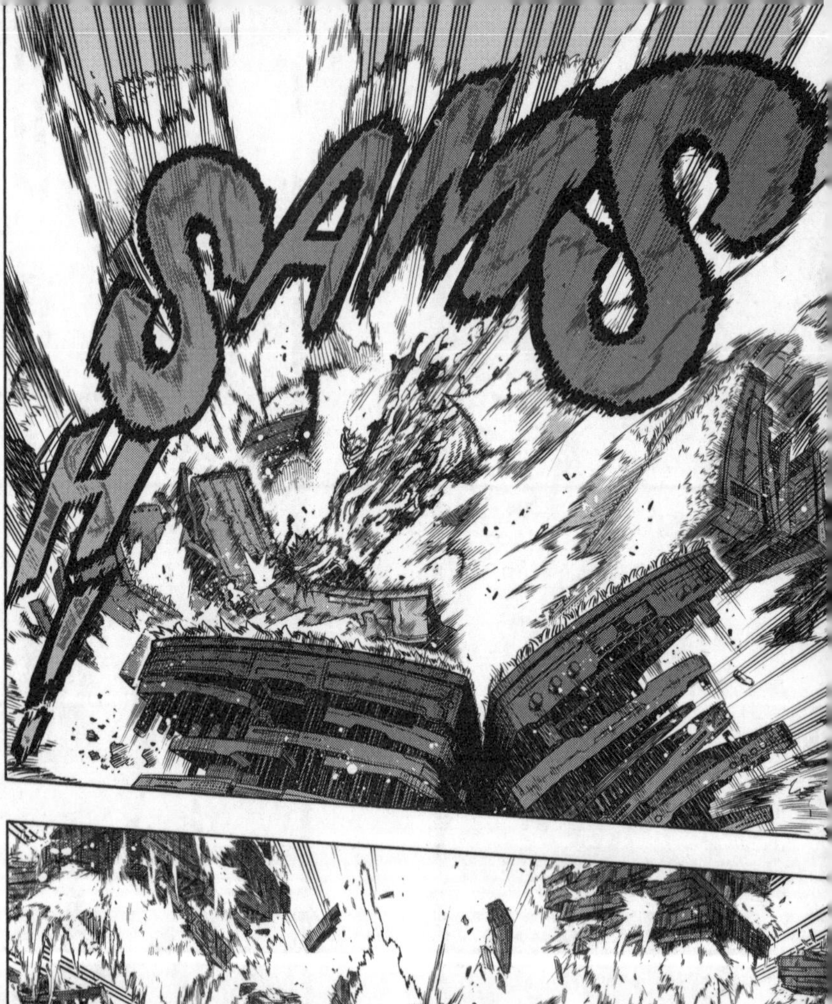

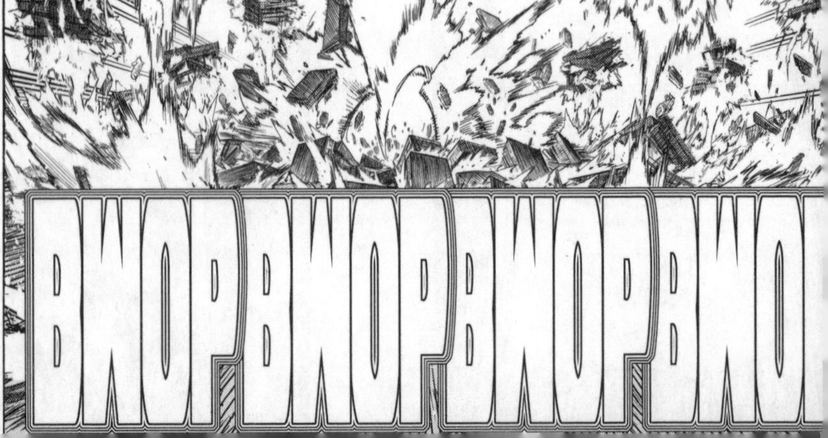
BWOP BWOP BWOP BWO

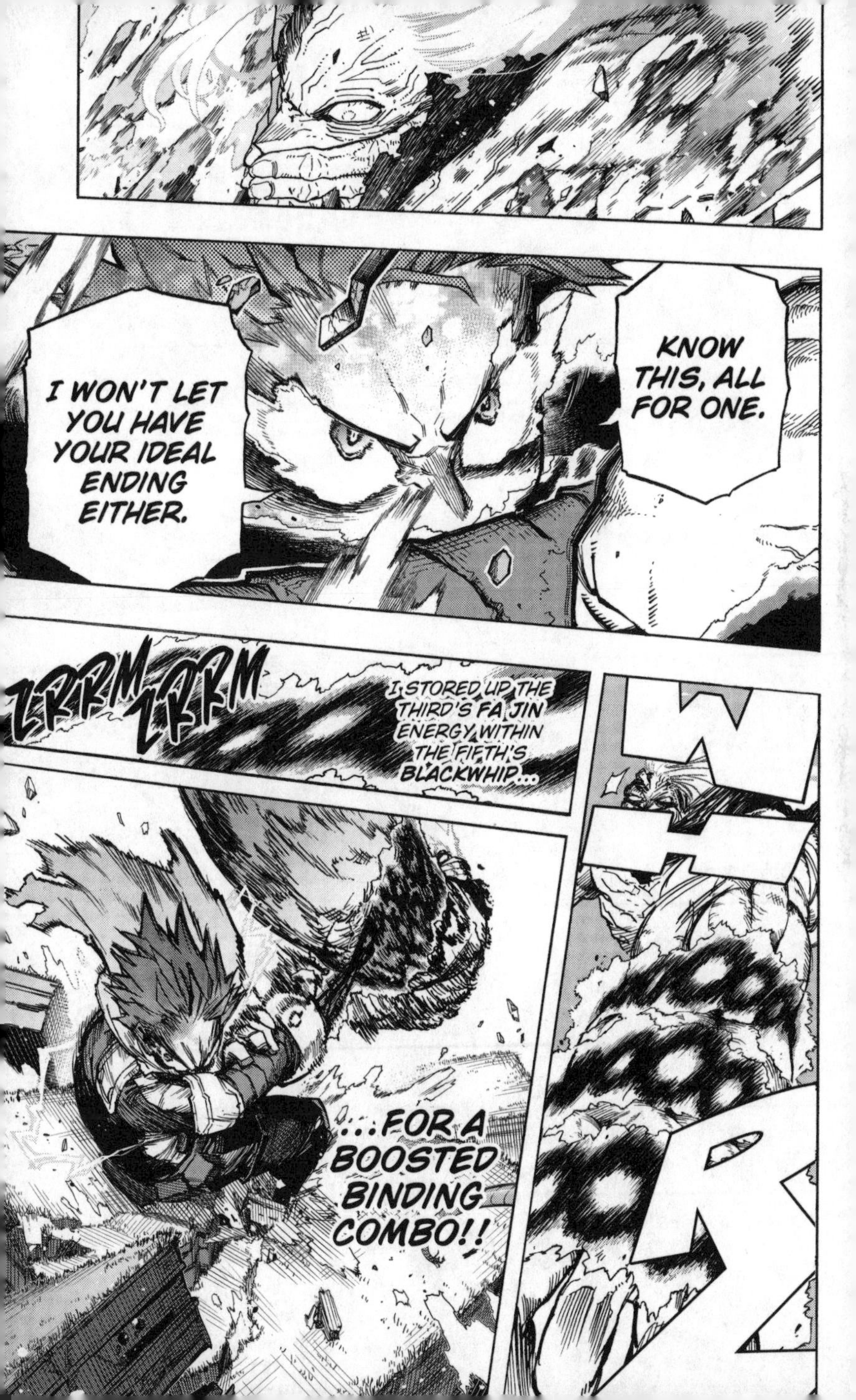
KNOW THIS, ALL FOR ONE.
I WON'T LET YOU HAVE YOUR IDEAL ENDING EITHER.
WHR
ZRRM ZRRM
I STORED UP THE THIRD'S FA JIN ENERGY WITHIN THE FIFTH'S BLACKWHIP...
...FOR A BOOSTED BINDING COMBO!!

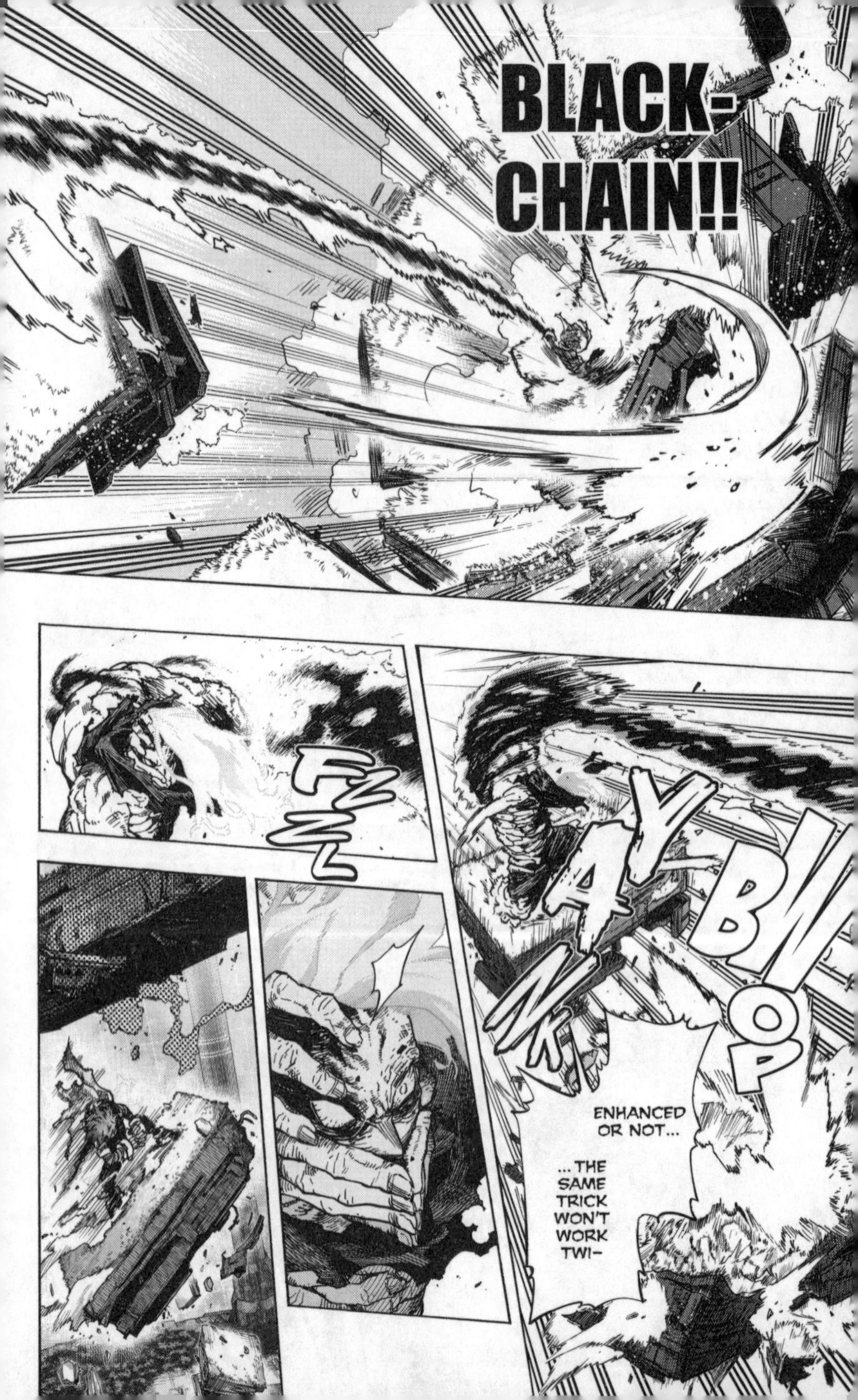
BLACK-CHAIN!!
BWOP
YANK
FZZL
ENHANCED OR NOT...
...THE SAME TRICK WON'T WORK TWI-

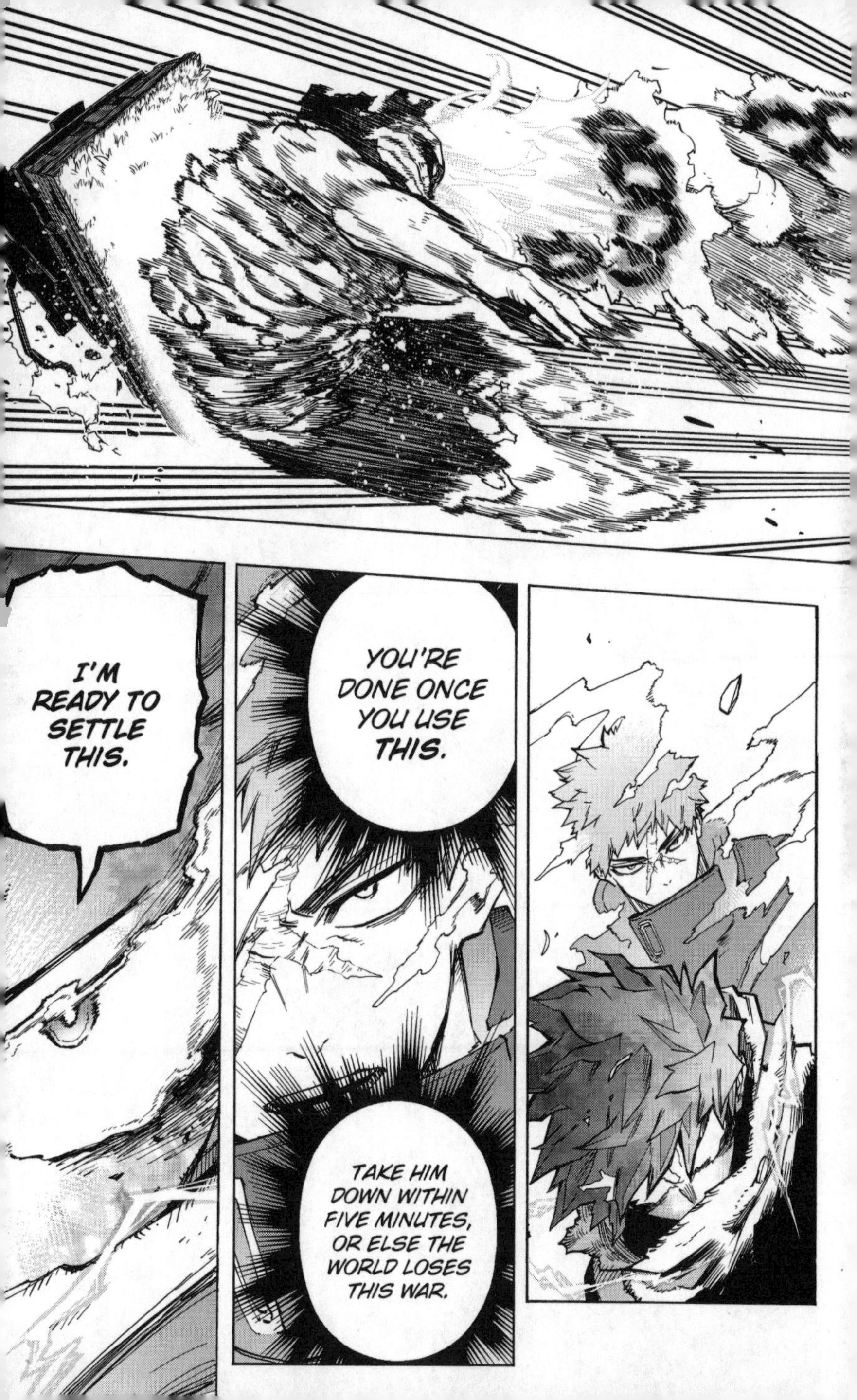
YOU'RE DONE ONCE YOU USE THIS.
TAKE HIM DOWN WITHIN FIVE MINUTES, OR ELSE THE WORLD LOSES THIS WAR.
I'M READY TO SETTLE THIS.

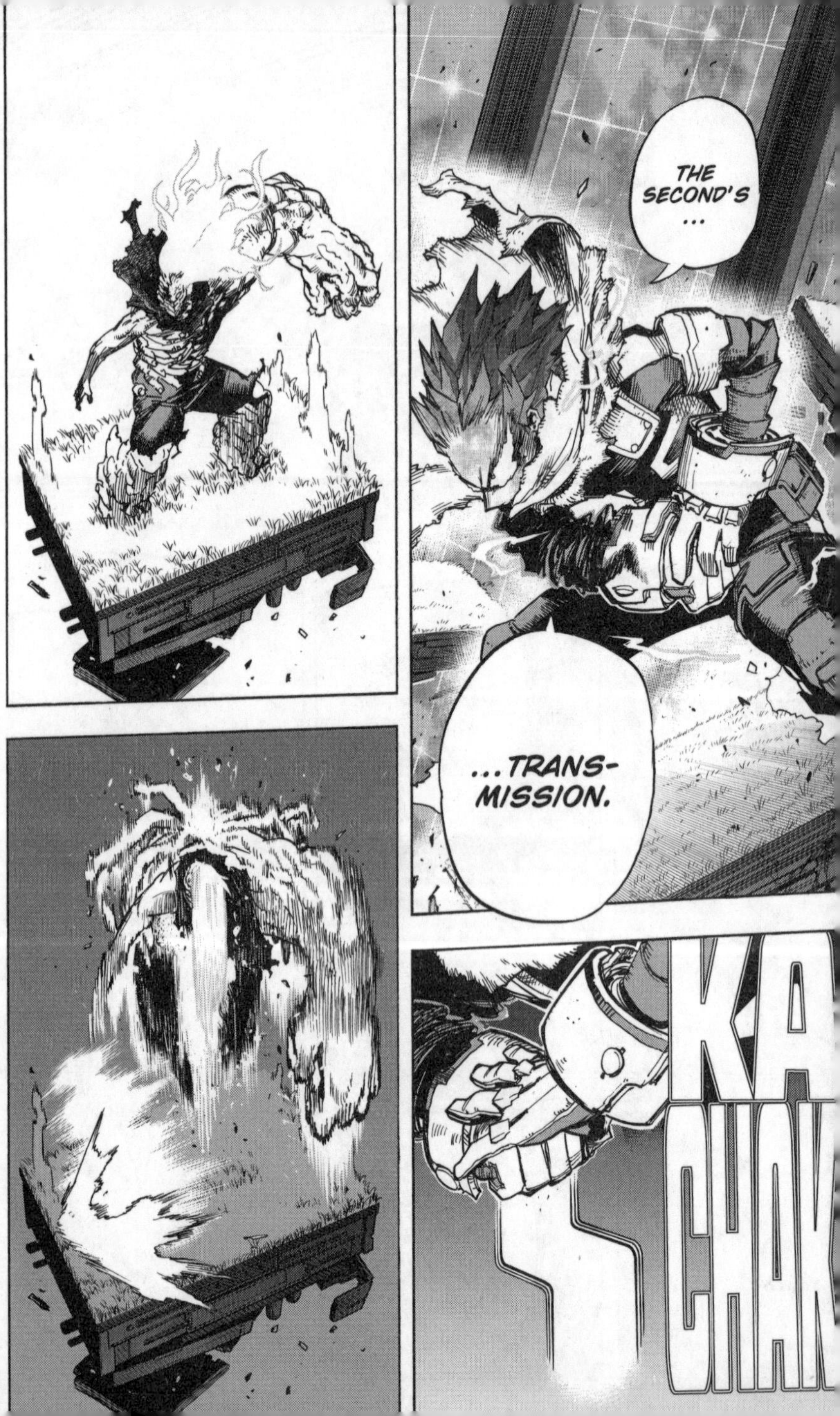
THE SECOND'S ...
...TRANS-MISSION.
KA
CHAK

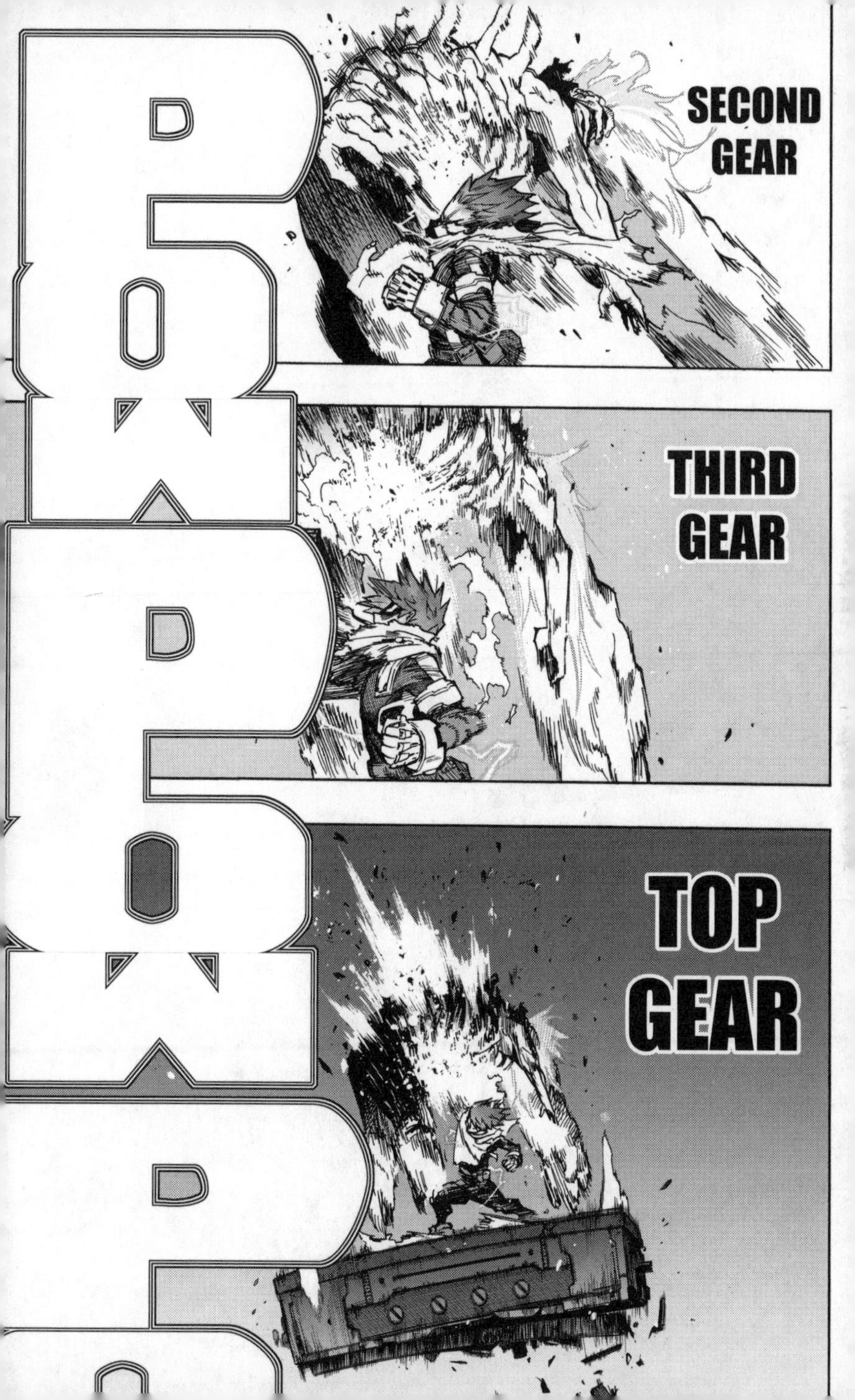
SECOND GEAR
THIRD GEAR
TOP GEAR

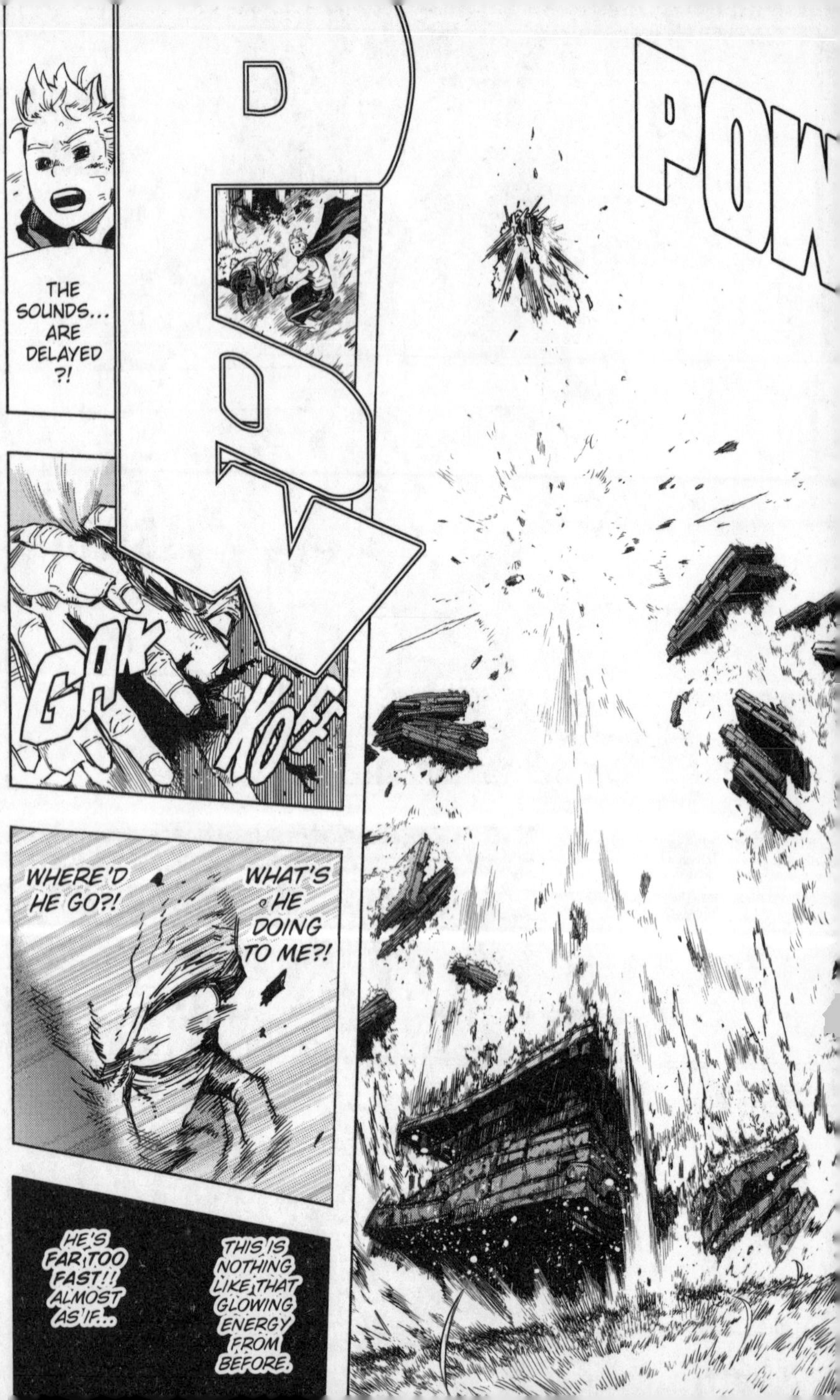
POW
THE SOUNDS... ARE DELAYED ?!
GAK KOFF
WHAT'S HE DOING TO ME?!
WHERE'D HE GO?!
THIS IS NOTHING LIKE THAT GLOWING ENERGY FROM BEFORE.
HE'S FAR TOO FAST!! ALMOST AS IF...

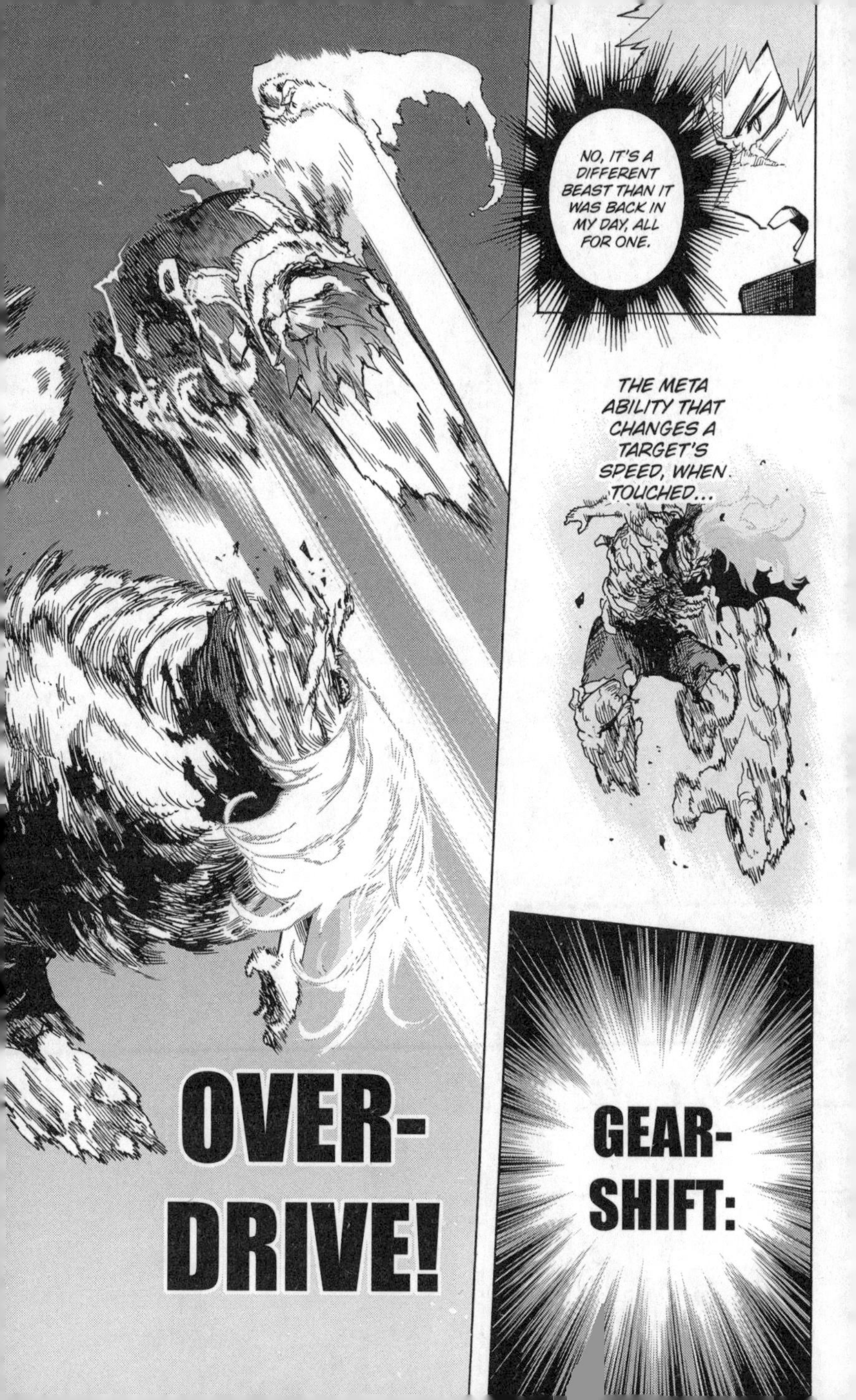
NO, IT'S A DIFFERENT BEAST THAN IT WAS BACK IN MY DAY, ALL FOR ONE.
THE META ABILITY THAT CHANGES A TARGET'S SPEED, WHEN TOUCHED...
GEAR-SHIFT:
OVER-DRIVE!

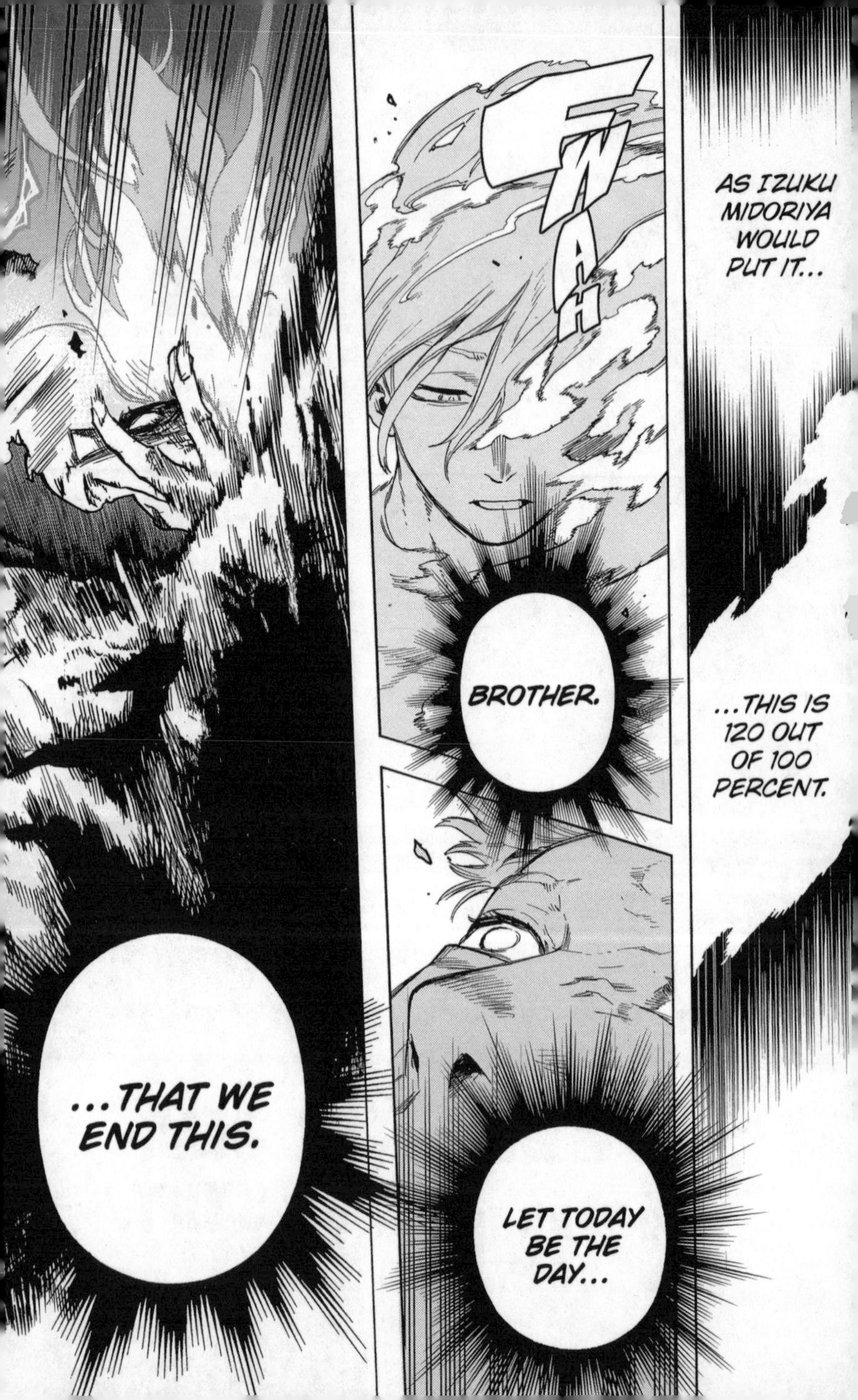
AS IZUKU MIDORIYA WOULD PUT IT...
...THIS IS 120 OUT OF 100 PERCENT.
FWAH
BROTHER.
LET TODAY BE THE DAY...
...THAT WE END THIS.

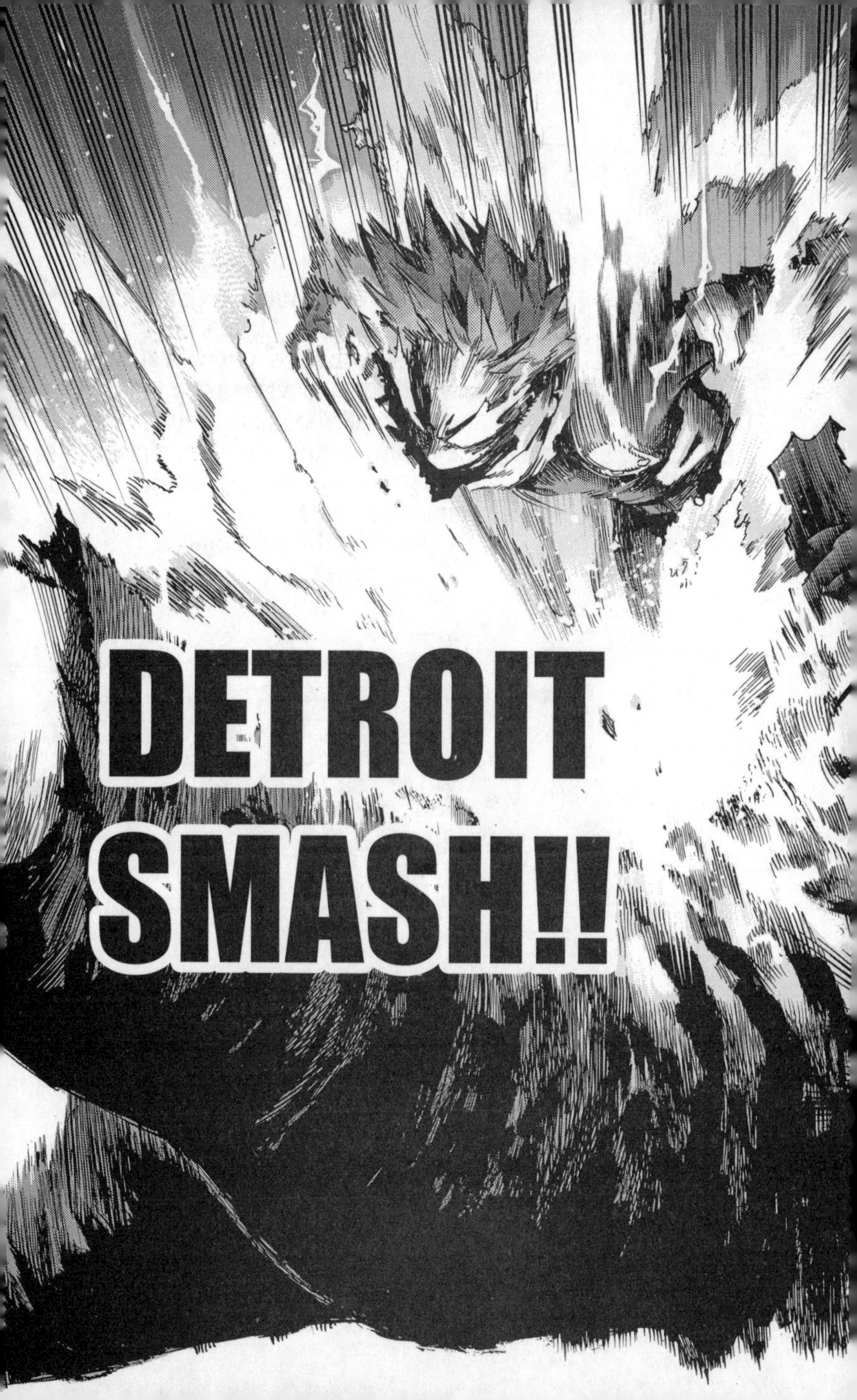
DETROIT
SMASH!!

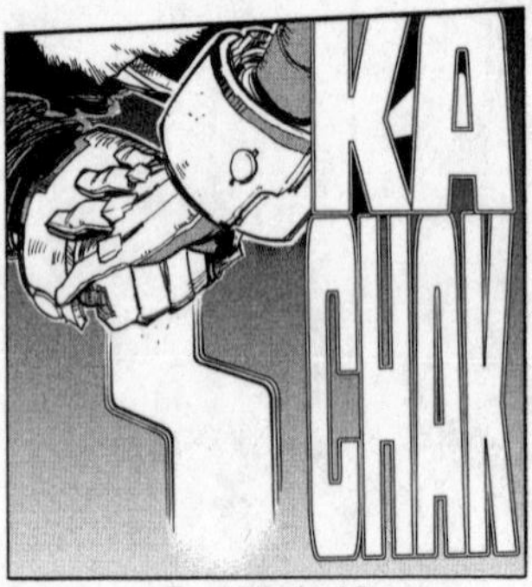
KA
CHAK
Page 94, panel 2

That "KACHAK" is supposed to be evocative of operating a gearshift lever in a vehicle. Deku's never driven a car before, but he still makes a point of visualizing the action. That's been his go-to method when training, ever since All Might made the point about coming up with handy visualizations back in volume 1.

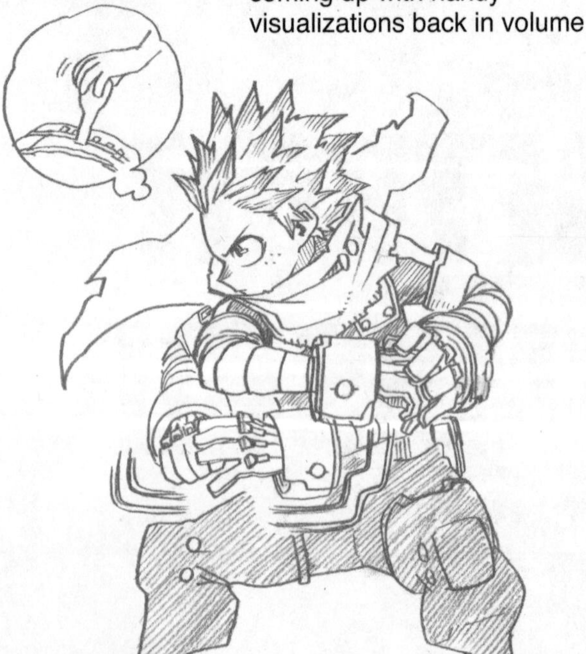

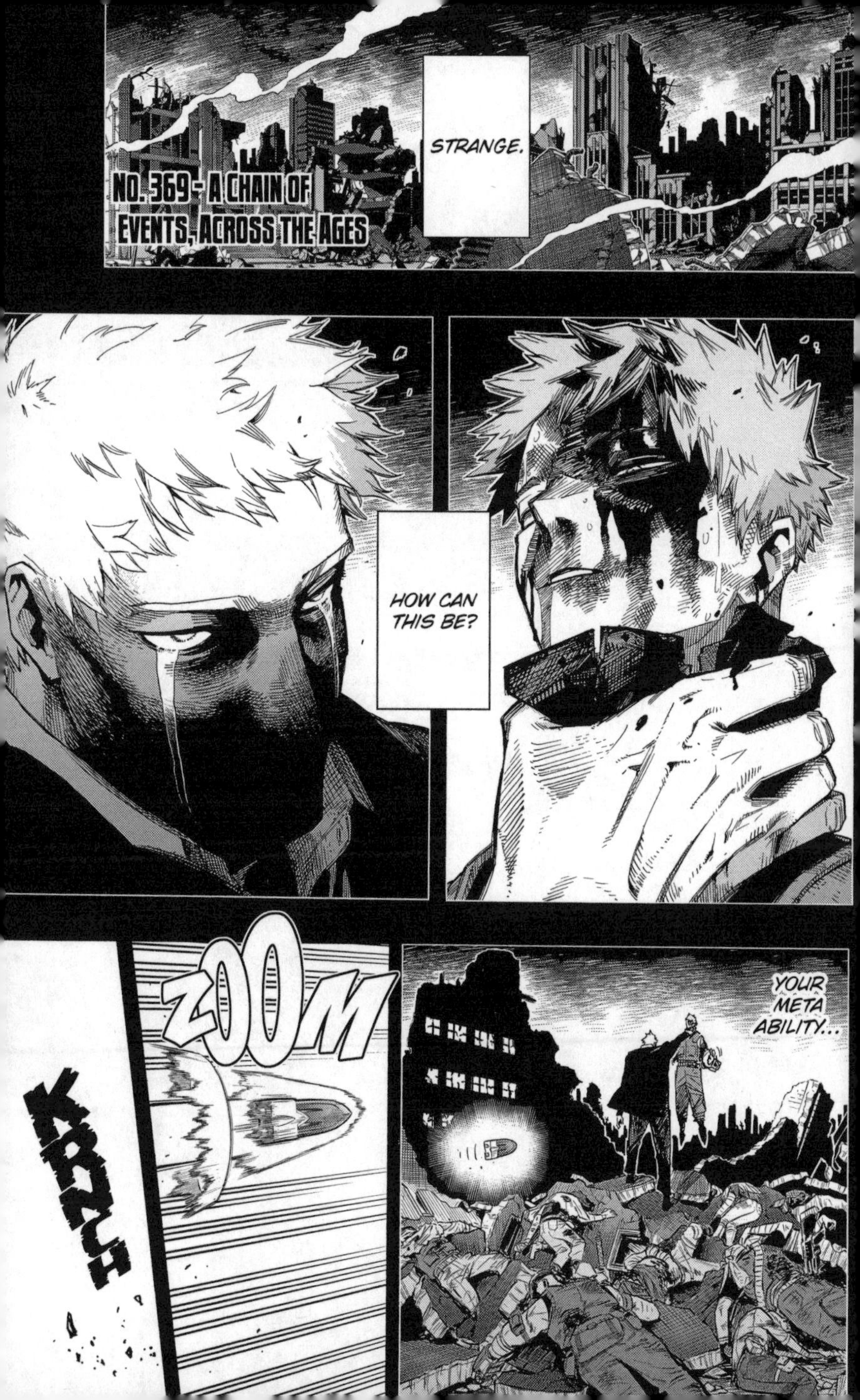
No. 369 - A Chain of Events, Across the Ages
STRANGE.
HOW CAN THIS BE?
YOUR META ABILITY...
ZOOM
KRACH

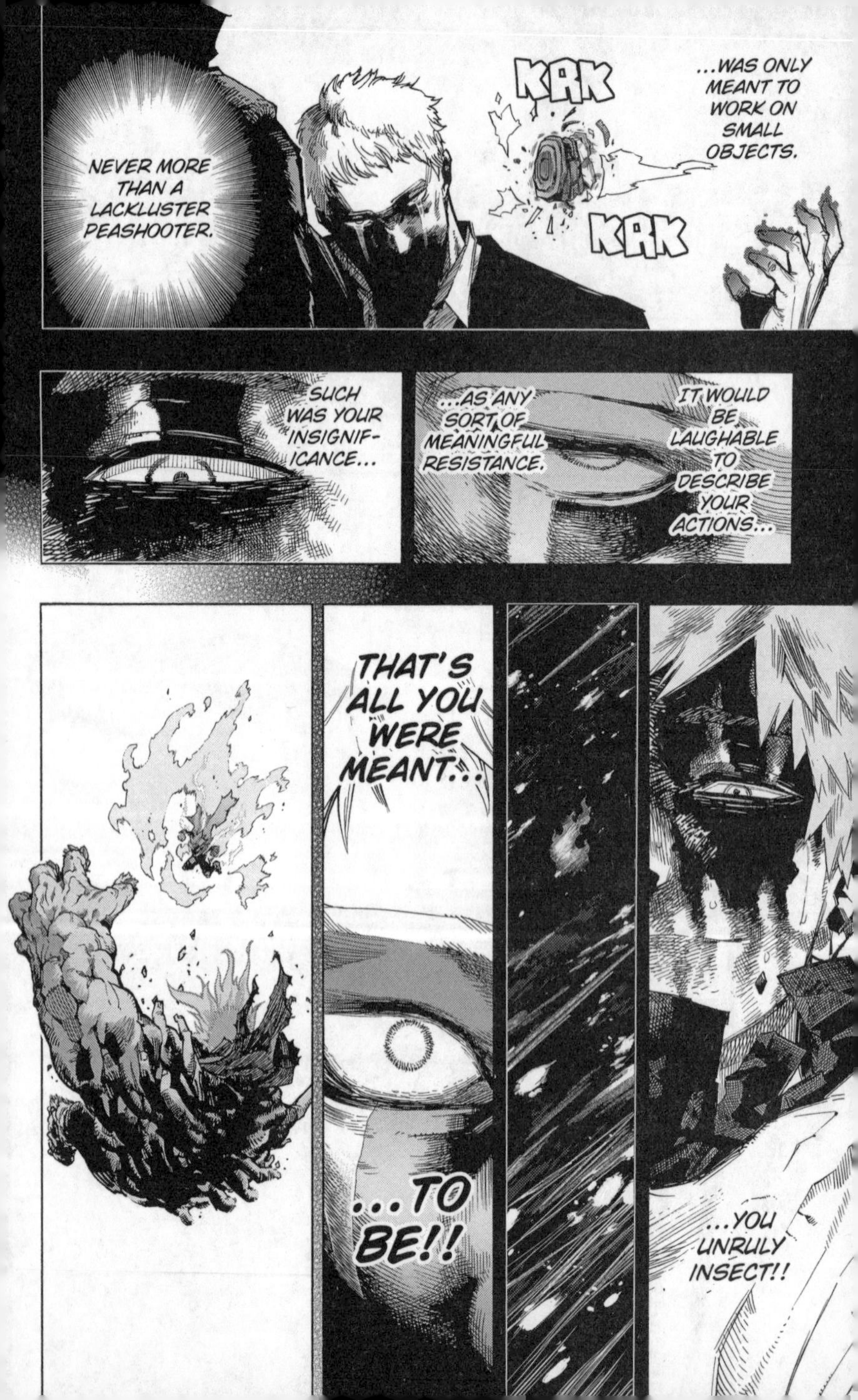
...WAS ONLY MEANT TO WORK ON SMALL OBJECTS.
KRK
KRK
NEVER MORE THAN A LACKLUSTER PEASHOOTER.
IT WOULD BE LAUGHABLE TO DESCRIBE YOUR ACTIONS...
...AS ANY SORT OF MEANINGFUL RESISTANCE.
SUCH WAS YOUR INSIGNIF-ICANCE...
...YOU UNRULY INSECT!!
THAT'S ALL YOU WERE MEANT...
...TO BE!!

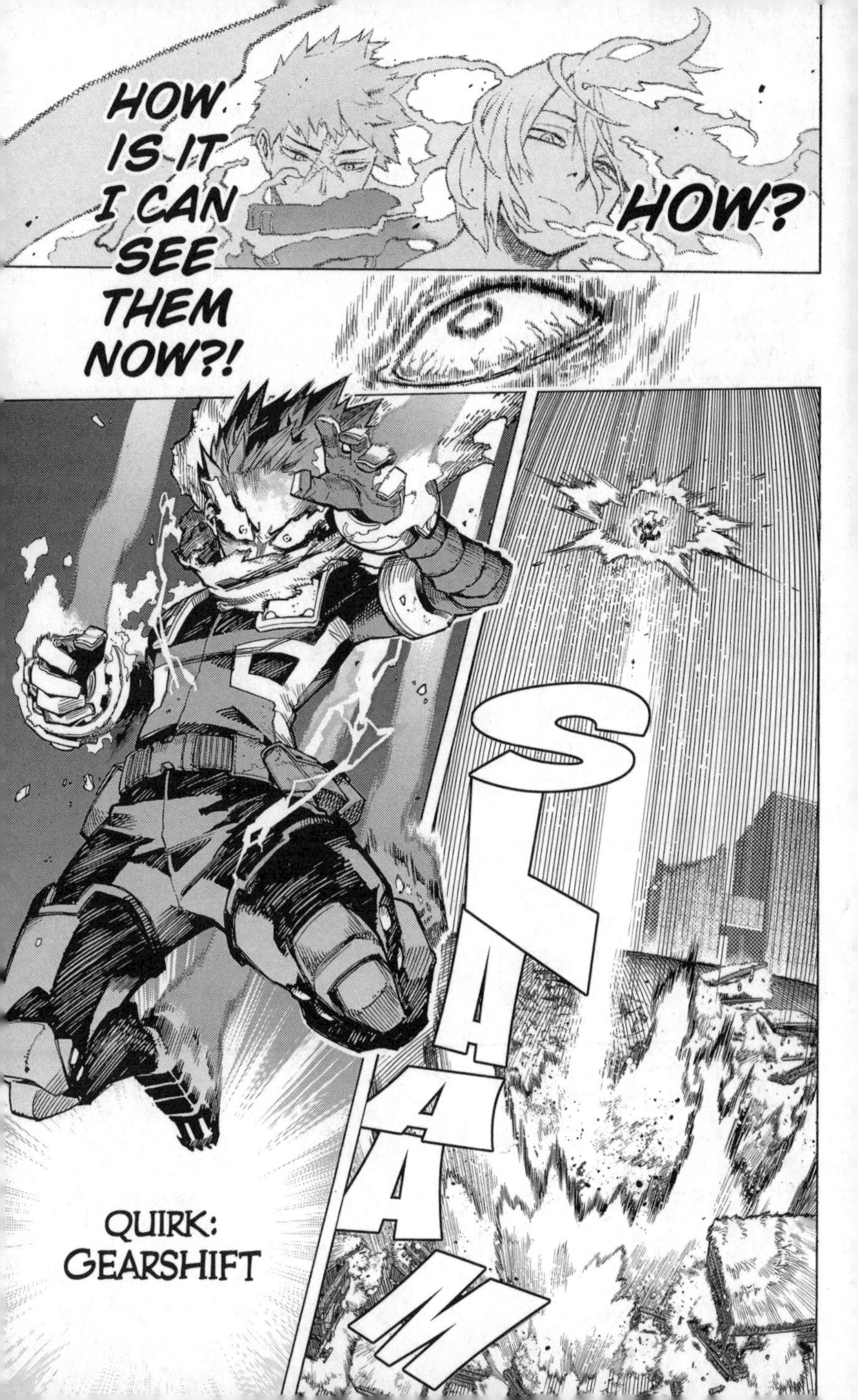
HOW?
HOW IS IT I CAN SEE THEM NOW?!
SLAAAAM
QUIRK: GEARSHIFT

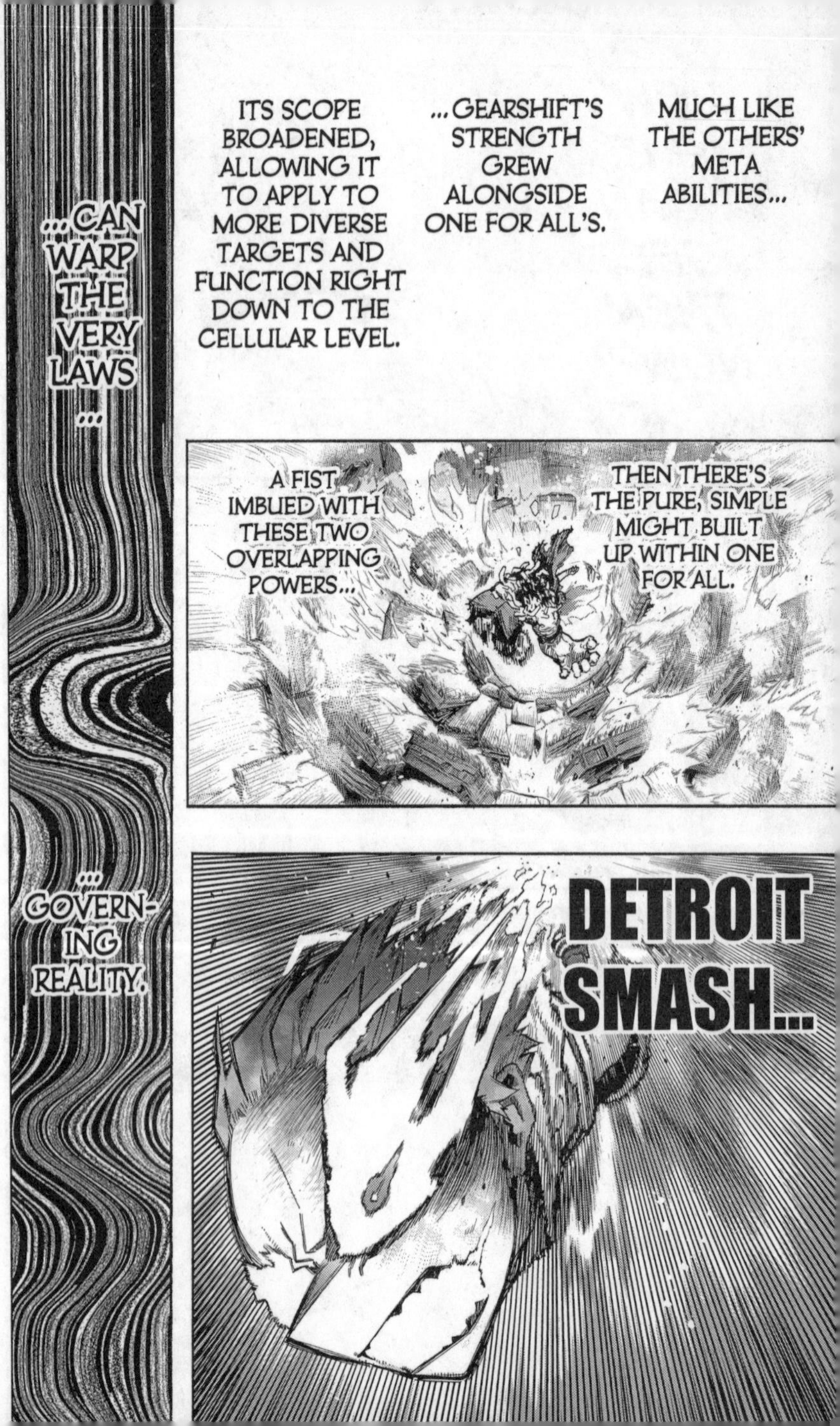
MUCH LIKE THE OTHERS' META ABILITIES...
...GEARSHIFT'S STRENGTH GREW ALONGSIDE ONE FOR ALL'S.
ITS SCOPE BROADENED, ALLOWING IT TO APPLY TO MORE DIVERSE TARGETS AND FUNCTION RIGHT DOWN TO THE CELLULAR LEVEL.
THEN THERE'S THE PURE, SIMPLE MIGHT BUILT UP WITHIN ONE FOR ALL.
A FIST IMBUED WITH THESE TWO OVERLAPPING POWERS...
DETROIT SMASH...
...CAN WARP THE VERY LAWS...
...GOVERNING REALITY.

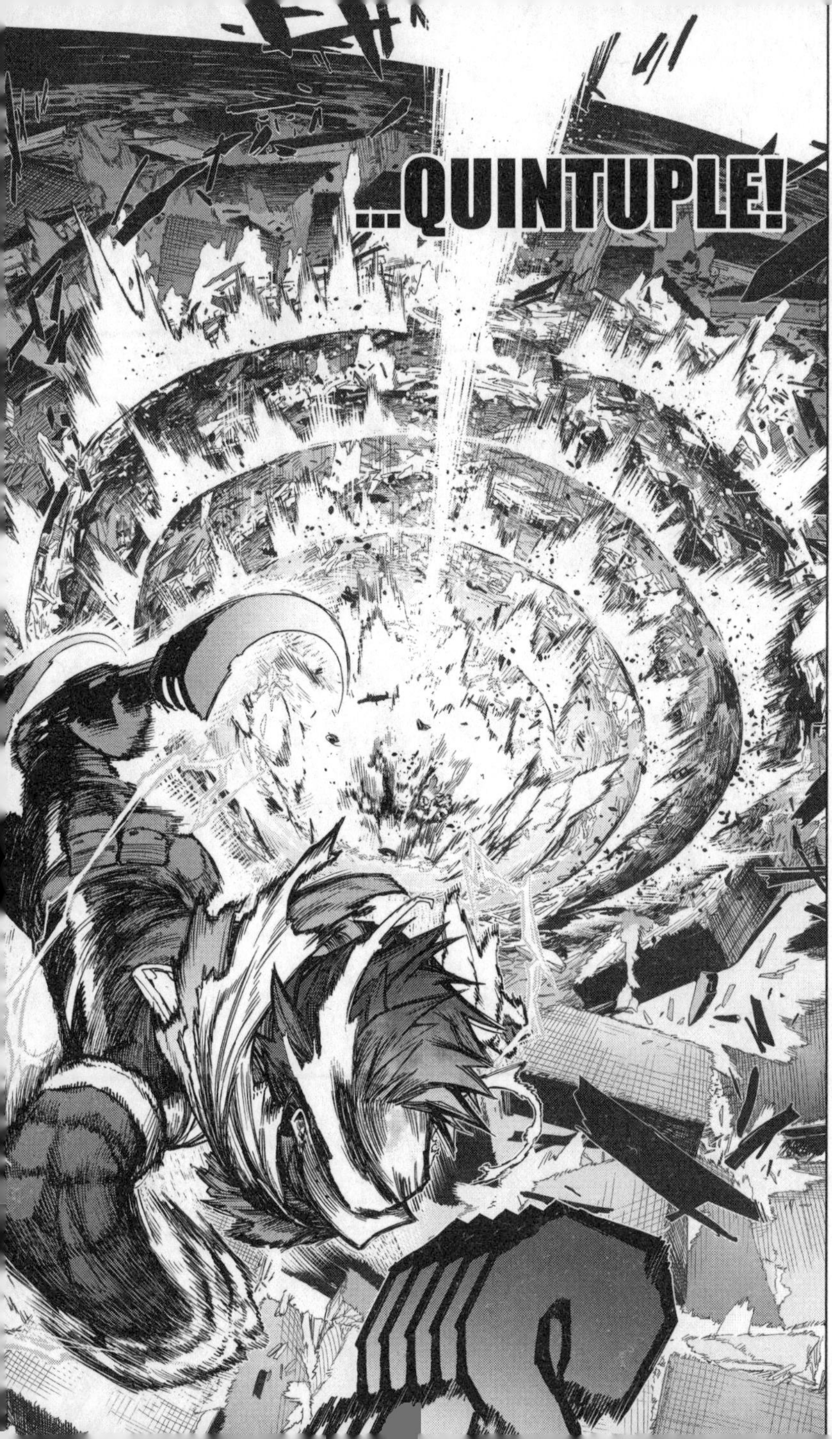
...QUINTUPLE!

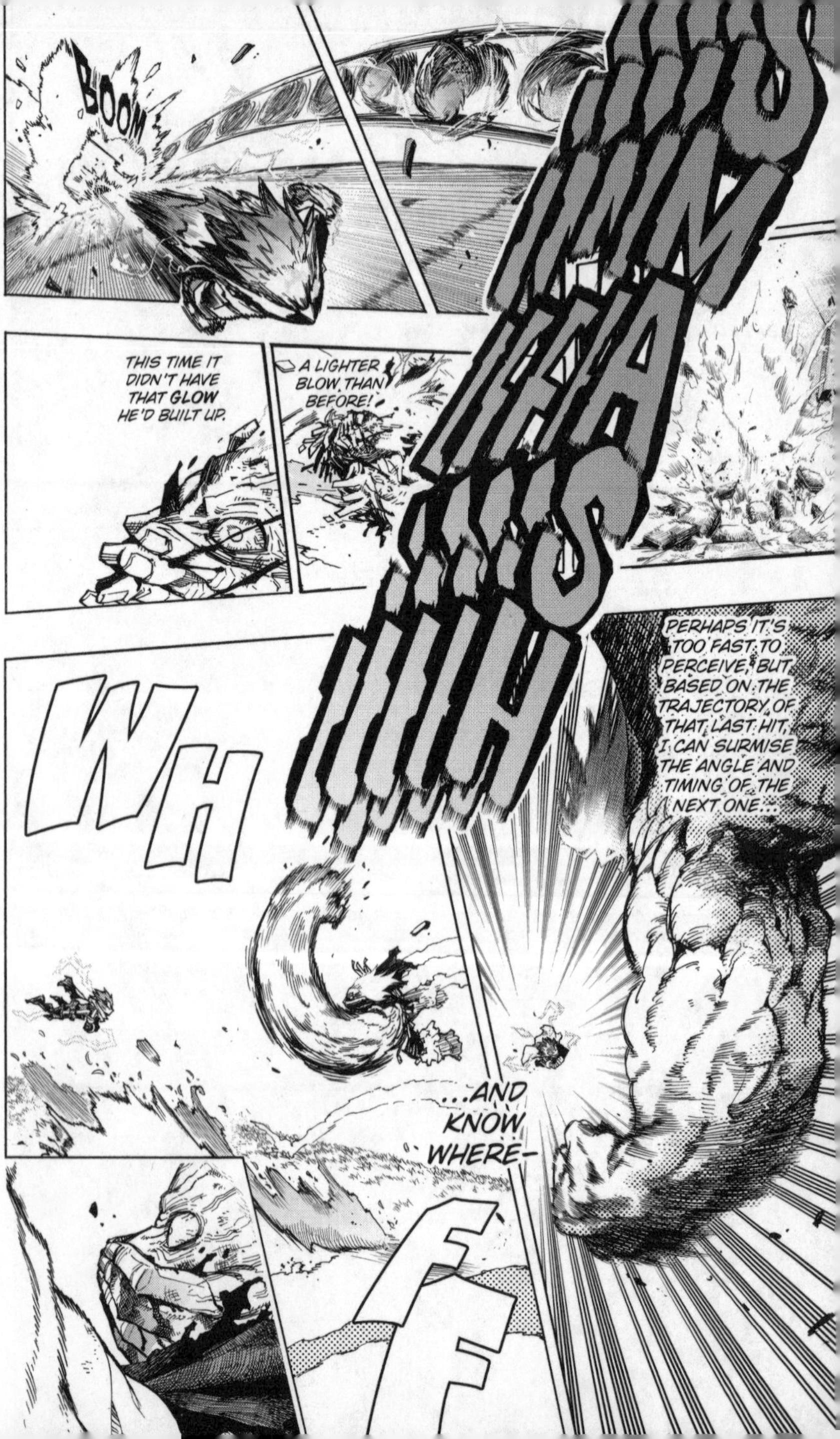
SMASH
BOOM
A LIGHTER BLOW THAN BEFORE!
THIS TIME IT DIDN'T HAVE THAT GLOW HE'D BUILT UP.
PERHAPS IT'S TOO FAST TO PERCEIVE, BUT BASED ON THE TRAJECTORY OF THAT LAST HIT, I CAN SURMISE THE ANGLE AND TIMING OF THE NEXT ONE...
WH
...AND KNOW WHERE-
FF

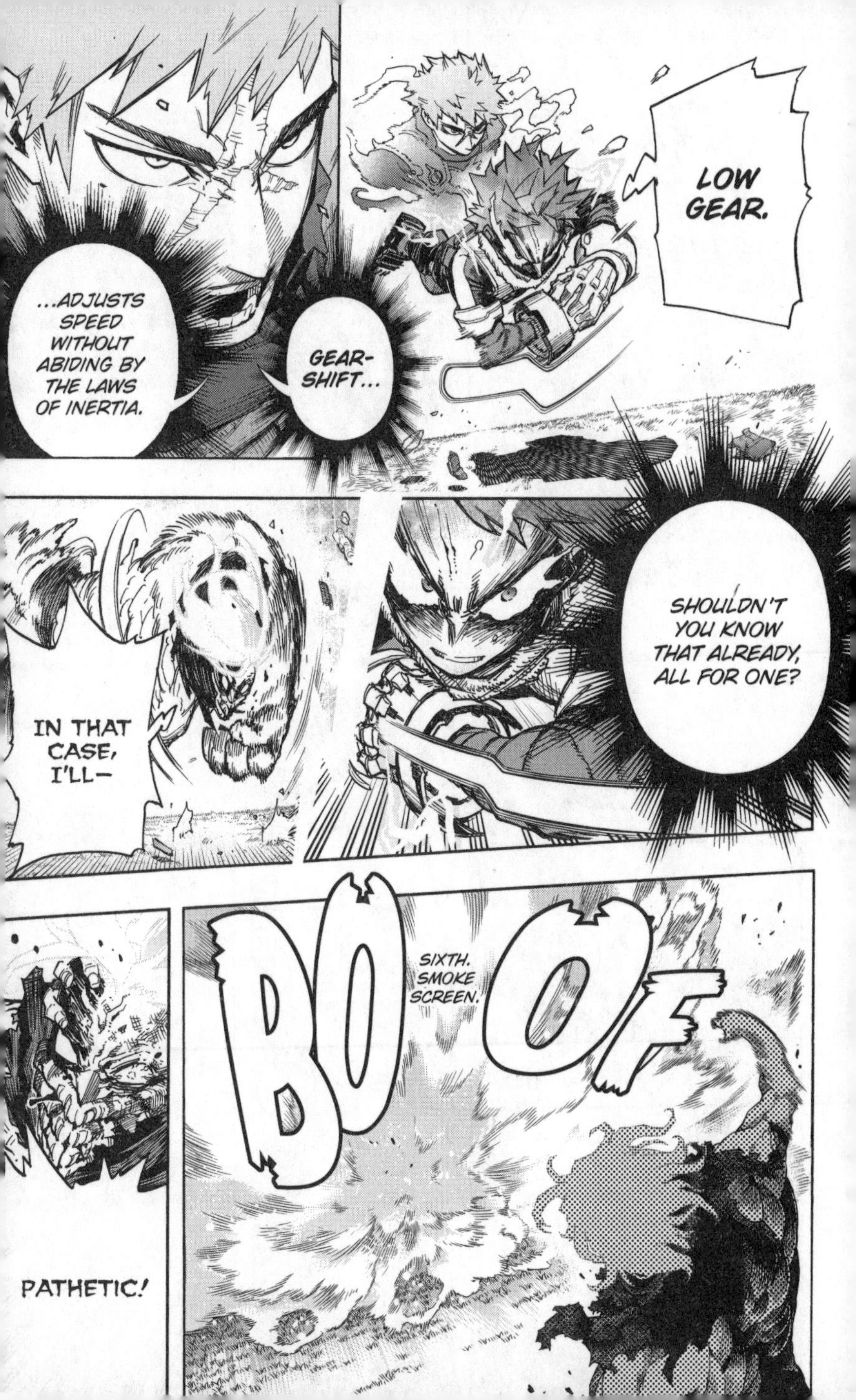
LOW GEAR.
GEAR-SHIFT...
...ADJUSTS SPEED WITHOUT ABIDING BY THE LAWS OF INERTIA.
SHOULDN'T YOU KNOW THAT ALREADY, ALL FOR ONE?
IN THAT CASE, I'LL—
SIXTH. SMOKE SCREEN.
BOOF
PATHETIC!

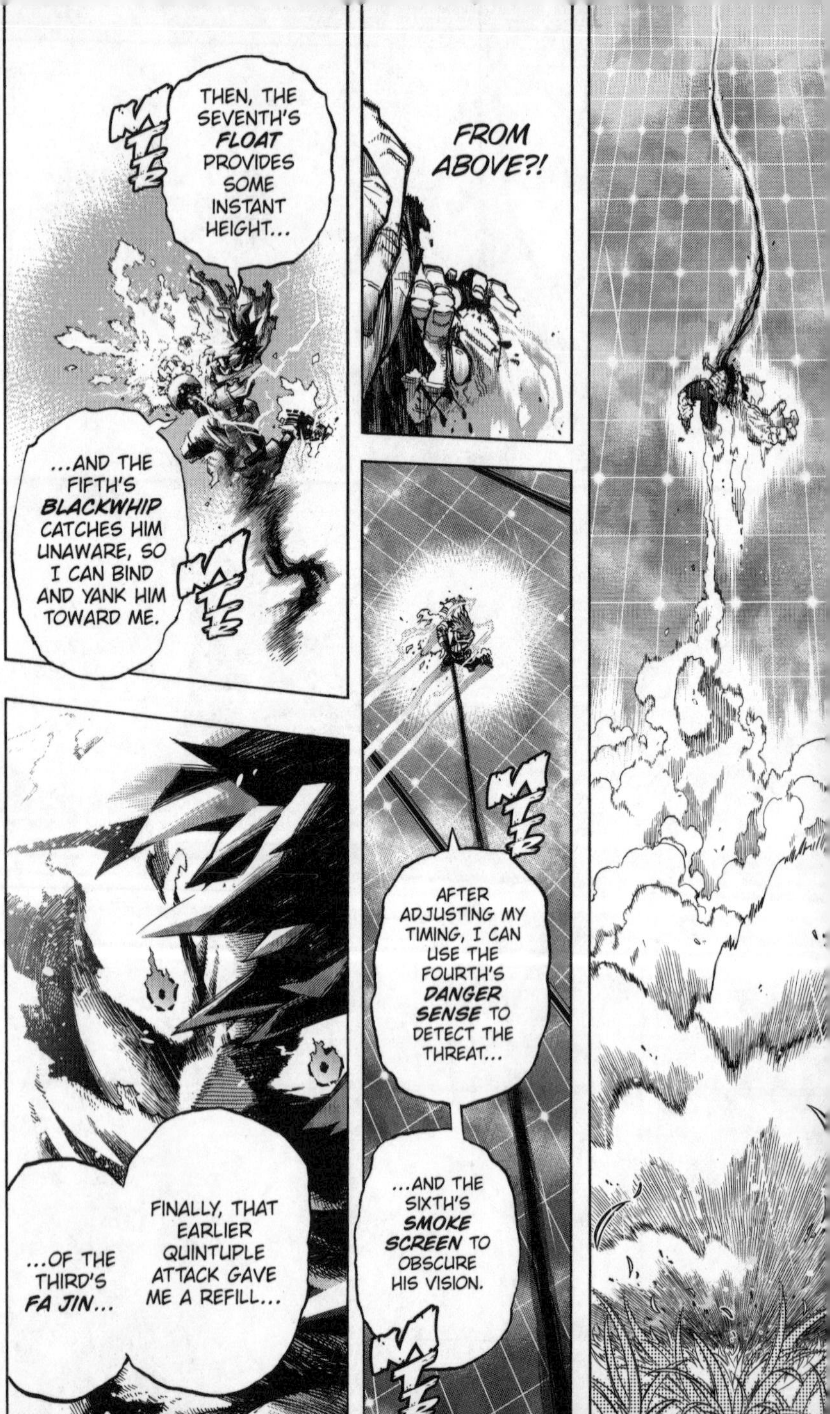
FROM ABOVE?!
AFTER ADJUSTING MY TIMING, I CAN USE THE FOURTH'S DANGER SENSE TO DETECT THE THREAT...
...AND THE SIXTH'S SMOKE SCREEN TO OBSCURE HIS VISION.
THEN, THE SEVENTH'S FLOAT PROVIDES SOME INSTANT HEIGHT...
...AND THE FIFTH'S BLACKWHIP CATCHES HIM UNAWARE, SO I CAN BIND AND YANK HIM TOWARD ME.
FINALLY, THAT EARLIER QUINTUPLE ATTACK GAVE ME A REFILL...
...OF THE THIRD'S FA JIN...

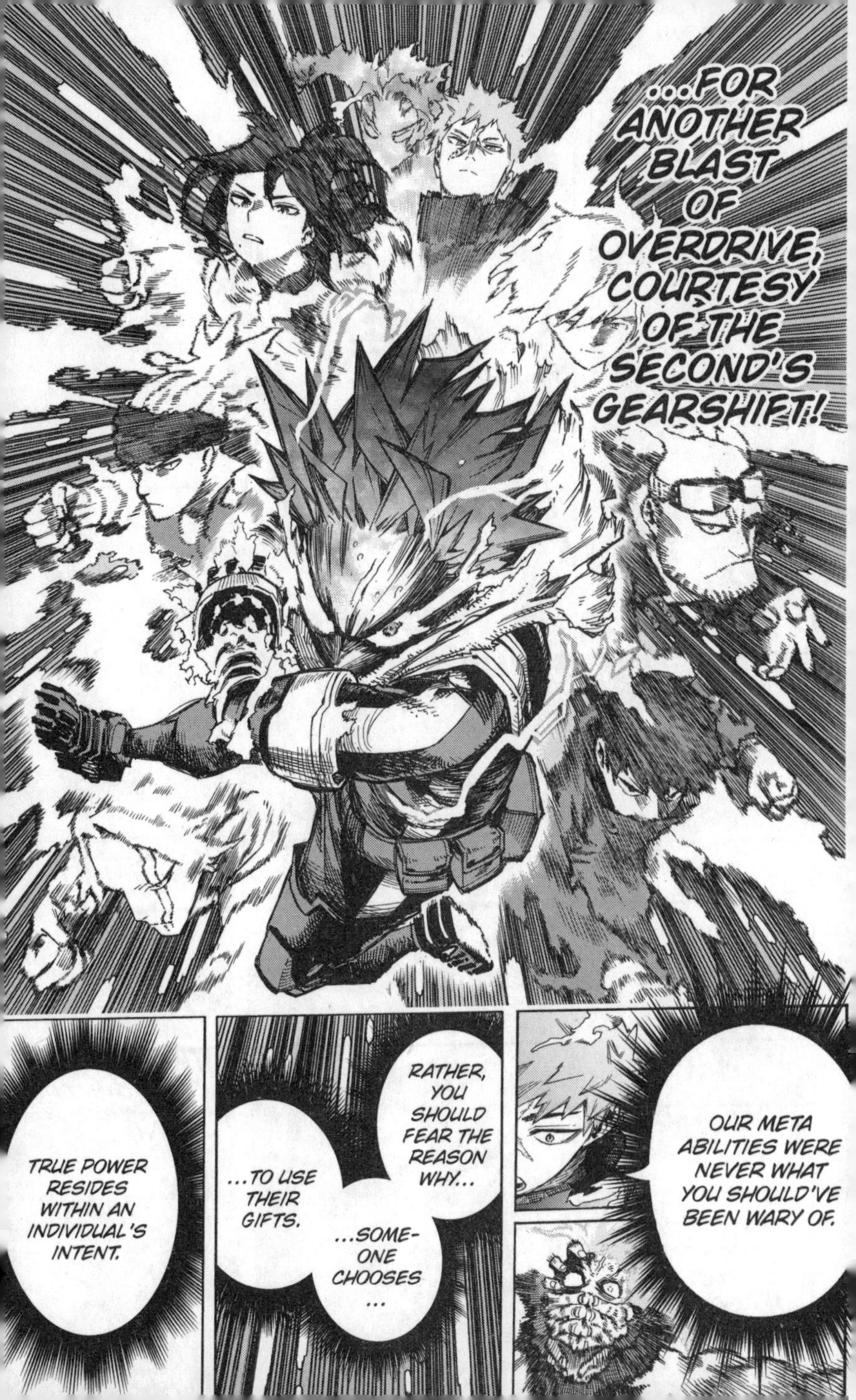
...FOR ANOTHER BLAST OF OVERDRIVE, COURTESY OF THE SECOND'S GEARSHIFT!
OUR META ABILITIES WERE NEVER WHAT YOU SHOULD'VE BEEN WARY OF.
RATHER, YOU SHOULD FEAR THE REASON WHY...
...SOME-ONE CHOOSES ...
...TO USE THEIR GIFTS.
TRUE POWER RESIDES WITHIN AN INDIVIDUAL'S INTENT.

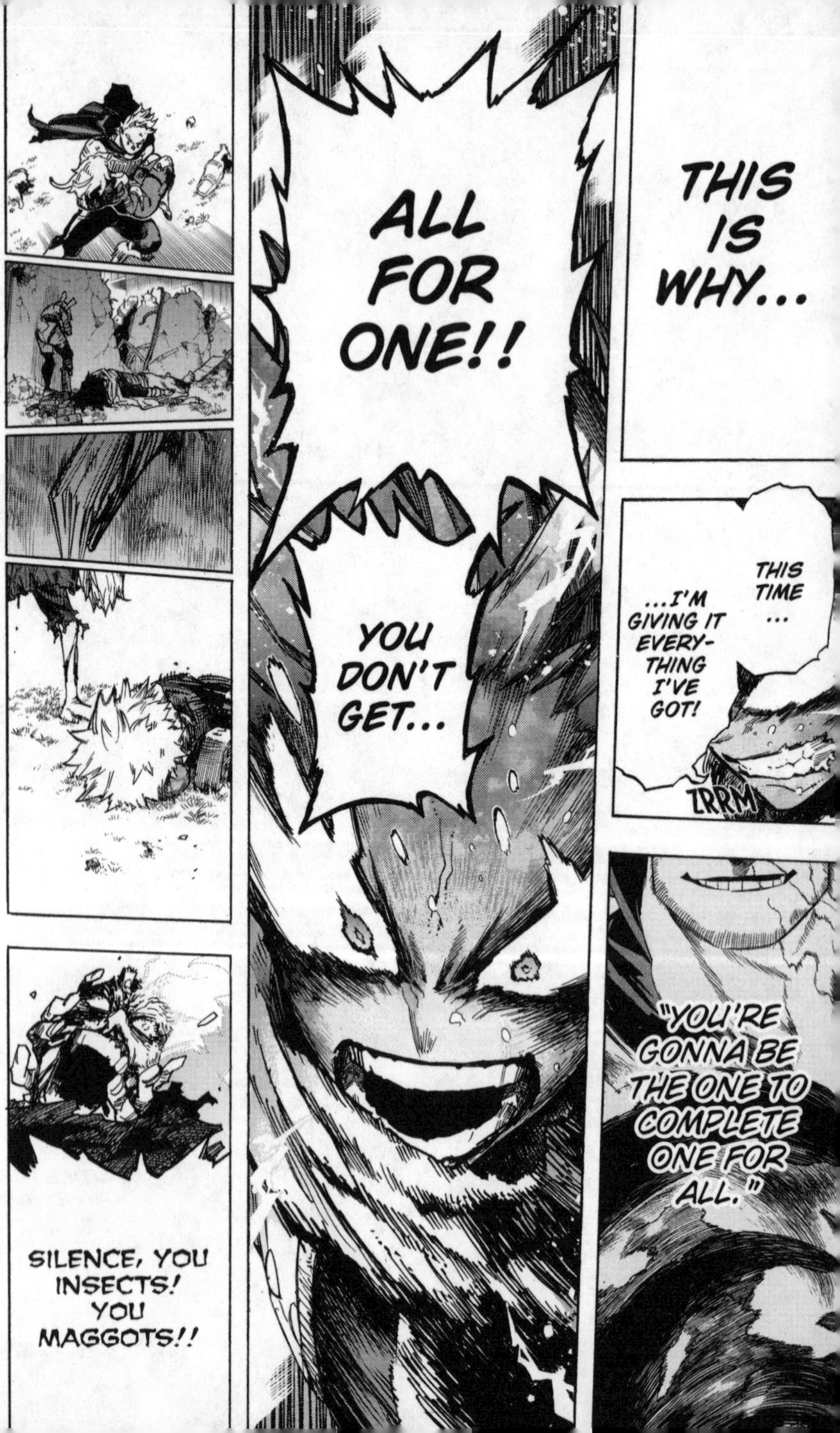
THIS IS WHY...
THIS TIME...
...I'M GIVING IT EVERY-THING I'VE GOT!
ZRRM
"YOU'RE GONNA BE THE ONE TO COMPLETE ONE FOR ALL."
ALL FOR ONE!!
YOU DON'T GET...
SILENCE, YOU INSECTS! YOU MAGGOTS!!

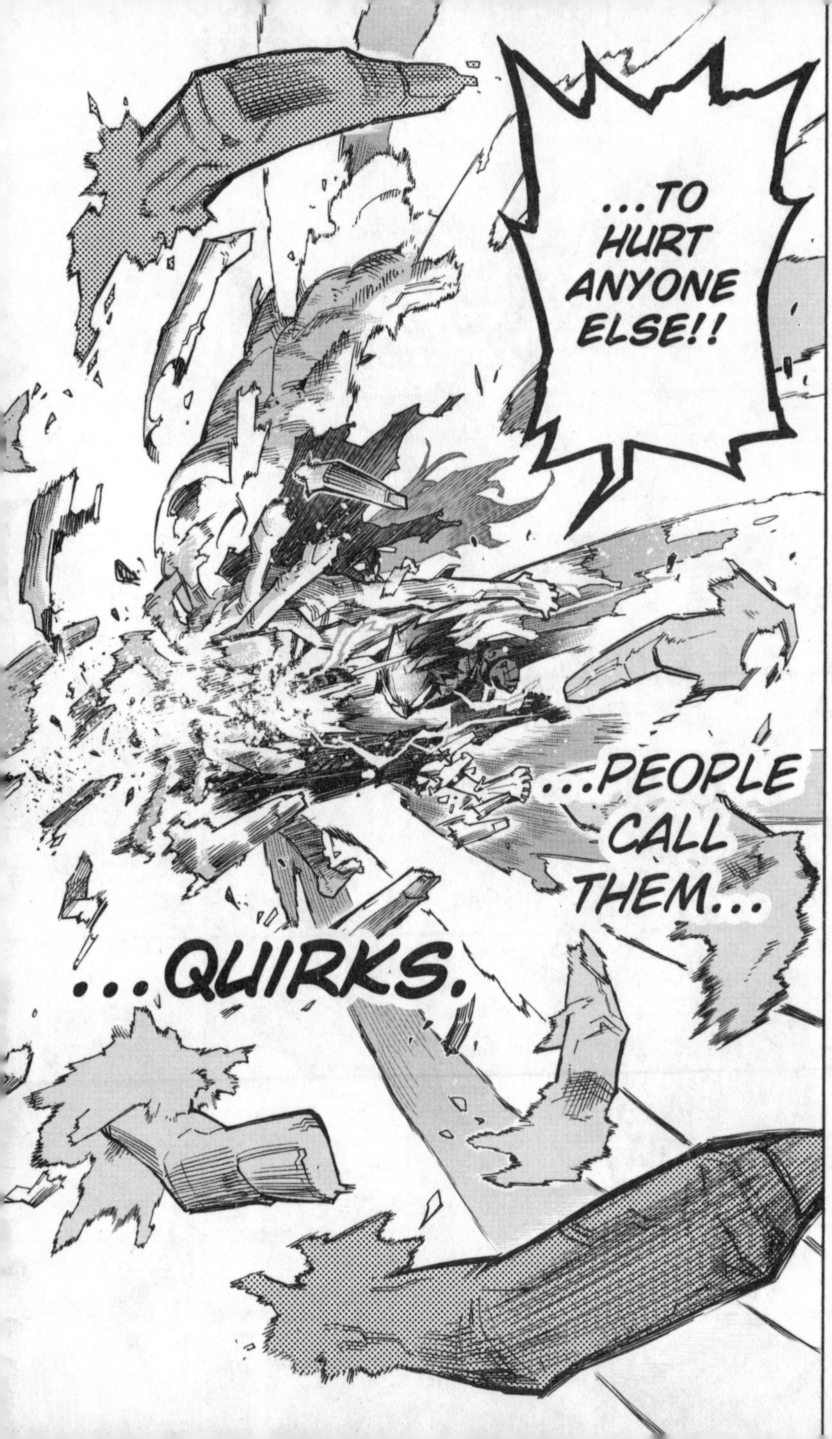
...TO HURT ANYONE ELSE!!
...PEOPLE CALL THEM...
...QUIRKS.

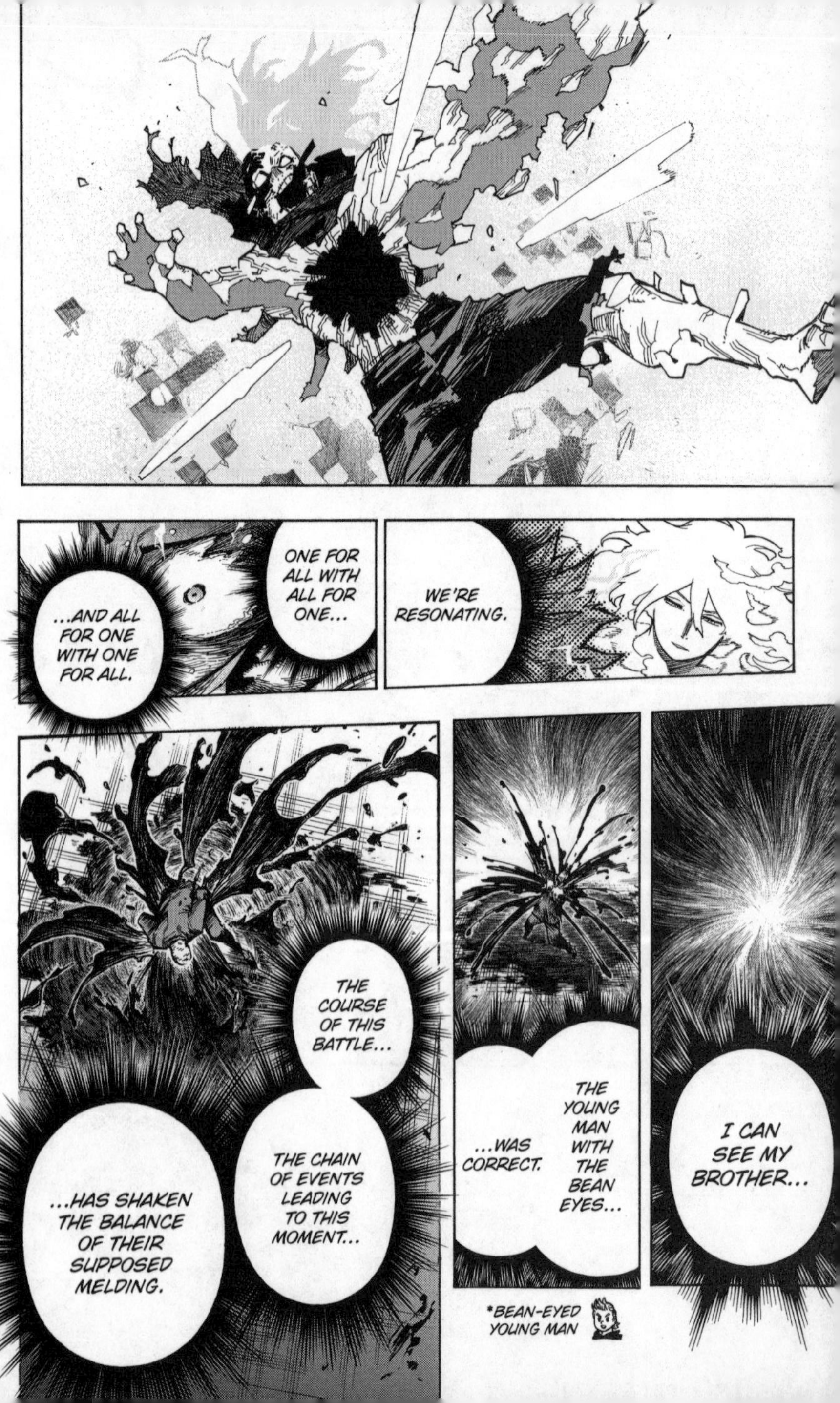
WE'RE RESONATING.
ONE FOR ALL WITH ALL FOR ONE...
...AND ALL FOR ONE WITH ONE FOR ALL.
I CAN SEE MY BROTHER...
THE YOUNG MAN WITH THE BEAN EYES...
...WAS CORRECT.
*BEAN-EYED YOUNG MAN
THE COURSE OF THIS BATTLE...
THE CHAIN OF EVENTS LEADING TO THIS MOMENT...
...HAS SHAKEN THE BALANCE OF THEIR SUPPOSED MELDING.

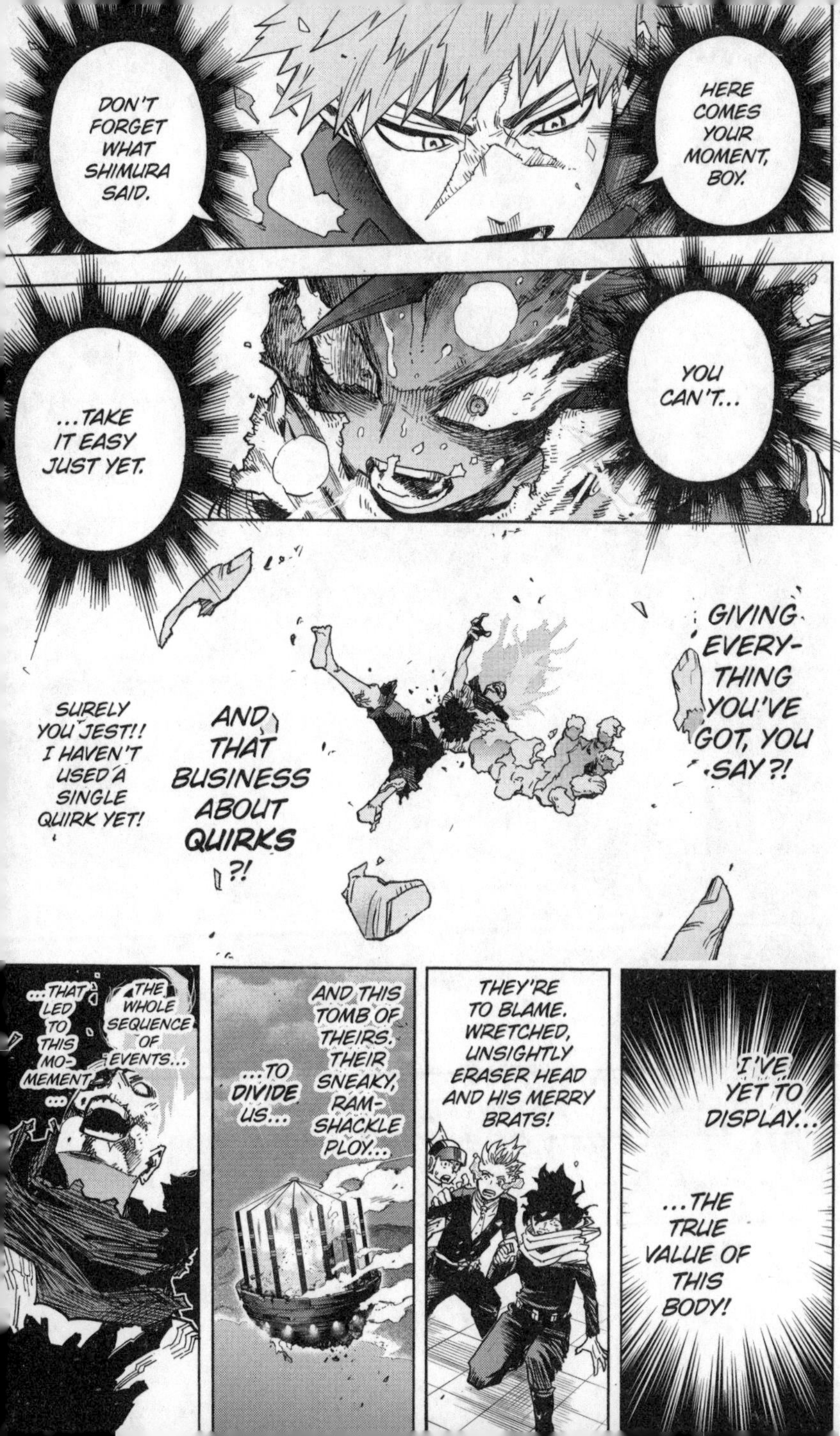
HERE COMES YOUR MOMENT, BOY.
DON'T FORGET WHAT SHIMURA SAID.
YOU CAN'T...
...TAKE IT EASY JUST YET.
GIVING EVERYTHING YOU'VE GOT, YOU SAY?!
AND THAT BUSINESS ABOUT QUIRKS?!
SURELY YOU JEST!! I HAVEN'T USED A SINGLE QUIRK YET!
I'VE YET TO DISPLAY...
...THE TRUE VALUE OF THIS BODY!
THEY'RE TO BLAME. WRETCHED, UNSIGHTLY ERASER HEAD AND HIS MERRY BRATS!
AND THIS TOMB OF THEIRS. THEIR SNEAKY, RAMSHACKLE PLOY...
...TO DIVIDE US...
THE WHOLE SEQUENCE OF EVENTS...
...THAT LED TO THIS MOMEMENT...

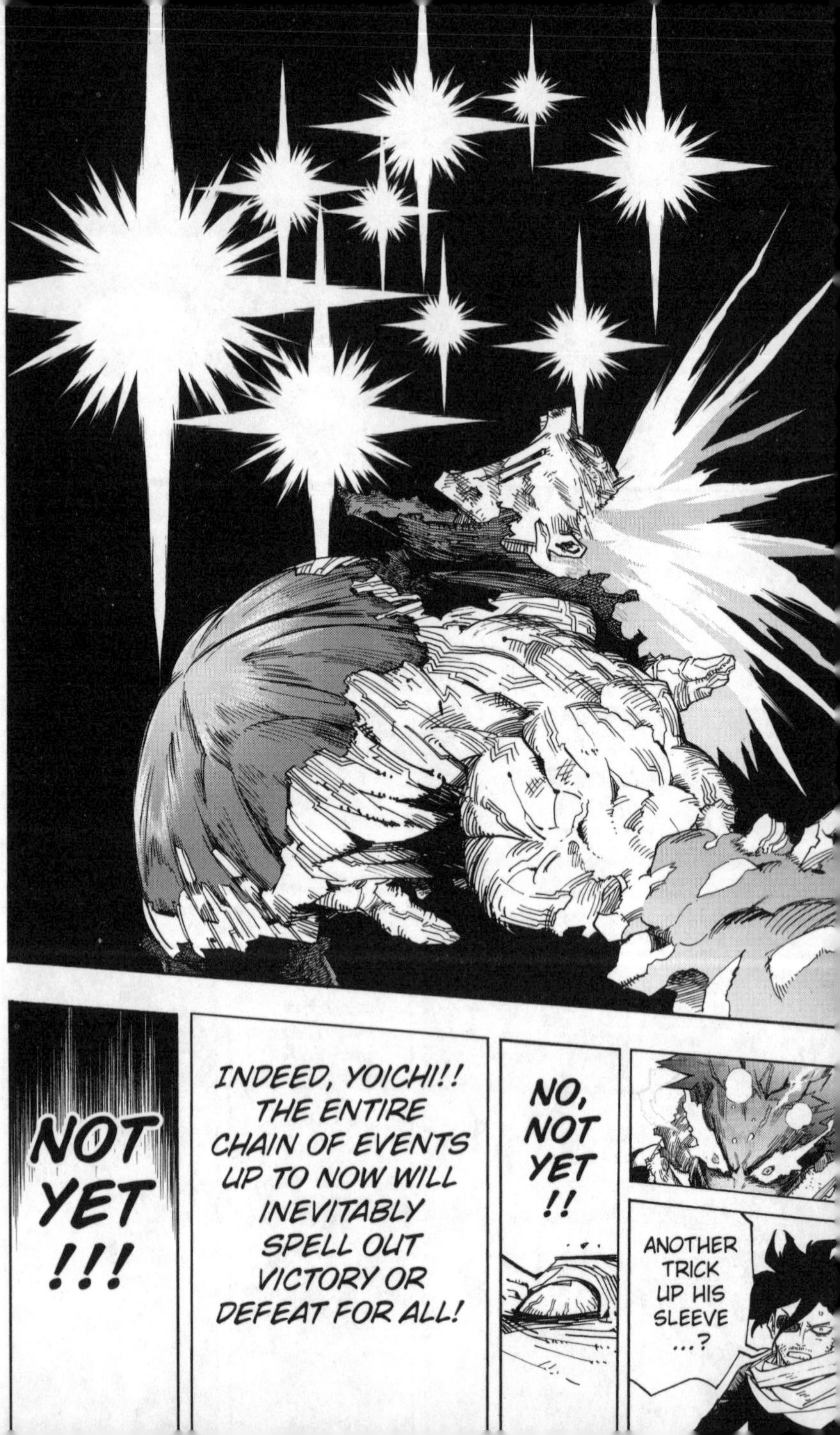
ANOTHER TRICK UP HIS SLEEVE ...?
NO, NOT YET!!
INDEED, YOICHI!! THE ENTIRE CHAIN OF EVENTS UP TO NOW WILL INEVITABLY SPELL OUT VICTORY OR DEFEAT FOR ALL!
NOT YET!!!

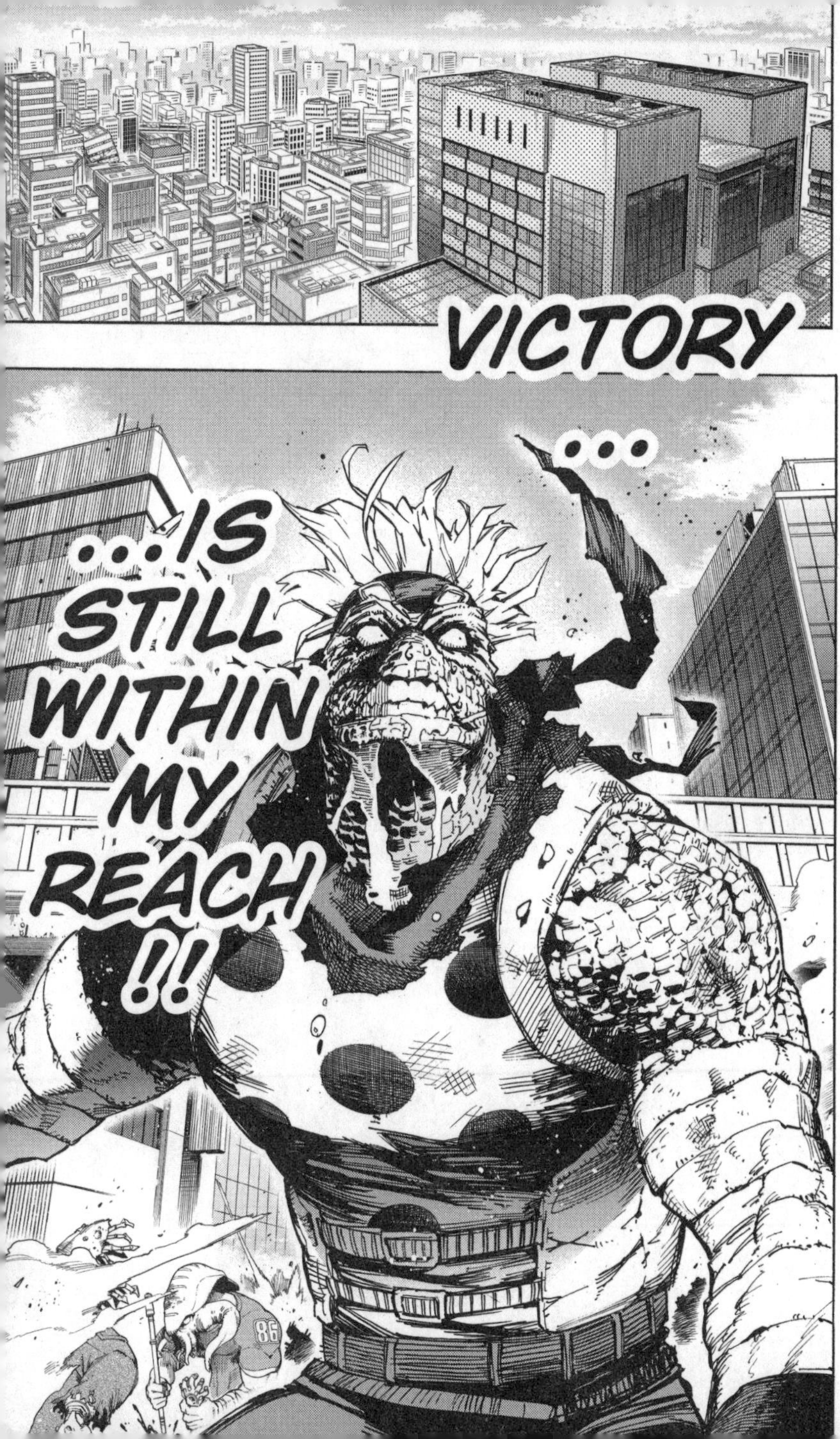
VICTORY
...
...IS STILL WITHIN MY REACH!!

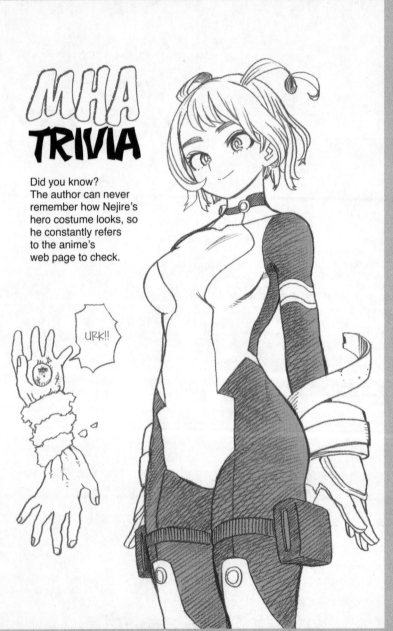

MHA TRIVIA

Did you know?
The author can never remember how Nejire's hero costume looks, so he constantly refers to the anime's web page to check.

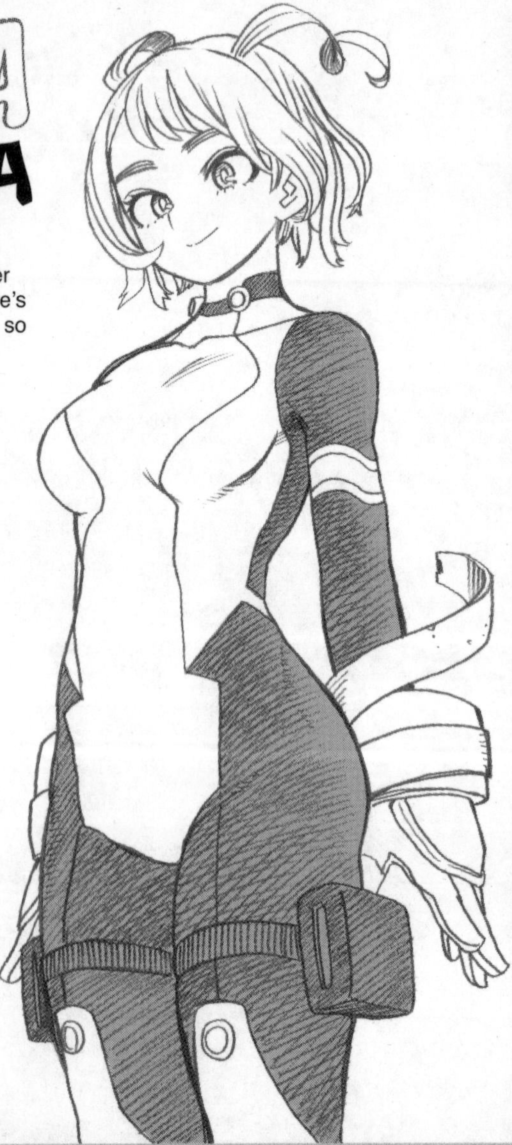

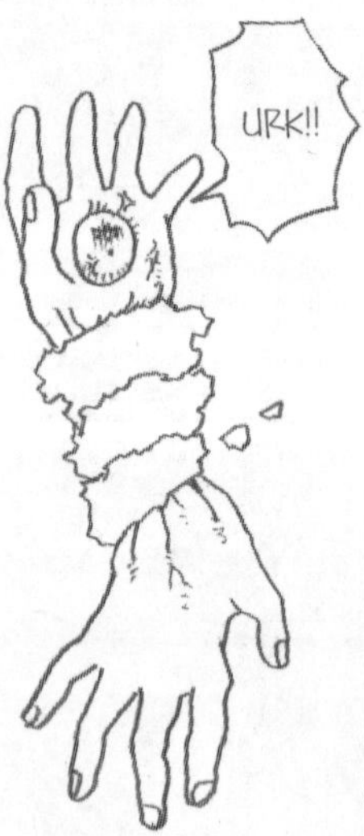
URK!!

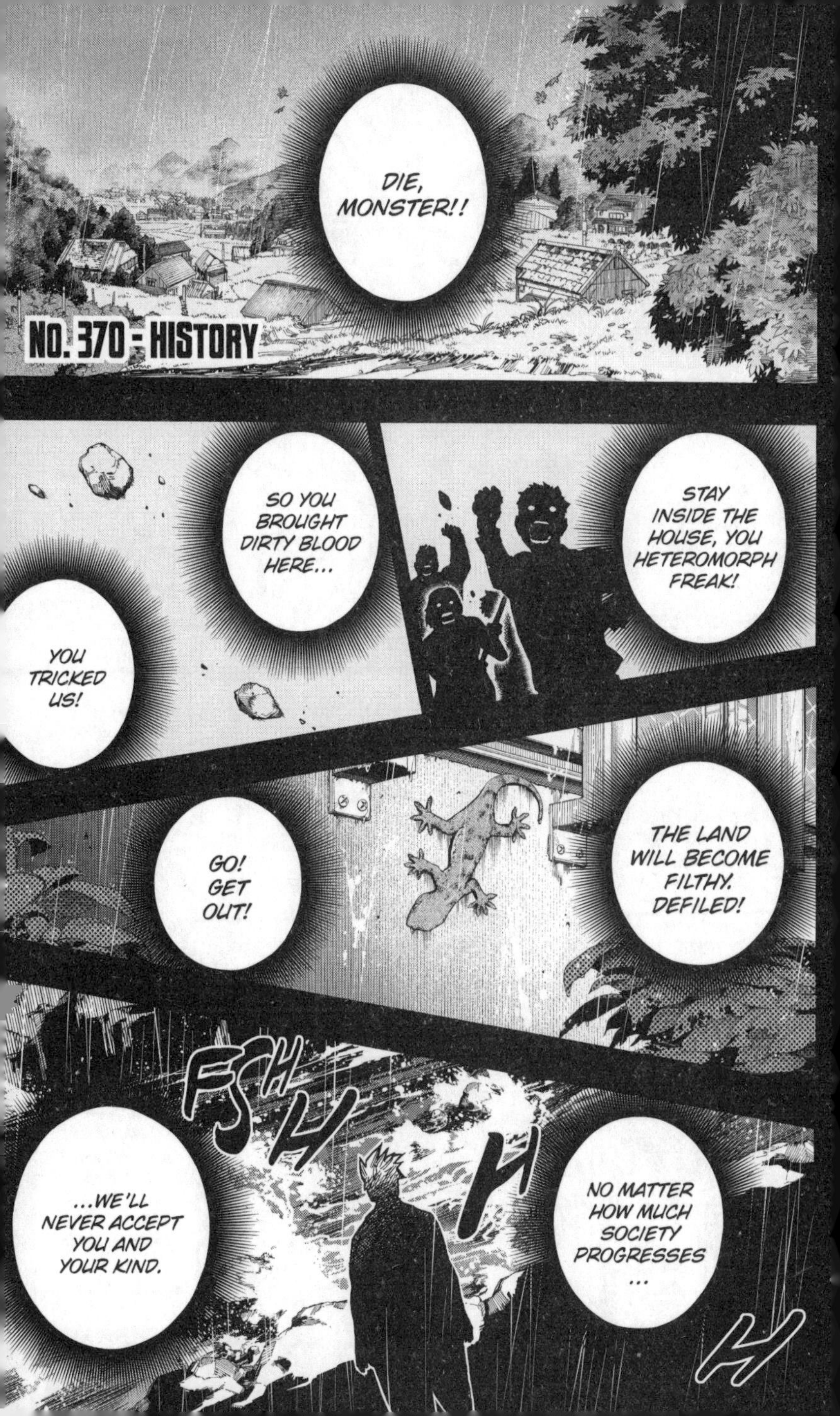
DIE, MONSTER!!
NO. 370 - HISTORY
STAY INSIDE THE HOUSE, YOU HETEROMORPH FREAK!
SO YOU BROUGHT DIRTY BLOOD HERE...
YOU TRICKED US!
THE LAND WILL BECOME FILTHY. DEFILED!
GO! GET OUT!
FSHHH
NO MATTER HOW MUCH SOCIETY PROGRESSES ...
...WE'LL NEVER ACCEPT YOU AND YOUR KIND.

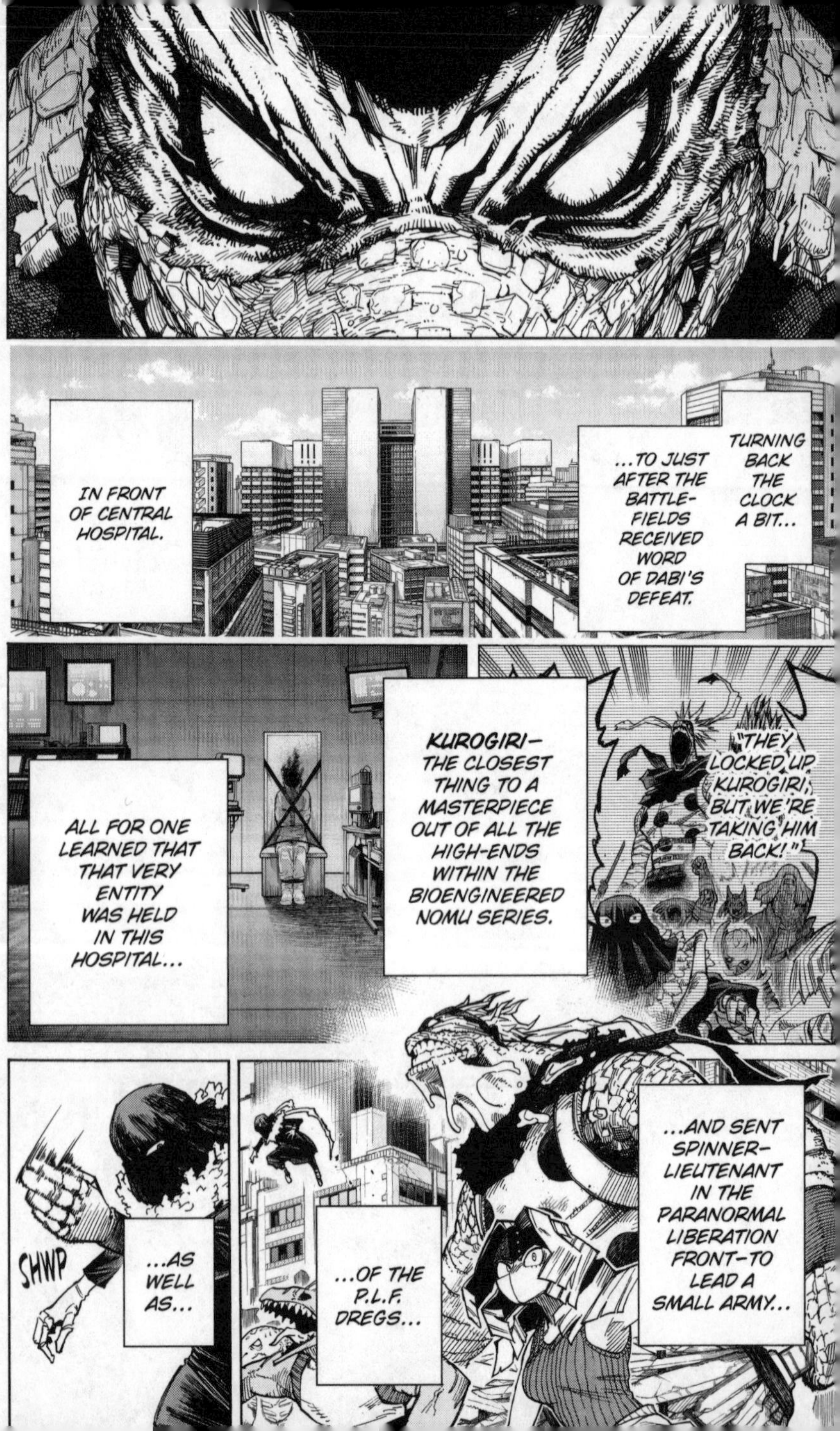
TURNING BACK THE CLOCK A BIT...
...TO JUST AFTER THE BATTLE-FIELDS RECEIVED WORD OF DABI'S DEFEAT.
IN FRONT OF CENTRAL HOSPITAL.
"THEY LOCKED UP KUROGIRI, BUT WE'RE TAKING HIM BACK!"
KUROGIRI—THE CLOSEST THING TO A MASTERPIECE OUT OF ALL THE HIGH-ENDS WITHIN THE BIOENGINEERED NOMU SERIES.
ALL FOR ONE LEARNED THAT THAT VERY ENTITY WAS HELD IN THIS HOSPITAL...
...AND SENT SPINNER-LIEUTENANT IN THE PARANORMAL LIBERATION FRONT—TO LEAD A SMALL ARMY...
...OF THE P.L.F. DREGS...
...AS WELL AS...
SHWP

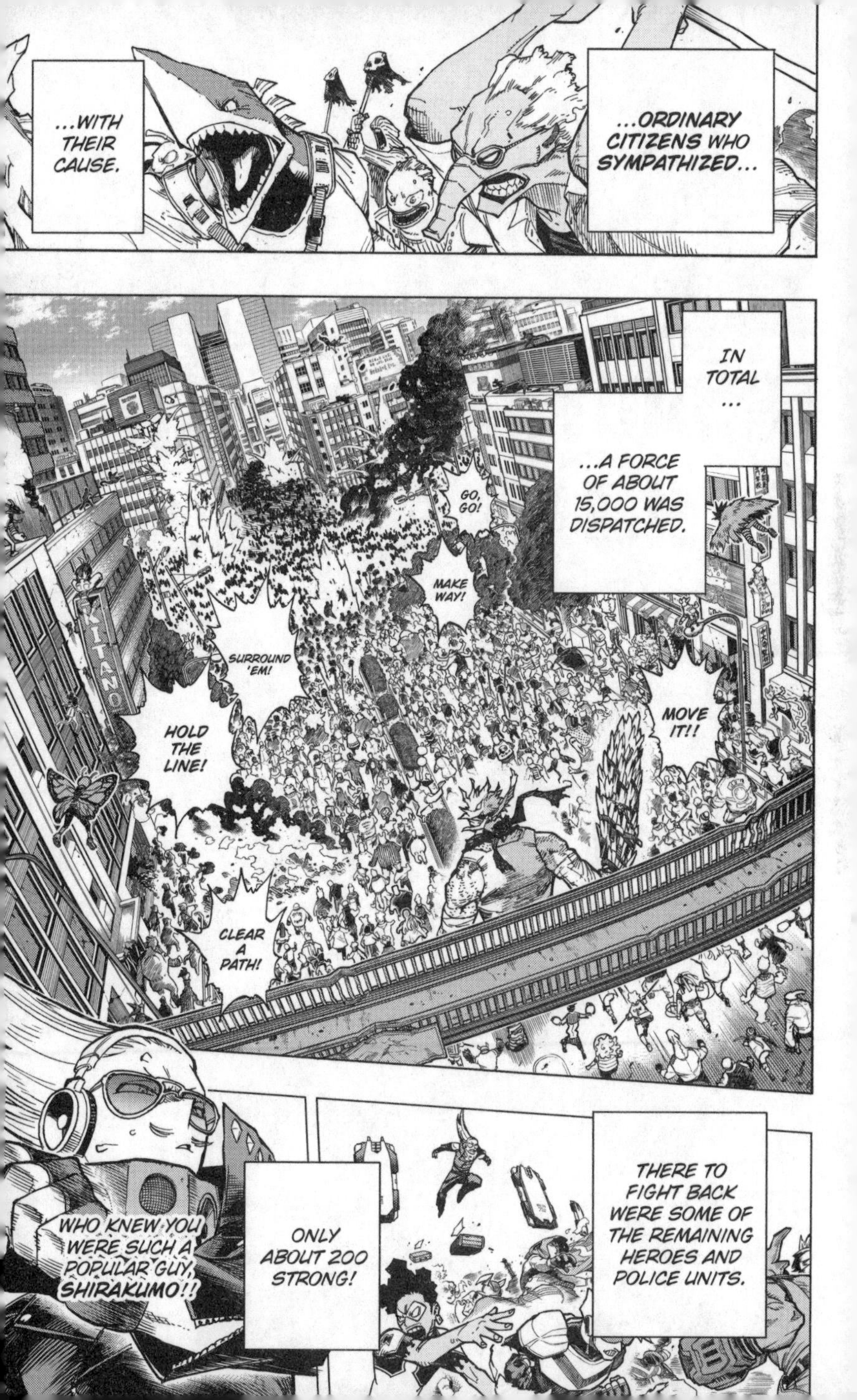
...ORDINARY CITIZENS WHO SYMPATHIZED...
...WITH THEIR CAUSE.
IN TOTAL...
...A FORCE OF ABOUT 15,000 WAS DISPATCHED.
GO, GO!
MAKE WAY!
MOVE IT!!
SURROUND 'EM!
HOLD THE LINE!
CLEAR A PATH!
THERE TO FIGHT BACK WERE SOME OF THE REMAINING HEROES AND POLICE UNITS.
ONLY ABOUT 200 STRONG!
WHO KNEW YOU WERE SUCH A POPULAR GUY, SHIRAKUMO!!

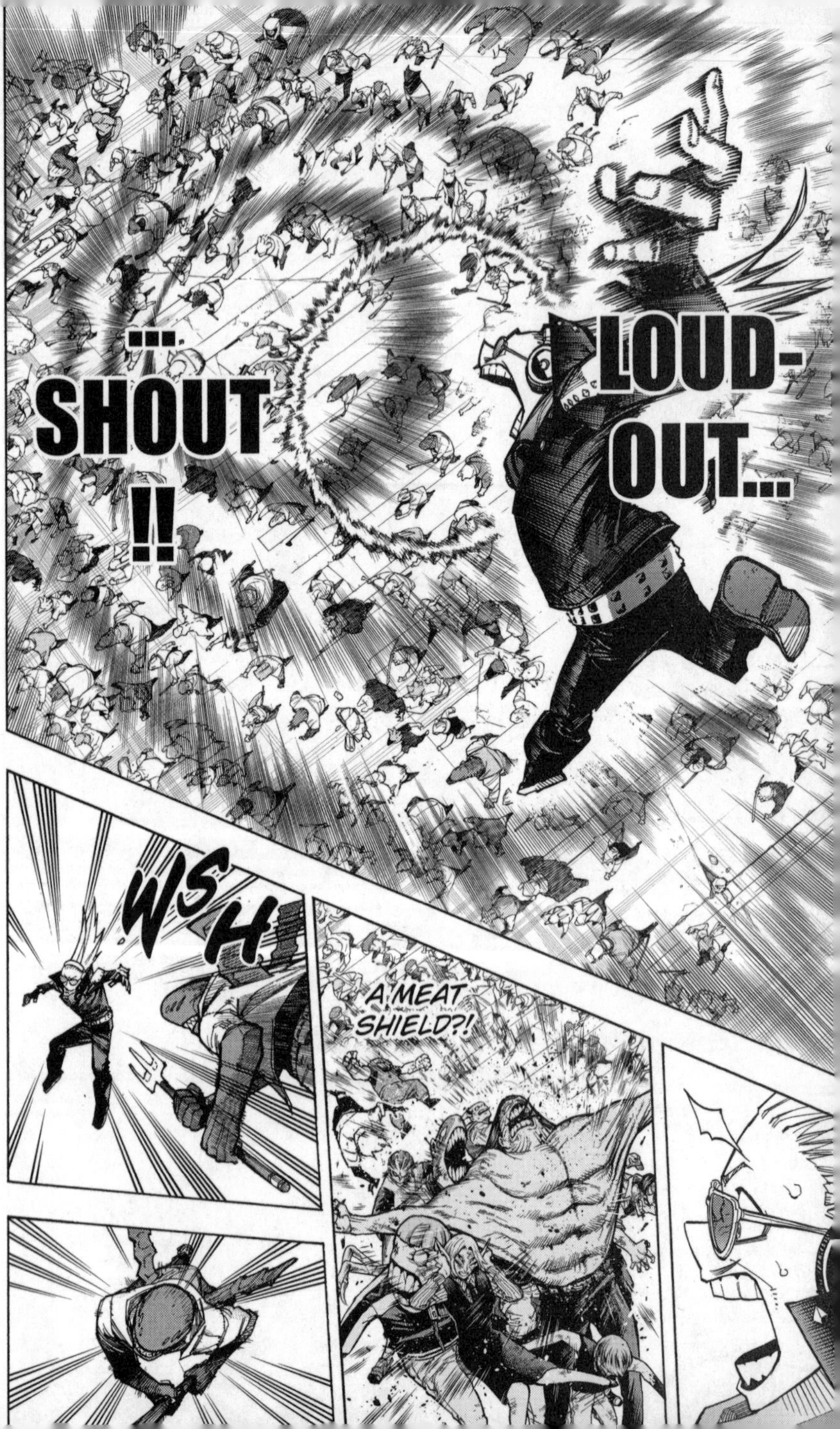
LOUD-
OUT...
...SHOUT!!
A MEAT SHIELD?!
WSH

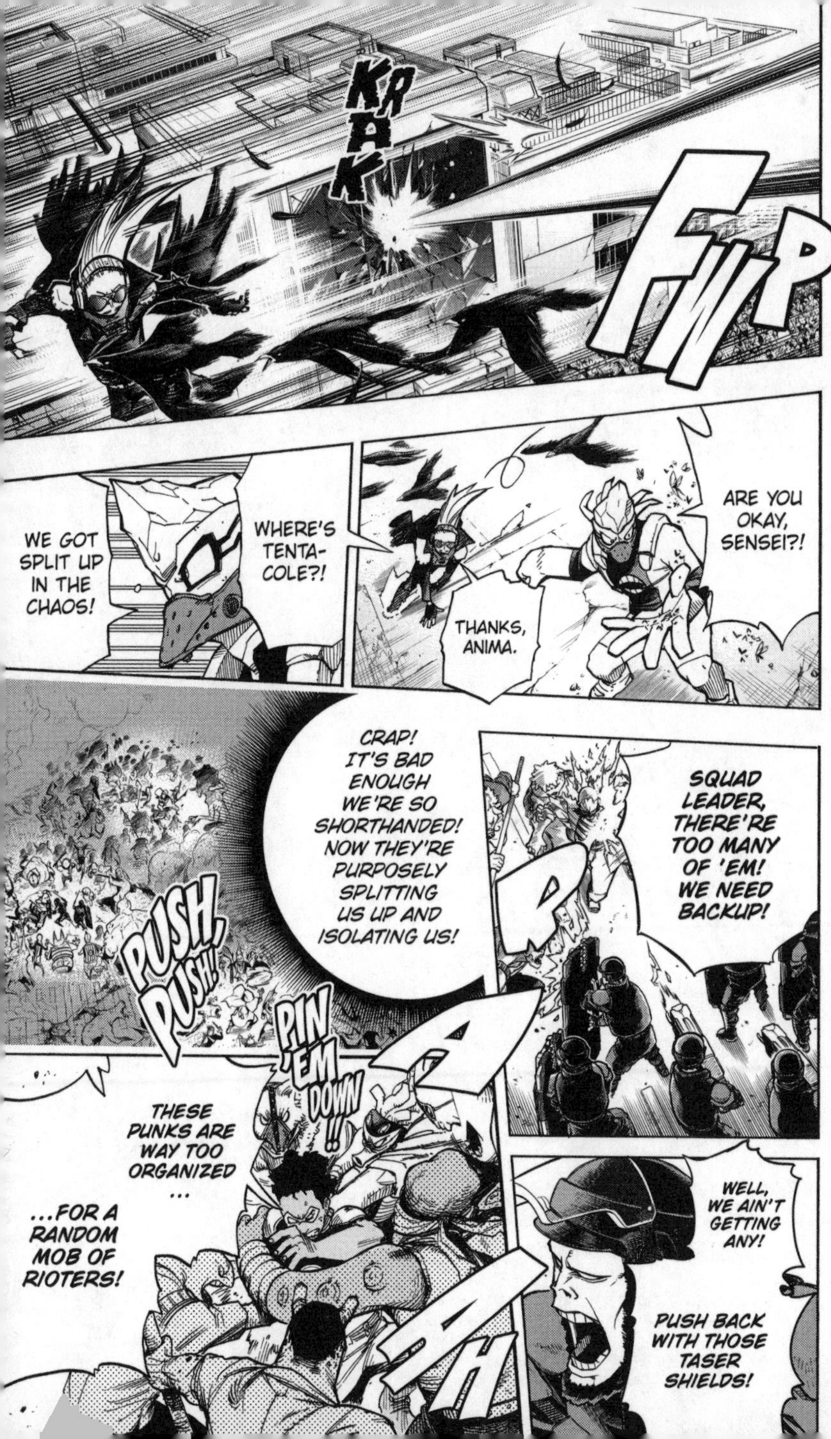
FWIP
KRAK
ARE YOU OKAY, SENSEI?!
THANKS, ANIMA.
WHERE'S TENTA-COLE?!
WE GOT SPLIT UP IN THE CHAOS!
SQUAD LEADER, THERE'RE TOO MANY OF 'EM! WE NEED BACKUP!
CRAP! IT'S BAD ENOUGH WE'RE SO SHORTHANDED! NOW THEY'RE PURPOSELY SPLITTING US UP AND ISOLATING US!
PUSH, PUSH!
PIN 'EM DOWN!!
WELL, WE AIN'T GETTING ANY!
PUSH BACK WITH THOSE TASER SHIELDS!
THESE PUNKS ARE WAY TOO ORGANIZED...
...FOR A RANDOM MOB OF RIOTERS!

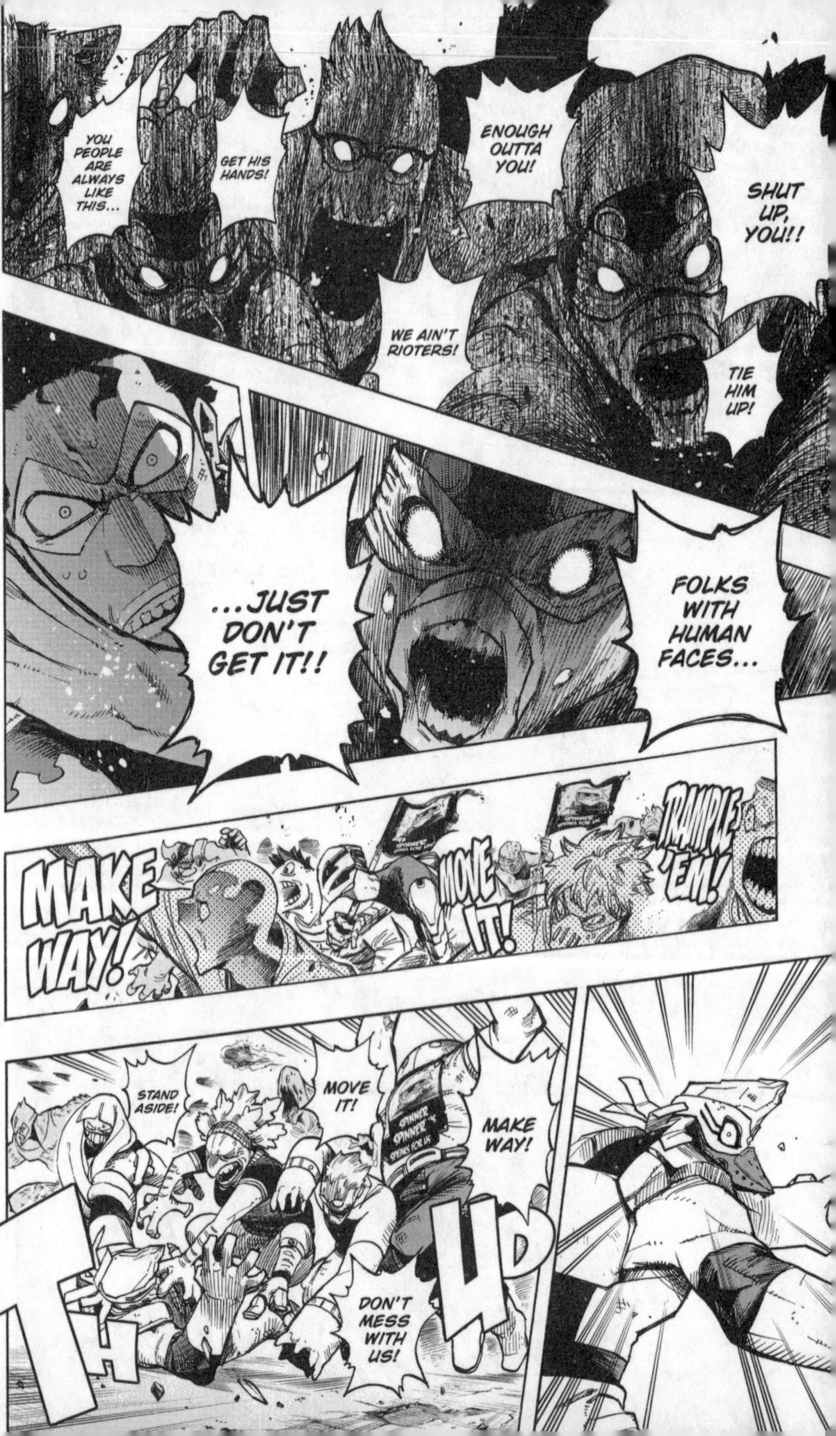
SHUT UP, YOU!!
ENOUGH OUTTA YOU!
GET HIS HANDS!
YOU PEOPLE ARE ALWAYS LIKE THIS...
TIE HIM UP!
WE AIN'T RIOTERS!
FOLKS WITH HUMAN FACES...
...JUST DON'T GET IT!!
TRAMPLE 'EM!
MOVE IT!
MAKE WAY!
MAKE WAY!
SPINNER
SPINNER
SPEAKS FOR US
MOVE IT!
STAND ASIDE!
THUD
DON'T MESS WITH US!

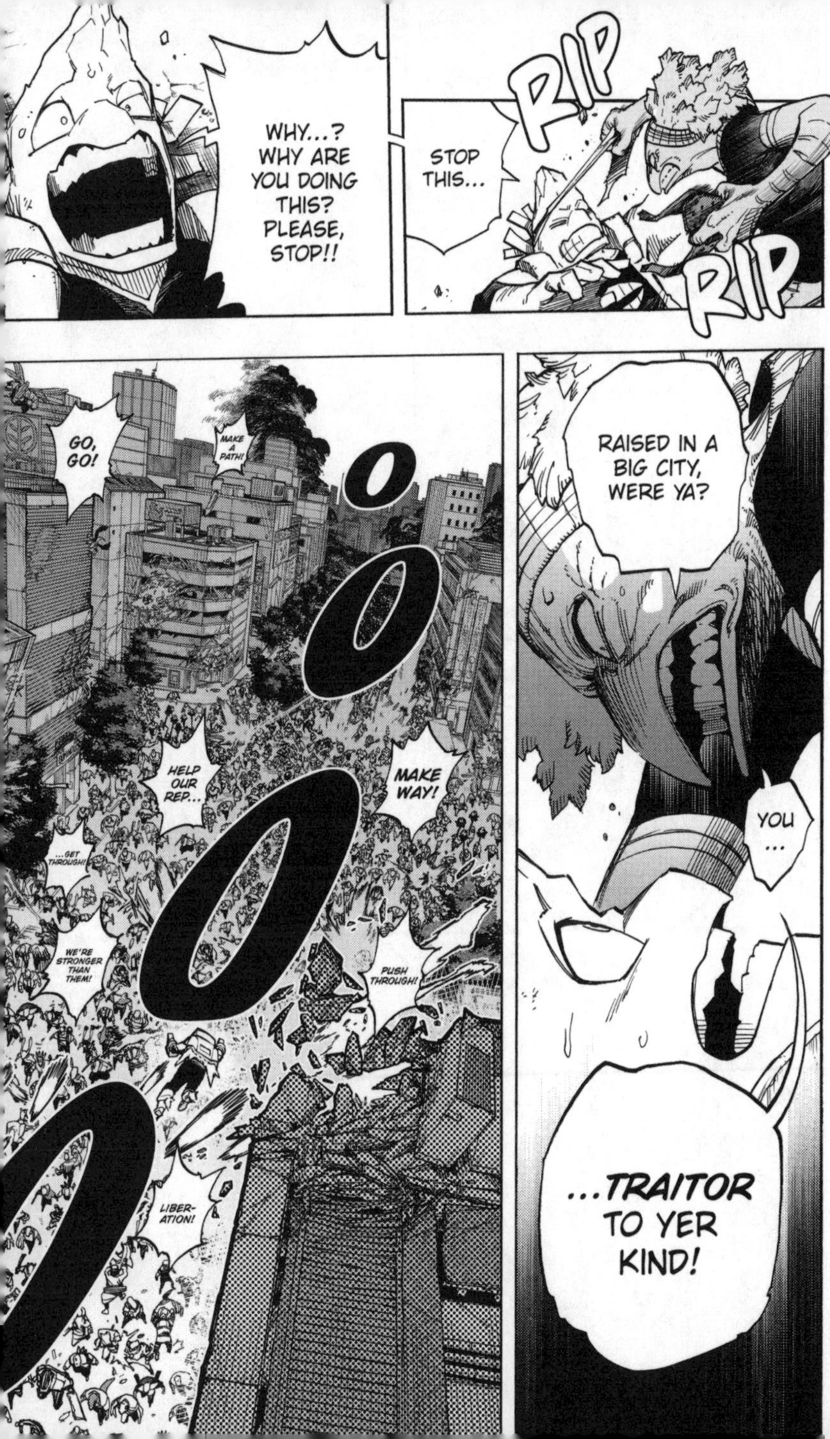
STOP THIS...
RIP
RIP
WHY...? WHY ARE YOU DOING THIS? PLEASE, STOP!!
RAISED IN A BIG CITY, WERE YA?
YOU...
...TRAITOR TO YER KIND!
MAKE A PATH!
GO, GO!
OOOO
MAKE WAY!
HELP OUR REP...
...GET THROUGH!
PUSH THROUGH!
WE'RE STRONGER THAN THEM!
LIBER-ATION!

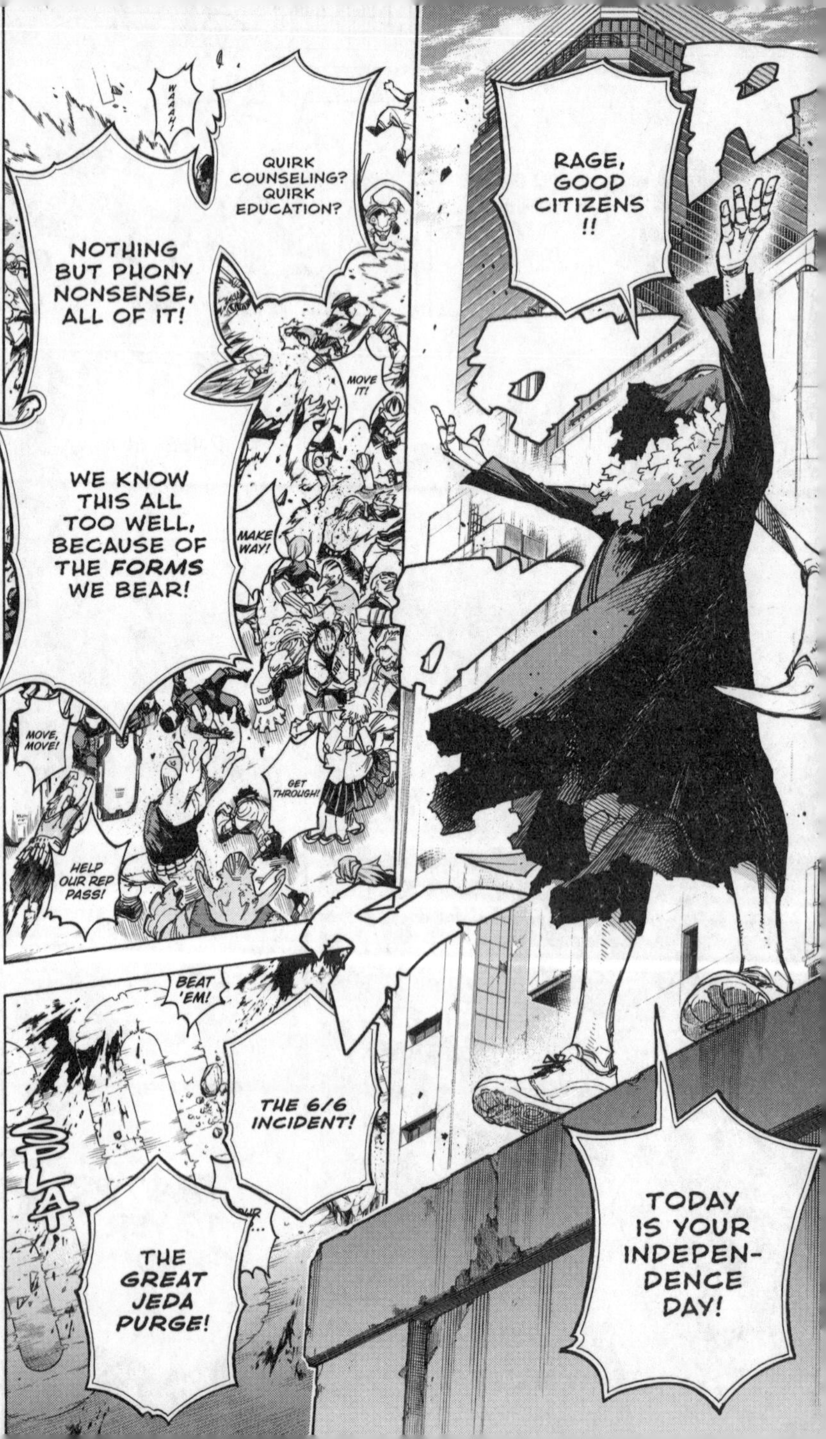
RAGE, GOOD CITIZENS !!
TODAY IS YOUR INDEPEN-DENCE DAY!
QUIRK COUNSELING? QUIRK EDUCATION?
NOTHING BUT PHONY NONSENSE, ALL OF IT!
MOVE IT!
WE KNOW THIS ALL TOO WELL, BECAUSE OF THE *FORMS* WE BEAR!
MAKE WAY!
MOVE, MOVE!
GET THROUGH!
HELP OUR REP PASS!
BEAT 'EM!
THE 6/6 INCIDENT!
THE GREAT JEDA PURGE!

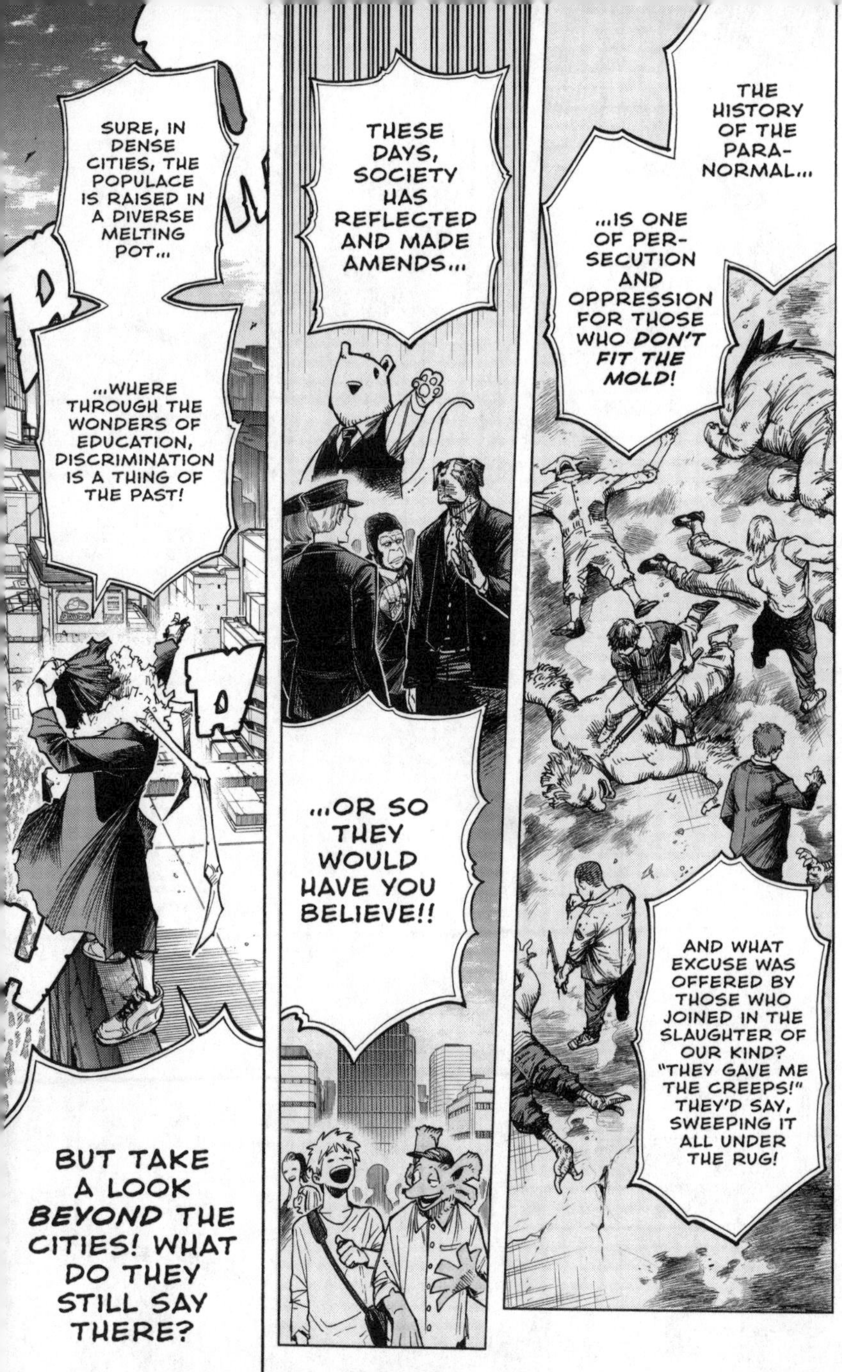

THE HISTORY OF THE PARA-NORMAL...
...IS ONE OF PER-SECUTION AND OPPRESSION FOR THOSE WHO *DON'T FIT THE MOLD!*
AND WHAT EXCUSE WAS OFFERED BY THOSE WHO JOINED IN THE SLAUGHTER OF OUR KIND? "THEY GAVE ME THE CREEPS!" THEY'D SAY, SWEEPING IT ALL UNDER THE RUG!
THESE DAYS, SOCIETY HAS REFLECTED AND MADE AMENDS...
...OR SO THEY WOULD HAVE YOU BELIEVE!!
SURE, IN DENSE CITIES, THE POPULACE IS RAISED IN A DIVERSE MELTING POT...
...WHERE THROUGH THE WONDERS OF EDUCATION, DISCRIMINATION IS A THING OF THE PAST!
BUT TAKE A LOOK *BEYOND* THE CITIES! WHAT DO THEY STILL SAY THERE?

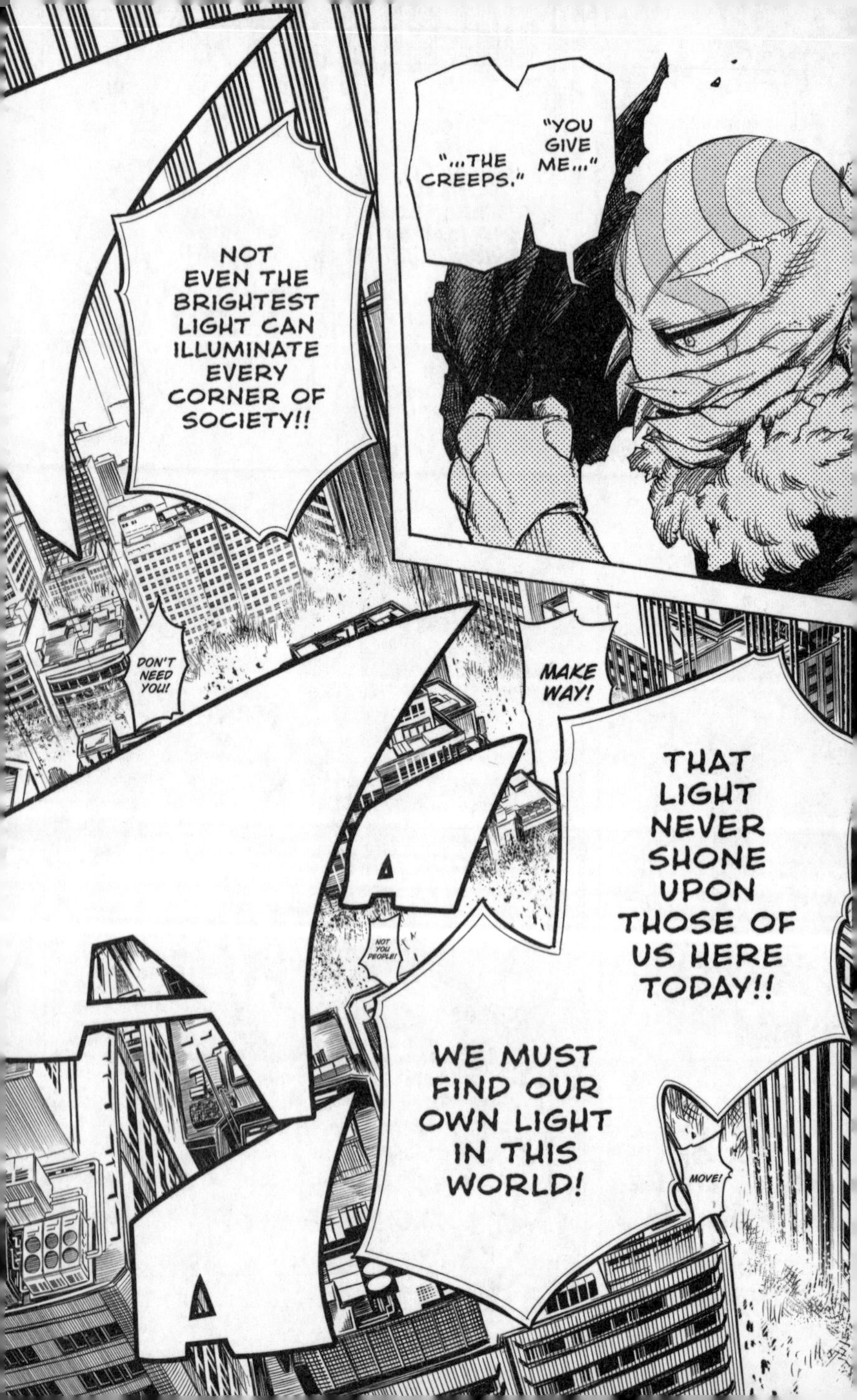
"YOU GIVE ME..."
"...THE CREEPS."
NOT EVEN THE BRIGHTEST LIGHT CAN ILLUMINATE EVERY CORNER OF SOCIETY!!
MAKE WAY!
DON'T NEED YOU!
THAT LIGHT NEVER SHONE UPON THOSE OF US HERE TODAY!!
NOT YOU PEOPLE!
WE MUST FIND OUR OWN LIGHT IN THIS WORLD!
MOVE!

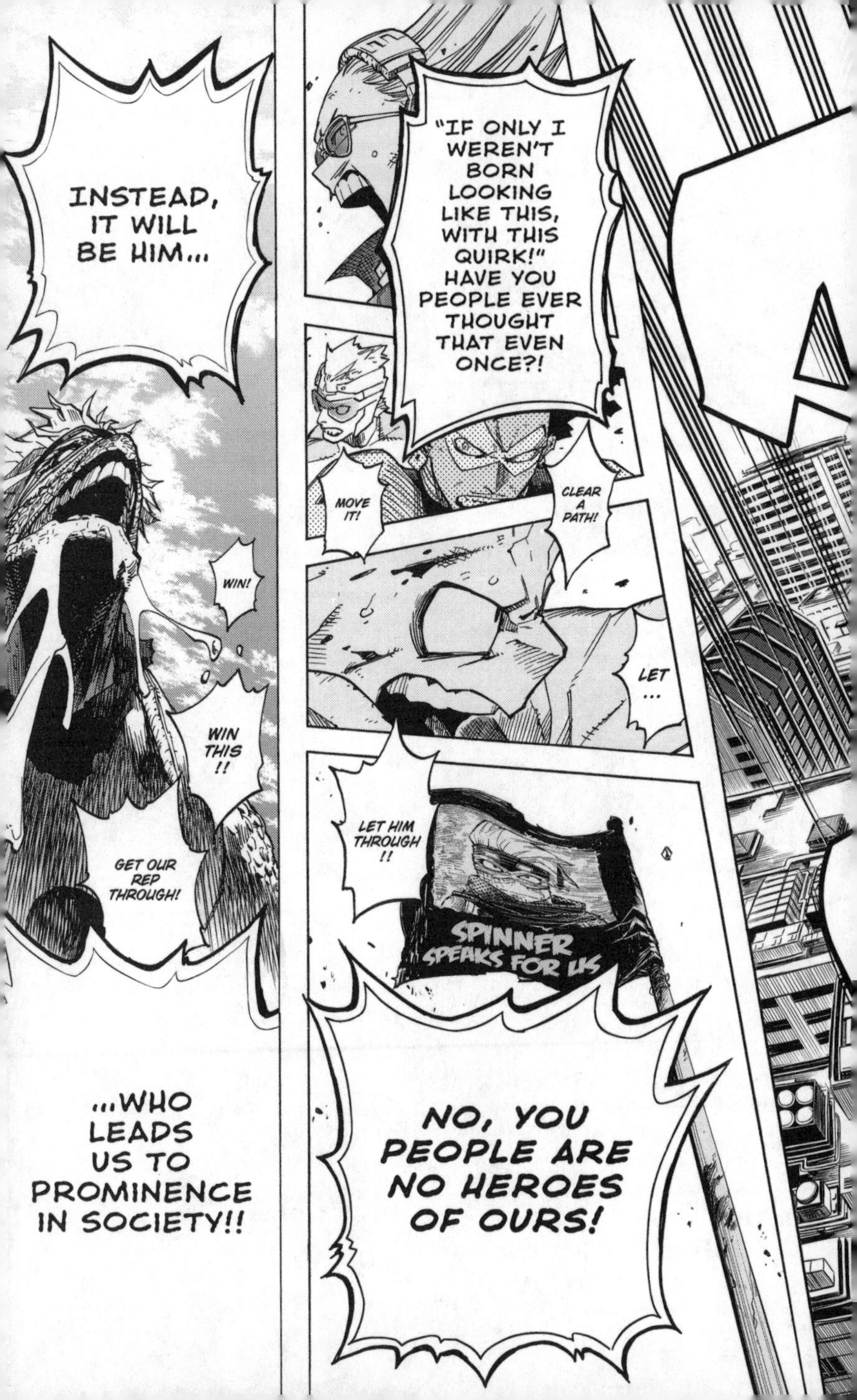
"IF ONLY I WEREN'T BORN LOOKING LIKE THIS, WITH THIS QUIRK!" HAVE YOU PEOPLE EVER THOUGHT THAT EVEN ONCE?!
CLEAR A PATH!
MOVE IT!
LET ...
LET HIM THROUGH!!
SPINNER SPEAKS FOR US
NO, YOU PEOPLE ARE NO HEROES OF OURS!
INSTEAD, IT WILL BE HIM...
WIN!
WIN THIS!!
GET OUR REP THROUGH!
...WHO LEADS US TO PROMINENCE IN SOCIETY!!

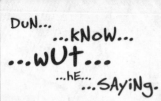
DUN...
...KNOW...
...WUt...
...hE...SAYiNG.

eVEr SinCE
AiL FOR One...
...GaVE mE
pOWer...
...hEAd
GETTinG...
...FUZziEr...

mE
JUST
...

whAT-
eVer.

GRIN

HEY.
GO ON,
REP.

WELP...

...do
WUt...

TAKE
BACK...

"..."
KURO-
GIRI!!

...mE
ToLD.

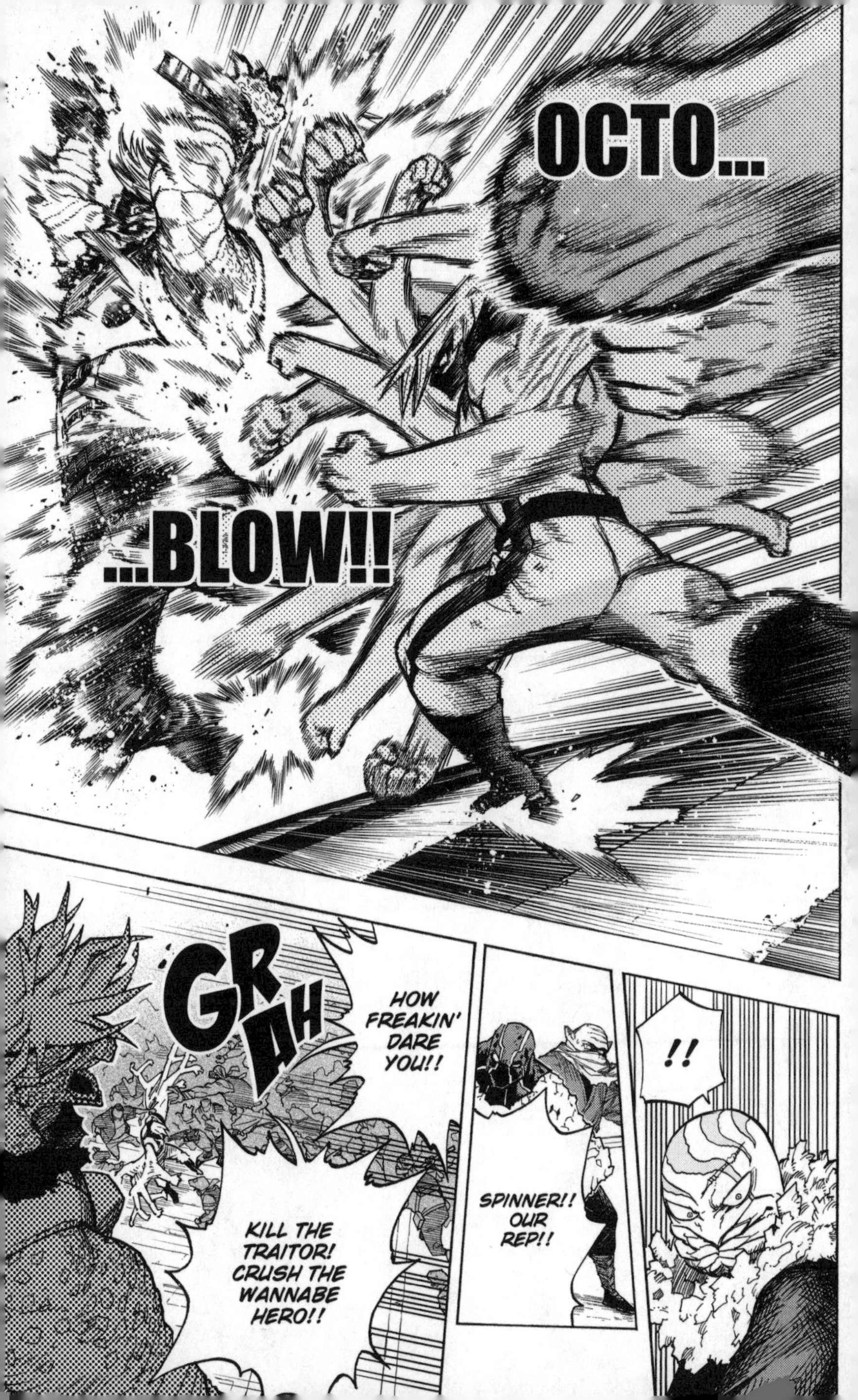
OCTO...
...BLOW!!
!!
SPINNER!! OUR REP!!
HOW FREAKIN' DARE YOU!!
GRAH
KILL THE TRAITOR! CRUSH THE WANNABE HERO!!

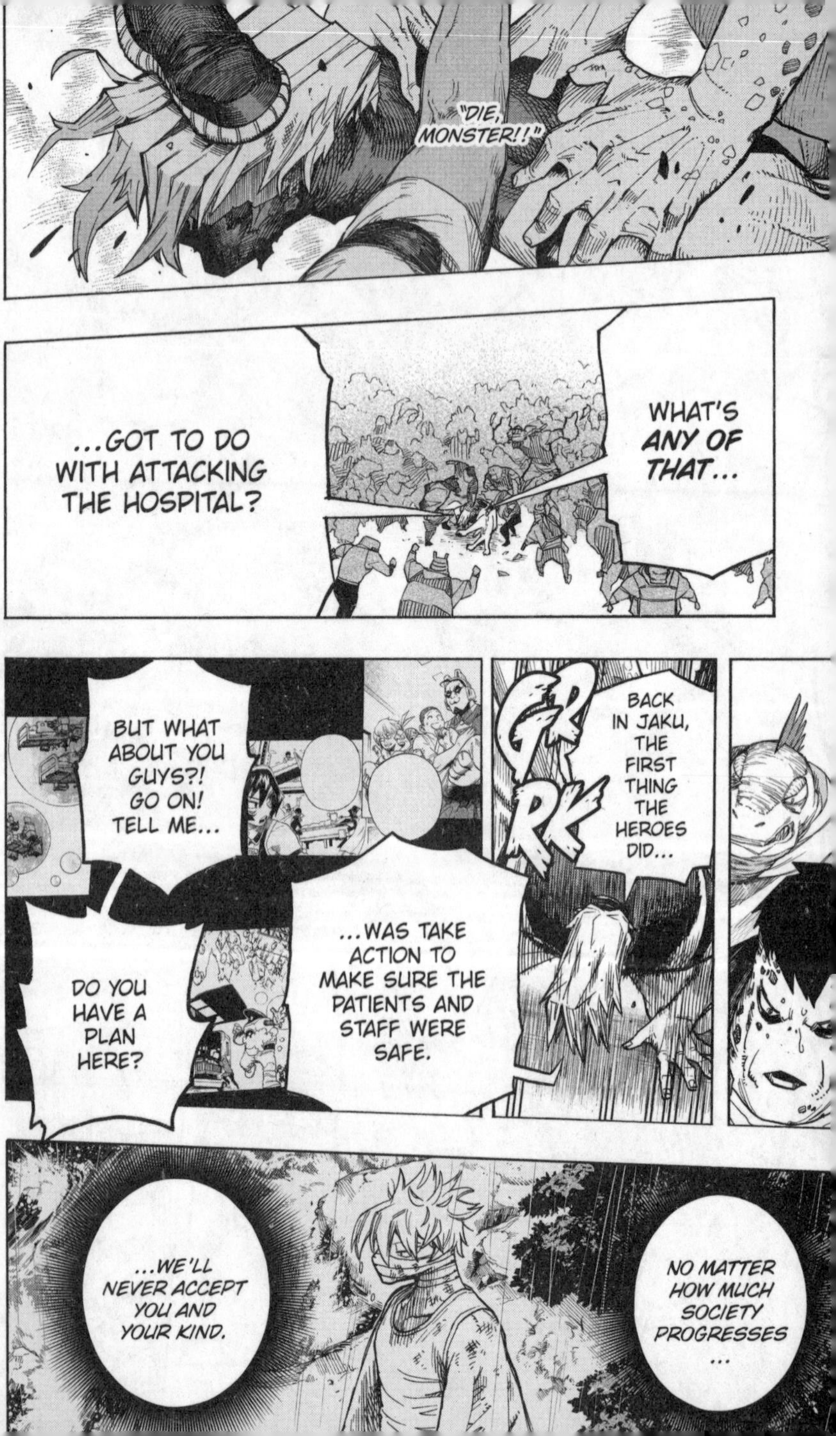
"DIE, MONSTER!!"
WHAT'S ANY OF THAT...
...GOT TO DO WITH ATTACKING THE HOSPITAL?
GRRK
BACK IN JAKU, THE FIRST THING THE HEROES DID...
...WAS TAKE ACTION TO MAKE SURE THE PATIENTS AND STAFF WERE SAFE.
BUT WHAT ABOUT YOU GUYS?! GO ON! TELL ME...
DO YOU HAVE A PLAN HERE?
NO MATTER HOW MUCH SOCIETY PROGRESSES ...
...WE'LL NEVER ACCEPT YOU AND YOUR KIND.

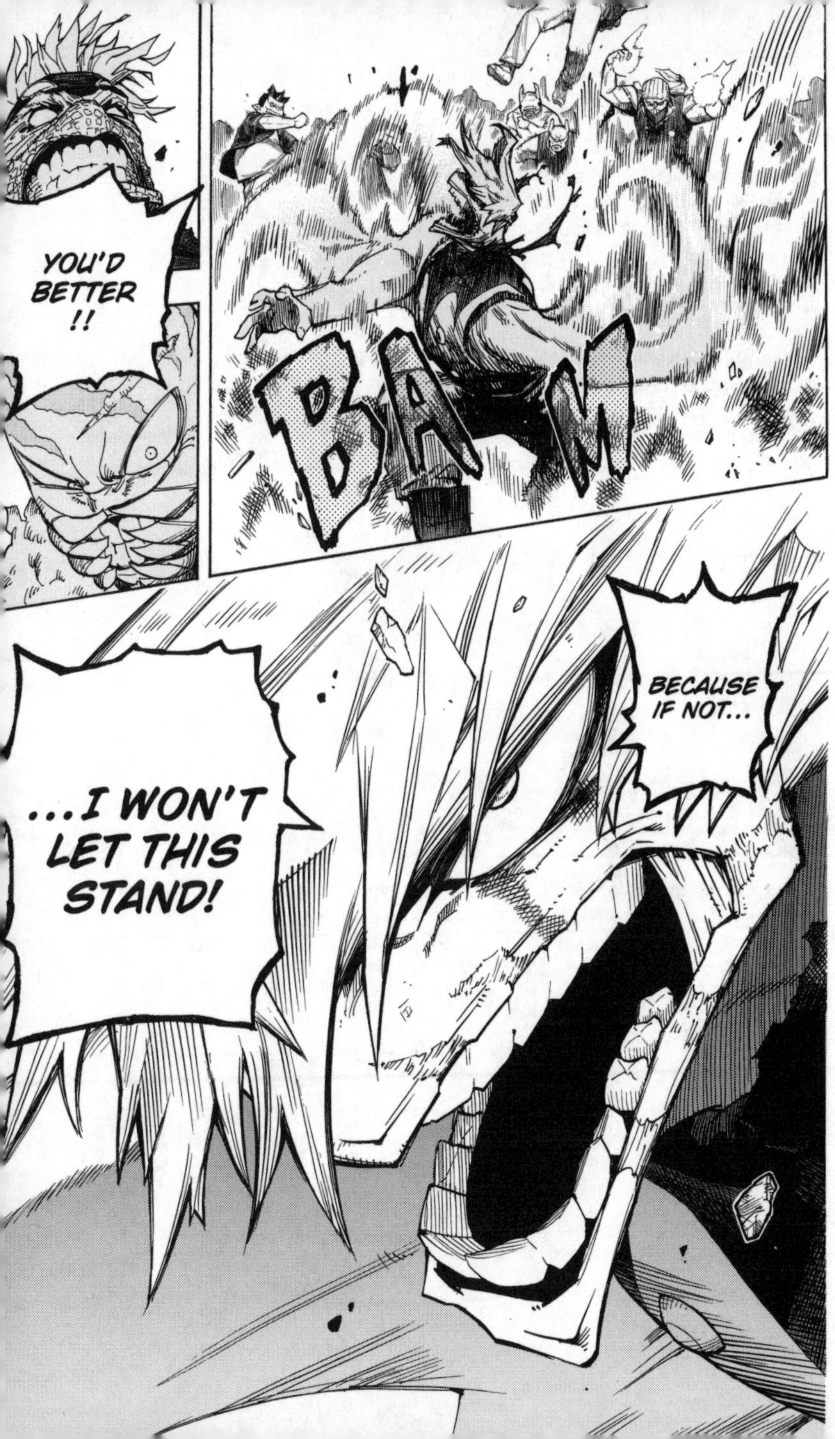
BAM
YOU'D BETTER !!
BECAUSE IF NOT...
...I WON'T LET THIS STAND!

Did you notice this gorilla man?
He appeared in volume 36, when he was
speaking with the captured doctor Garaki.

Did he use instant teleportation, or what?!
Naw, not quite.

There are a number of police bases near
the hospital at the moment, and the gorilla
guy was guarding detainees at one of them.
When the villains started to march on the
hospital, he switched over to riot duty.

Page 121, panel 5

As for Central Hospital…

THANKS TO CUTTING-EDGE MEDICAL TREATMENT
AND RECOVERY GIRL'S ARRIVAL AT THE HOSPITAL,
A LARGE NUMBER OF PATIENTS RECOVERED AND WERE
DISCHARGED. IZUKU MIDORIYA WASN'T FAR BEHIND…

Volume 32, page 51

As explained, many of the hospital patients were healed,
discharged, and escorted to safety, but some patients in
particularly bad shape didn't even have the stamina to
receive Recovery Girl's healing boost. They never got
discharged, so they're still in the hospital.

Volume 35, page 50
Extra wrinkly Recovery Girl

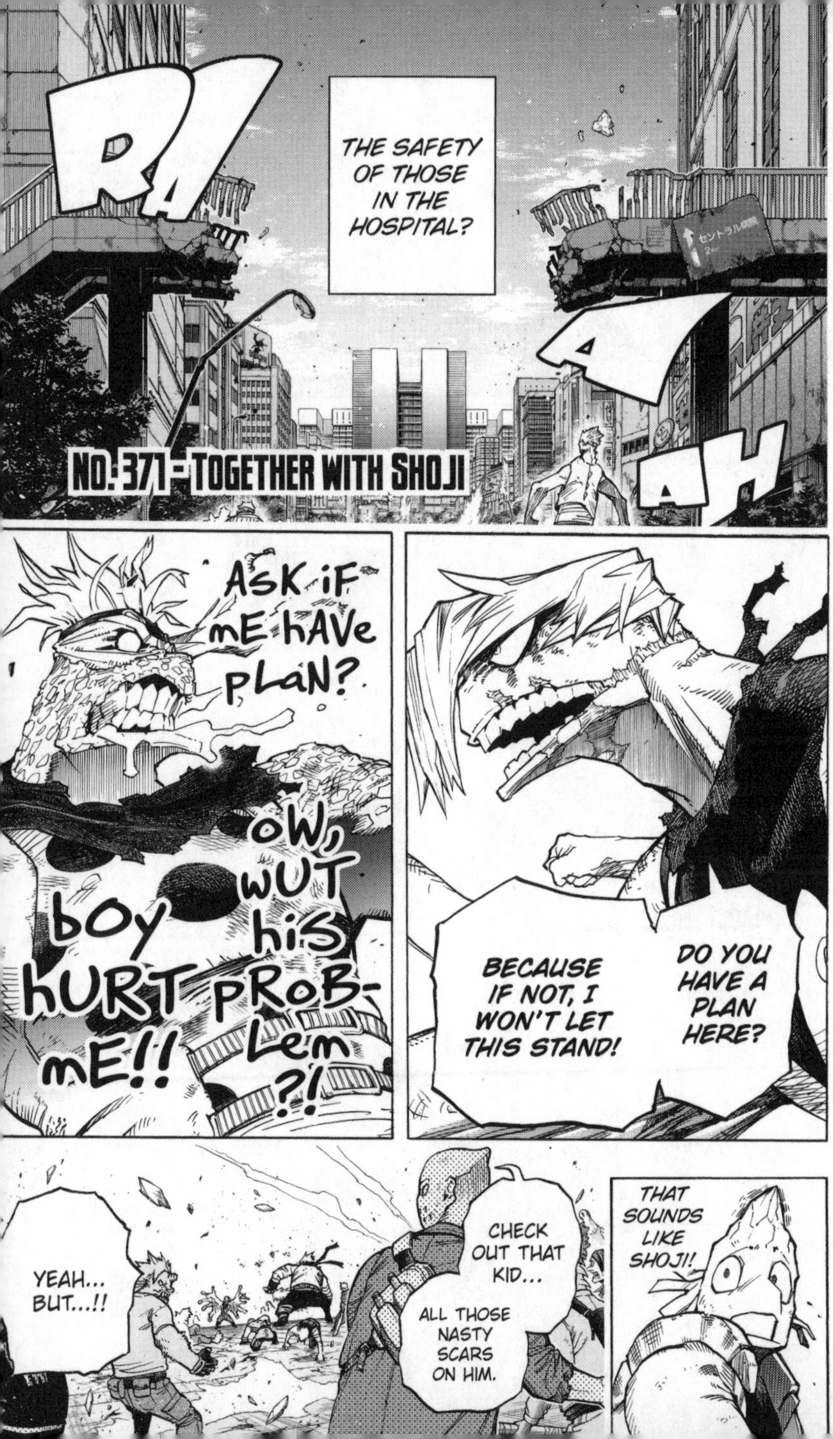
THE SAFETY OF THOSE IN THE HOSPITAL?
RA
A
AH
No. 371 - Together with Shoji
DO YOU HAVE A PLAN HERE?
BECAUSE IF NOT, I WON'T LET THIS STAND!
ASK IF ME HAVE PLAN?
OW, WUT HIS PROB-LEM?!
BOY HURT ME!!
THAT SOUNDS LIKE SHOJI!
CHECK OUT THAT KID...
ALL THOSE NASTY SCARS ON HIM.
YEAH... BUT...!!

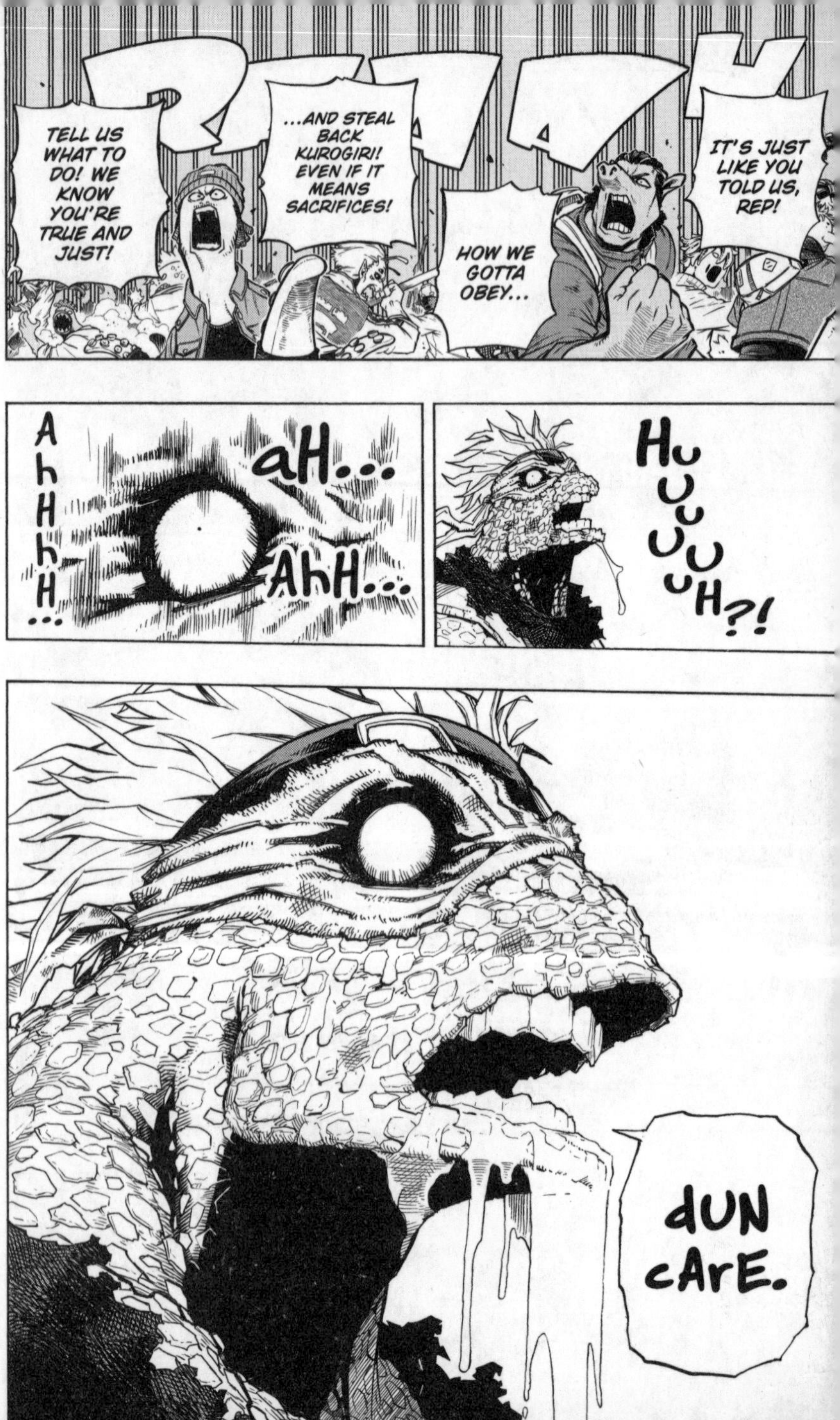
IT'S JUST LIKE YOU TOLD US, REP!
HOW WE GOTTA OBEY...
...AND STEAL BACK KUROGIRI! EVEN IF IT MEANS SACRIFICES!
TELL US WHAT TO DO! WE KNOW YOU'RE TRUE AND JUST!
HuUUUUUH?!
AhHhH...
aH...
AhH...
dUN cArE.

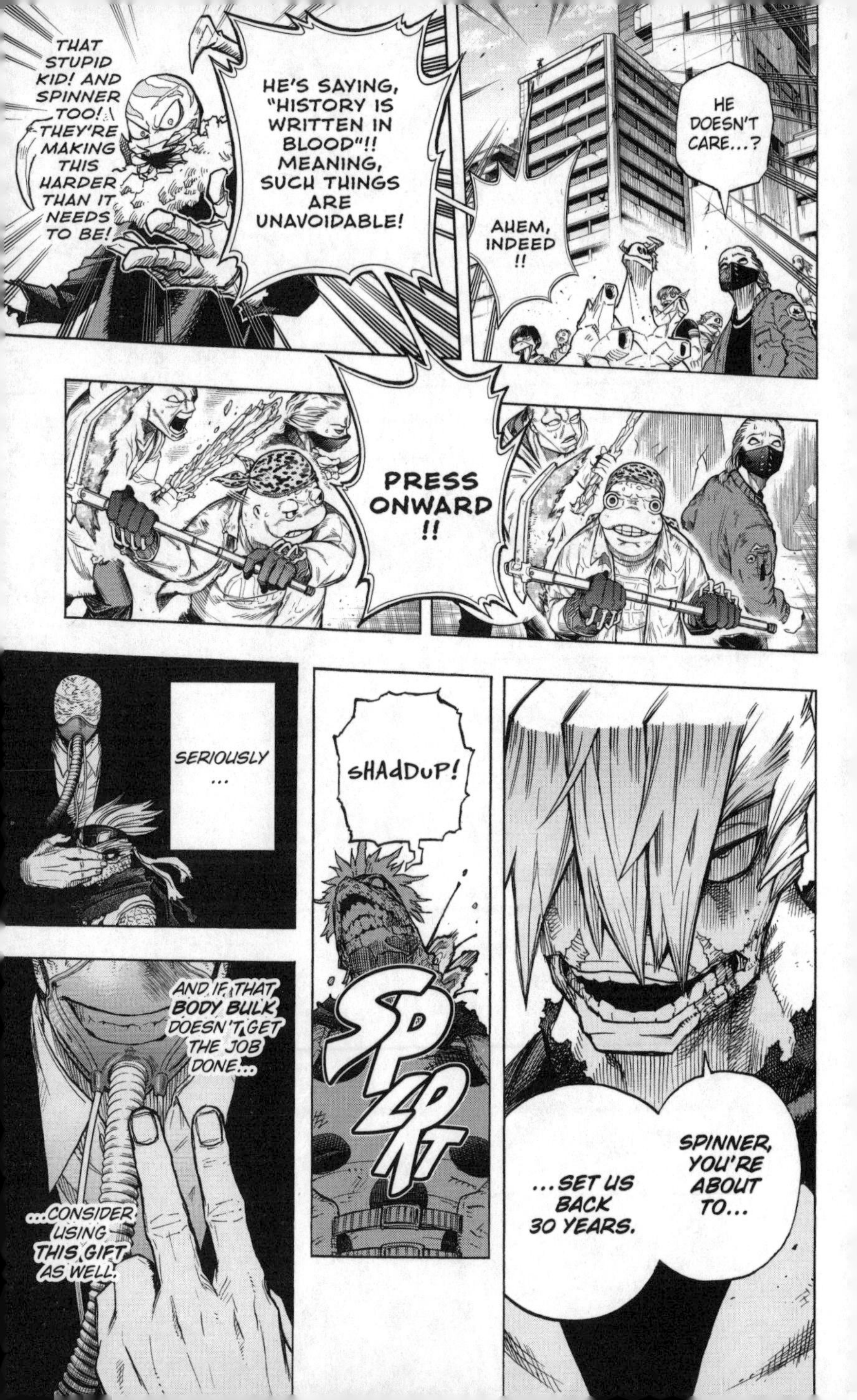
HE DOESN'T CARE...?
AHEM, INDEED!!
HE'S SAYING, "HISTORY IS WRITTEN IN BLOOD"!! MEANING, SUCH THINGS ARE UNAVOIDABLE!
THAT STUPID KID! AND SPINNER TOO! THEY'RE MAKING THIS HARDER THAN IT NEEDS TO BE!
PRESS ONWARD!!
SPINNER, YOU'RE ABOUT TO...
...SET US BACK 30 YEARS.
SHADDUP!
SERIOUSLY...
AND IF THAT BODY BULK DOESN'T GET THE JOB DONE...
...CONSIDER USING THIS GIFT AS WELL.

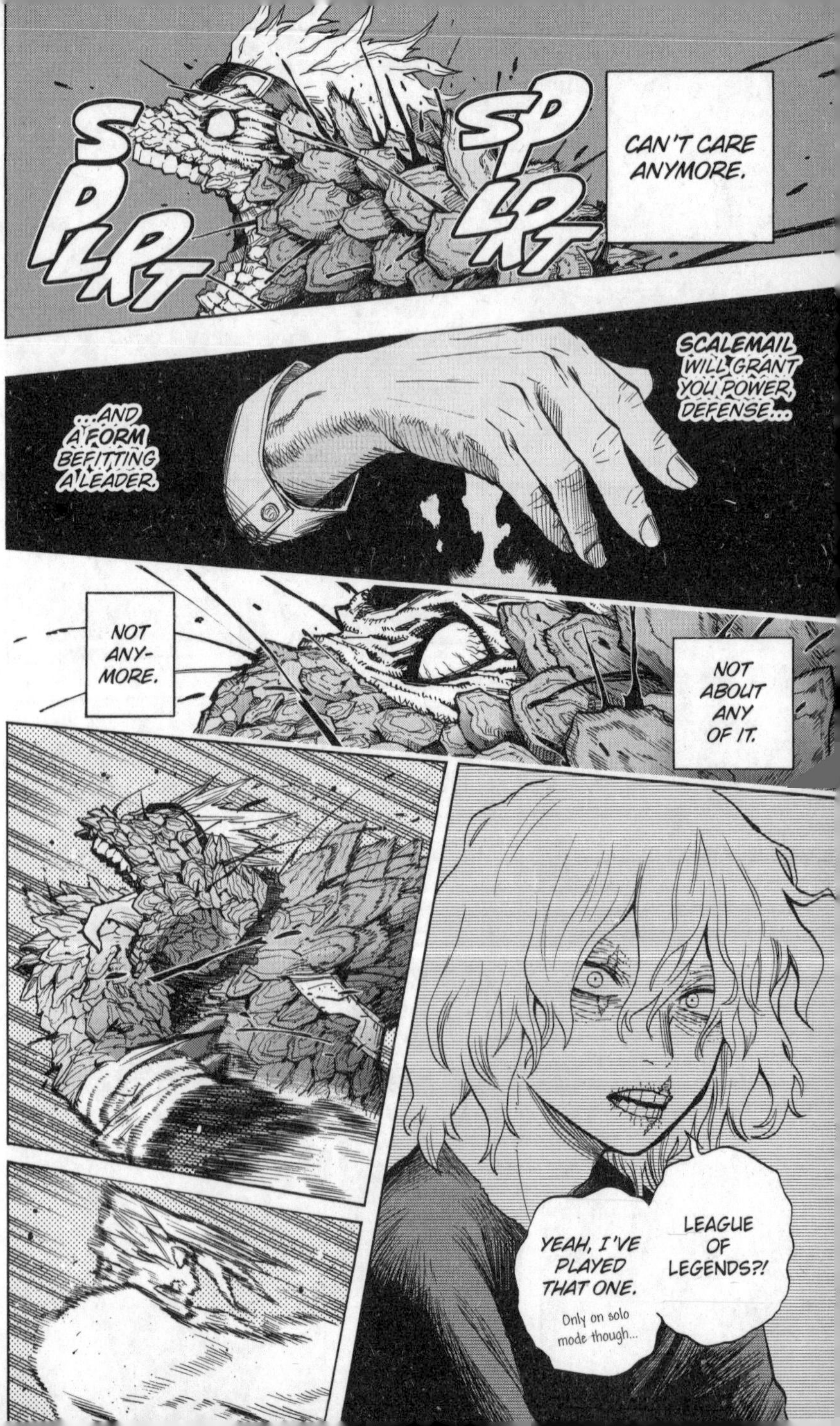
CAN'T CARE ANYMORE.
SCALEMAIL WILL GRANT YOU POWER, DEFENSE...
...AND A FORM BEFITTING A LEADER.
NOT ANYMORE.
NOT ABOUT ANY OF IT.
LEAGUE OF LEGENDS?!
YEAH, I'VE PLAYED THAT ONE.
Only on solo mode though...

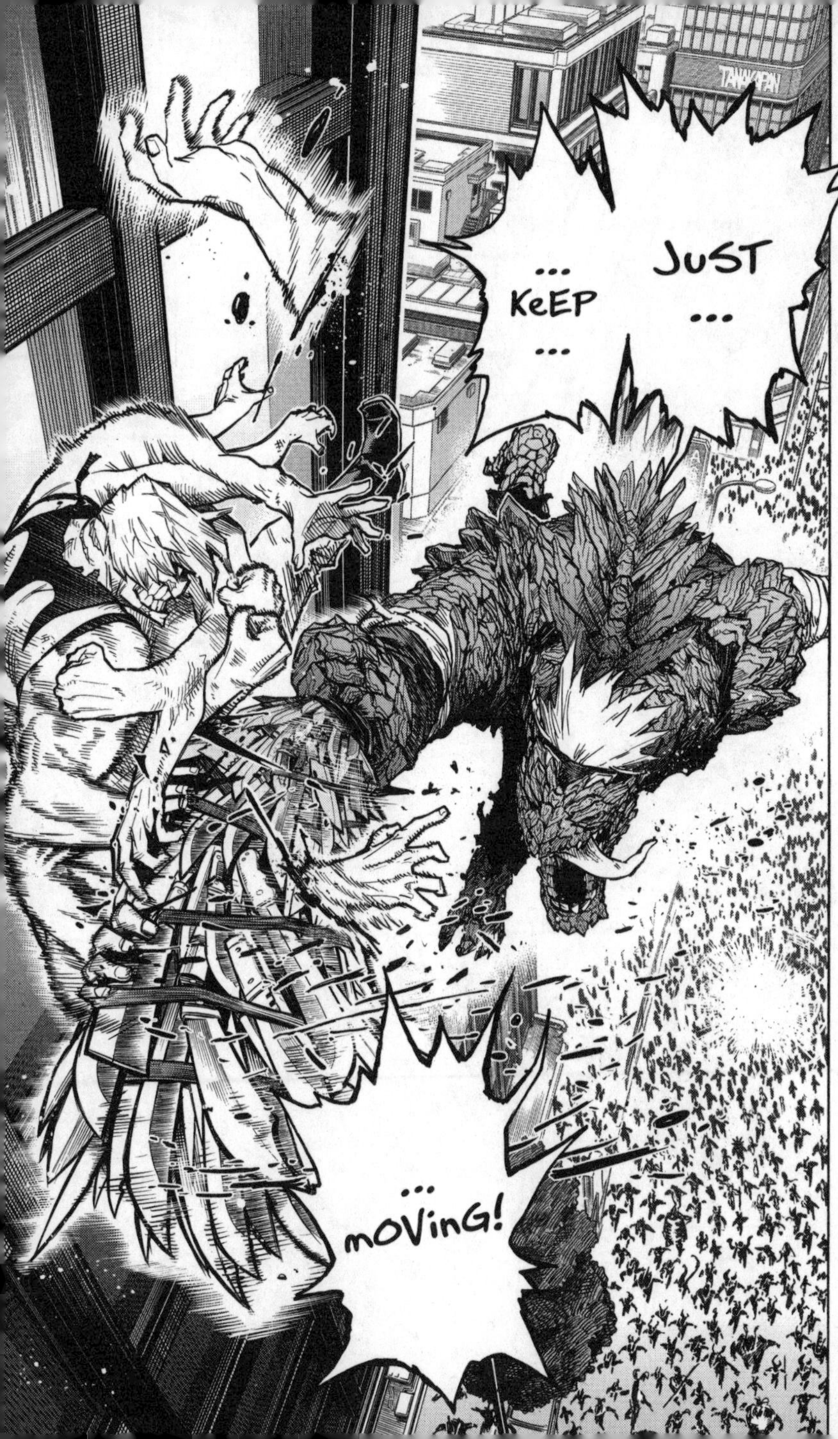

JUST ... ... KEEP ...
... MOVING!
TANAKAPAN

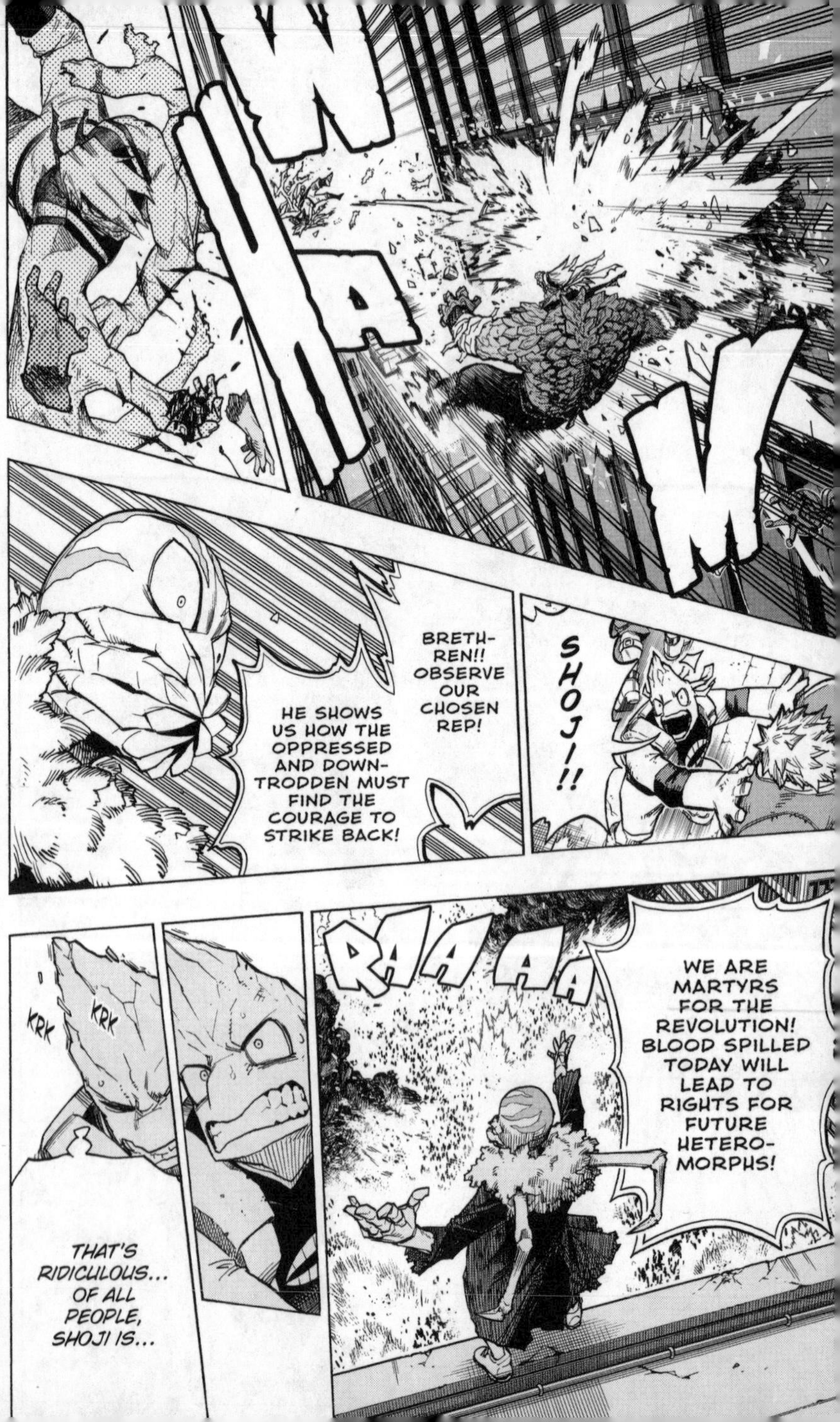
WHAAM
SHOJI!!
BRETH-REN!! OBSERVE OUR CHOSEN REP!
HE SHOWS US HOW THE OPPRESSED AND DOWN-TRODDEN MUST FIND THE COURAGE TO STRIKE BACK!
RAAAA
WE ARE MARTYRS FOR THE REVOLUTION! BLOOD SPILLED TODAY WILL LEAD TO RIGHTS FOR FUTURE HETERO-MORPHS!
KRK
KRK
THAT'S RIDICULOUS... OF ALL PEOPLE, SHOJI IS...

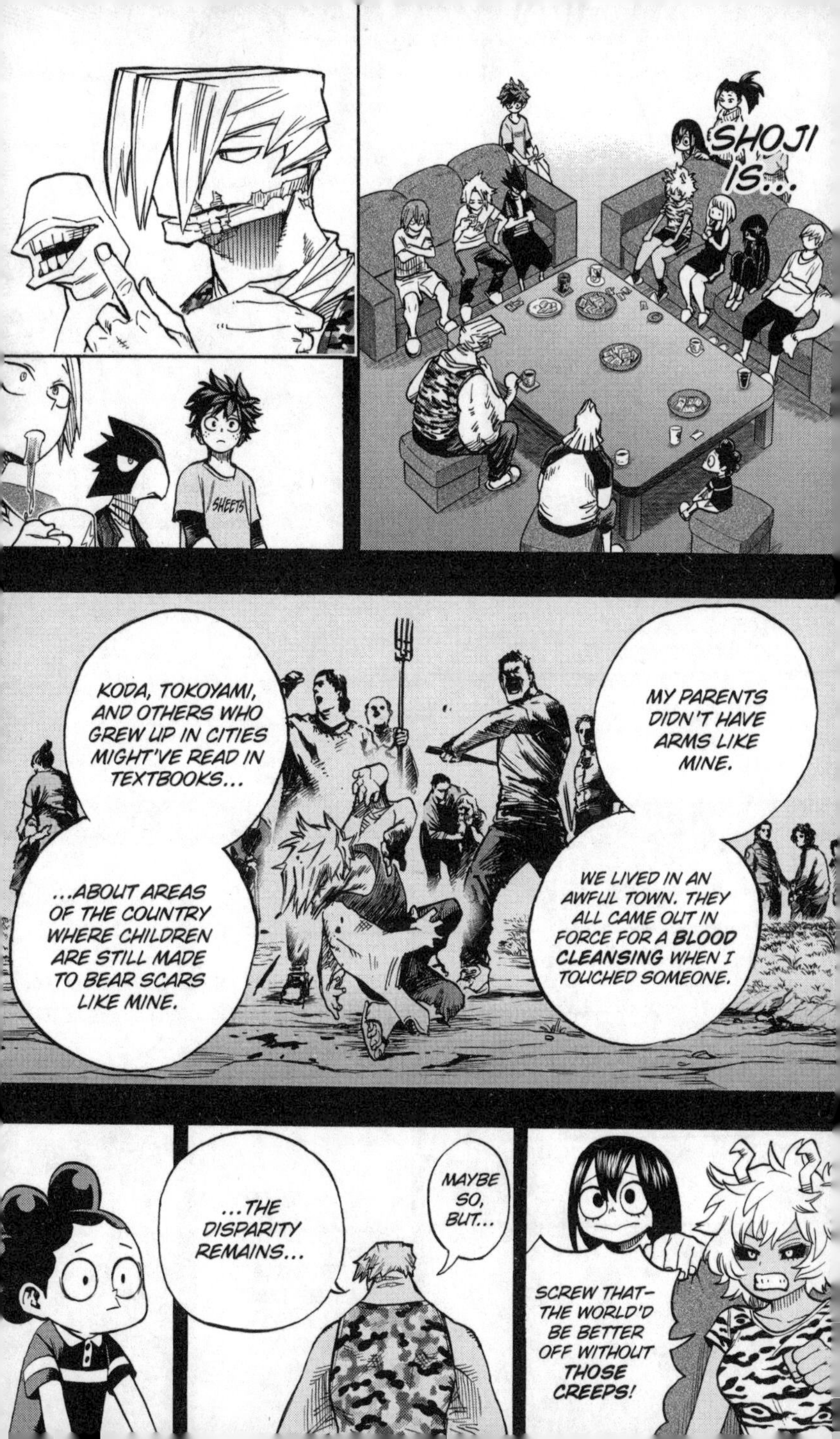
SHOJI IS...
MY PARENTS DIDN'T HAVE ARMS LIKE MINE.
WE LIVED IN AN AWFUL TOWN. THEY ALL CAME OUT IN FORCE FOR A **BLOOD CLEANSING** WHEN I TOUCHED SOMEONE.
KODA, TOKOYAMI, AND OTHERS WHO GREW UP IN CITIES MIGHT'VE READ IN TEXTBOOKS...
...ABOUT AREAS OF THE COUNTRY WHERE CHILDREN ARE STILL MADE TO BEAR SCARS LIKE MINE.
SCREW THAT— THE WORLD'D BE BETTER OFF WITHOUT **THOSE CREEPS!**
MAYBE SO, BUT...
...THE DISPARITY REMAINS...
SHEETS

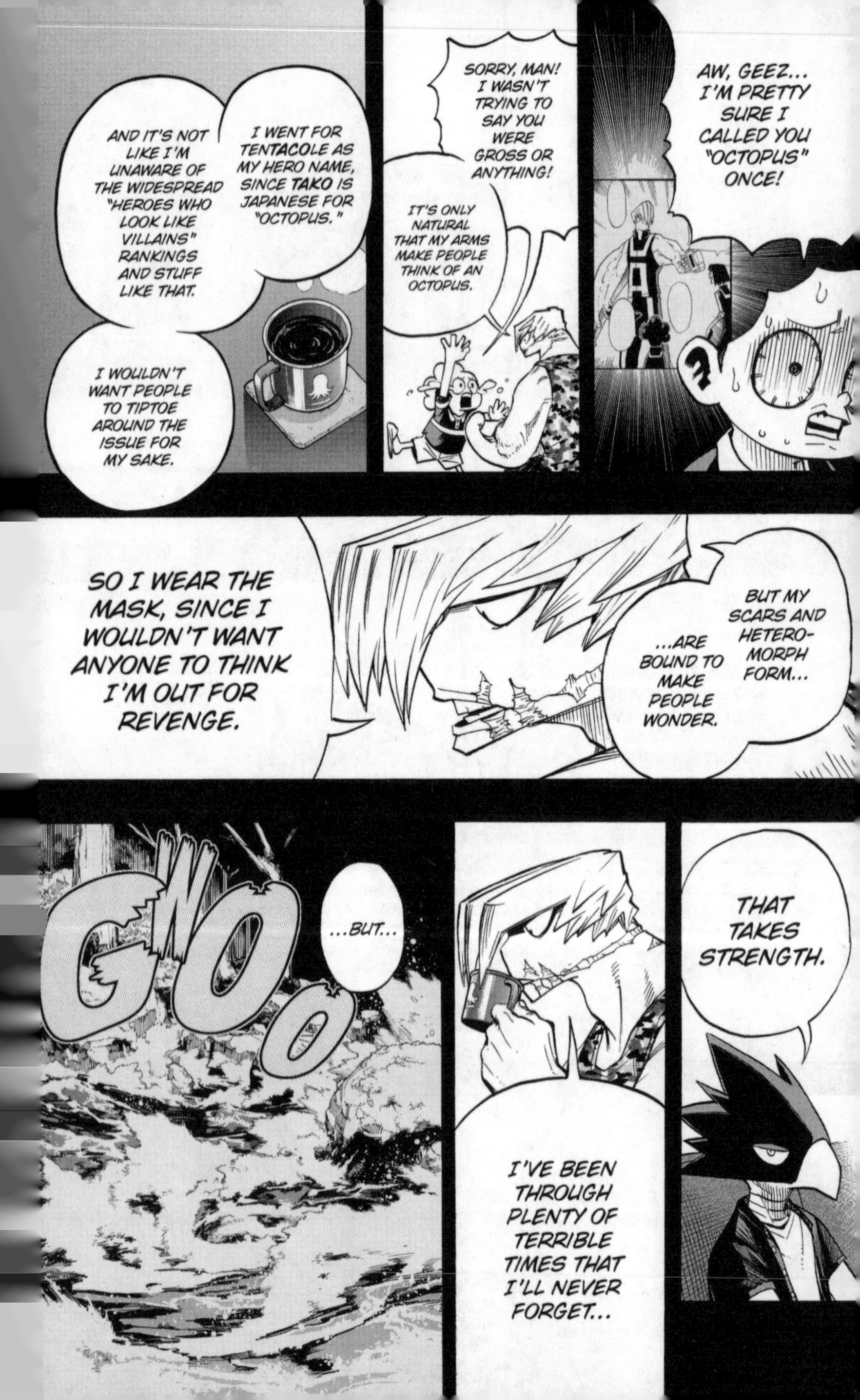
AW, GEEZ... I'M PRETTY SURE I CALLED YOU "OCTOPUS" ONCE!
SORRY, MAN! I WASN'T TRYING TO SAY YOU WERE GROSS OR ANYTHING!
IT'S ONLY NATURAL THAT MY ARMS MAKE PEOPLE THINK OF AN OCTOPUS.
I WENT FOR TENTACOLE AS MY HERO NAME, SINCE TAKO IS JAPANESE FOR "OCTOPUS."
AND IT'S NOT LIKE I'M UNAWARE OF THE WIDESPREAD "HEROES WHO LOOK LIKE VILLAINS" RANKINGS AND STUFF LIKE THAT.
I WOULDN'T WANT PEOPLE TO TIPTOE AROUND THE ISSUE FOR MY SAKE.
BUT MY SCARS AND HETERO-MORPH FORM...
...ARE BOUND TO MAKE PEOPLE WONDER.
SO I WEAR THE MASK, SINCE I WOULDN'T WANT ANYONE TO THINK I'M OUT FOR REVENGE.
THAT TAKES STRENGTH.
I'VE BEEN THROUGH PLENTY OF TERRIBLE TIMES THAT I'LL NEVER FORGET...
...BUT...
GNOO

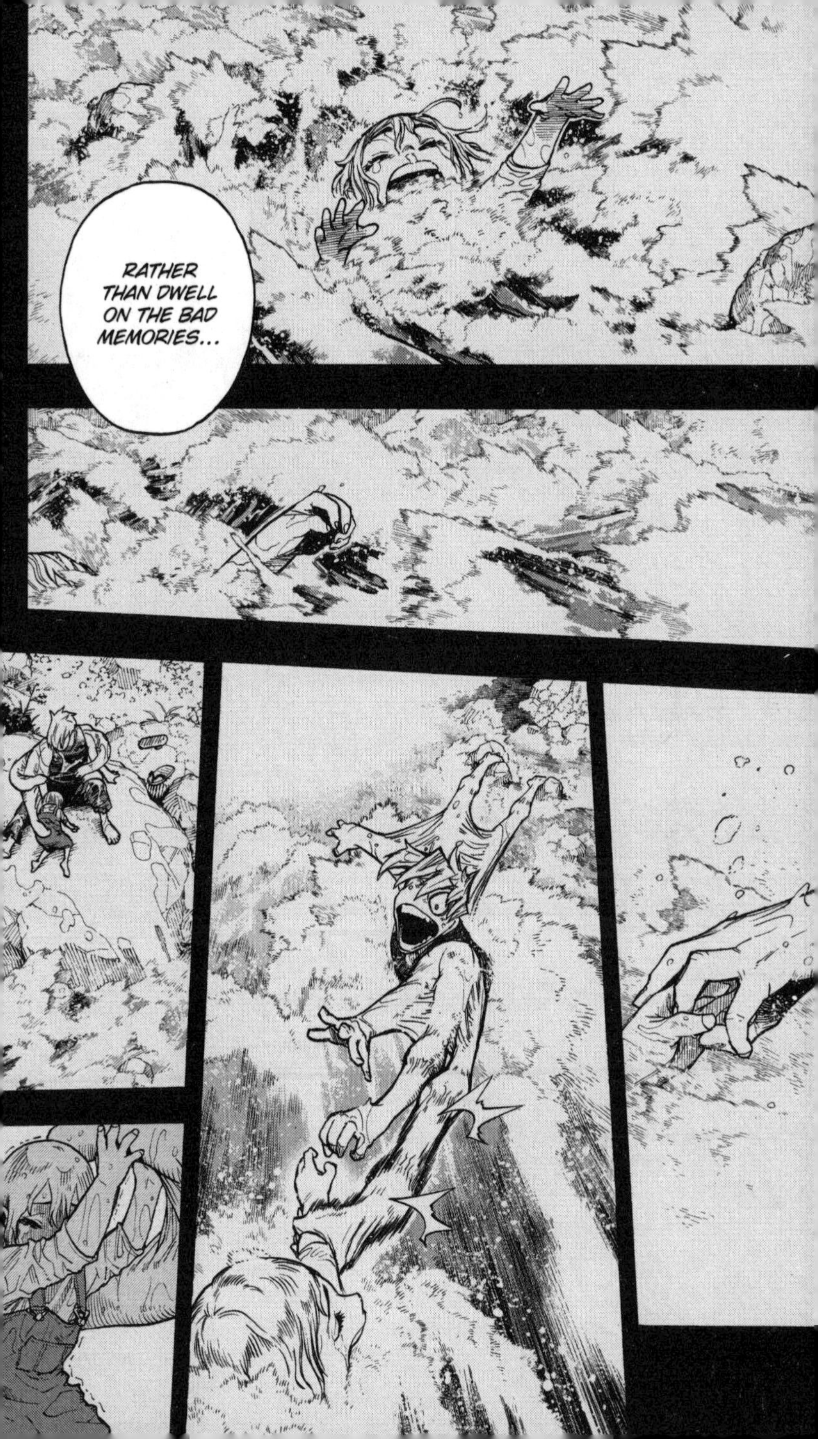
RATHER THAN DWELL ON THE BAD MEMORIES...

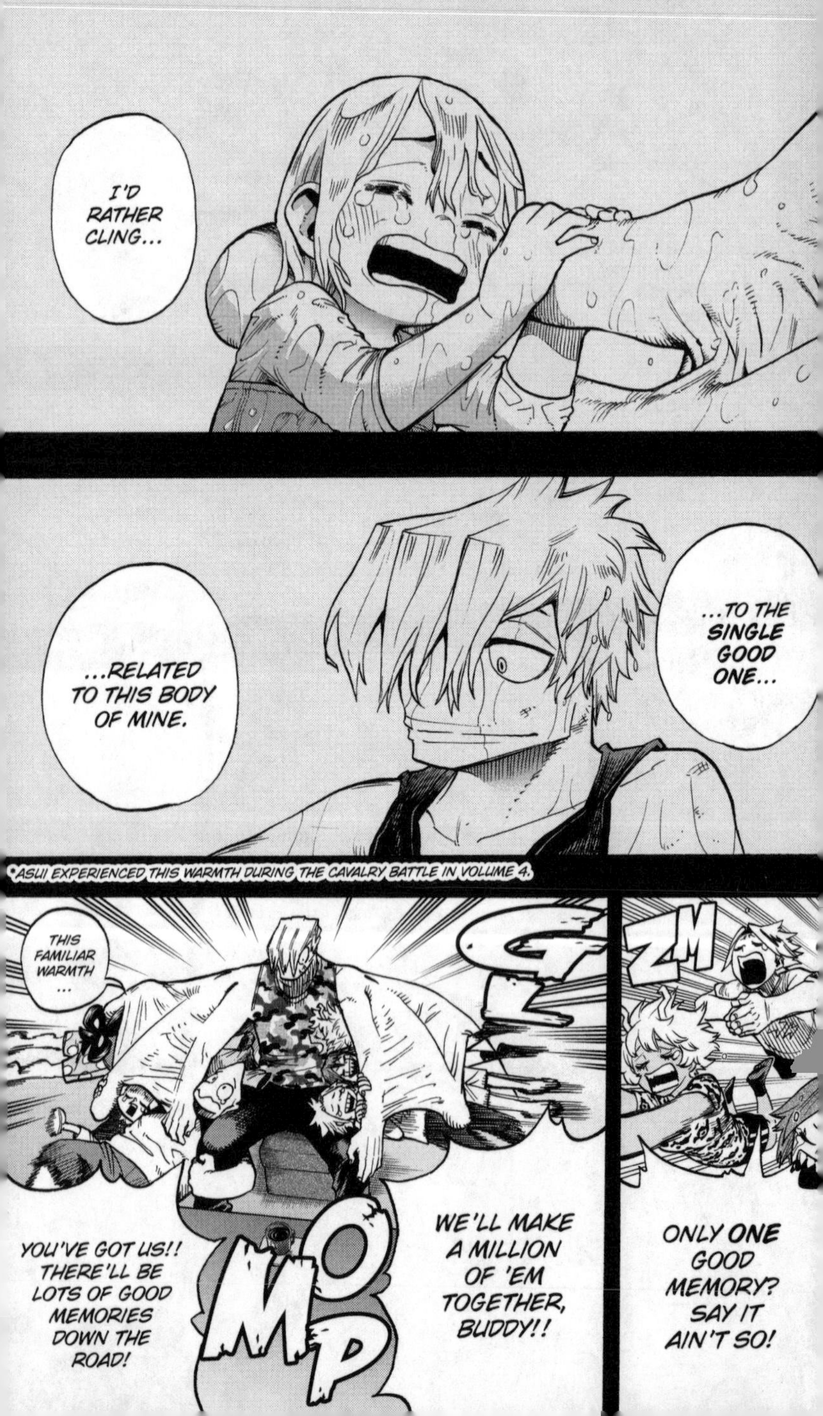
I'D RATHER CLING...
...TO THE SINGLE GOOD ONE...
...RELATED TO THIS BODY OF MINE.
*ASUI EXPERIENCED THIS WARMTH DURING THE CAVALRY BATTLE IN VOLUME 4.
ZM
ONLY ONE GOOD MEMORY? SAY IT AIN'T SO!
THIS FAMILIAR WARMTH ...
WE'LL MAKE A MILLION OF 'EM TOGETHER, BUDDY!!
YOU'VE GOT US!! THERE'LL BE LOTS OF GOOD MEMORIES DOWN THE ROAD!

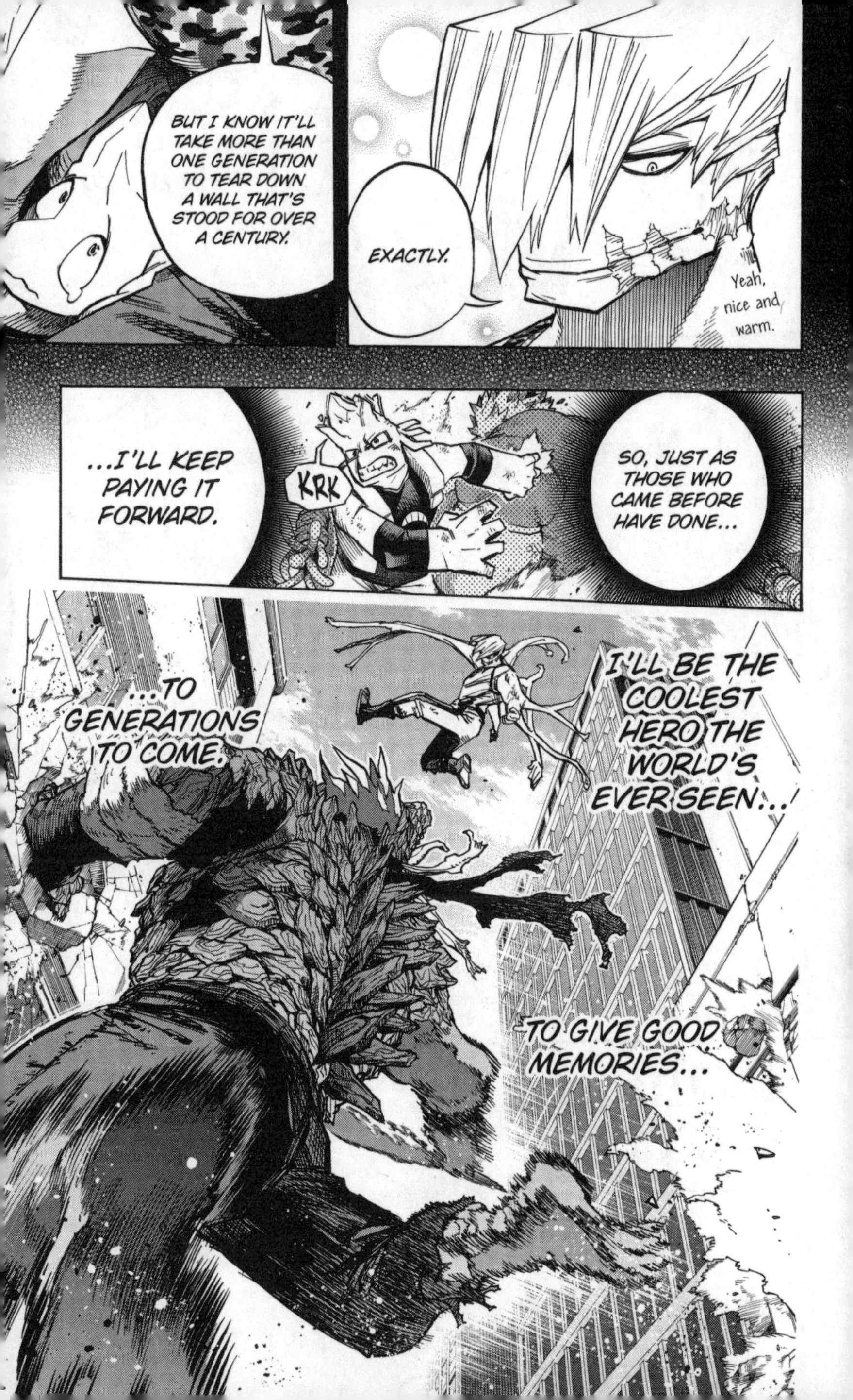
EXACTLY.
Yeah, nice and warm.
BUT I KNOW IT'LL TAKE MORE THAN ONE GENERATION TO TEAR DOWN A WALL THAT'S STOOD FOR OVER A CENTURY.
SO, JUST AS THOSE WHO CAME BEFORE HAVE DONE...
KRK
...I'LL KEEP PAYING IT FORWARD.
I'LL BE THE COOLEST HERO THE WORLD'S EVER SEEN...
TO GIVE GOOD MEMORIES...
...TO GENERATIONS TO COME.

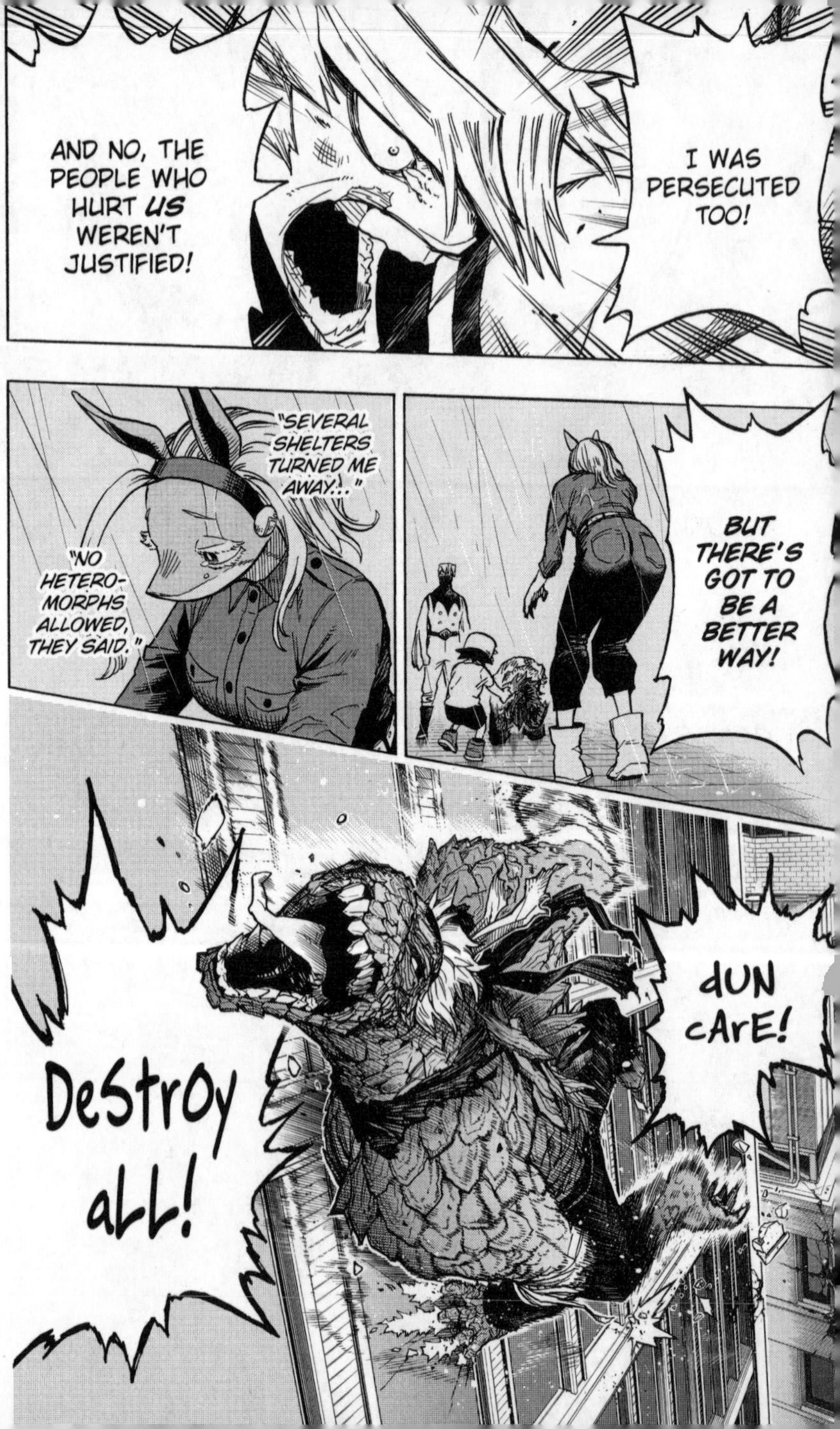
I WAS PERSECUTED TOO!
AND NO, THE PEOPLE WHO HURT US WEREN'T JUSTIFIED!
BUT THERE'S GOT TO BE A BETTER WAY!
"SEVERAL SHELTERS TURNED ME AWAY..."
"NO HETERO-MORPHS ALLOWED, THEY SAID."
DUN CArE!
DeStrOy aLL!

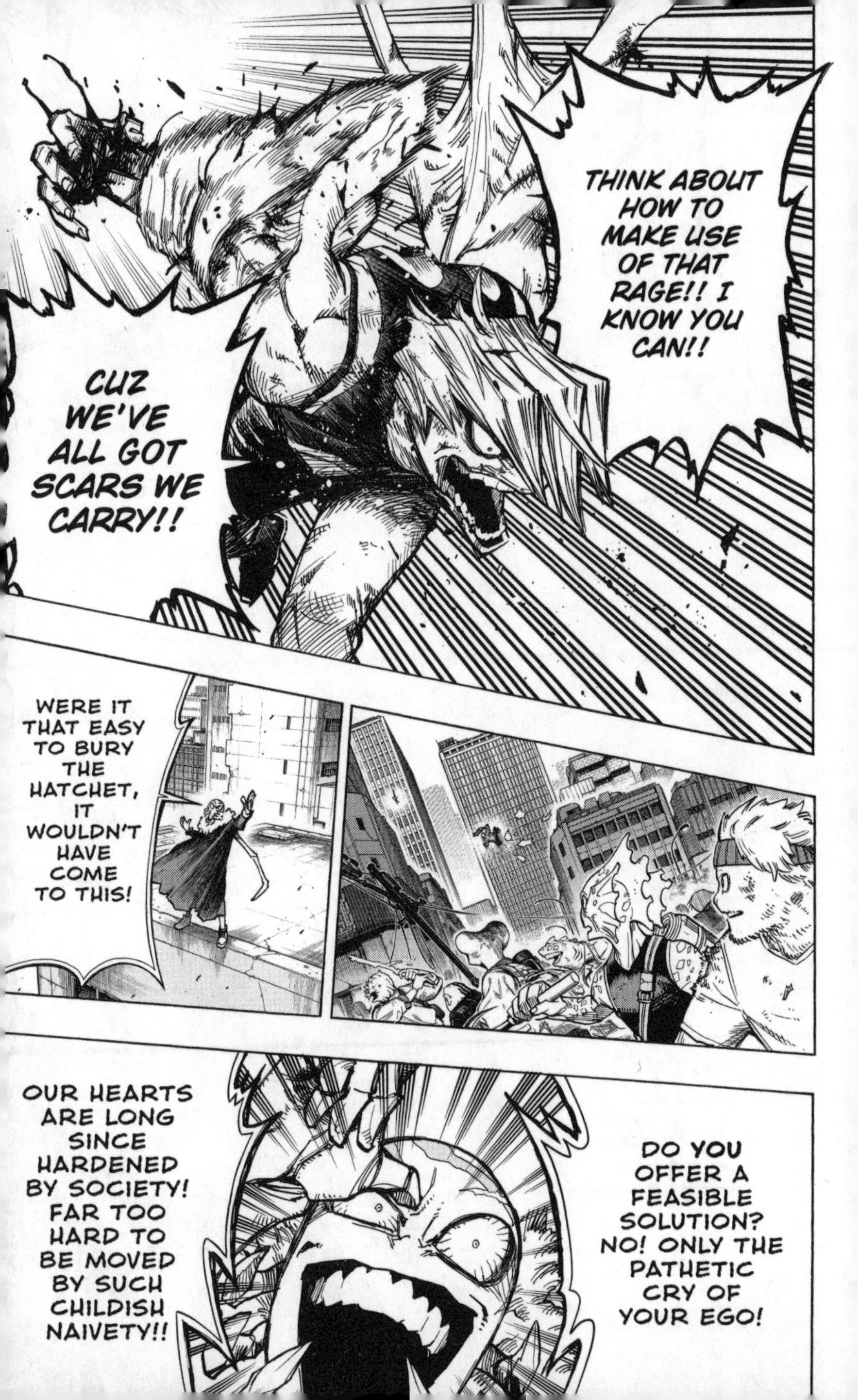
THINK ABOUT HOW TO MAKE USE OF THAT RAGE!! I KNOW YOU CAN!!
CUZ WE'VE ALL GOT SCARS WE CARRY!!
WERE IT THAT EASY TO BURY THE HATCHET, IT WOULDN'T HAVE COME TO THIS!
DO YOU OFFER A FEASIBLE SOLUTION? NO! ONLY THE PATHETIC CRY OF YOUR EGO!
OUR HEARTS ARE LONG SINCE HARDENED BY SOCIETY! FAR TOO HARD TO BE MOVED BY SUCH CHILDISH NAIVETY!!

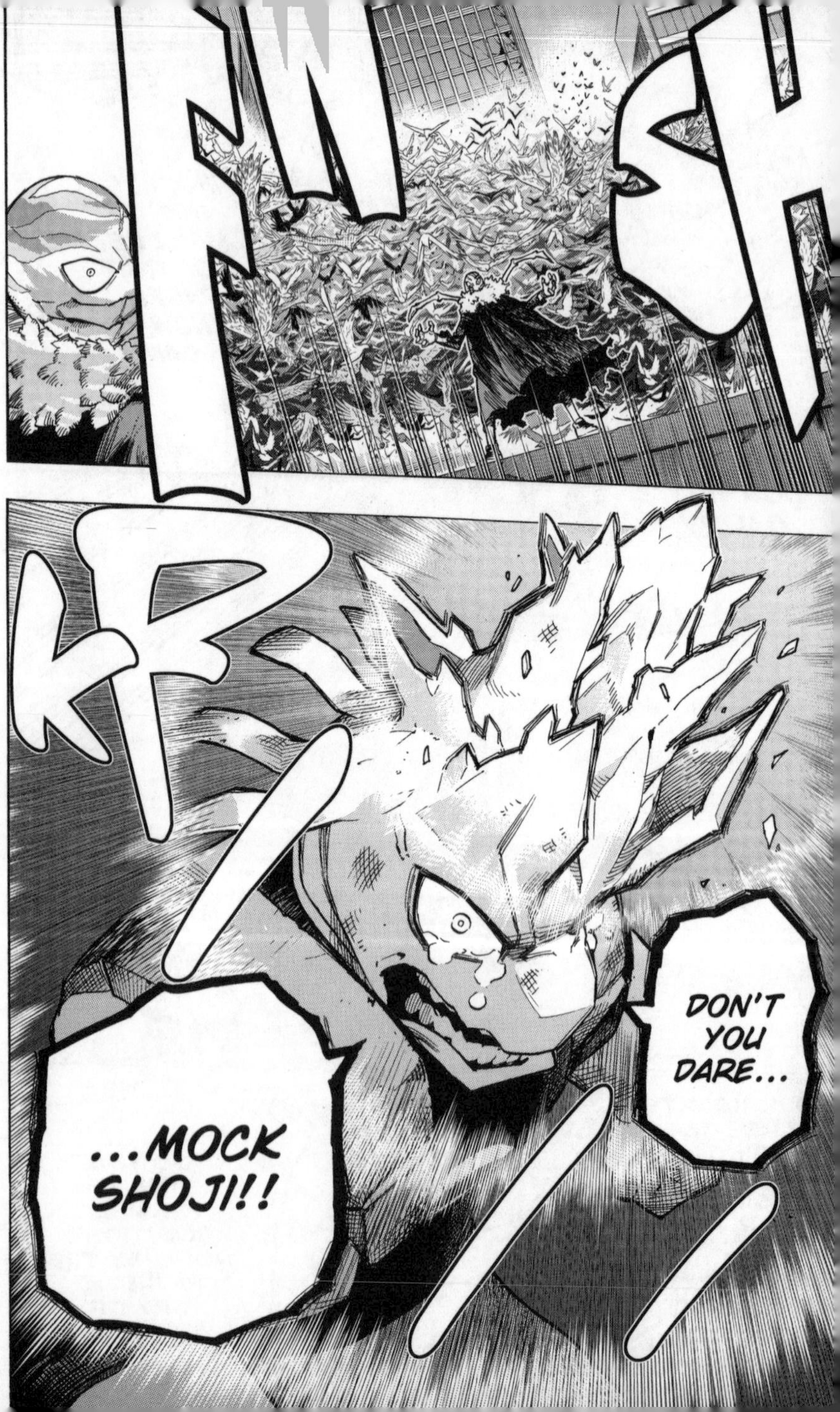
DON'T YOU DARE...
...MOCK SHOJI!!

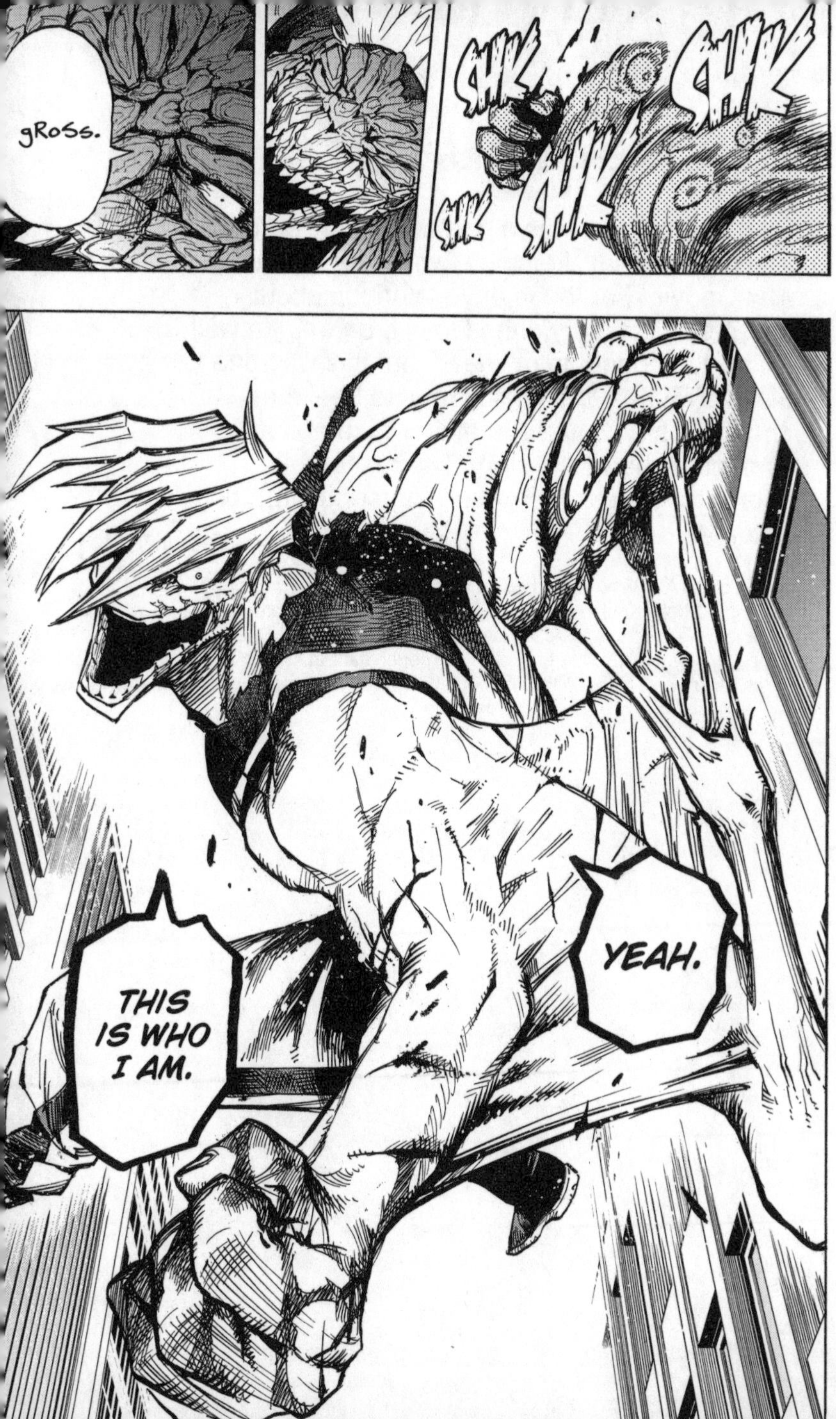
SHK
SHK
SHK
SHK
gRoSs.
YEAH.
THIS IS WHO I AM.

TOGETHER WITH SHOJI

That chapter title was a phrase I used years ago, in a promotional sketch on Twitter for the second *MHA* movie. For those of you curious about chapter titles—very often I toss a dart at the wall without a thought in my head, but this was one I always wanted to use, so I'm glad I got that chance. There's just something I like about it. And that's the whole story. The rest of this interstitial page is Horikoshi's personal grab bag notepad.

Within class A's "Who looks best in traditional Japanese clothing?" rankings, Shoji came in first place by a landslide. His inscrutable comment was "I'd like to do my duties in this garb, without petty conceit in my heart." Way to flaunt your nonchalant attitude and talent for playing along in the moment.

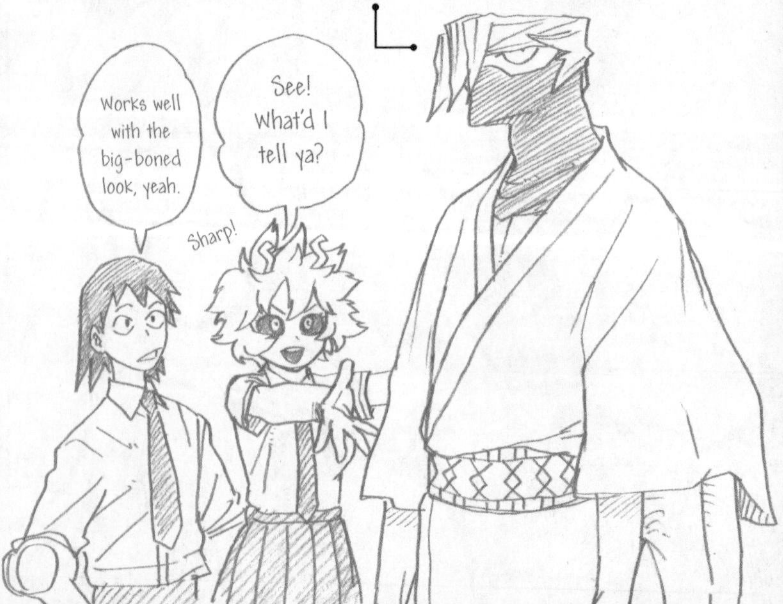
See! What'd I tell ya?
Works well with the big-boned look, yeah.
Sharp!

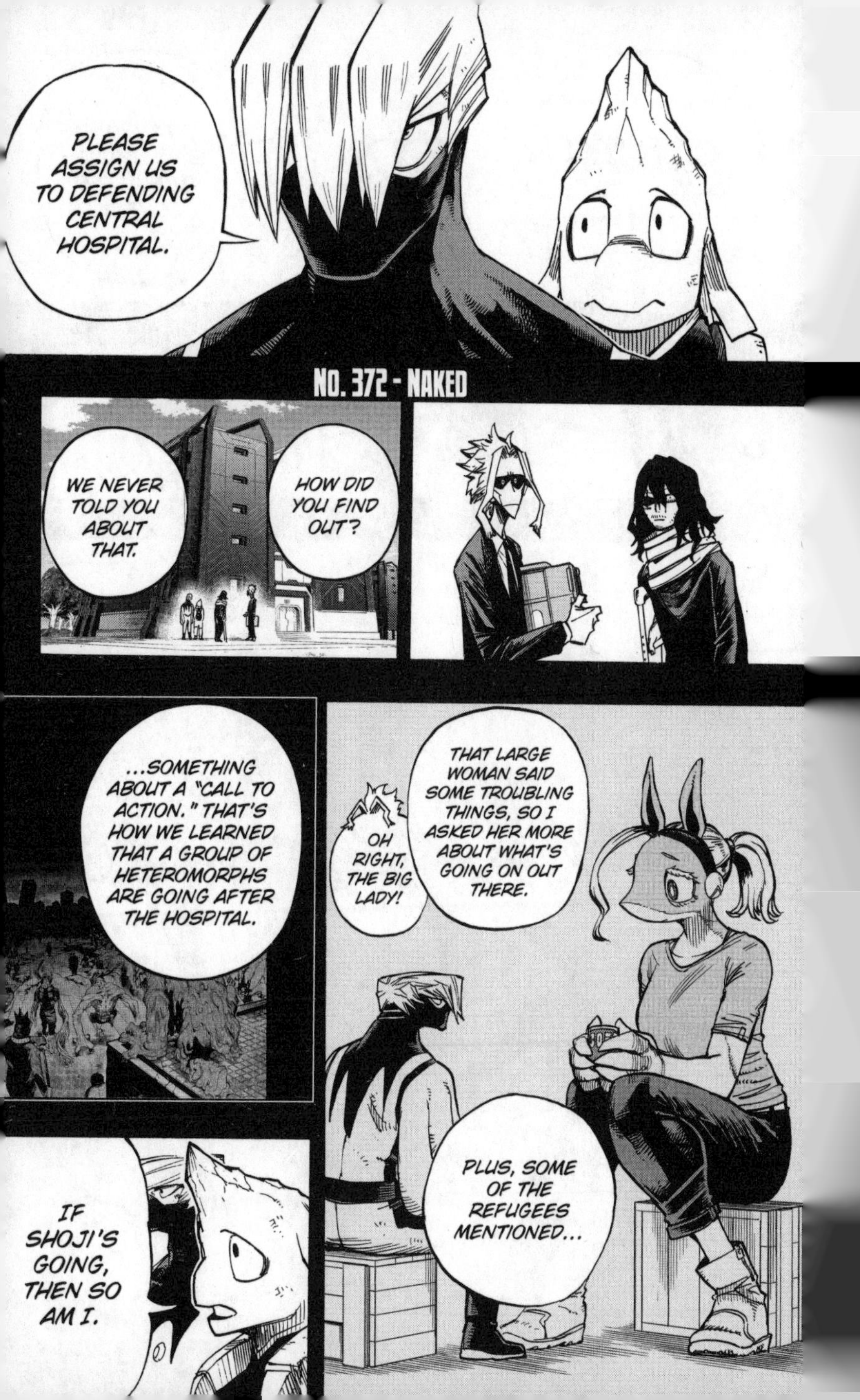
PLEASE ASSIGN US TO DEFENDING CENTRAL HOSPITAL.
NO. 372 - NAKED
HOW DID YOU FIND OUT?
WE NEVER TOLD YOU ABOUT THAT.
THAT LARGE WOMAN SAID SOME TROUBLING THINGS, SO I ASKED HER MORE ABOUT WHAT'S GOING ON OUT THERE.
OH RIGHT, THE BIG LADY!
PLUS, SOME OF THE REFUGEES MENTIONED...
...SOMETHING ABOUT A "CALL TO ACTION." THAT'S HOW WE LEARNED THAT A GROUP OF HETEROMORPHS ARE GOING AFTER THE HOSPITAL.
IF SHOJI'S GOING, THEN SO AM I.

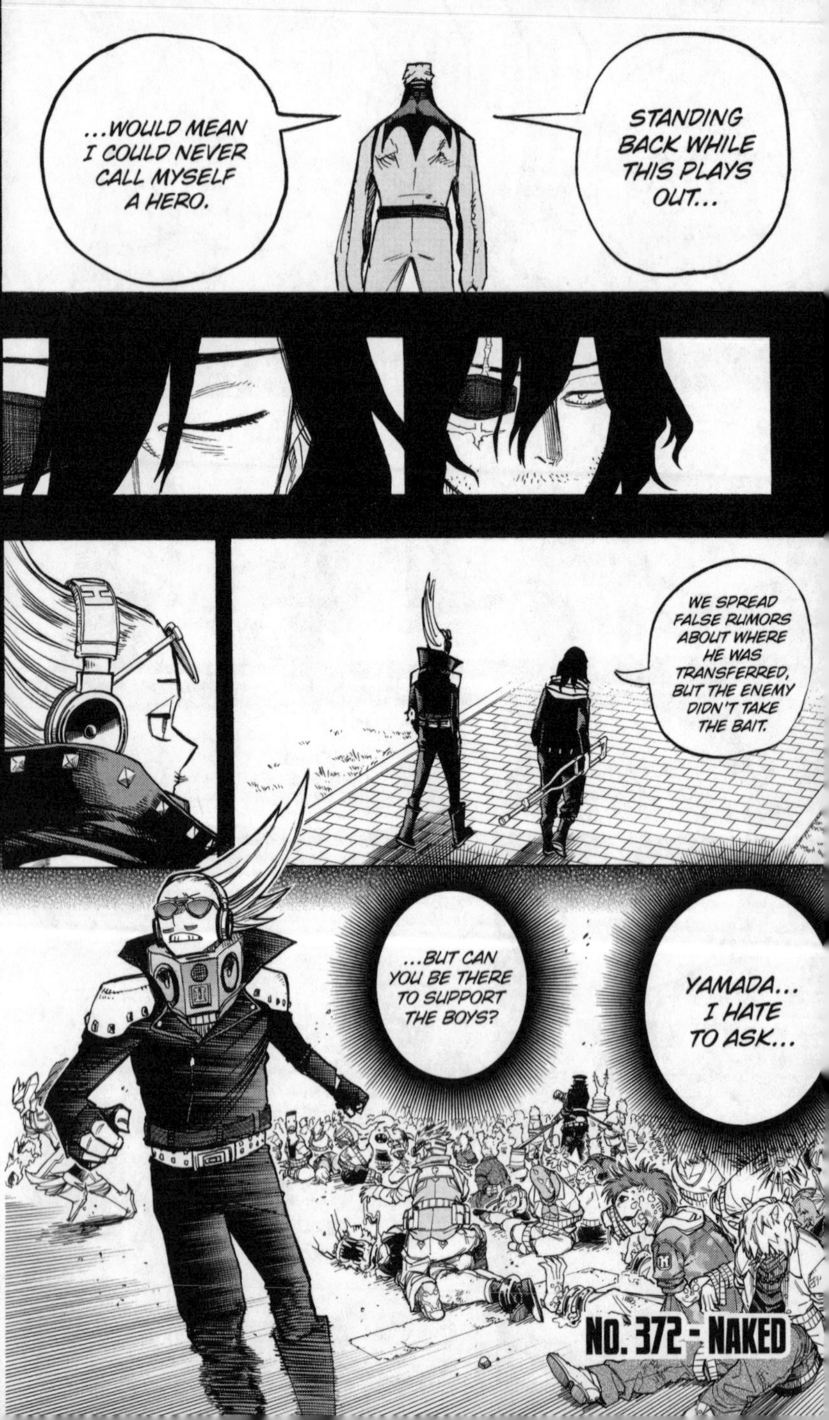
STANDING BACK WHILE THIS PLAYS OUT...
...WOULD MEAN I COULD NEVER CALL MYSELF A HERO.
WE SPREAD FALSE RUMORS ABOUT WHERE HE WAS TRANSFERRED, BUT THE ENEMY DIDN'T TAKE THE BAIT.
YAMADA... I HATE TO ASK...
...BUT CAN YOU BE THERE TO SUPPORT THE BOYS?
NO. 372 - NAKED

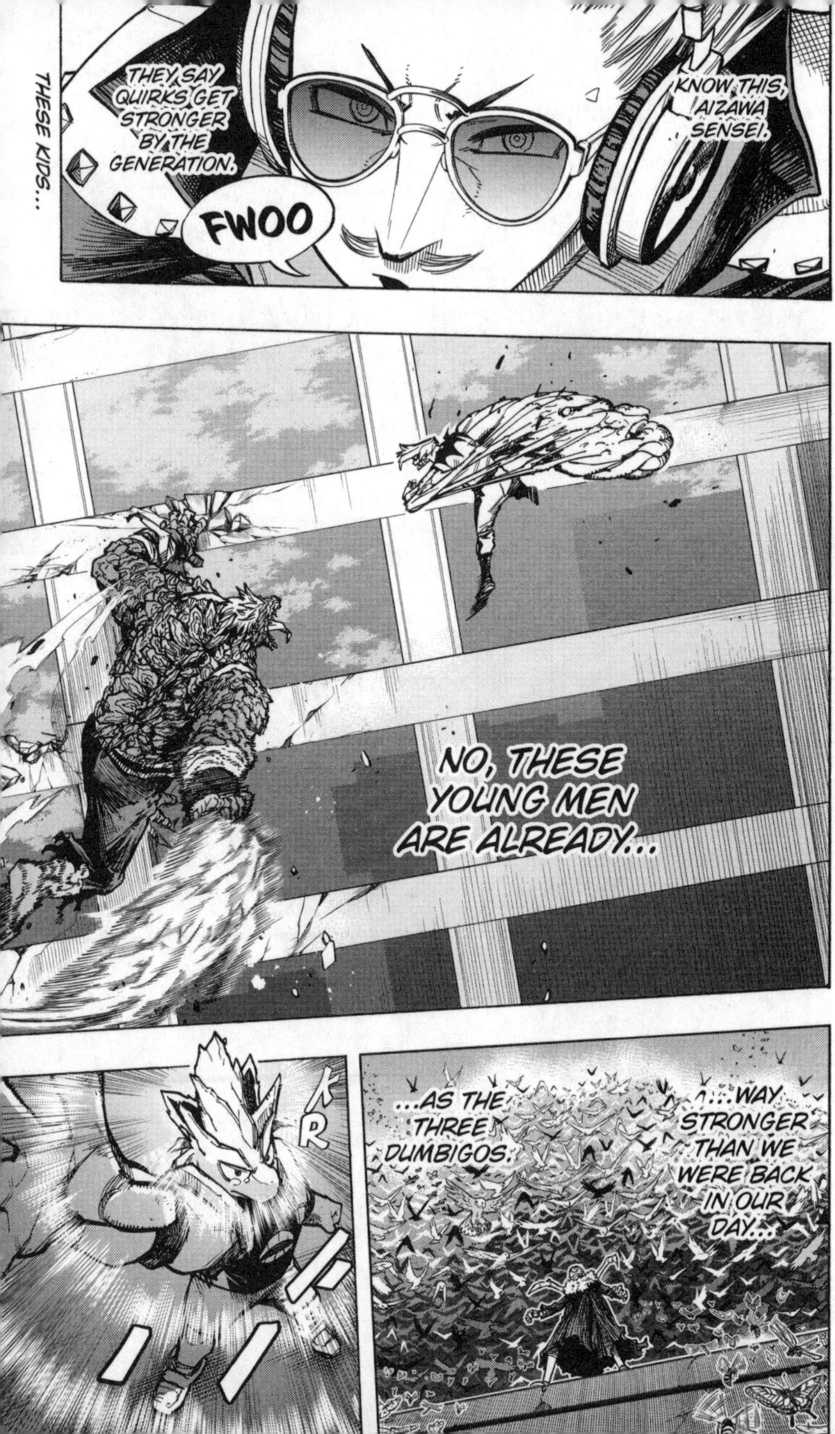
KNOW THIS, AIZAWA SENSEI.
THEY SAY QUIRKS GET STRONGER BY THE GENERATION.
FWOO
THESE KIDS...
NO, THESE YOUNG MEN ARE ALREADY...
...WAY STRONGER THAN WE WERE BACK IN OUR DAY...
...AS THE THREE DUMBIGOS.
KR

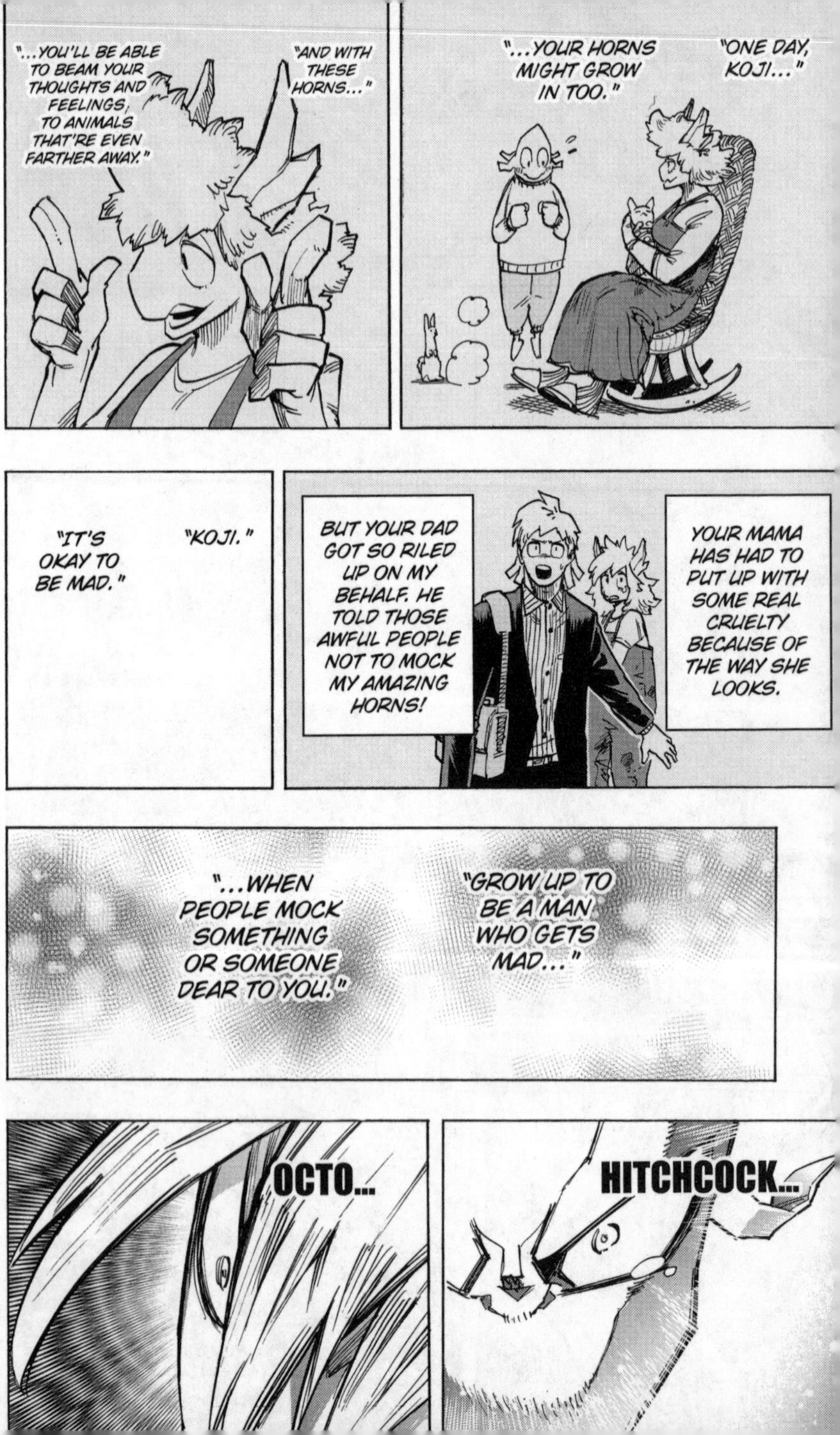
"ONE DAY, KOJI..."
"...YOUR HORNS MIGHT GROW IN TOO."
"AND WITH THESE HORNS..."
"...YOU'LL BE ABLE TO BEAM YOUR THOUGHTS AND FEELINGS, TO ANIMALS THAT'RE EVEN FARTHER AWAY."
YOUR MAMA HAS HAD TO PUT UP WITH SOME REAL CRUELTY BECAUSE OF THE WAY SHE LOOKS.
BUT YOUR DAD GOT SO RILED UP ON MY BEHALF. HE TOLD THOSE AWFUL PEOPLE NOT TO MOCK MY AMAZING HORNS!
"KOJI."
"IT'S OKAY TO BE MAD."
"GROW UP TO BE A MAN WHO GETS MAD..."
"...WHEN PEOPLE MOCK SOMETHING OR SOMEONE DEAR TO YOU."
HITCHCOCK...
OCTO...

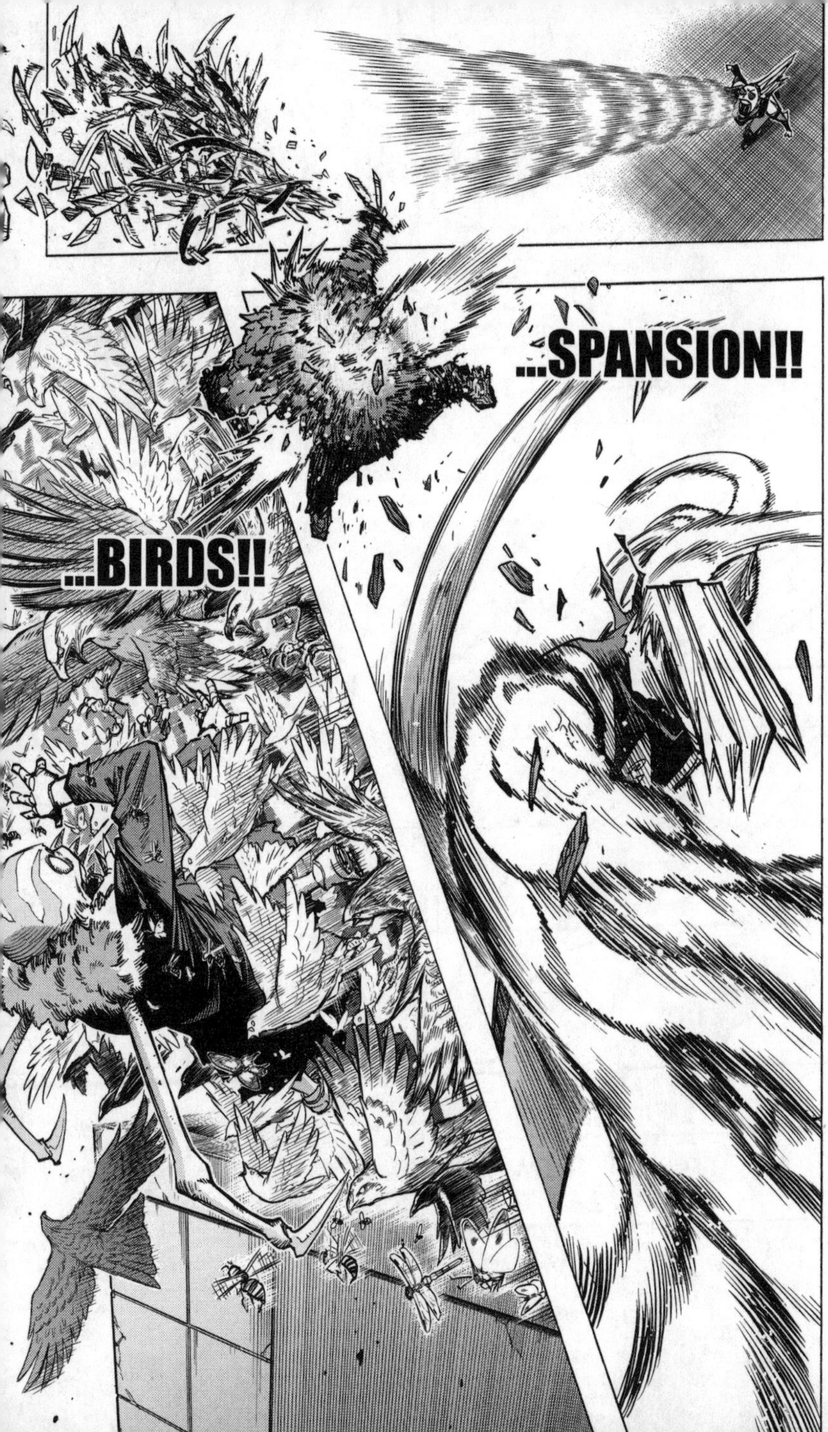
...SPANSION!!
...BIRDS!!

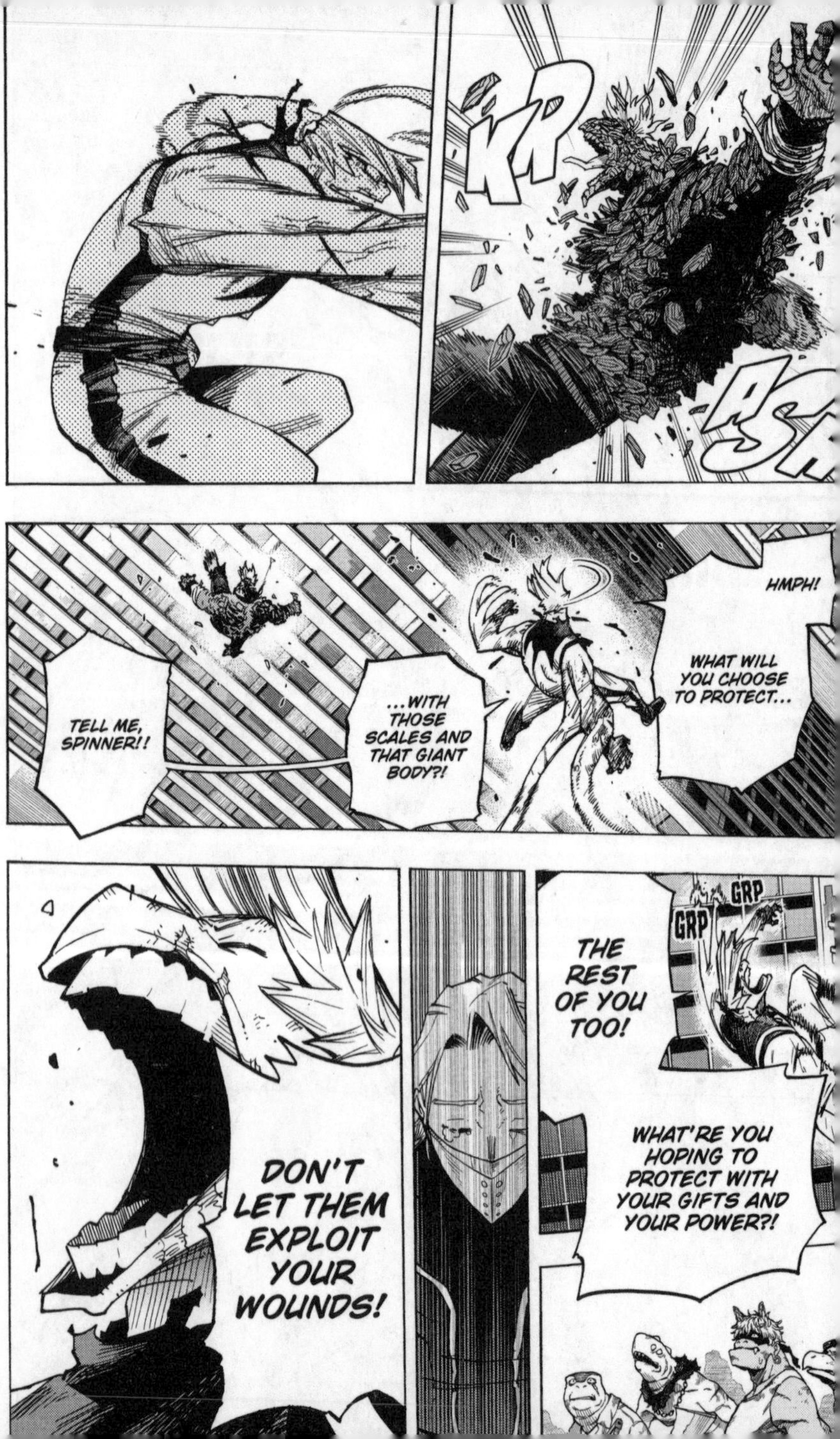
HMPH!
WHAT WILL YOU CHOOSE TO PROTECT...
...WITH THOSE SCALES AND THAT GIANT BODY?!
TELL ME, SPINNER!!
GRP
GRP
THE REST OF YOU TOO!
WHAT'RE YOU HOPING TO PROTECT WITH YOUR GIFTS AND YOUR POWER?!
DON'T LET THEM EXPLOIT YOUR WOUNDS!

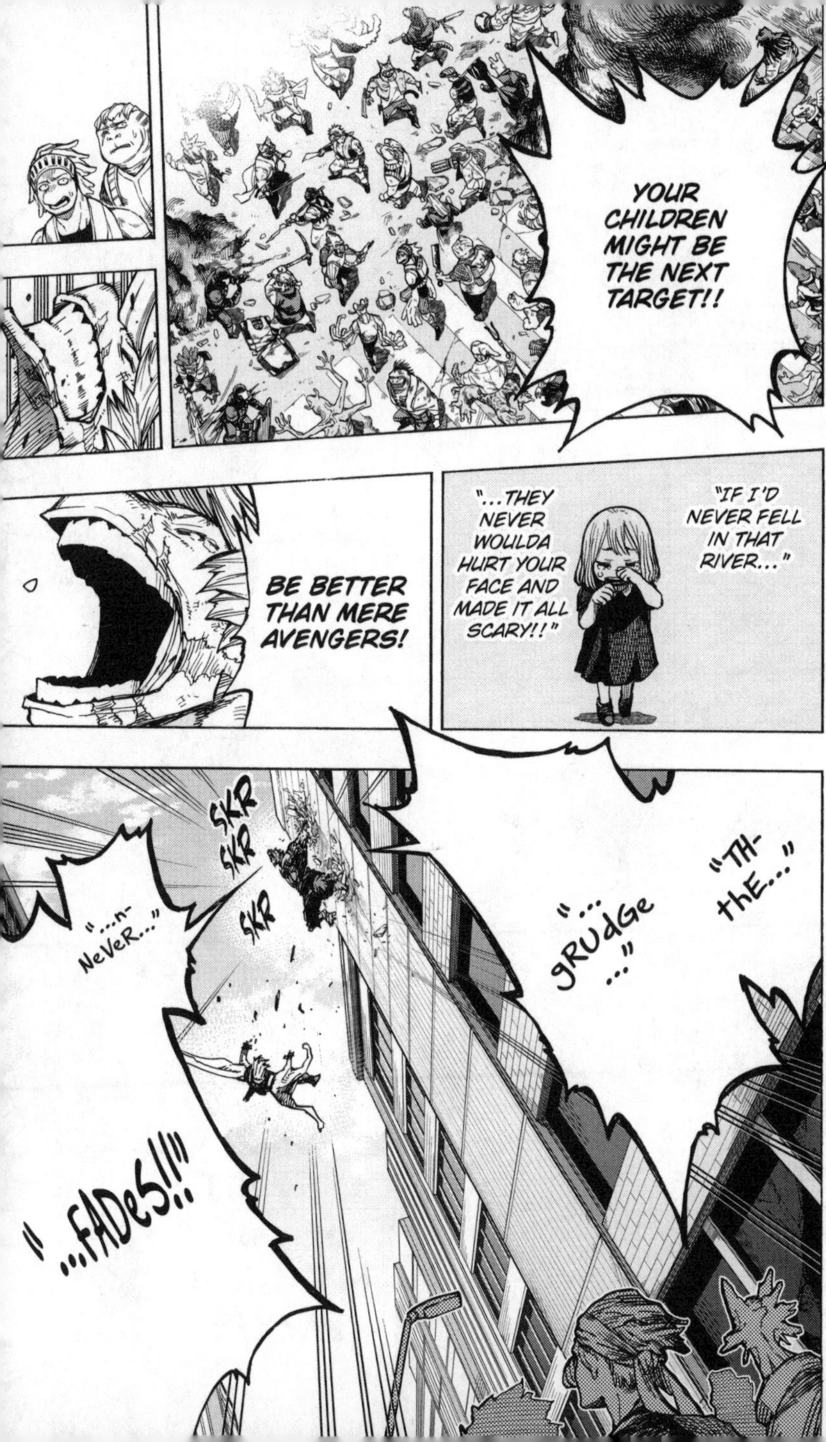
YOUR CHILDREN MIGHT BE THE NEXT TARGET!!
"IF I'D NEVER FELL IN THAT RIVER..."
"...THEY NEVER WOULDA HURT YOUR FACE AND MADE IT ALL SCARY!!"
BE BETTER THAN MERE AVENGERS!
"TH- thE..."
"...gRUdge..."
SKR SKR
SKR
"...n- NeVeR..."
"...FADeS!!"

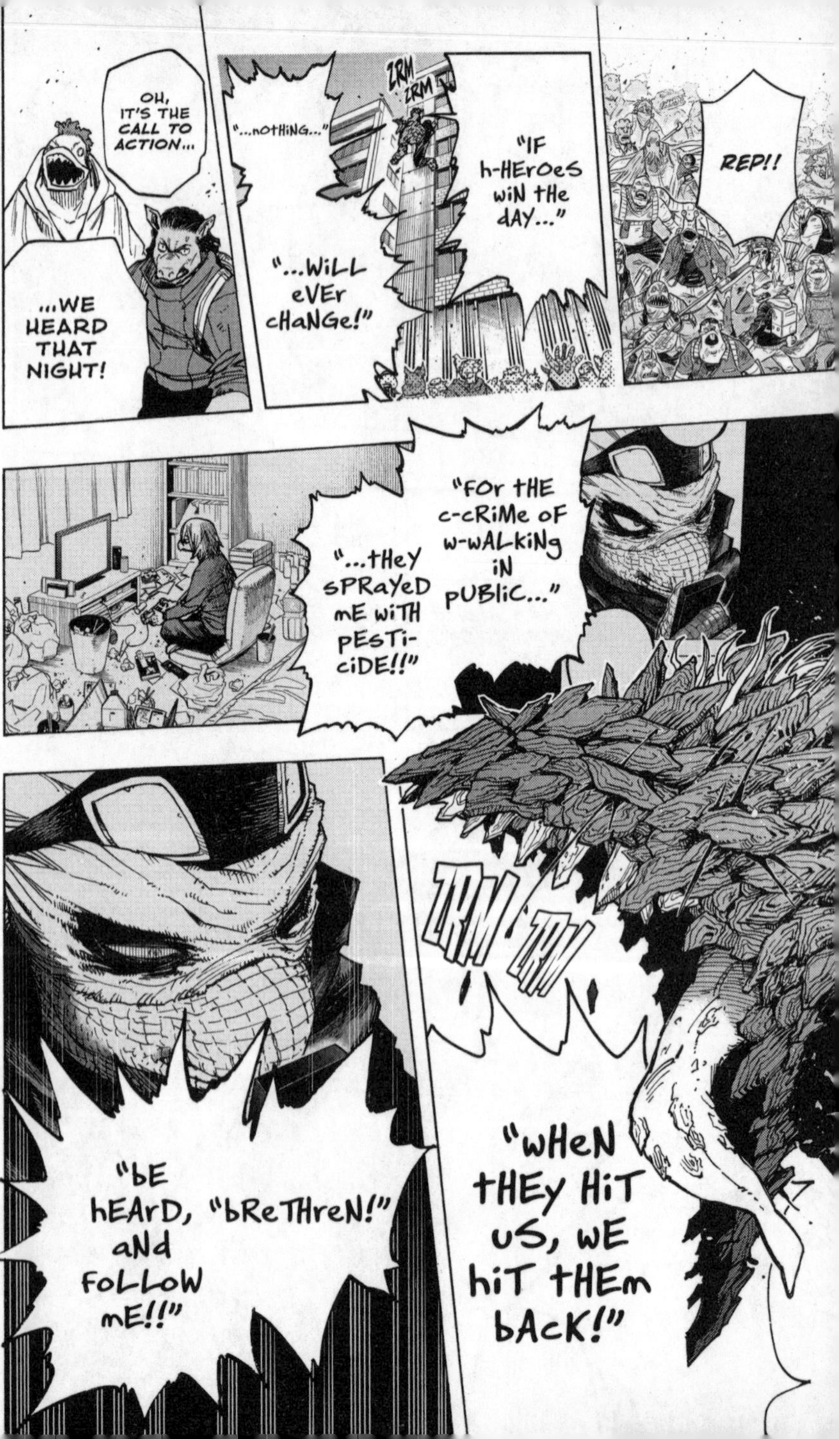
REP!!
ZRM ZRM
"IF h-HEroes wiN the day..."
"...nothing..."
"...will ever change!"
OH, IT'S THE CALL TO ACTION...
...WE HEARD THAT NIGHT!
"For the c-crime of w-walking in public..."
"...they sprayed me with pesti-cide!!"
ZRM ZRM
"when they hit us, we hit them back!"
"be heard, "brethren!" and follow me!!"

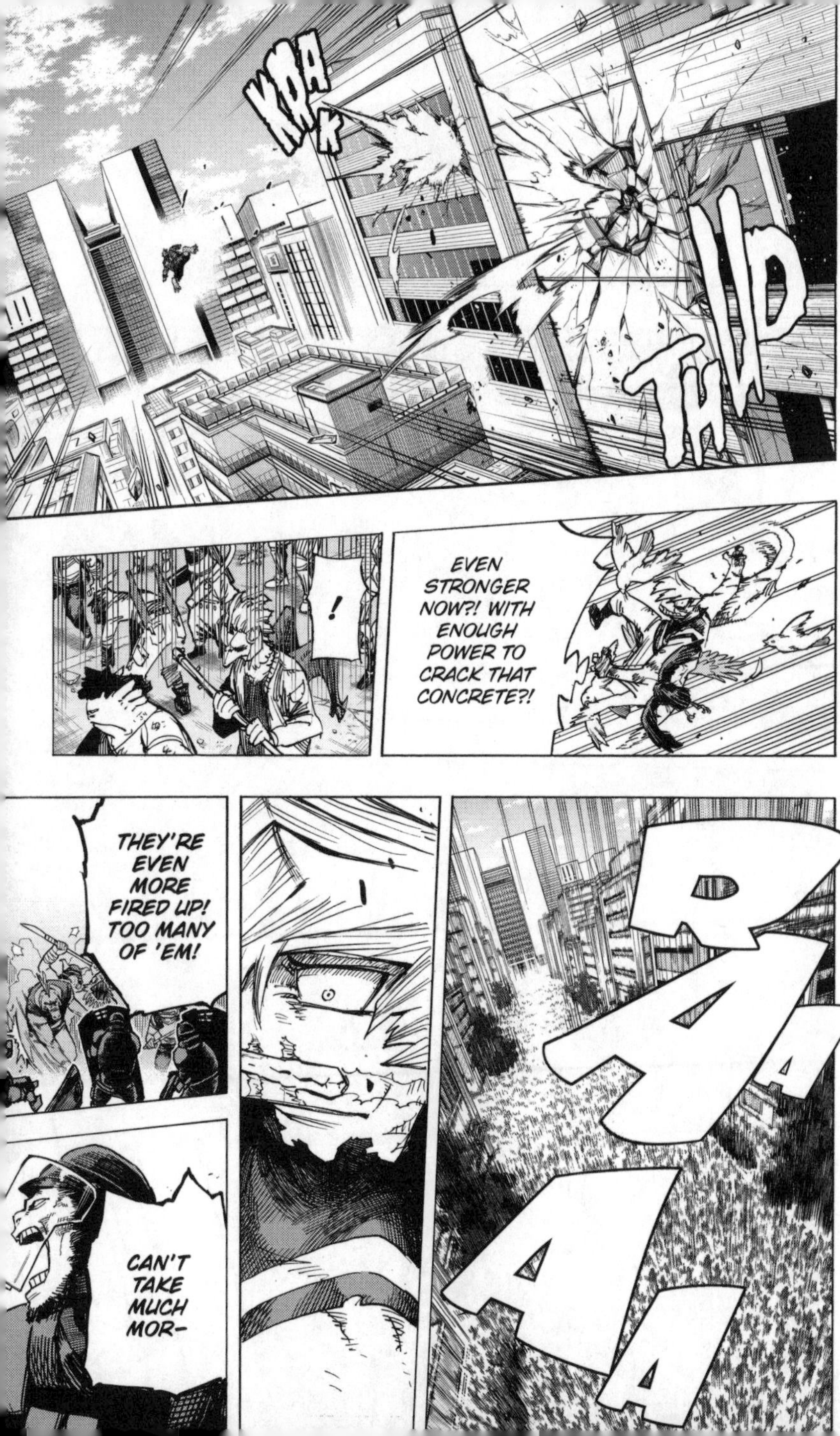
KRAK
THUD
EVEN STRONGER NOW?! WITH ENOUGH POWER TO CRACK THAT CONCRETE?!
!
RAAAAA
!
THEY'RE EVEN MORE FIRED UP! TOO MANY OF 'EM!
CAN'T TAKE MUCH MOR-

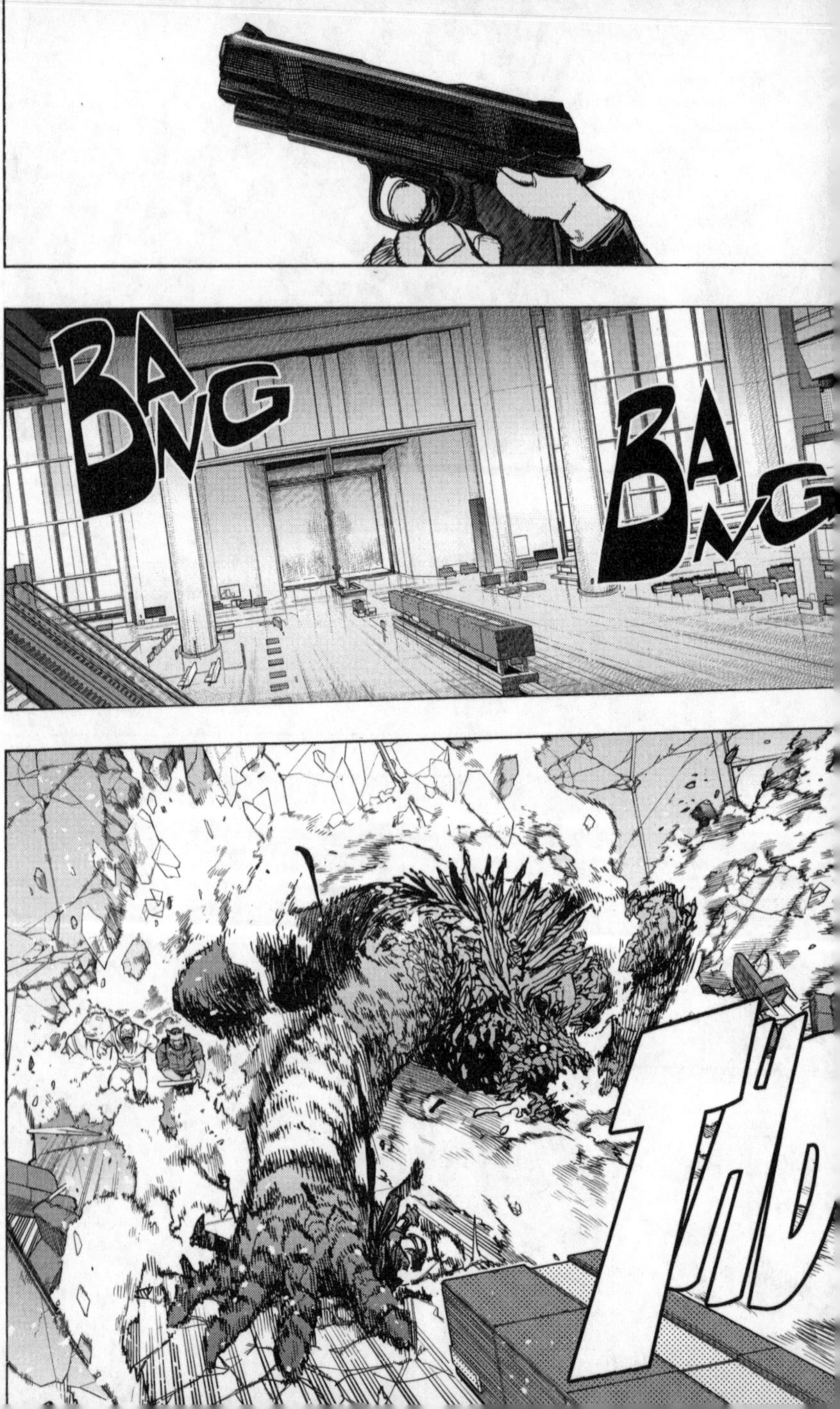
BANG
BANG

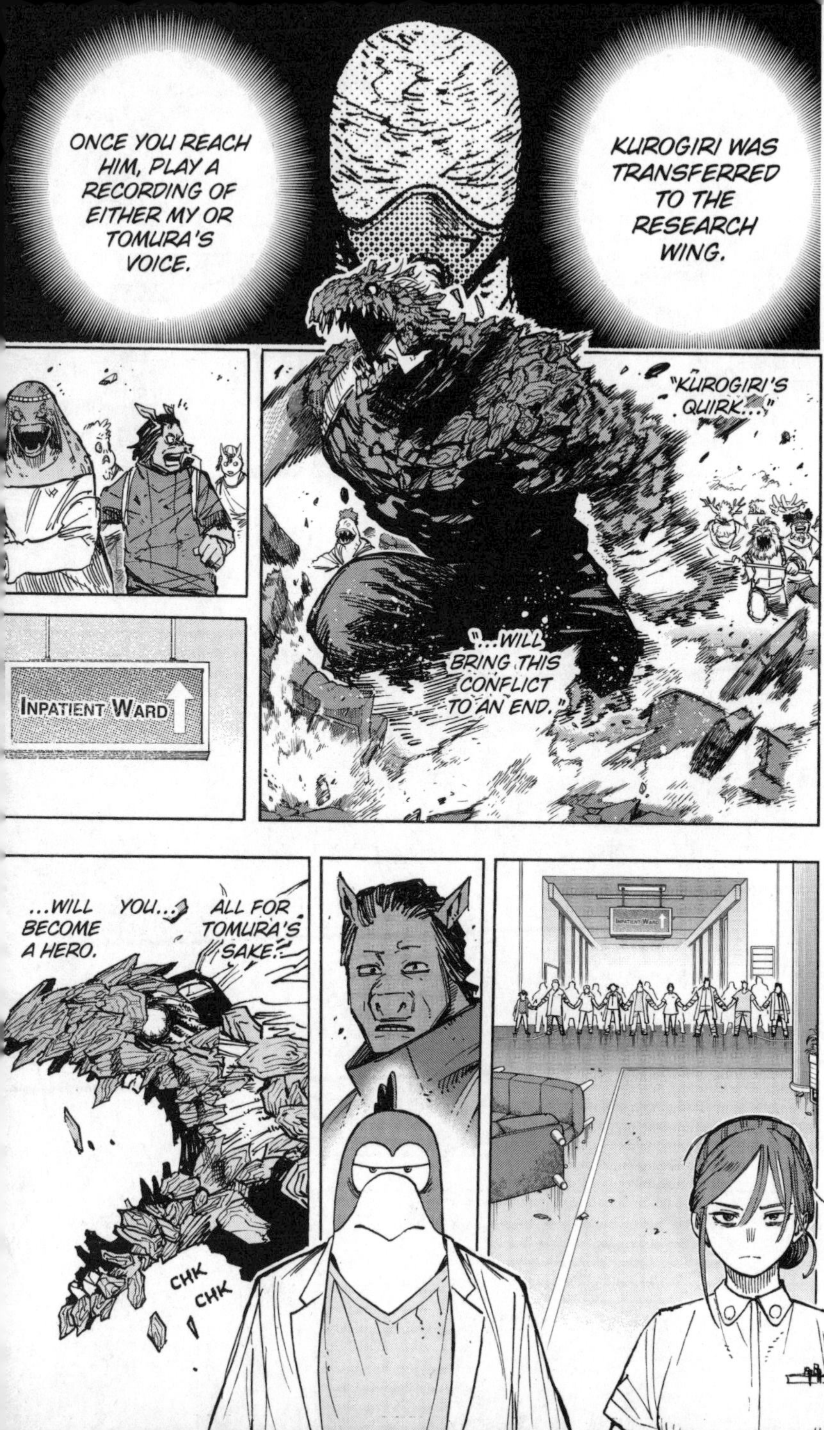
KUROGIRI WAS TRANSFERRED TO THE RESEARCH WING.
ONCE YOU REACH HIM, PLAY A RECORDING OF EITHER MY OR TOMURA'S VOICE.
"KUROGIRI'S QUIRK..."
"...WILL BRING THIS CONFLICT TO AN END."
INPATIENT WARD
ALL FOR TOMURA'S SAKE?
YOU...
...WILL BECOME A HERO.
CHK CHK

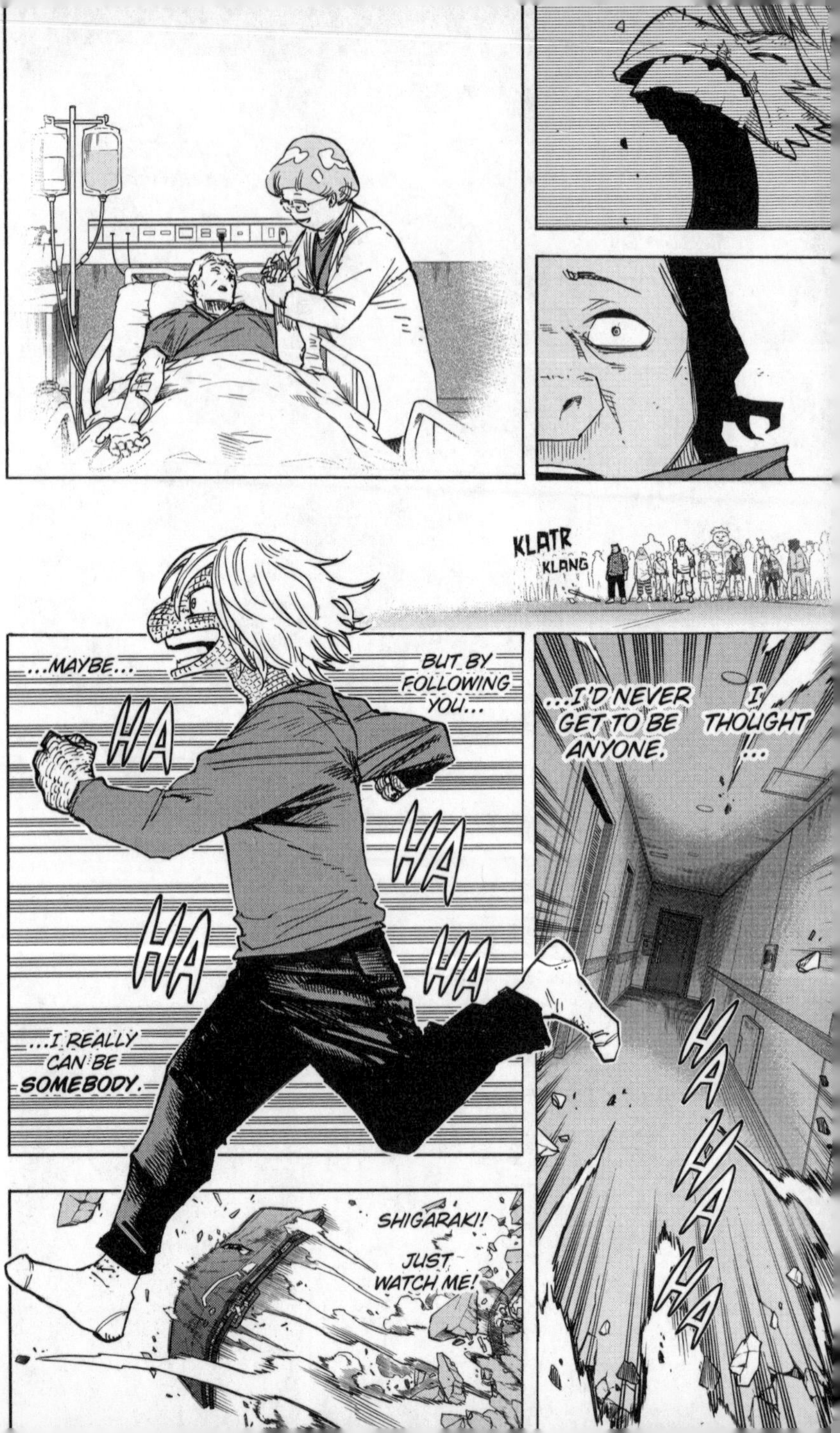
KLATR
KLANG
I THOUGHT...
...I'D NEVER GET TO BE ANYONE.
HAHAHAHAHA
BUT BY FOLLOWING YOU...
...MAYBE...
HA
HA
HA
HA
...I REALLY CAN BE SOMEBODY.
SHIGARAKI!
JUST WATCH ME!

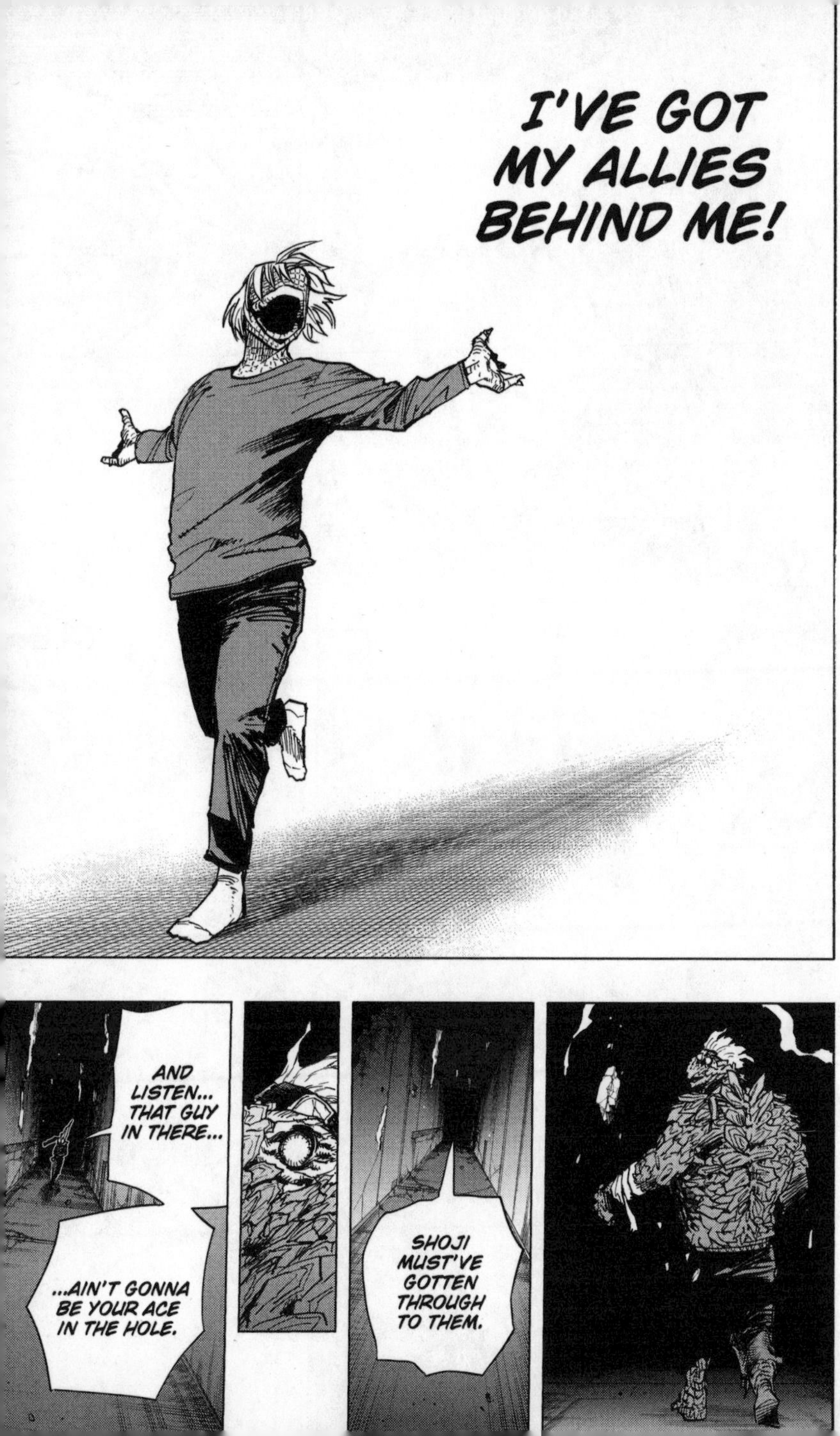
I'VE GOT MY ALLIES BEHIND ME!
SHOJI MUST'VE GOTTEN THROUGH TO THEM.
AND LISTEN... THAT GUY IN THERE...
...AIN'T GONNA BE YOUR ACE IN THE HOLE.

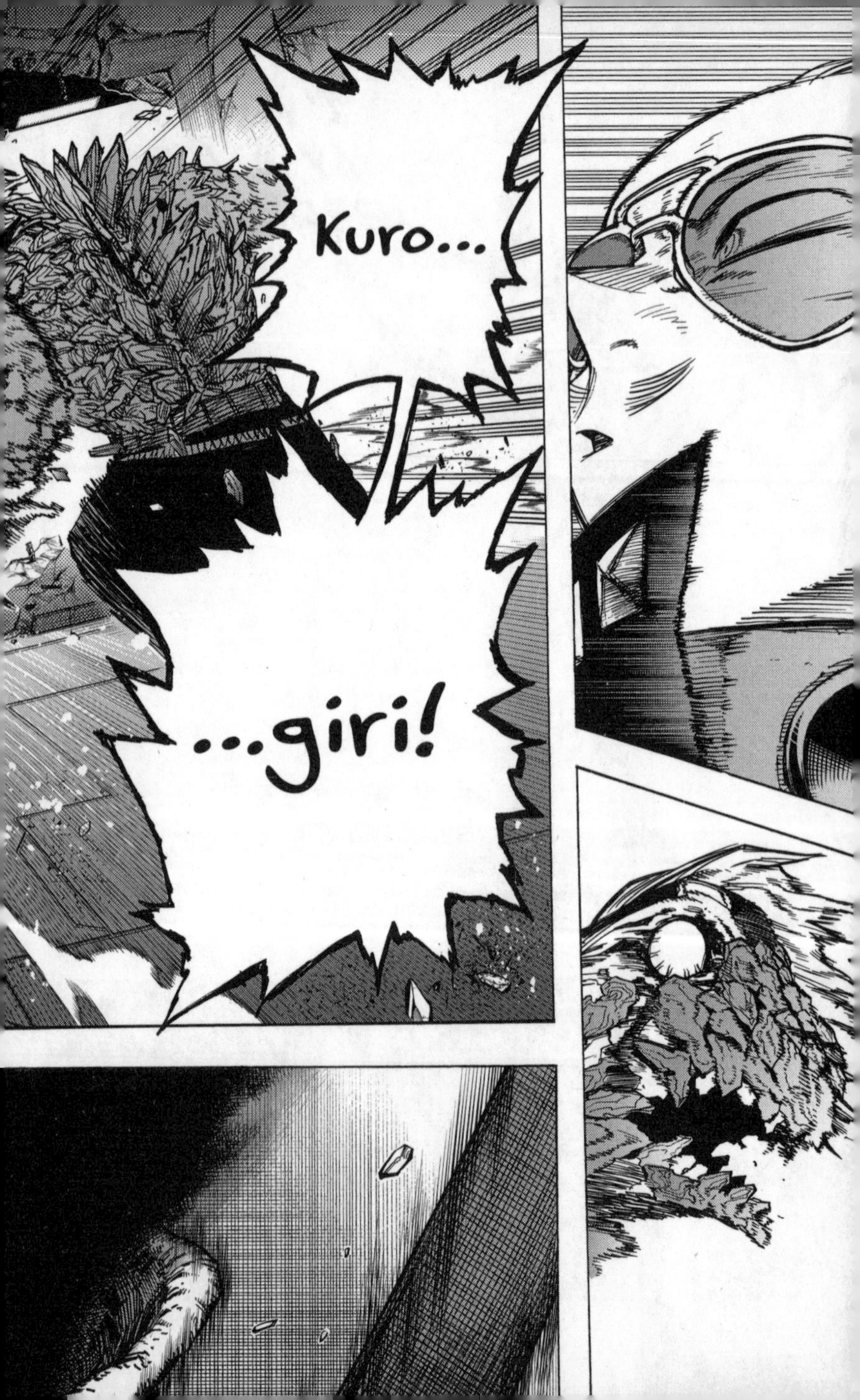
Kuro...
...giri!

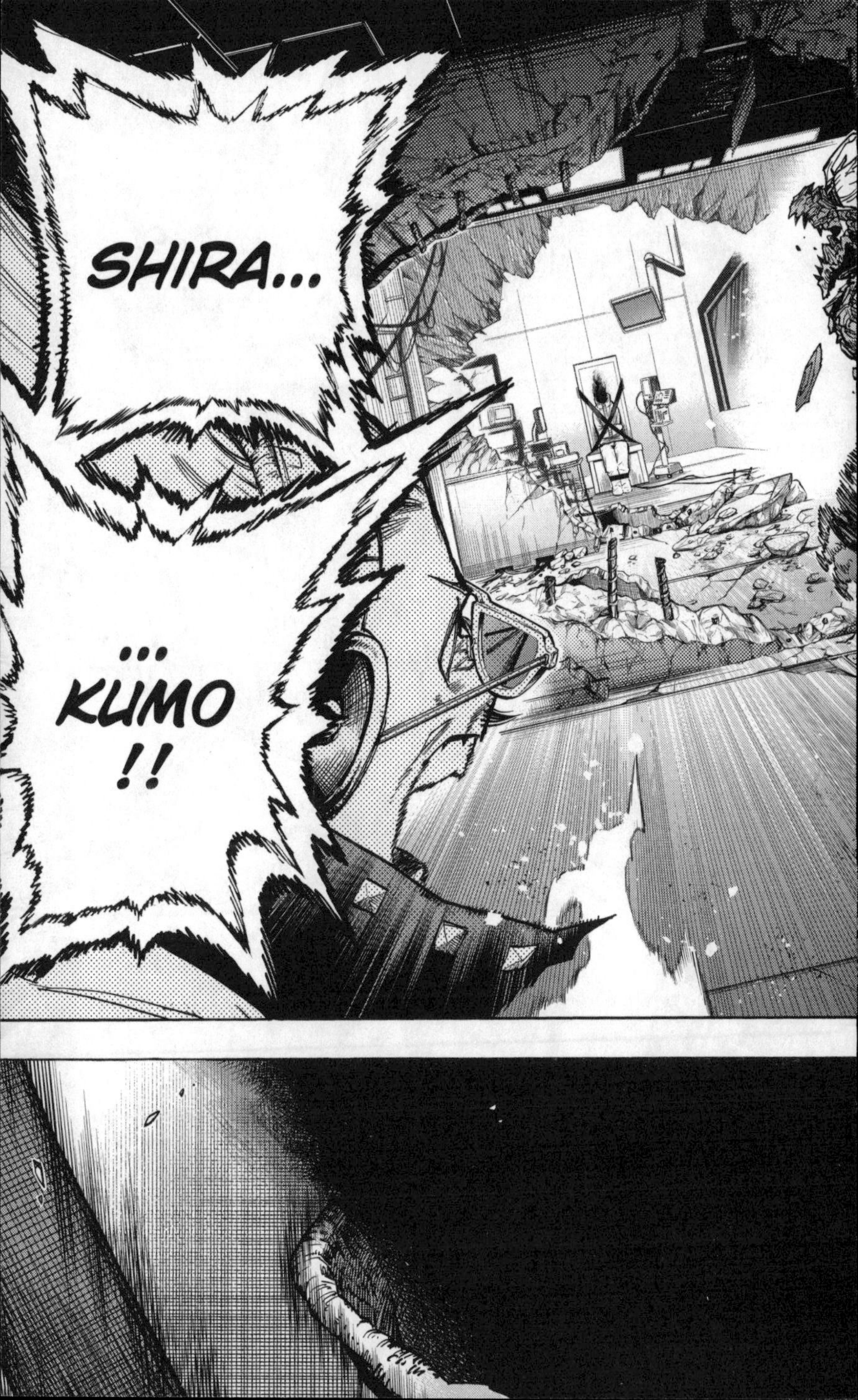
SHIRA...
...KUMO!!

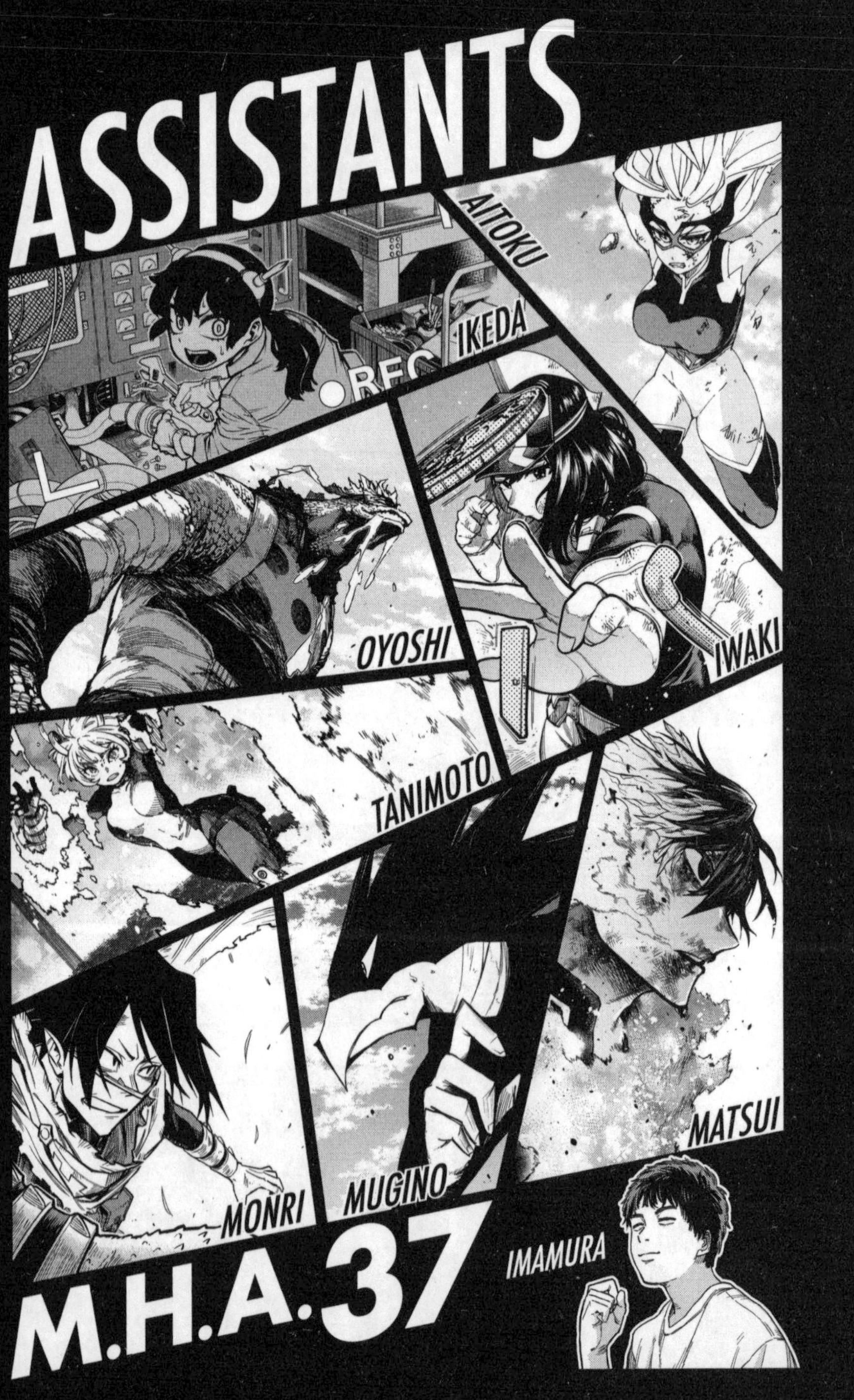

ASSISTANTS
AITOKU
IKEDA
IWAKI
OYOSHI
TANIMOTO
MATSUI
MUGINO
MONRI
IMAMURA
M.H.A. 37

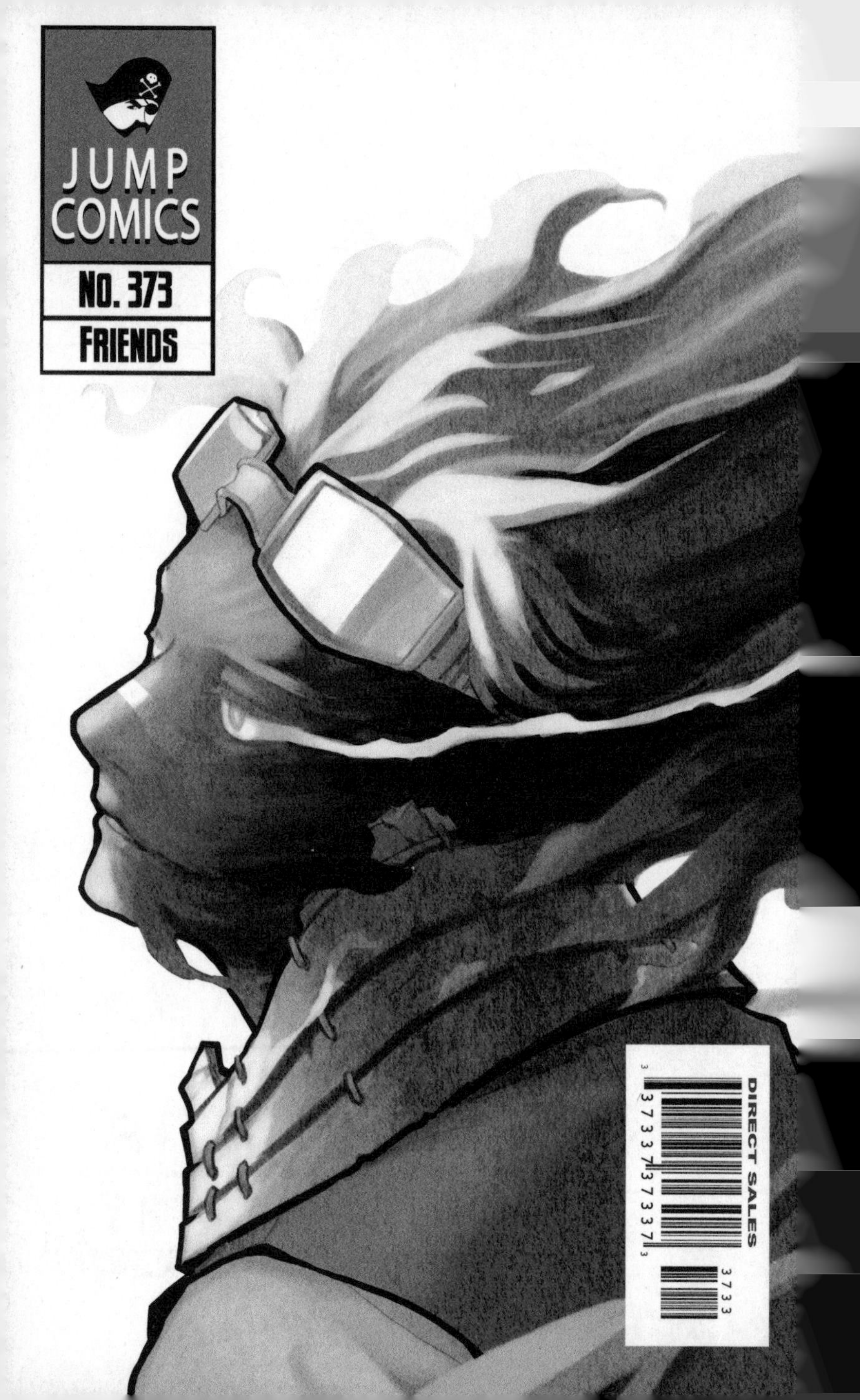
JUMP COMICS
NO. 373
FRIENDS
DIRECT SALES

MY HERO ACADEMIA

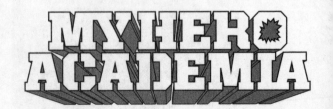

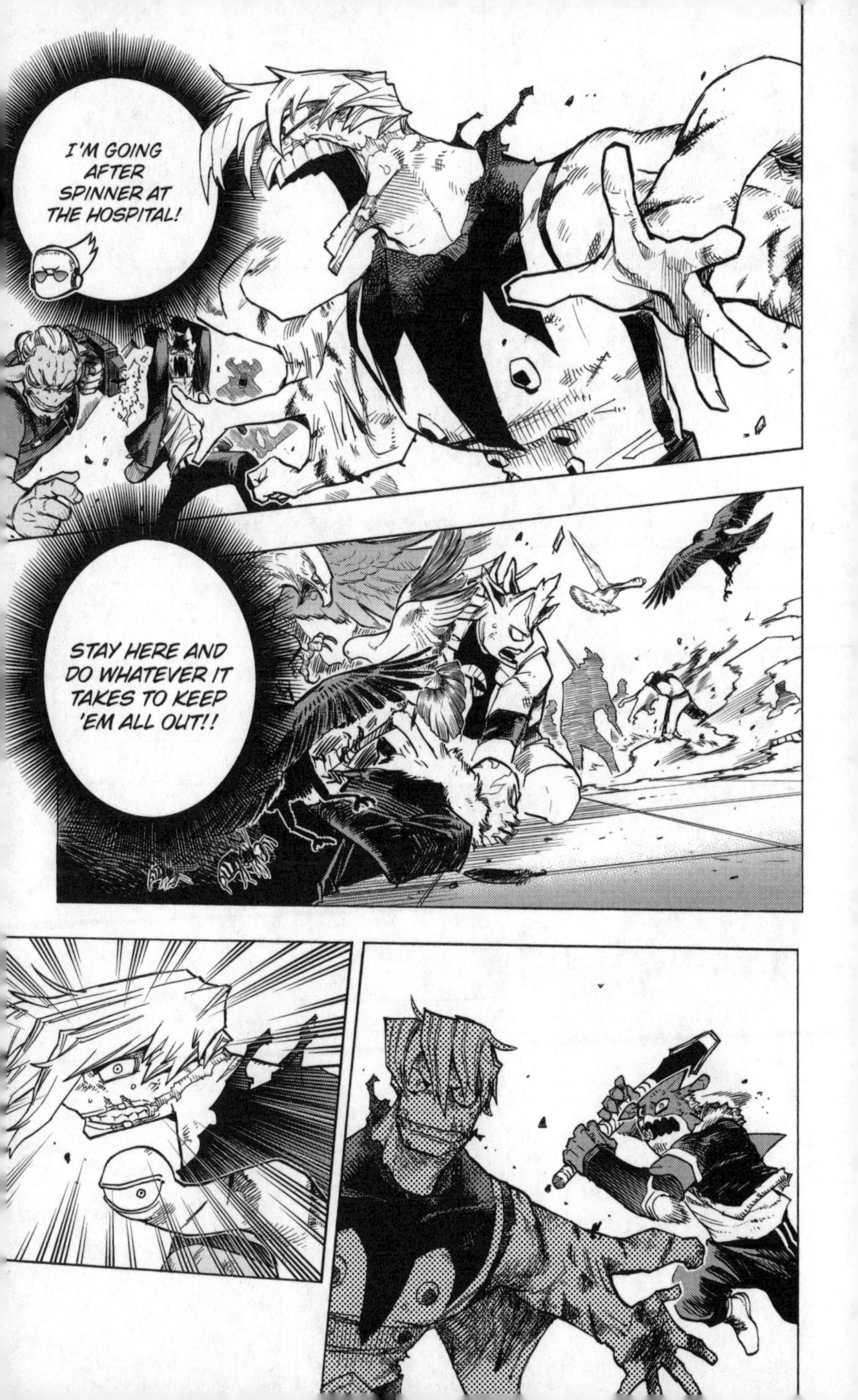
I'M GOING AFTER SPINNER AT THE HOSPITAL!
STAY HERE AND DO WHATEVER IT TAKES TO KEEP 'EM ALL OUT!!

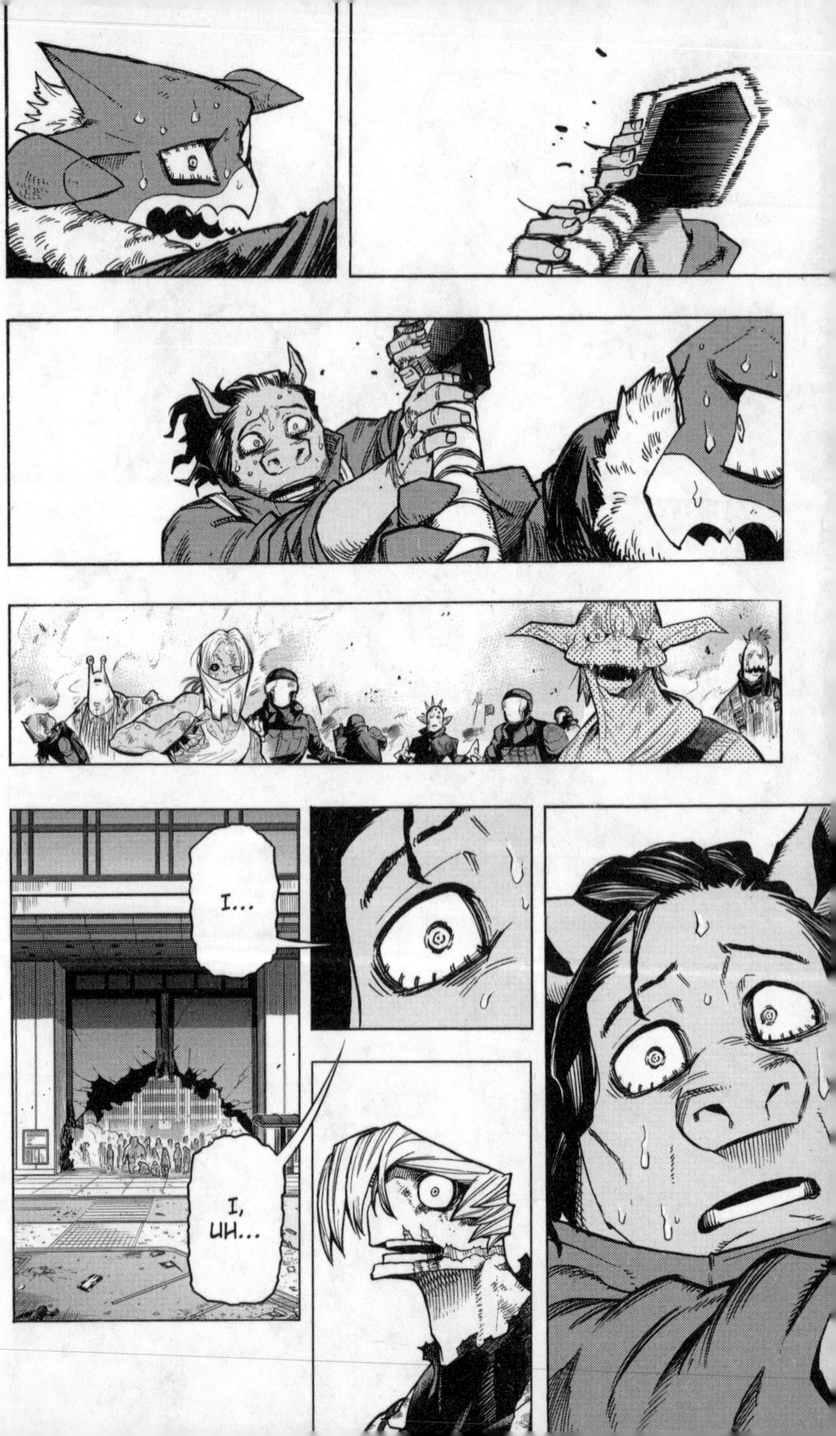
I...
I, UH...

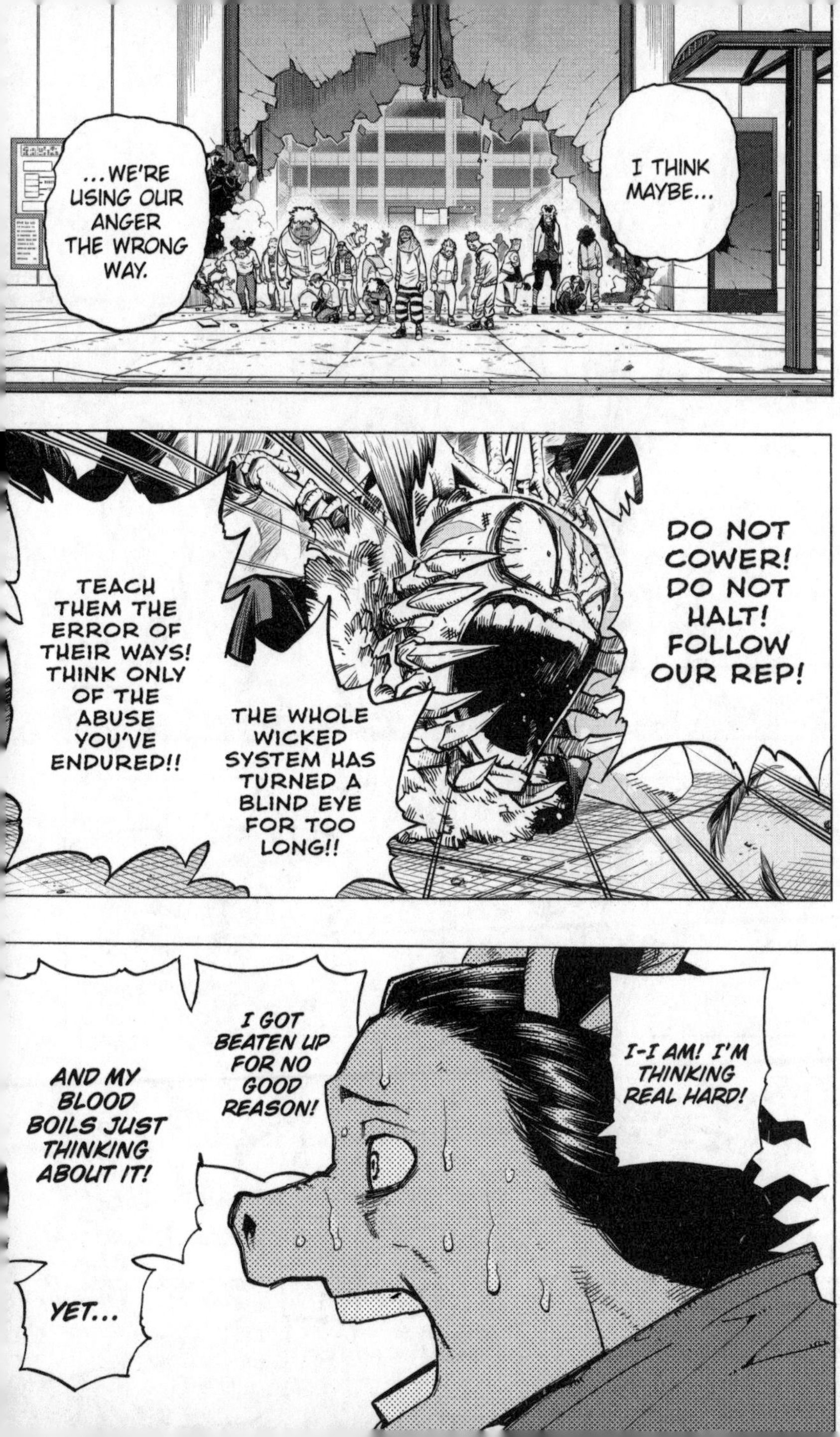
I THINK MAYBE...
...WE'RE USING OUR ANGER THE WRONG WAY.
DO NOT COWER! DO NOT HALT! FOLLOW OUR REP!
THE WHOLE WICKED SYSTEM HAS TURNED A BLIND EYE FOR TOO LONG!!
TEACH THEM THE ERROR OF THEIR WAYS! THINK ONLY OF THE ABUSE YOU'VE ENDURED!!
I-I AM! I'M THINKING REAL HARD!
I GOT BEATEN UP FOR NO GOOD REASON!
AND MY BLOOD BOILS JUST THINKING ABOUT IT!
YET...

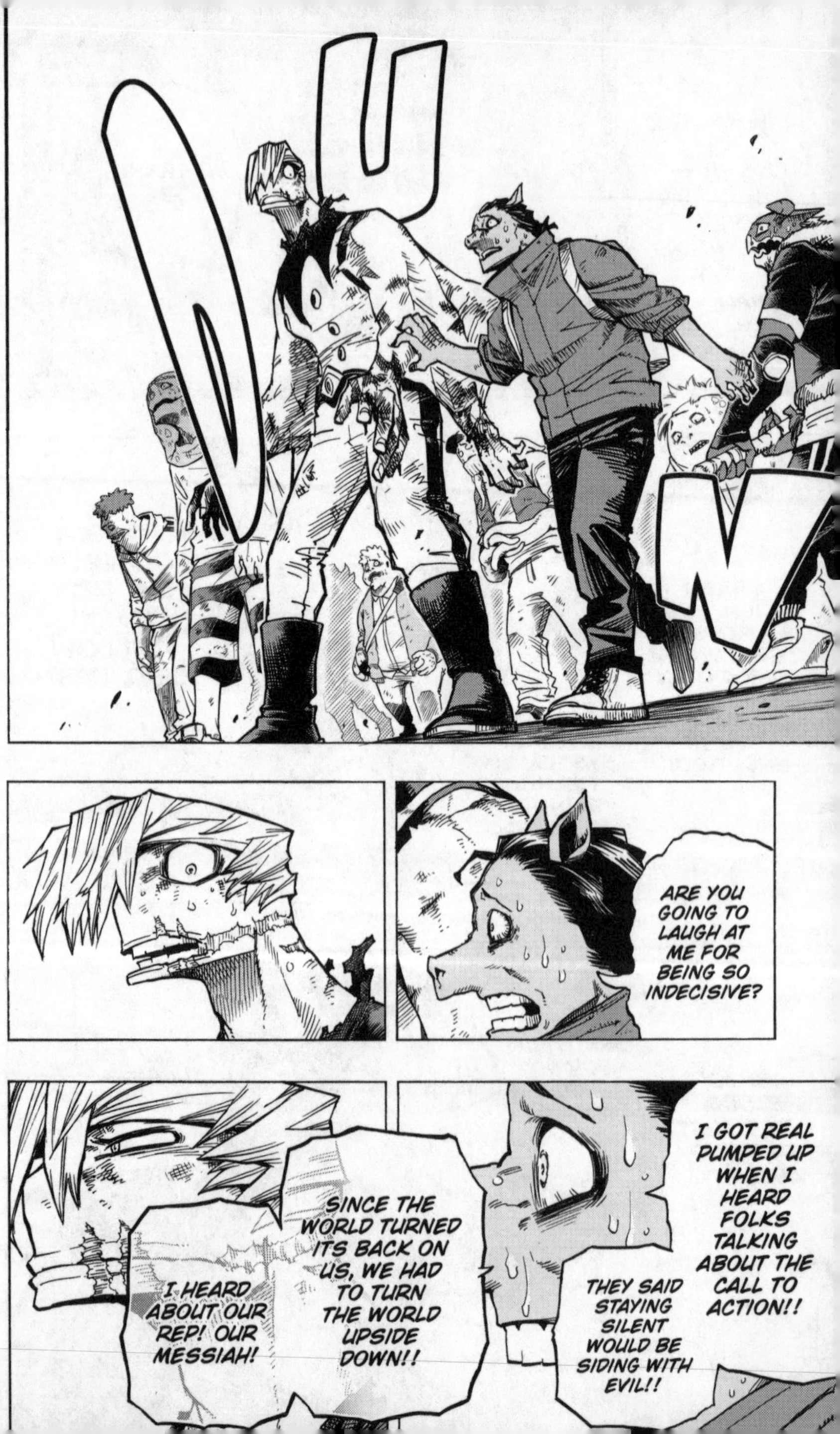
ARE YOU GOING TO LAUGH AT ME FOR BEING SO INDECISIVE?
I GOT REAL PUMPED UP WHEN I HEARD FOLKS TALKING ABOUT THE CALL TO ACTION!!
THEY SAID STAYING SILENT WOULD BE SIDING WITH EVIL!!
SINCE THE WORLD TURNED ITS BACK ON US, WE HAD TO TURN THE WORLD UPSIDE DOWN!!
I HEARD ABOUT OUR REP! OUR MESSIAH!

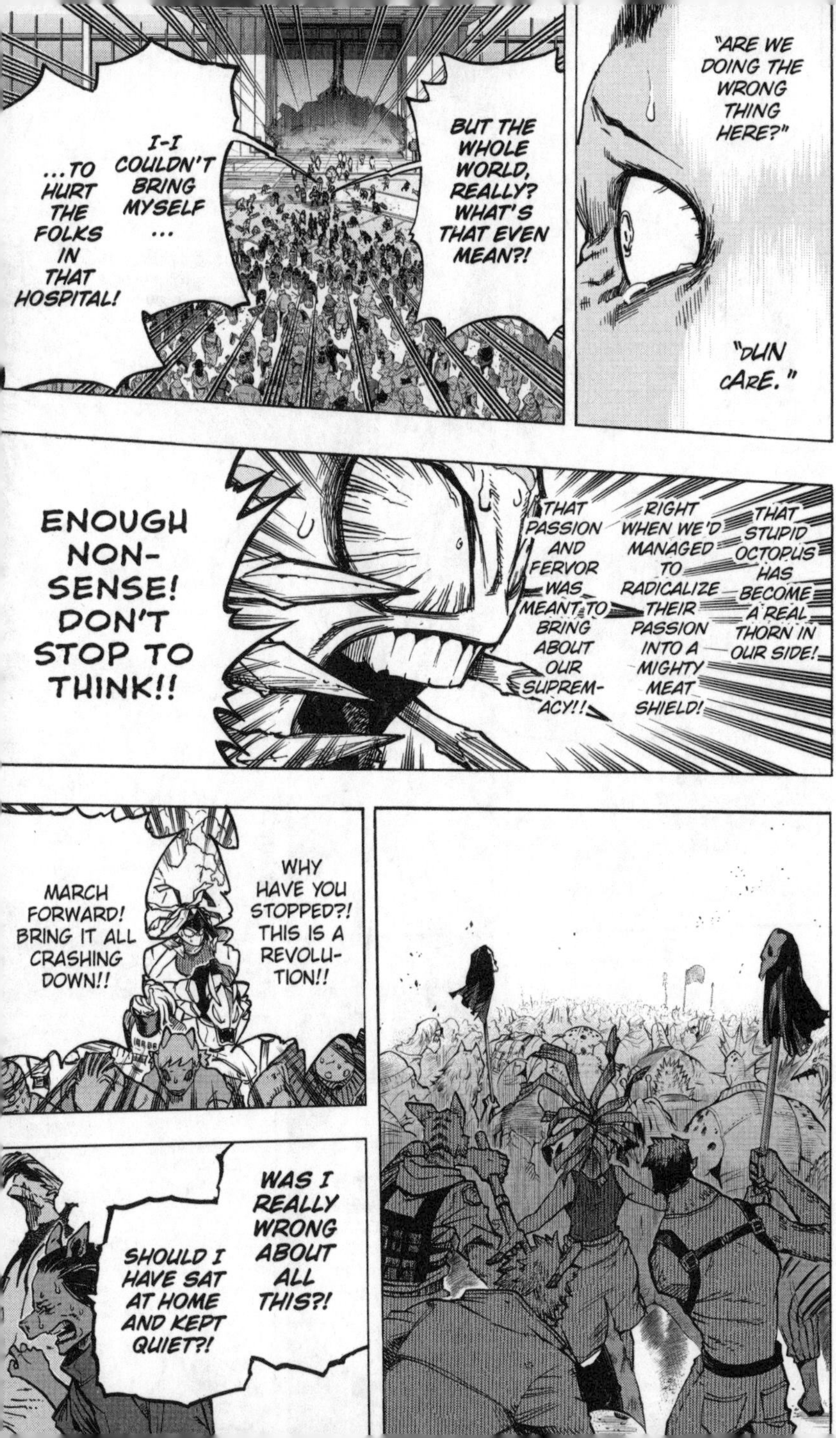
"ARE WE DOING THE WRONG THING HERE?"
"DUN CARE."
BUT THE WHOLE WORLD, REALLY? WHAT'S THAT EVEN MEAN?!
I-I COULDN'T BRING MYSELF...
...TO HURT THE FOLKS IN THAT HOSPITAL!
THAT STUPID OCTOPUS HAS BECOME A REAL THORN IN OUR SIDE!
RIGHT WHEN WE'D MANAGED TO RADICALIZE THEIR PASSION INTO A MIGHTY MEAT SHIELD!
THAT PASSION AND FERVOR WAS MEANT TO BRING ABOUT OUR SUPREM-ACY!!
ENOUGH NON-SENSE! DON'T STOP TO THINK!!
WHY HAVE YOU STOPPED?! THIS IS A REVOLU-TION!!
MARCH FORWARD! BRING IT ALL CRASHING DOWN!!
WAS I REALLY WRONG ABOUT ALL THIS?!
SHOULD I HAVE SAT AT HOME AND KEPT QUIET?!

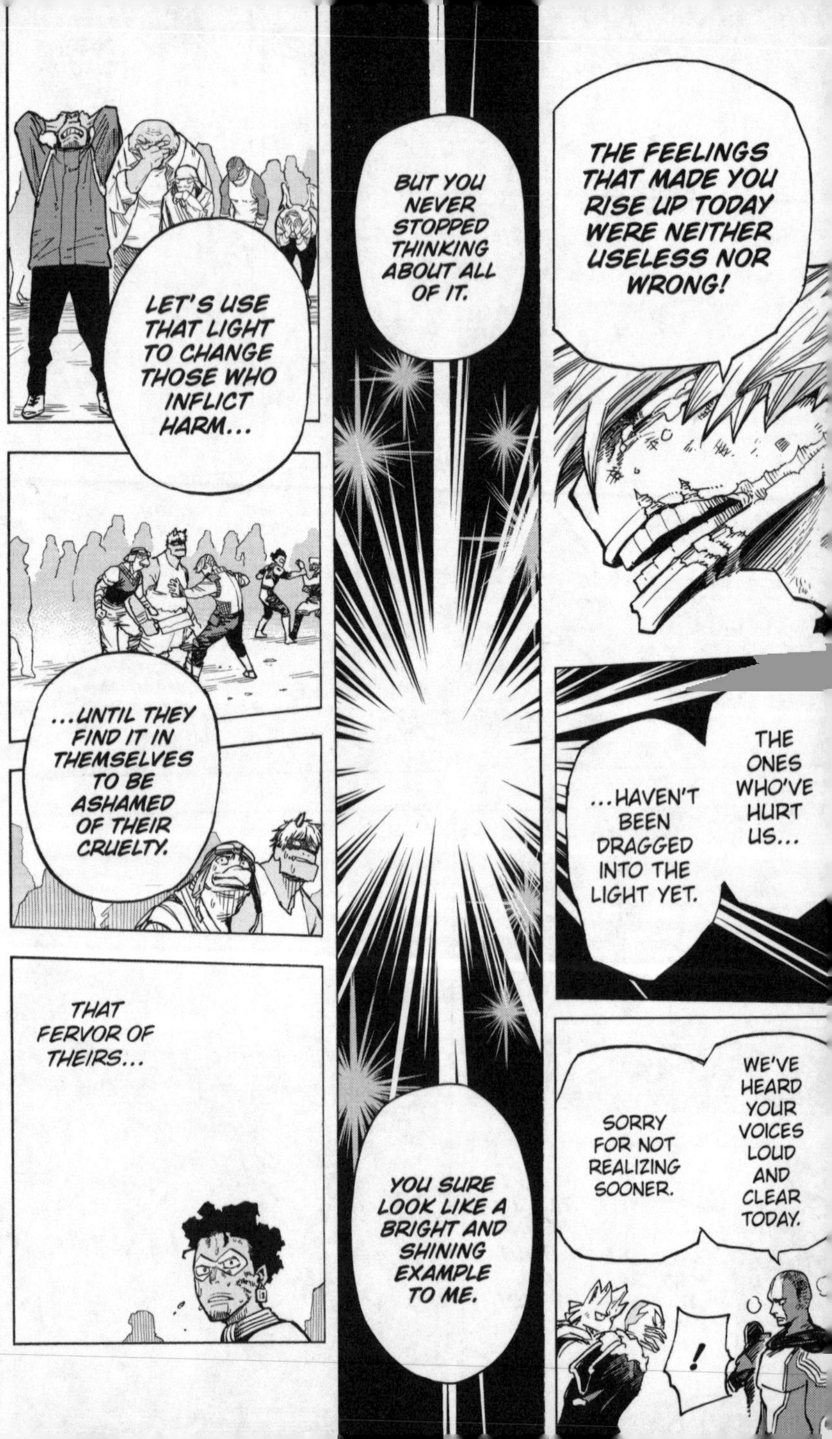
THE FEELINGS THAT MADE YOU RISE UP TODAY WERE NEITHER USELESS NOR WRONG!
THE ONES WHO'VE HURT US...
...HAVEN'T BEEN DRAGGED INTO THE LIGHT YET.
WE'VE HEARD YOUR VOICES LOUD AND CLEAR TODAY.
SORRY FOR NOT REALIZING SOONER.
!
BUT YOU NEVER STOPPED THINKING ABOUT ALL OF IT.
YOU SURE LOOK LIKE A BRIGHT AND SHINING EXAMPLE TO ME.
LET'S USE THAT LIGHT TO CHANGE THOSE WHO INFLICT HARM...
...UNTIL THEY FIND IT IN THEMSELVES TO BE ASHAMED OF THEIR CRUELTY.
THAT FERVOR OF THEIRS...

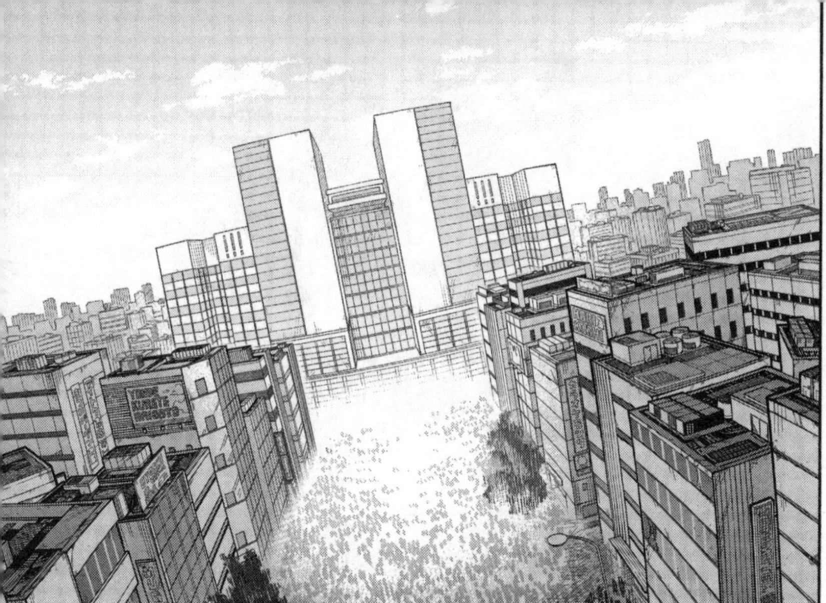

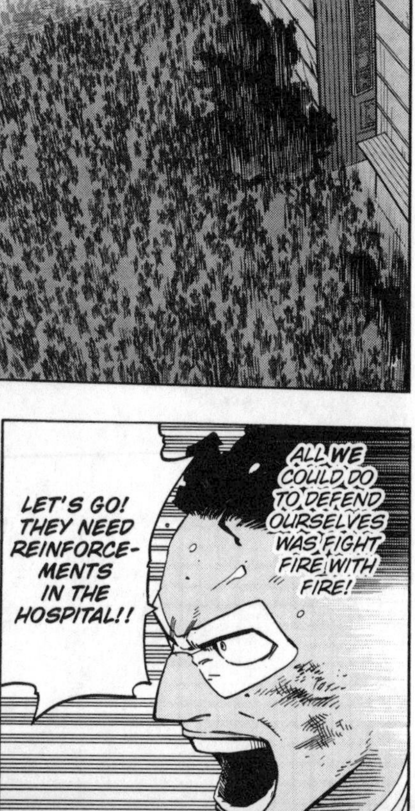
ALL WE COULD DO TO DEFEND OURSELVES WAS FIGHT FIRE WITH FIRE!
LET'S GO! THEY NEED REINFORCE-MENTS IN THE HOSPITAL!!

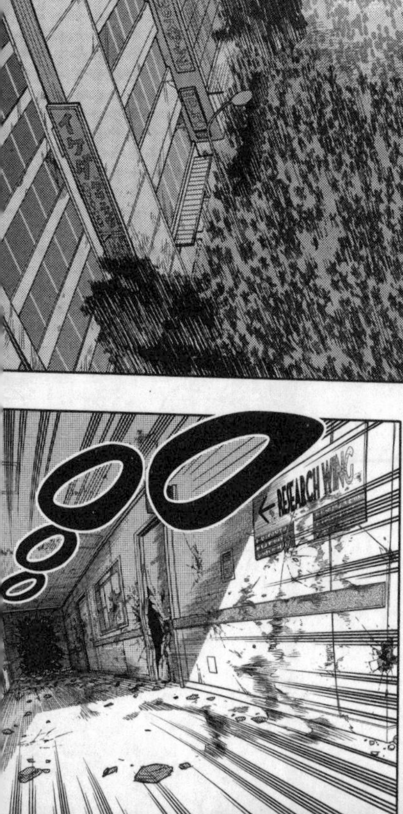
RESEARCH WING

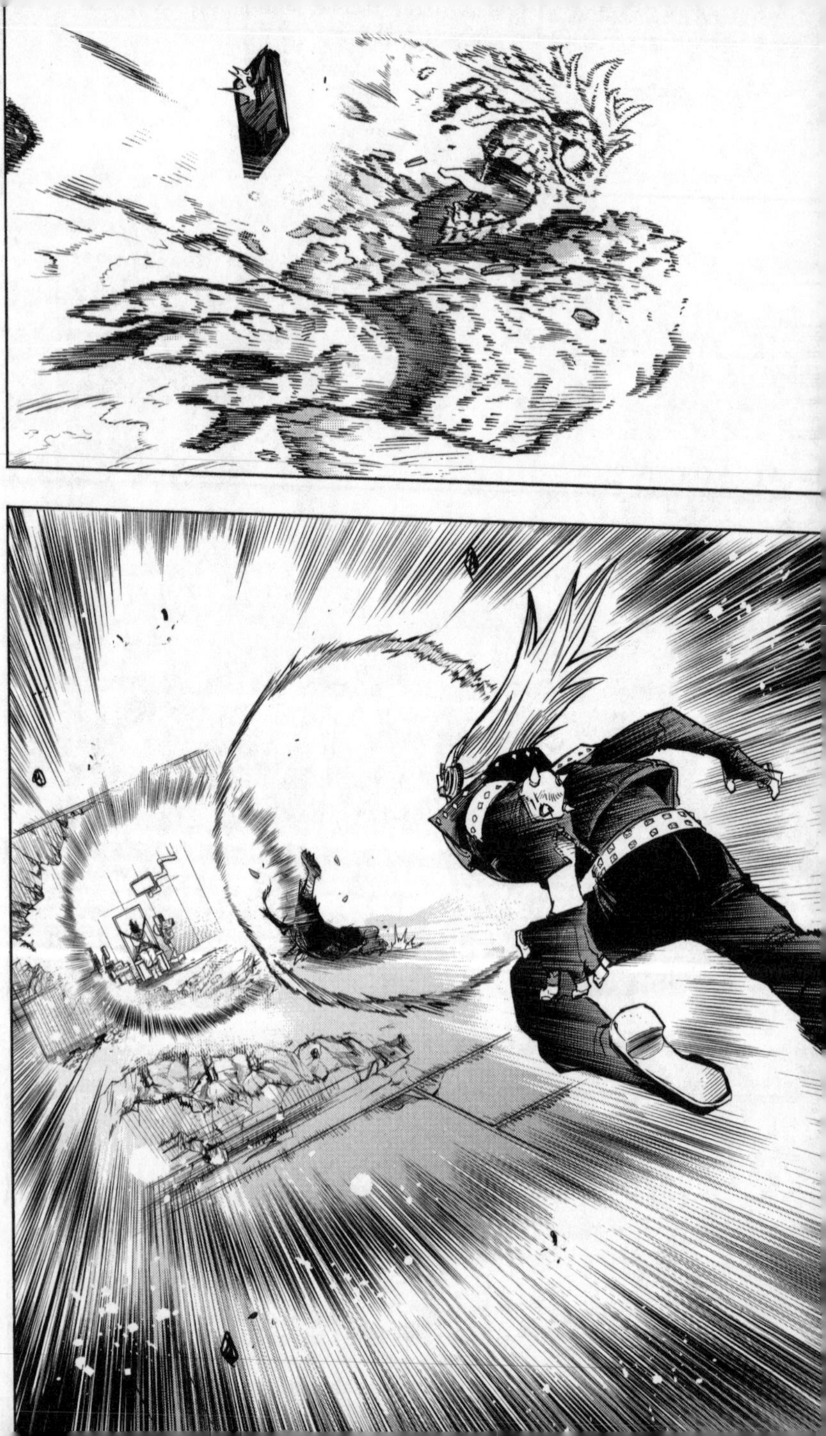

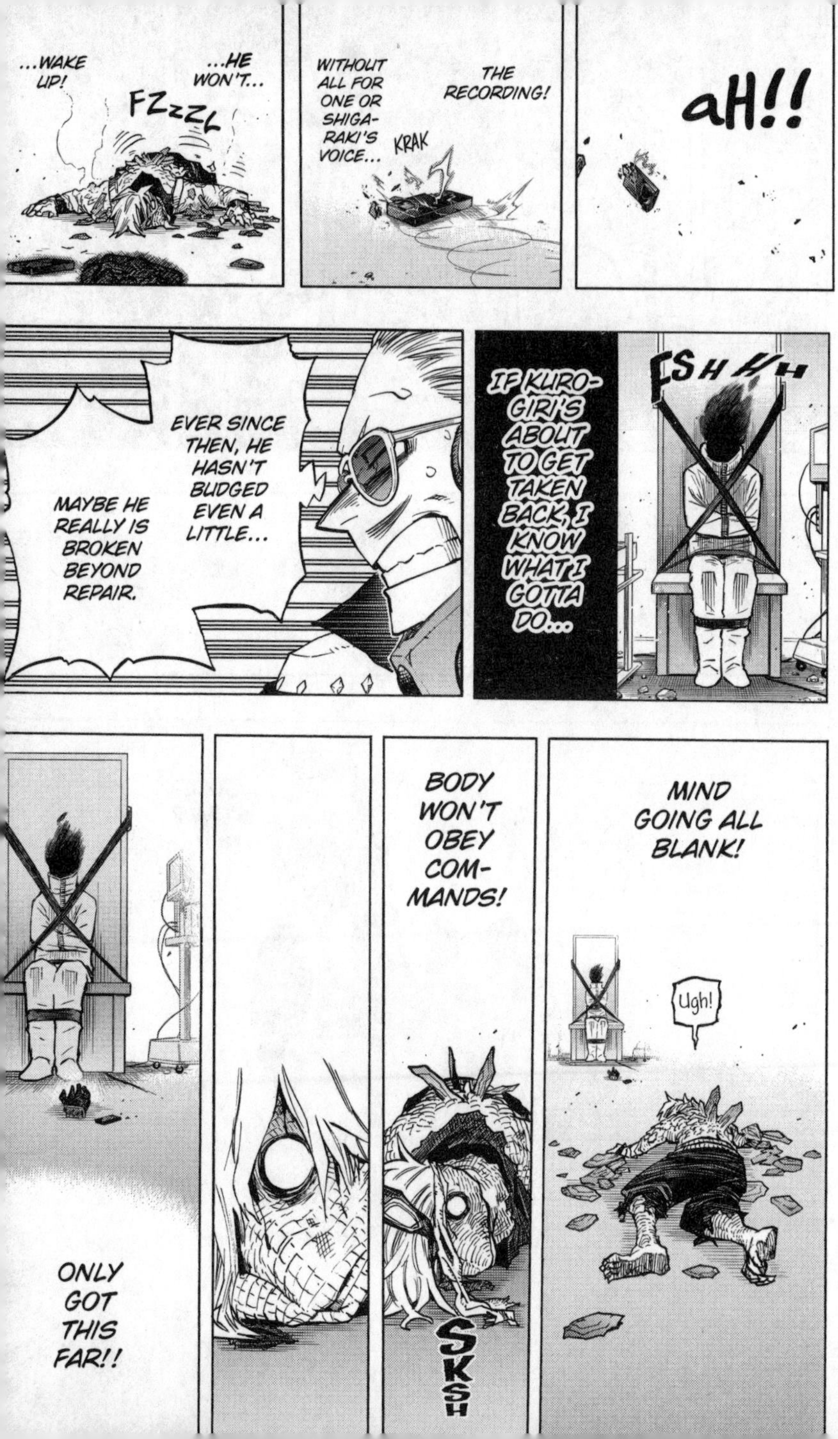
aH!!
THE RECORDING!
WITHOUT ALL FOR ONE OR SHIGA-RAKI'S VOICE...
KRAK
...HE WON'T...
...WAKE UP!
FZzZZ
FSHHHH
IF KURO-GIRI'S ABOUT TO GET TAKEN BACK, I KNOW WHAT I GOTTA DO...
EVER SINCE THEN, HE HASN'T BUDGED EVEN A LITTLE...
MAYBE HE REALLY IS BROKEN BEYOND REPAIR.
MIND GOING ALL BLANK!
Ugh!
BODY WON'T OBEY COM-MANDS!
SKSH
ONLY GOT THIS FAR!!

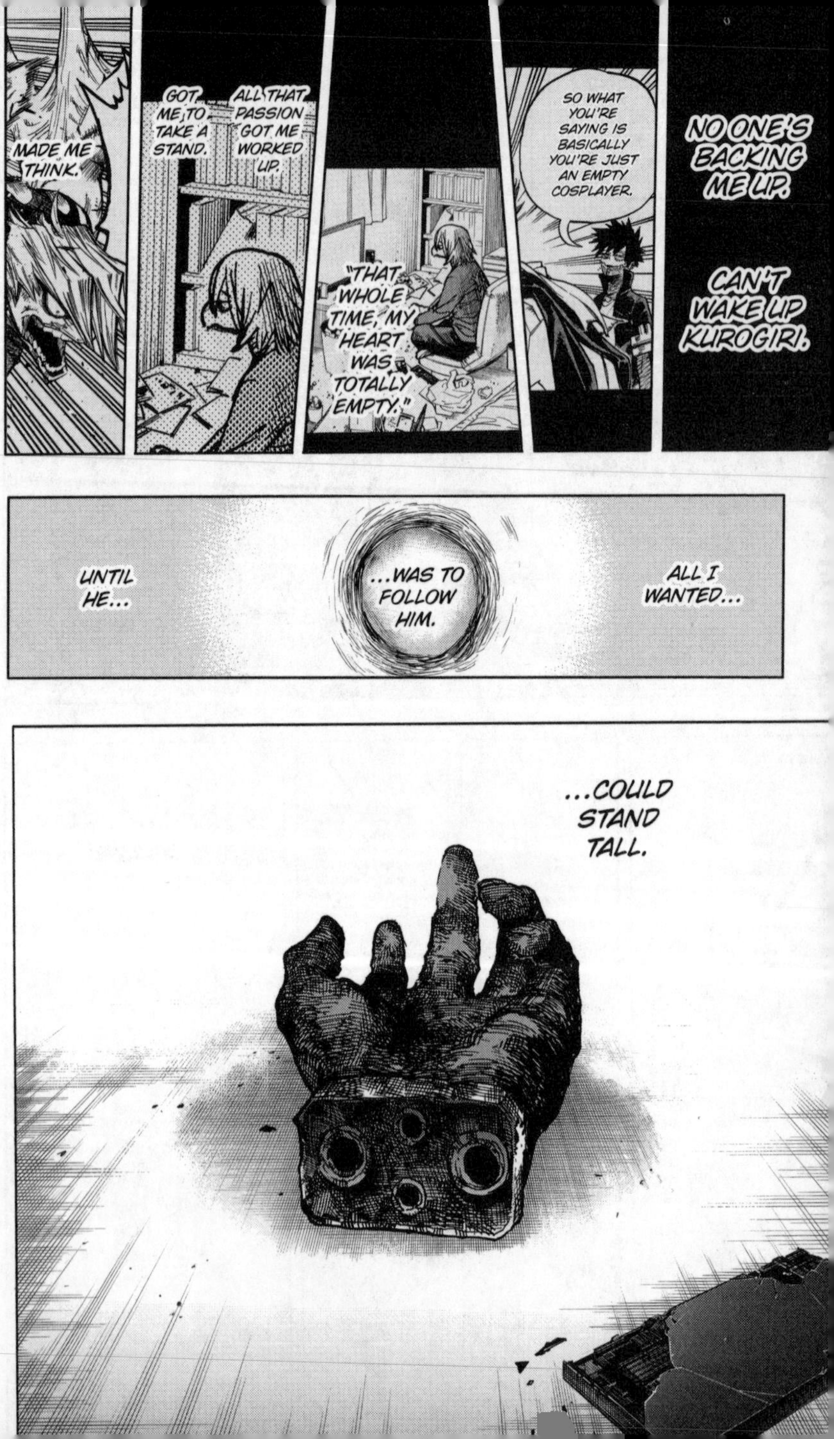
NO ONE'S BACKING ME UP.
CAN'T WAKE UP KUROGIRI.
SO WHAT YOU'RE SAYING IS BASICALLY YOU'RE JUST AN EMPTY COSPLAYER.
"THAT WHOLE TIME, MY HEART WAS TOTALLY EMPTY."
ALL THAT PASSION GOT ME WORKED UP.
GOT ME TO TAKE A STAND.
MADE ME THINK.
ALL I WANTED...
...WAS TO FOLLOW HIM.
UNTIL HE...
...COULD STAND TALL.

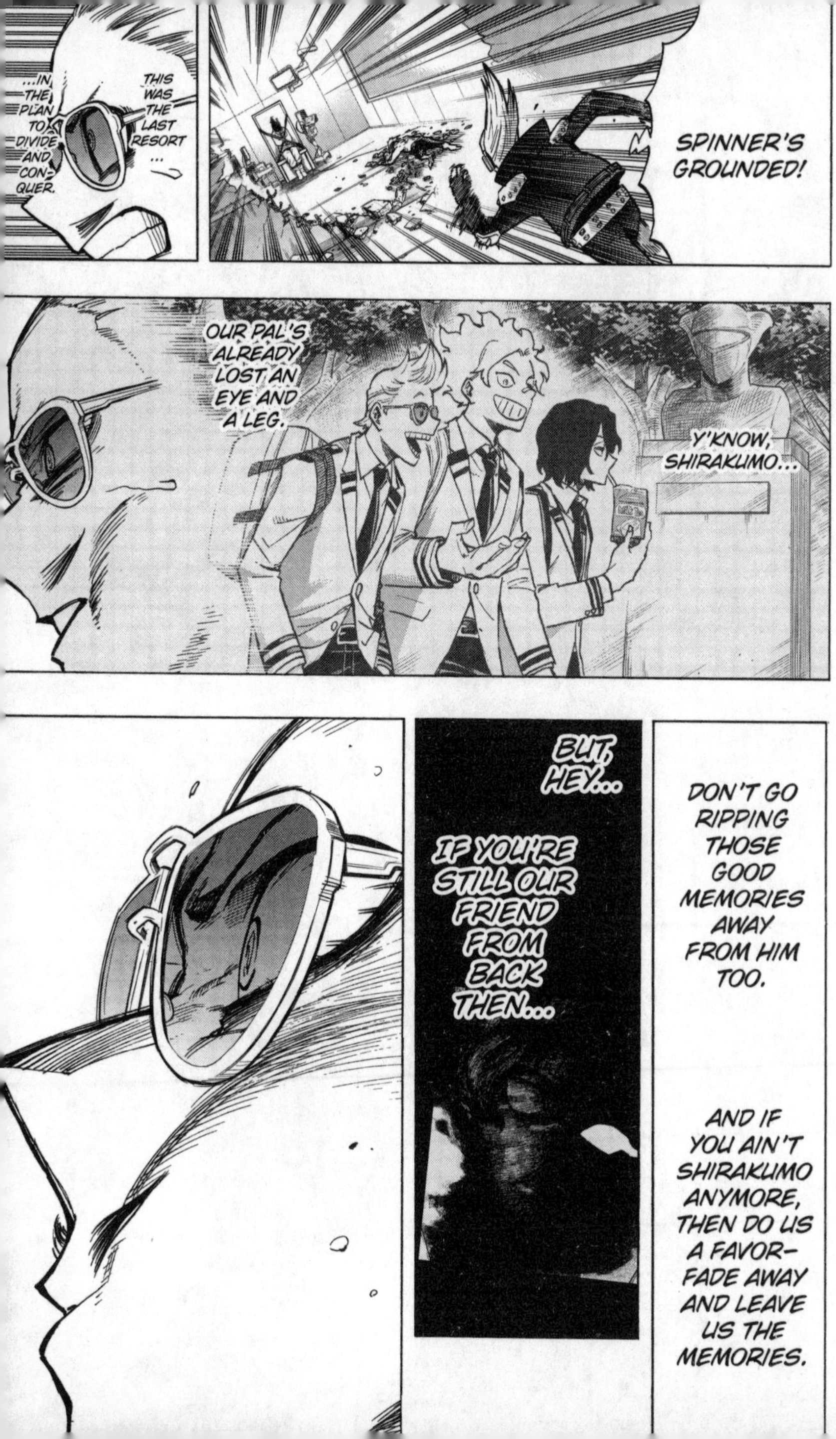
SPINNER'S GROUNDED!
THIS WAS THE LAST RESORT...
...IN THE PLAN TO DIVIDE AND CONQUER.
Y'KNOW, SHIRAKUMO...
OUR PAL'S ALREADY LOST AN EYE AND A LEG.
DON'T GO RIPPING THOSE GOOD MEMORIES AWAY FROM HIM TOO.
AND IF YOU AIN'T SHIRAKUMO ANYMORE, THEN DO US A FAVOR-FADE AWAY AND LEAVE US THE MEMORIES.
BUT, HEY...
IF YOU'RE STILL OUR FRIEND FROM BACK THEN...

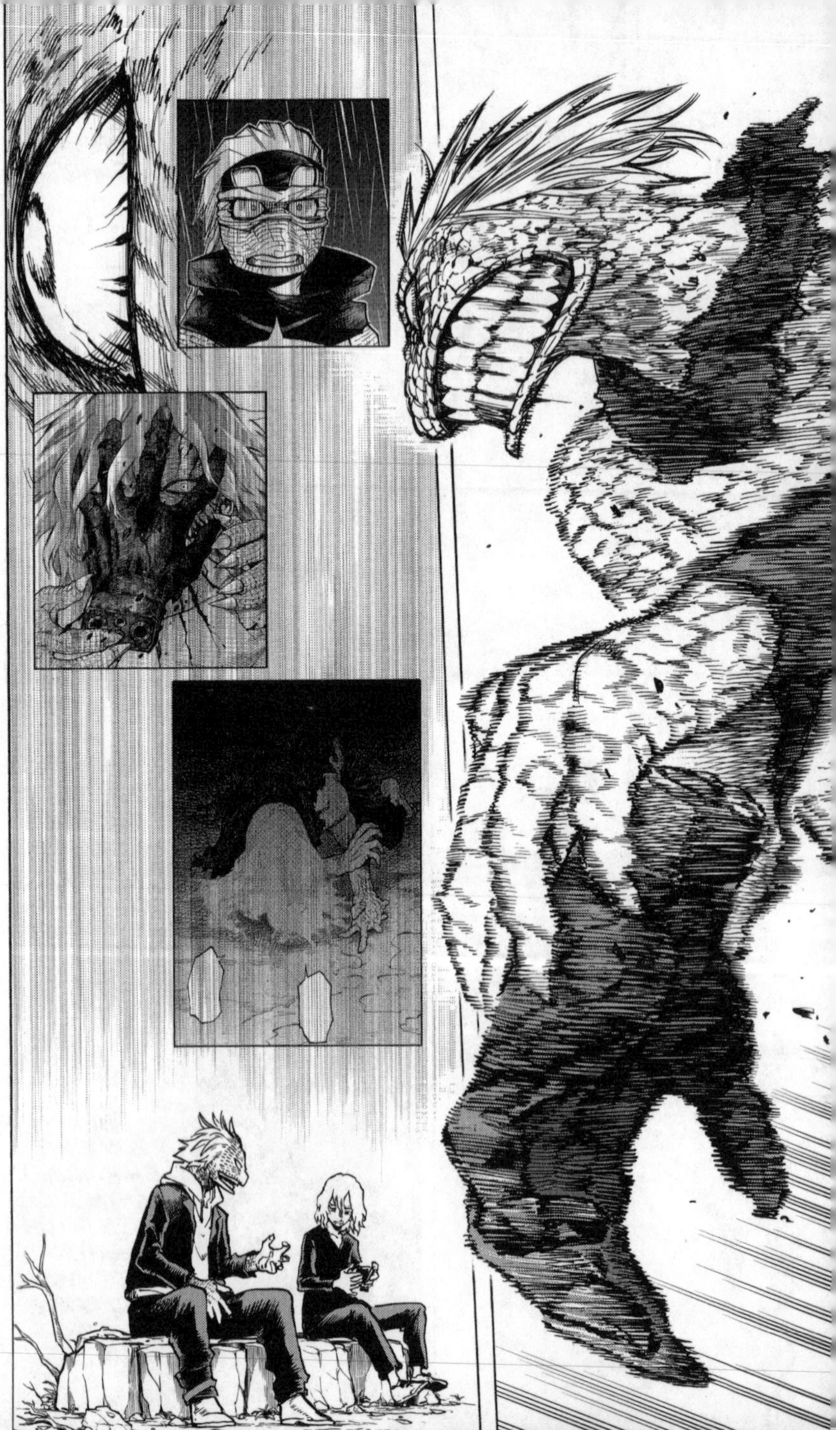

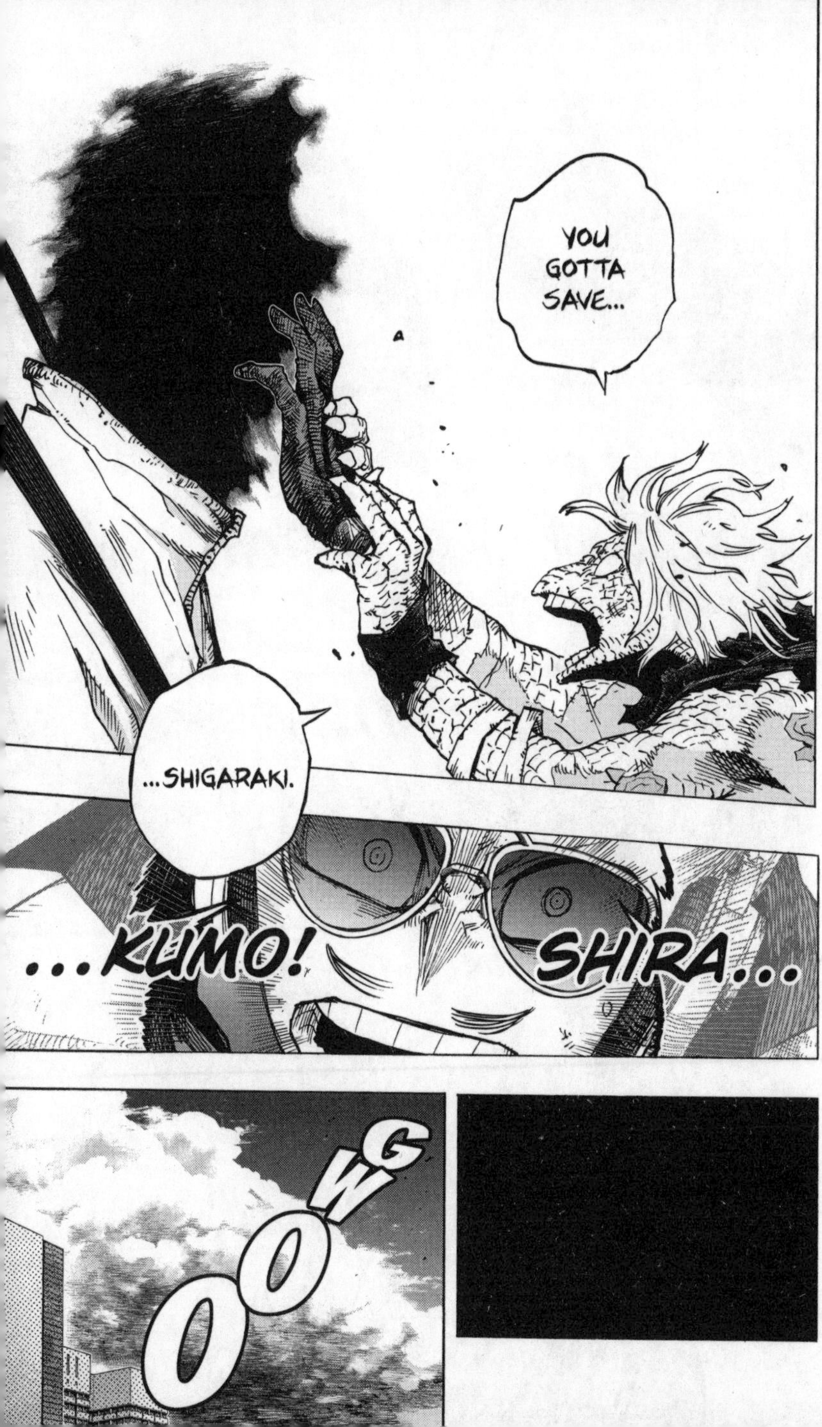
YOU GOTTA SAVE...
...SHIGARAKI.
SHIRA...
...KUMO!
GWOOO

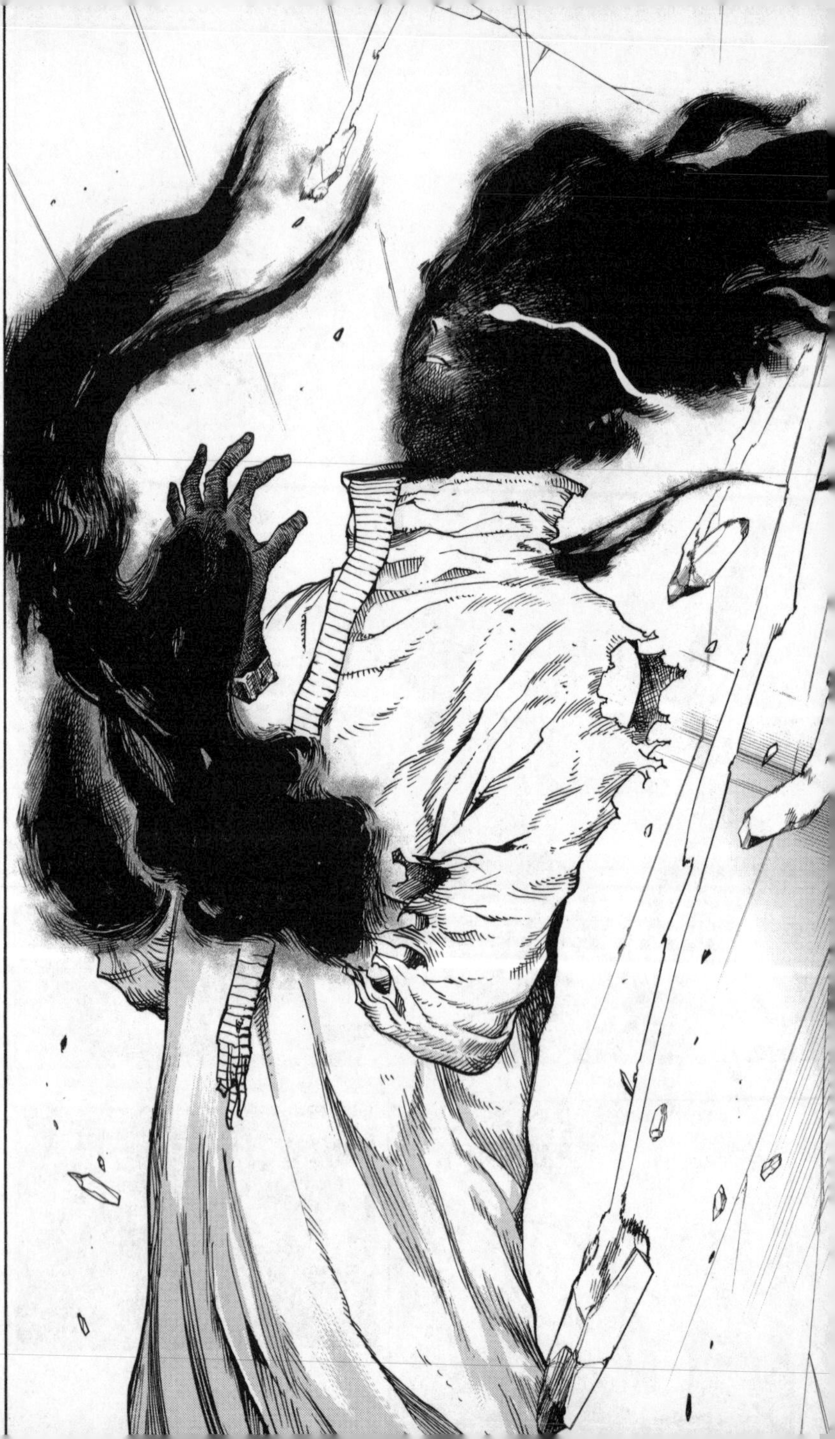

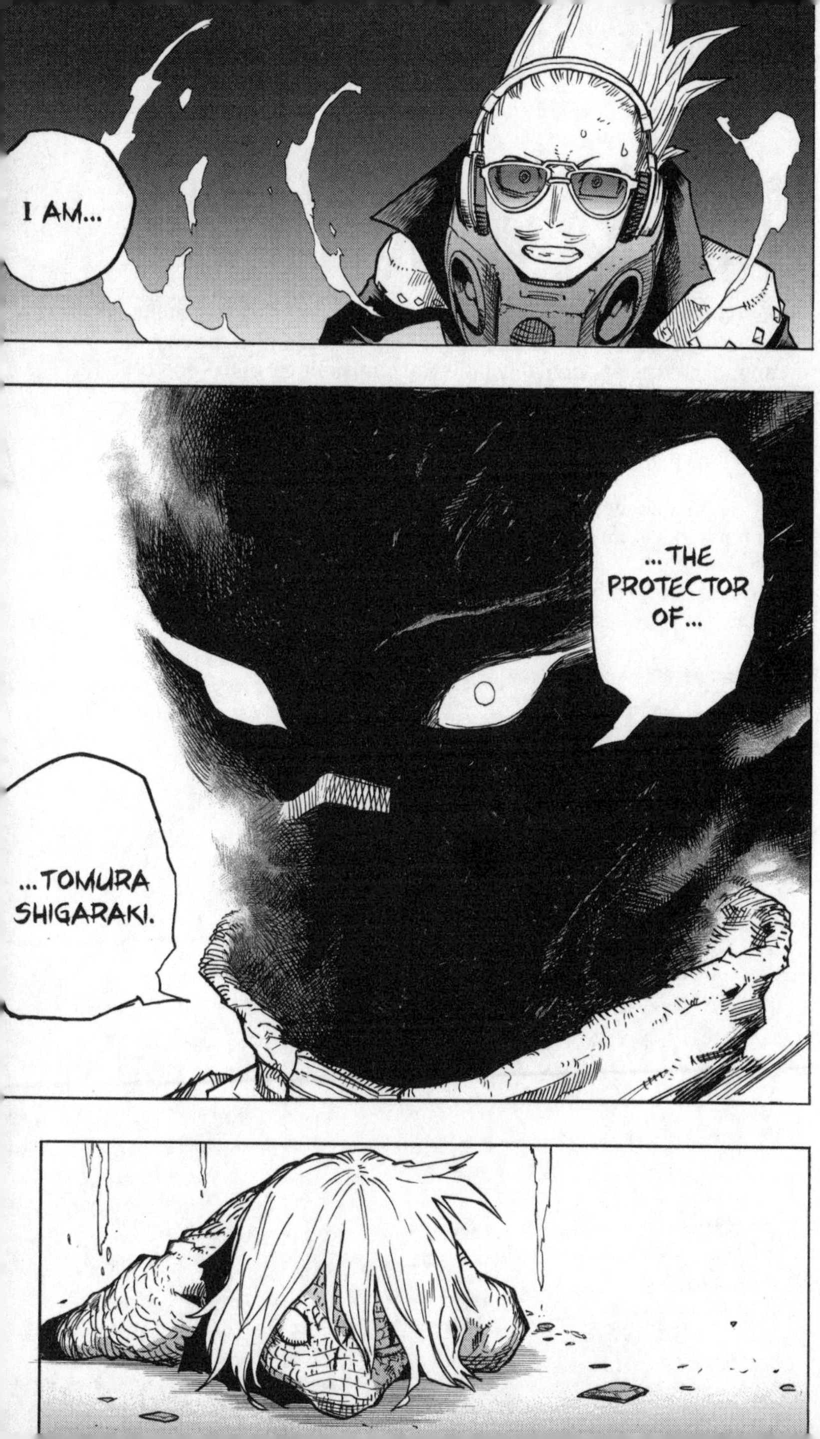
I AM...
...THE PROTECTOR OF...
...TOMURA SHIGARAKI.

THE POPULARITY POLL

As both sides duke it out to the death in the brutal battles of the current storyline, I'm pleased to present the results of the eighth annual character popularity poll. You can see it all at the end of the book.

Thank you for all the votes and support!

This may very well be the final popularity poll, but it sure was fun to have this yearly event to look forward to!

On that note, I'd better say thank you again! Ahem—thank you so much for your support!!

THANKS FOR ALL THE VOTES!

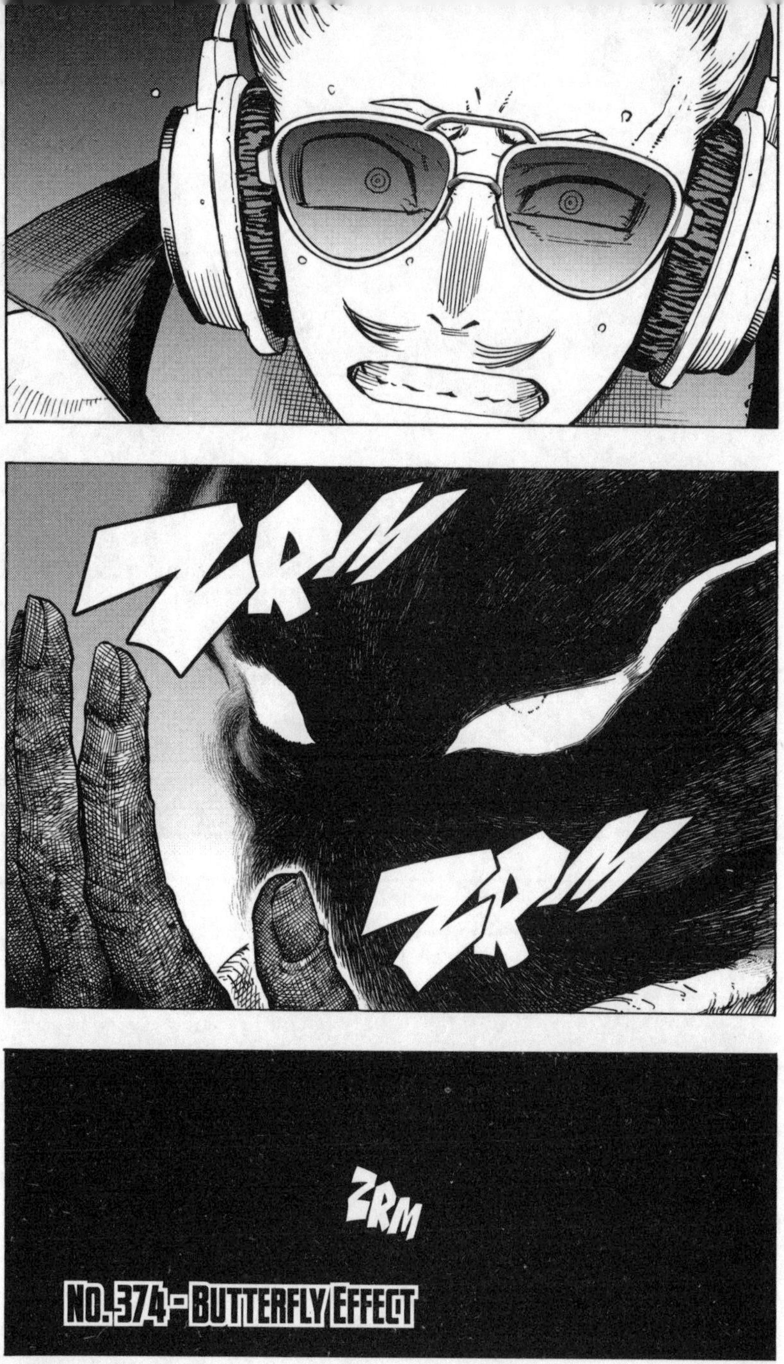
ZRM
ZRM
ZRM
No. 374 - Butterfly Effect

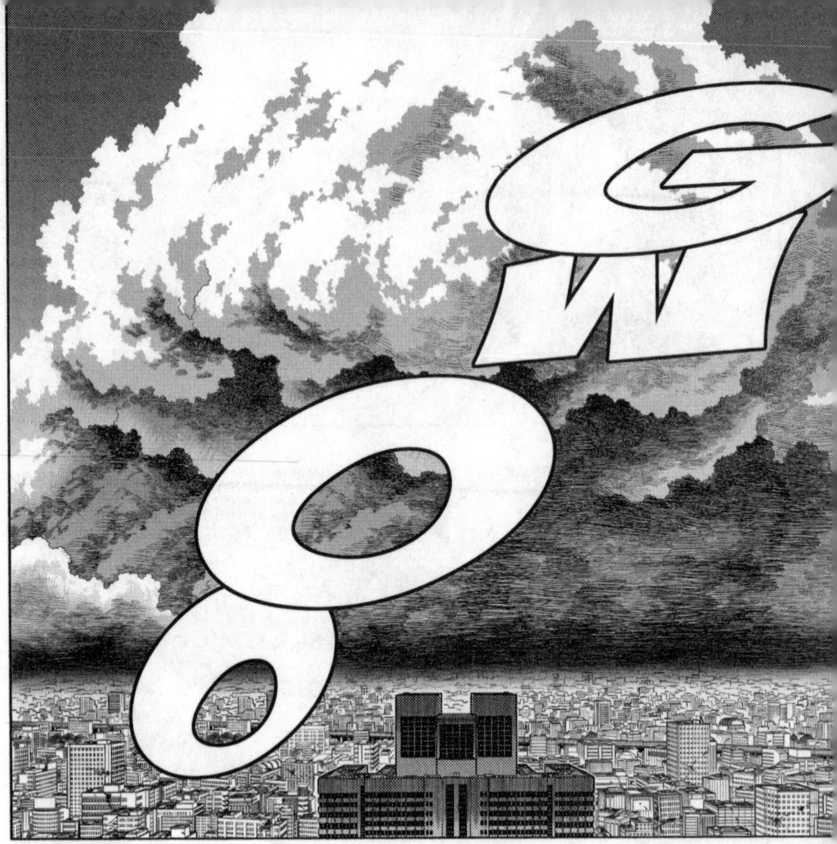
GWOO

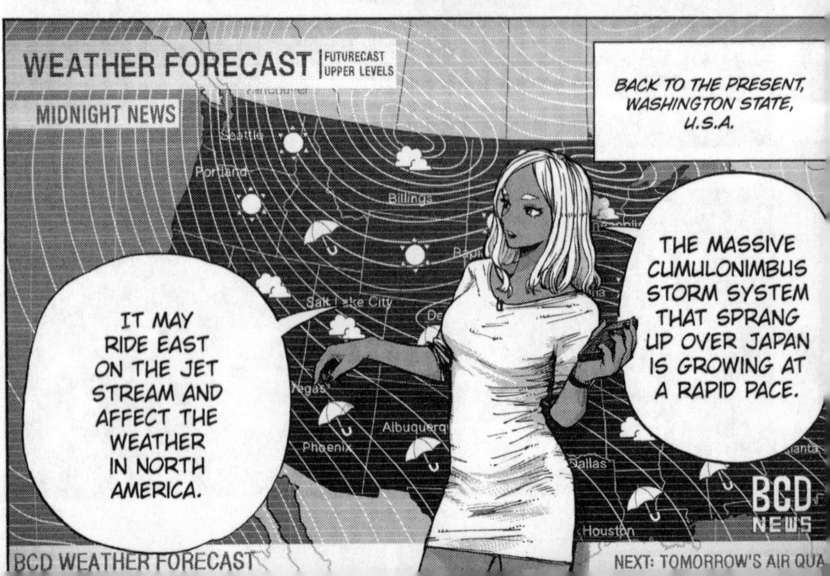
BACK TO THE PRESENT, WASHINGTON STATE, U.S.A.
THE MASSIVE CUMULONIMBUS STORM SYSTEM THAT SPRANG UP OVER JAPAN IS GROWING AT A RAPID PACE.
IT MAY RIDE EAST ON THE JET STREAM AND AFFECT THE WEATHER IN NORTH AMERICA.
WEATHER FORECAST
FUTURECAST UPPER LEVELS
MIDNIGHT NEWS
Seattle
Portland
Billings
Salt Lake City
Albuquerque
Phoenix
Dallas
Houston
BCD NEWS
BCD WEATHER FORECAST
NEXT: TOMORROW'S AIR QUA

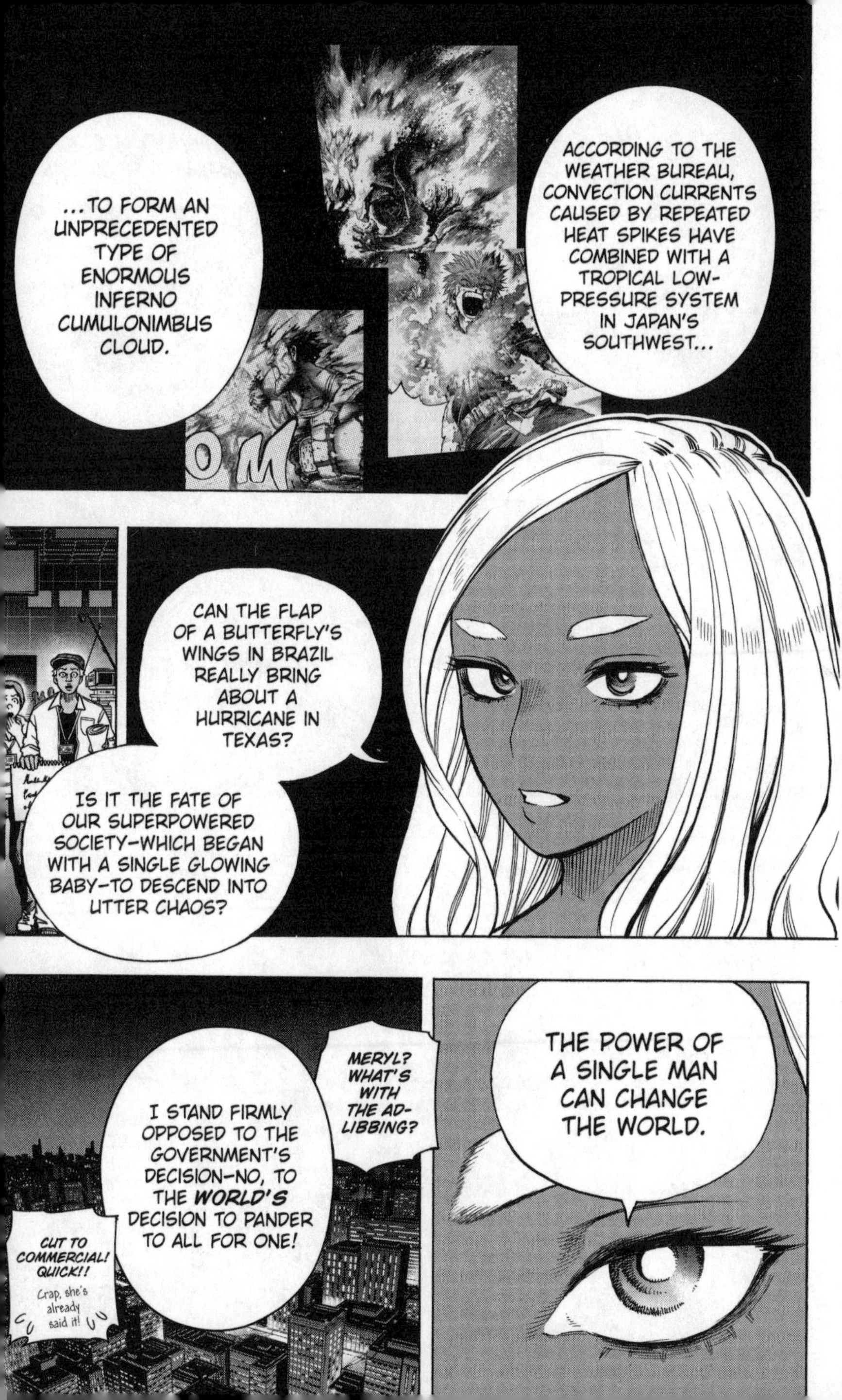
ACCORDING TO THE WEATHER BUREAU, CONVECTION CURRENTS CAUSED BY REPEATED HEAT SPIKES HAVE COMBINED WITH A TROPICAL LOW-PRESSURE SYSTEM IN JAPAN'S SOUTHWEST...
...TO FORM AN UNPRECEDENTED TYPE OF ENORMOUS INFERNO CUMULONIMBUS CLOUD.
CAN THE FLAP OF A BUTTERFLY'S WINGS IN BRAZIL REALLY BRING ABOUT A HURRICANE IN TEXAS?
IS IT THE FATE OF OUR SUPERPOWERED SOCIETY—WHICH BEGAN WITH A SINGLE GLOWING BABY—TO DESCEND INTO UTTER CHAOS?
THE POWER OF A SINGLE MAN CAN CHANGE THE WORLD.
MERYL? WHAT'S WITH THE AD-LIBBING?
I STAND FIRMLY OPPOSED TO THE GOVERNMENT'S DECISION—NO, TO THE ***WORLD'S*** DECISION TO PANDER TO ALL FOR ONE!
CUT TO COMMERCIAL! QUICK!!
Crap, she's already said it!

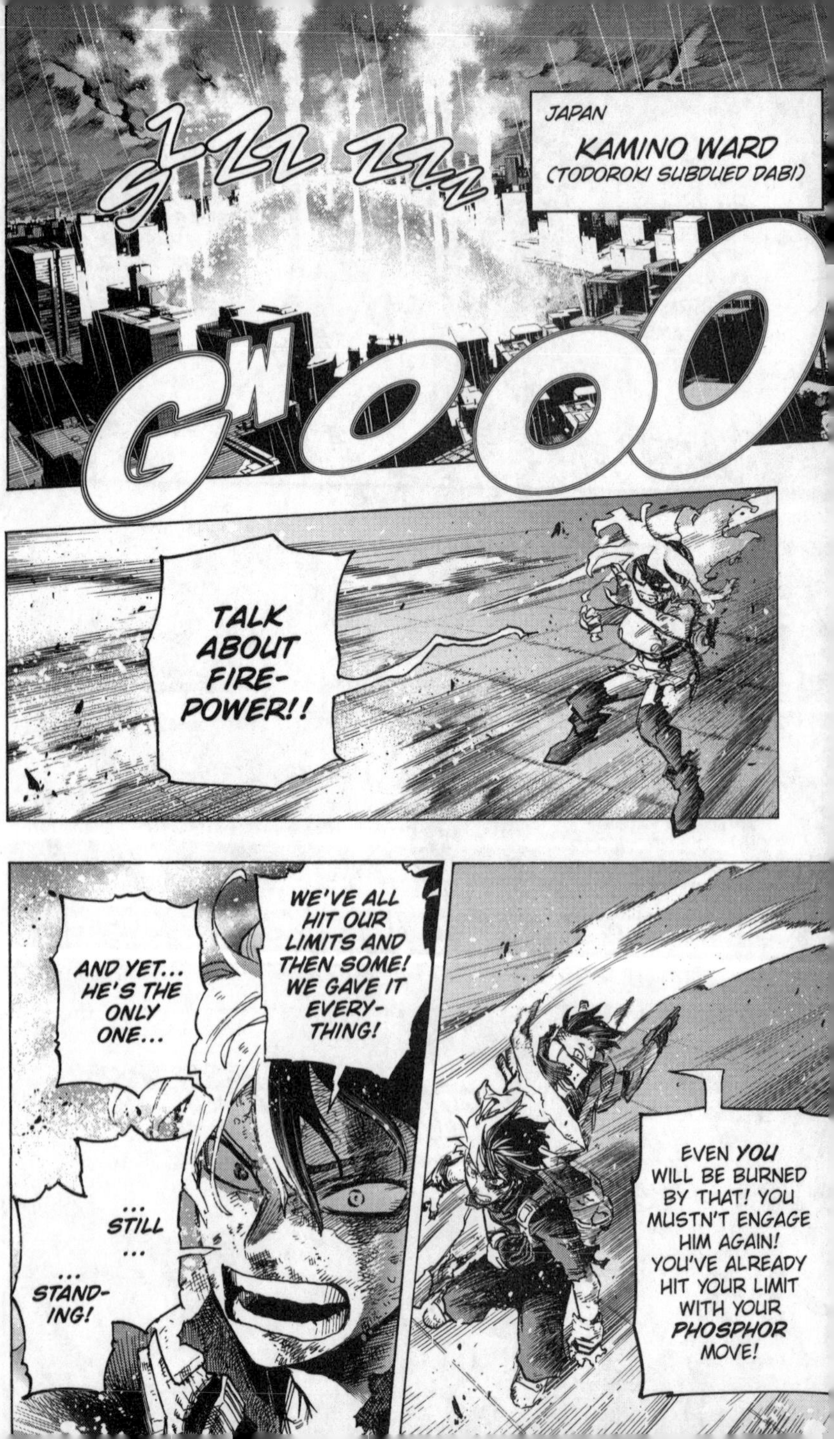
JAPAN
KAMINO WARD
(TODOROKI SUBDUED DABI)
SZZZ ZZZZ
GWOOOO
TALK ABOUT FIRE-POWER!!
EVEN YOU WILL BE BURNED BY THAT! YOU MUSTN'T ENGAGE HIM AGAIN! YOU'VE ALREADY HIT YOUR LIMIT WITH YOUR PHOSPHOR MOVE!
WE'VE ALL HIT OUR LIMITS AND THEN SOME! WE GAVE IT EVERY-THING!
AND YET... HE'S THE ONLY ONE...
... STILL ...
... STAND-ING!

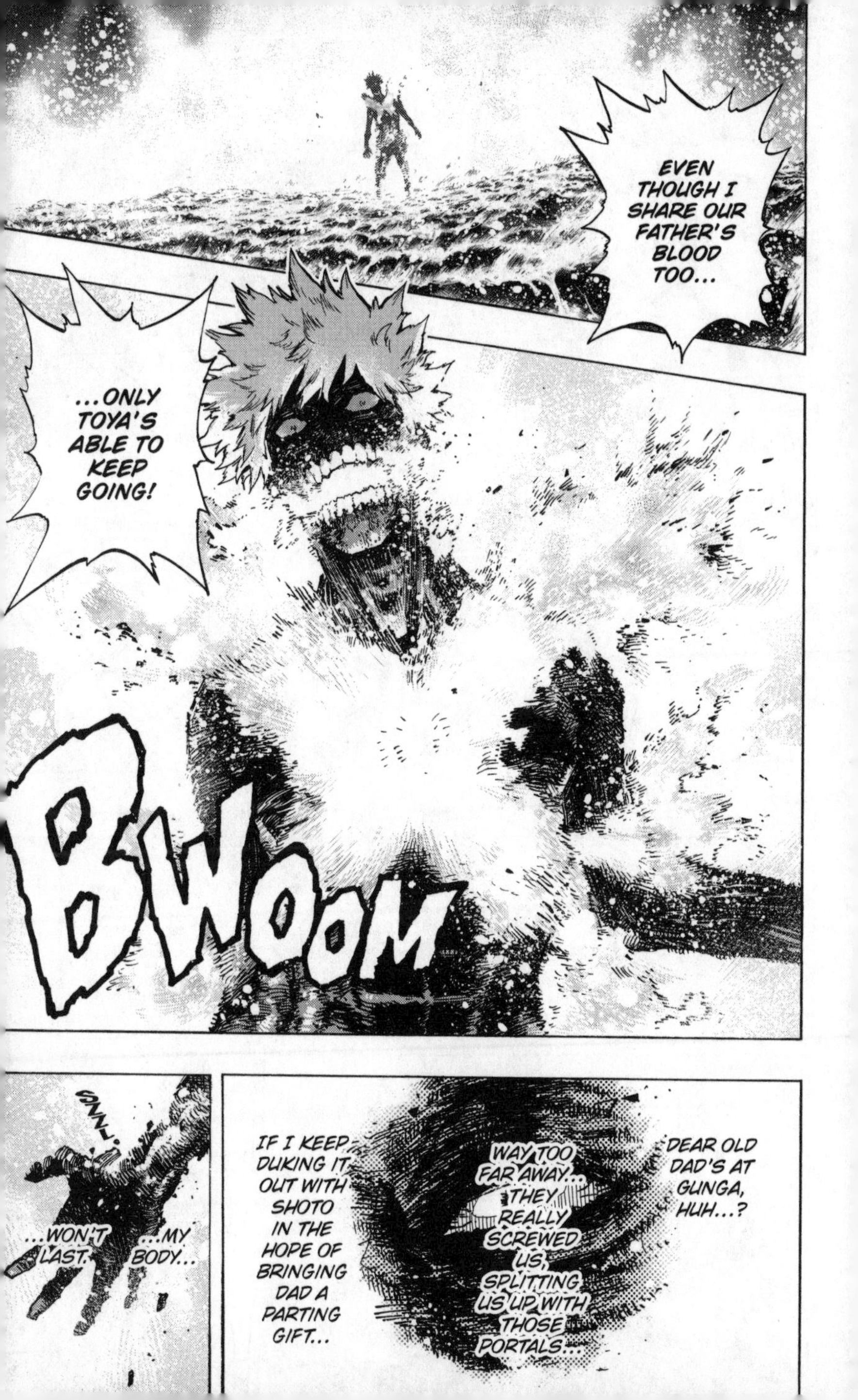
EVEN THOUGH I SHARE OUR FATHER'S BLOOD TOO...
...ONLY TOYA'S ABLE TO KEEP GOING!
BWOOM
DEAR OLD DAD'S AT GUNGA, HUH...?
WAY TOO FAR AWAY... THEY REALLY SCREWED US, SPLITTING US UP WITH THOSE PORTALS...
IF I KEEP DUKING IT OUT WITH SHOTO IN THE HOPE OF BRINGING DAD A PARTING GIFT...
SNNL
...MY BODY...
...WON'T LAST.

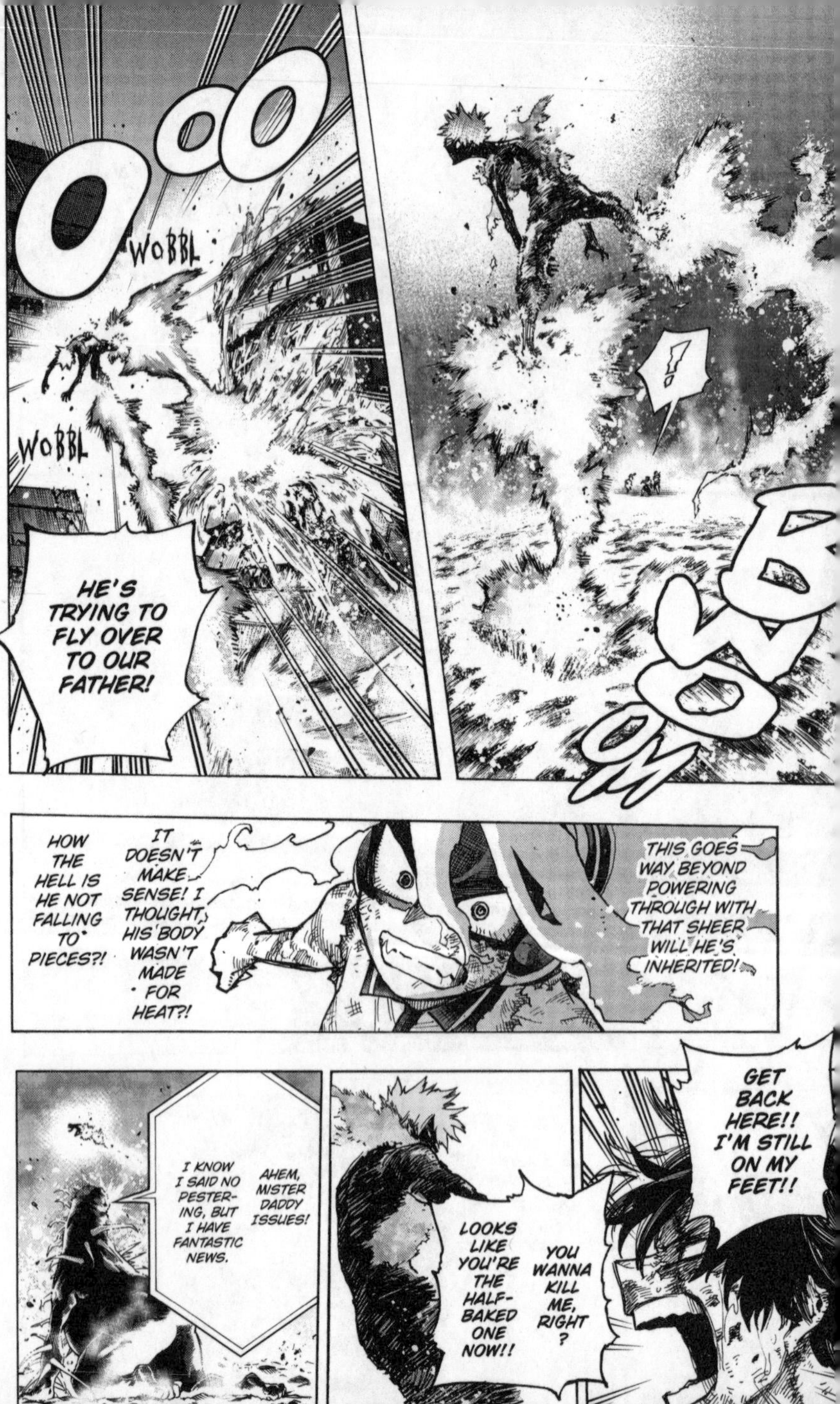
!?
BOOOM
OOOO
WOBBL
WOBBL
HE'S TRYING TO FLY OVER TO OUR FATHER!
THIS GOES WAY BEYOND POWERING THROUGH WITH THAT SHEER WILL HE'S INHERITED!
IT DOESN'T MAKE SENSE! I THOUGHT HIS BODY WASN'T MADE FOR HEAT?!
HOW THE HELL IS HE NOT FALLING TO PIECES?!
GET BACK HERE!! I'M STILL ON MY FEET!!
YOU WANNA KILL ME, RIGHT?
LOOKS LIKE YOU'RE THE HALF-BAKED ONE NOW!!
AHEM, MISTER DADDY ISSUES!
I KNOW I SAID NO PESTERING, BUT I HAVE FANTASTIC NEWS.

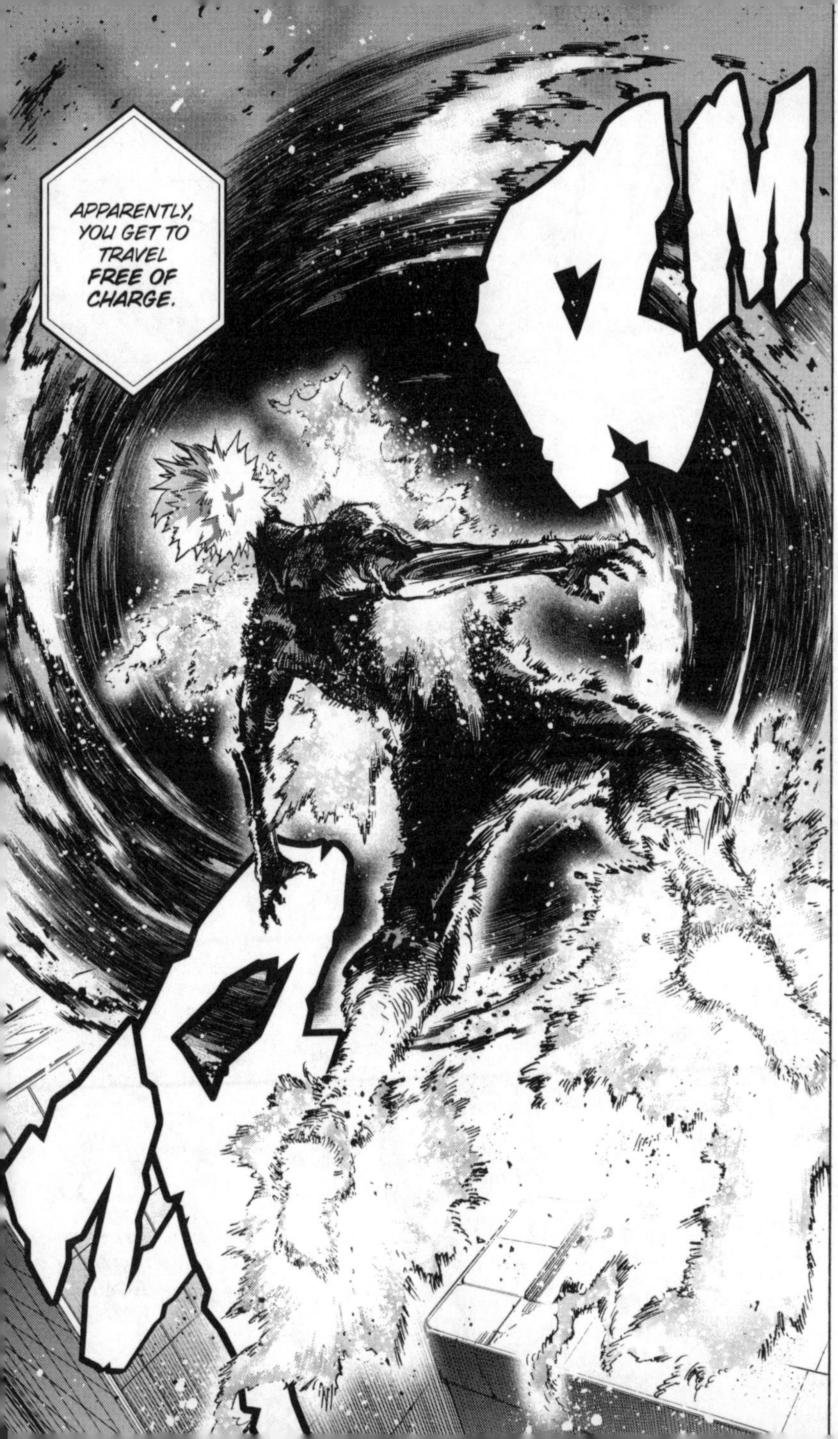
APPARENTLY, YOU GET TO TRAVEL FREE OF CHARGE.

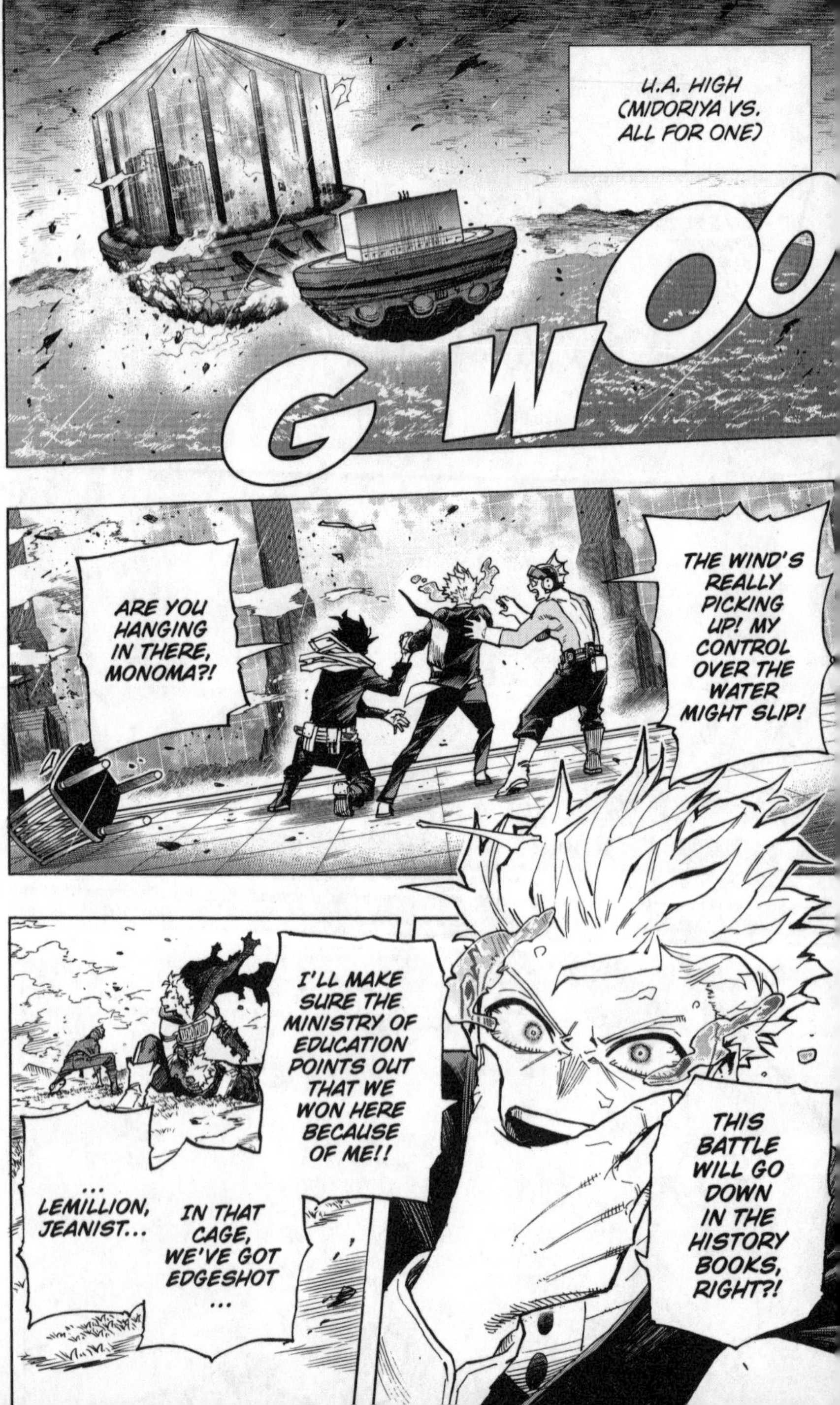
U.A. HIGH (MIDORIYA VS. ALL FOR ONE)
GWOOO
THE WIND'S REALLY PICKING UP! MY CONTROL OVER THE WATER MIGHT SLIP!
ARE YOU HANGING IN THERE, MONOMA?!
THIS BATTLE WILL GO DOWN IN THE HISTORY BOOKS, RIGHT?!
I'LL MAKE SURE THE MINISTRY OF EDUCATION POINTS OUT THAT WE WON HERE BECAUSE OF ME!!
... LEMILLION, JEANIST...
IN THAT CAGE, WE'VE GOT EDGESHOT ...

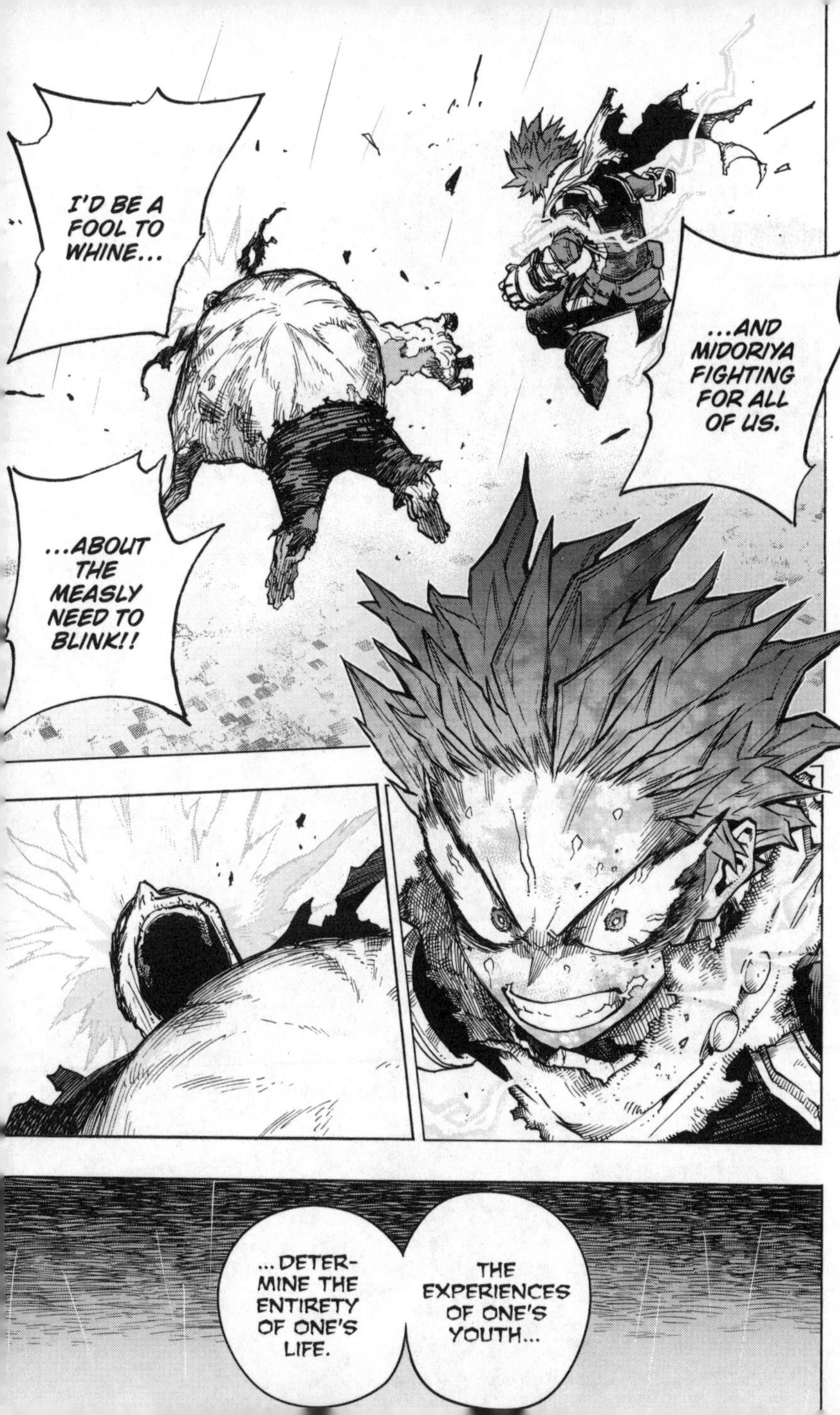
...AND MIDORIYA FIGHTING FOR ALL OF US.
I'D BE A FOOL TO WHINE...
...ABOUT THE MEASLY NEED TO BLINK!!
THE EXPERIENCES OF ONE'S YOUTH...
...DETERMINE THE ENTIRETY OF ONE'S LIFE.

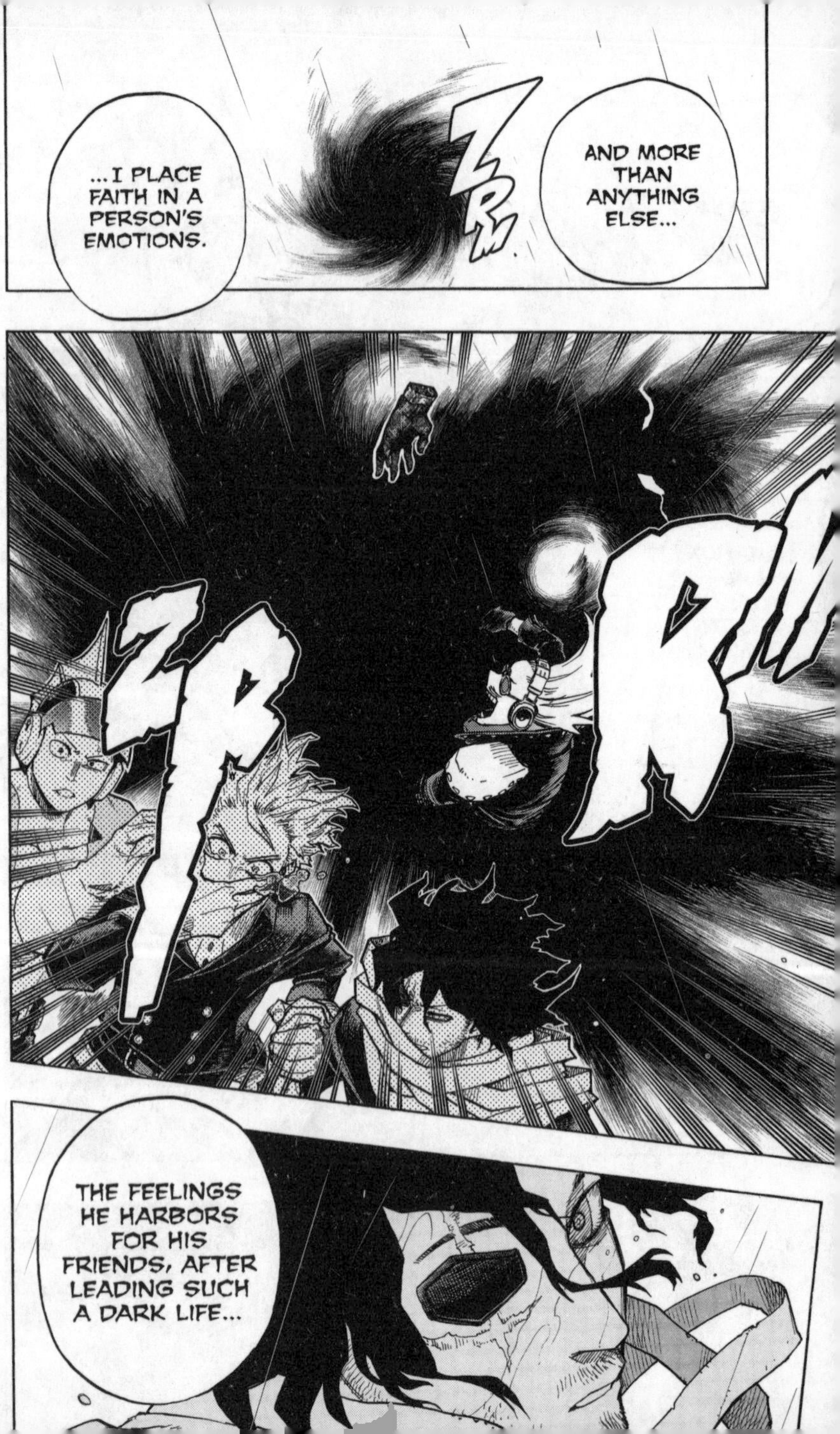
AND MORE THAN ANYTHING ELSE...
ZRM
...I PLACE FAITH IN A PERSON'S EMOTIONS.
ZR
RM
THE FEELINGS HE HARBORS FOR HIS FRIENDS, AFTER LEADING SUCH A DARK LIFE...

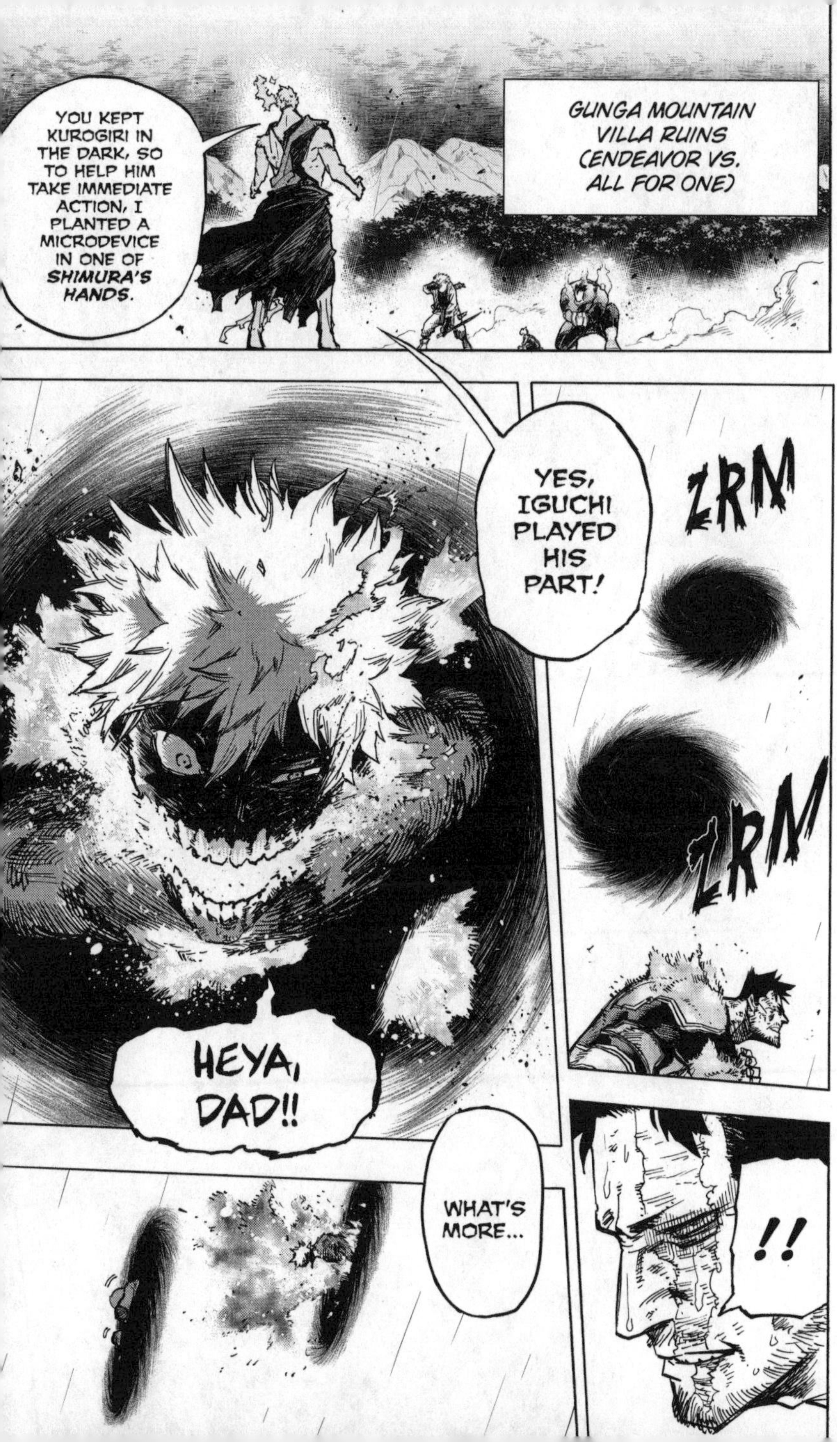
GUNGA MOUNTAIN VILLA RUINS (ENDEAVOR VS. ALL FOR ONE)
YOU KEPT KUROGIRI IN THE DARK, SO TO HELP HIM TAKE IMMEDIATE ACTION, I PLANTED A MICRODEVICE IN ONE OF SHIMURA'S HANDS.
YES, IGUCHI PLAYED HIS PART!
ZRM
ZRM
HEYA, DAD!!
!!
WHAT'S MORE...

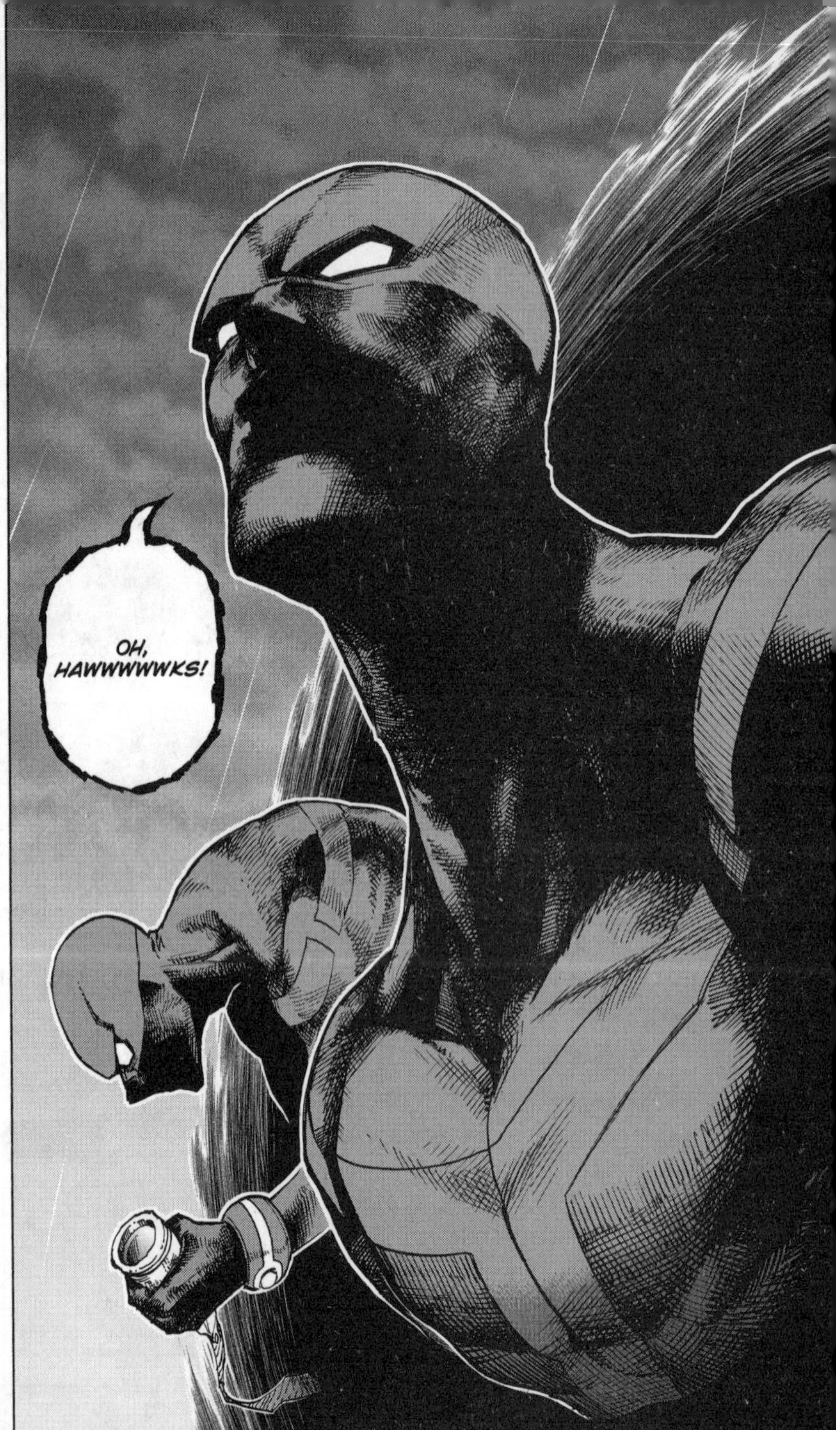
OH, HAWWWWWKS!

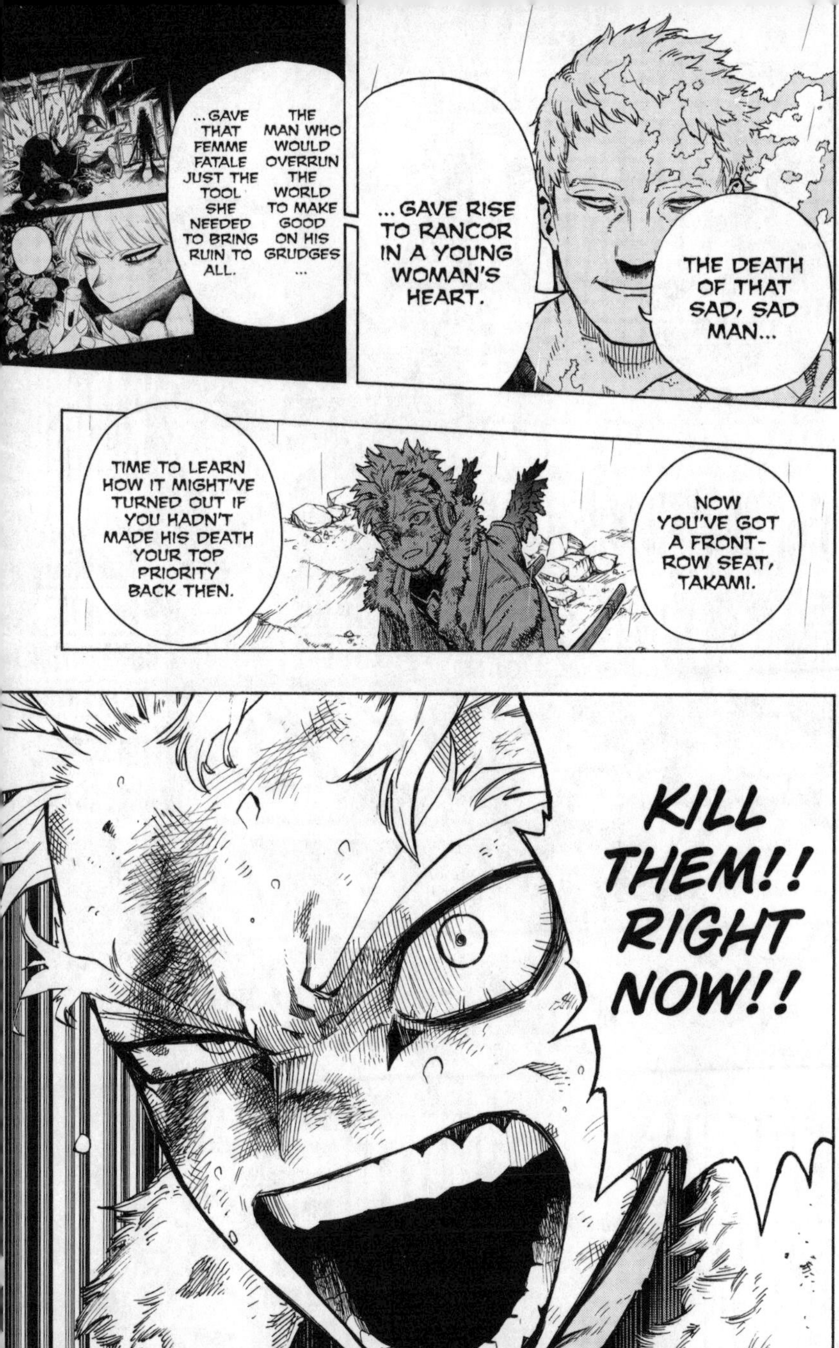
THE DEATH OF THAT SAD, SAD MAN...
...GAVE RISE TO RANCOR IN A YOUNG WOMAN'S HEART.
THE MAN WHO WOULD OVERRUN THE WORLD TO MAKE GOOD ON HIS GRUDGES...
...GAVE THAT FEMME FATALE JUST THE TOOL SHE NEEDED TO BRING RUIN TO ALL.
NOW YOU'VE GOT A FRONT-ROW SEAT, TAKAMI.
TIME TO LEARN HOW IT MIGHT'VE TURNED OUT IF YOU HADN'T MADE HIS DEATH YOUR TOP PRIORITY BACK THEN.
KILL THEM!! RIGHT NOW!!

VOLUME 37 - THOSE WHO DEFEND, THOSE WHO VIOLATE (END)

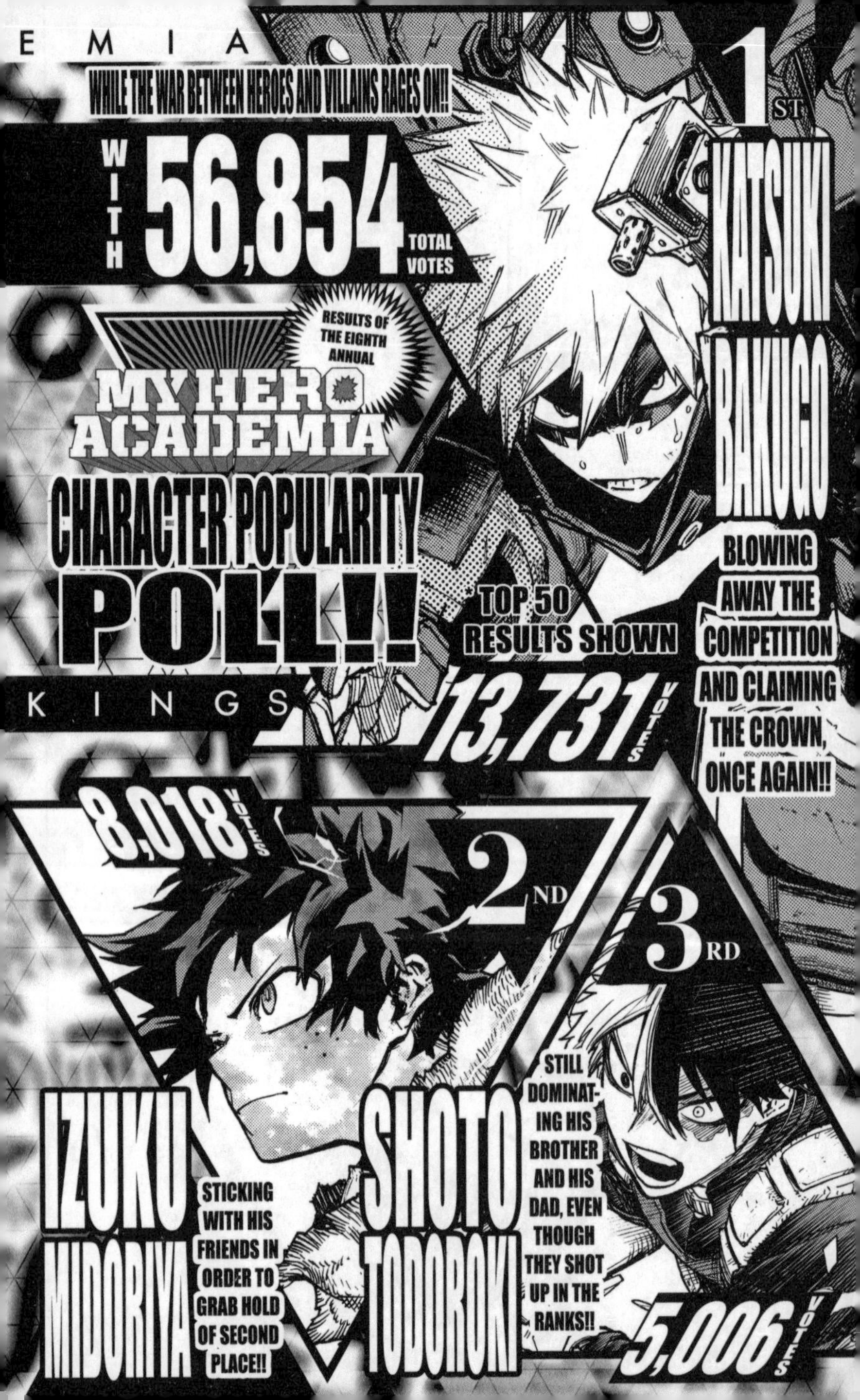
E M I A
WHILE THE WAR BETWEEN HEROES AND VILLAINS RAGES ON!!
WITH 56,854 TOTAL VOTES
RESULTS OF THE EIGHTH ANNUAL
MY HERO ACADEMIA
CHARACTER POPULARITY POLL!!
K I N G S
TOP 50 RESULTS SHOWN
1ST
KATSUKI BAKUGO
BLOWING AWAY THE COMPETITION AND CLAIMING THE CROWN, ONCE AGAIN!!
13,731 VOTES
2ND
8,018 VOTES
IZUKU MIDORIYA
STICKING WITH HIS FRIENDS IN ORDER TO GRAB HOLD OF SECOND PLACE!!
3RD
SHOTO TODOROKI
STILL DOMINATING HIS BROTHER AND HIS DAD, EVEN THOUGH THEY SHOT UP IN THE RANKS!!
5,006 VOTES

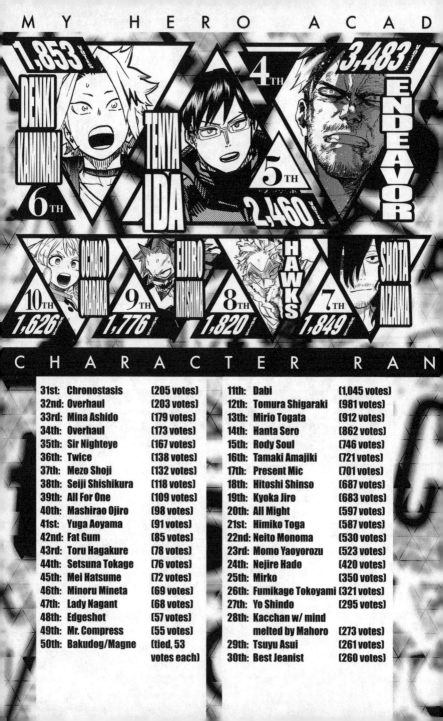

M Y H E R O A C A D

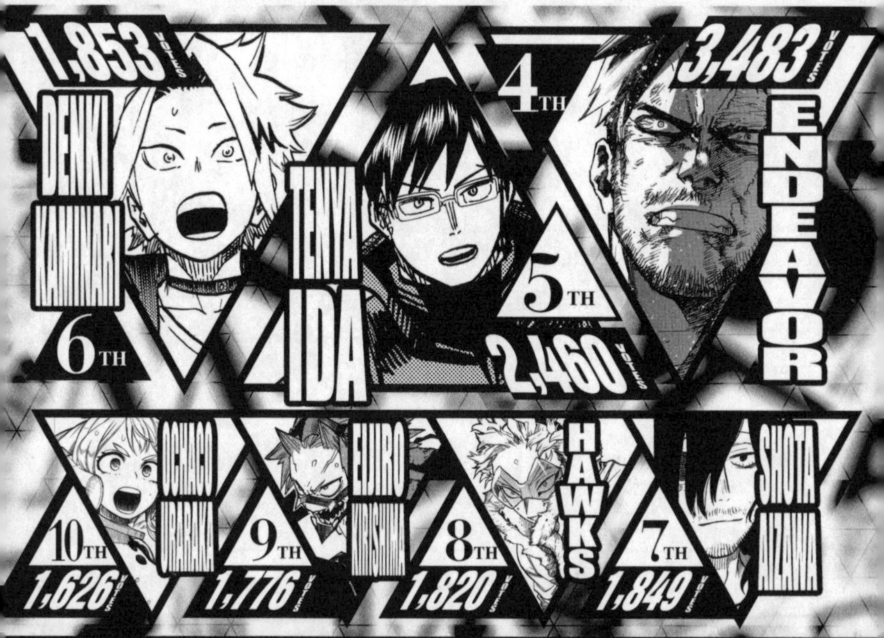

4TH
3,483 VOTES
ENDEAVOR
5TH
2,460 VOTES
TENYA IDA
1,853 VOTES
DENKI KAMINARI
6TH
SHOTA AIZAWA
7TH
1,849 VOTES
HAWKS
8TH
1,820 VOTES
EIJIRO KIRISHIMA
9TH
1,776 VOTES
OCHACO URARAKA
10TH
1,626 VOTES

C H A R A C T E R R A N

11th: Dabi (1,045 votes)
12th: Tomura Shigaraki (981 votes)
13th: Mirio Togata (912 votes)
14th: Hanta Sero (862 votes)
15th: Rody Soul (746 votes)
16th: Tamaki Amajiki (721 votes)
17th: Present Mic (701 votes)
18th: Hitoshi Shinso (687 votes)
19th: Kyoka Jiro (683 votes)
20th: All Might (597 votes)
21st: Himiko Toga (587 votes)
22nd: Neito Monoma (530 votes)
23rd: Momo Yaoyorozu (523 votes)
24th: Nejire Hado (420 votes)
25th: Mirko (350 votes)
26th: Fumikage Tokoyami (321 votes)
27th: Yo Shindo (295 votes)
28th: Kacchan w/ mind melted by Mahoro (273 votes)
29th: Tsuyu Asui (261 votes)
30th: Best Jeanist (260 votes)

31st: Chronostasis (205 votes)
32nd: Overhaul (203 votes)
33rd: Mina Ashido (179 votes)
34th: Overhaul (173 votes)
35th: Sir Nighteye (167 votes)
36th: Twice (138 votes)
37th: Mezo Shoji (132 votes)
38th: Seiji Shishikura (118 votes)
39th: All For One (109 votes)
40th: Mashirao Ojiro (98 votes)
41st: Yuga Aoyama (91 votes)
42nd: Fat Gum (85 votes)
43rd: Toru Hagakure (78 votes)
44th: Setsuna Tokage (76 votes)
45th: Mei Hatsume (72 votes)
46th: Minoru Mineta (69 votes)
47th: Lady Nagant (68 votes)
48th: Edgeshot (57 votes)
49th: Mr. Compress (55 votes)
50th: Bakudog/Magne (tied, 53 votes each)

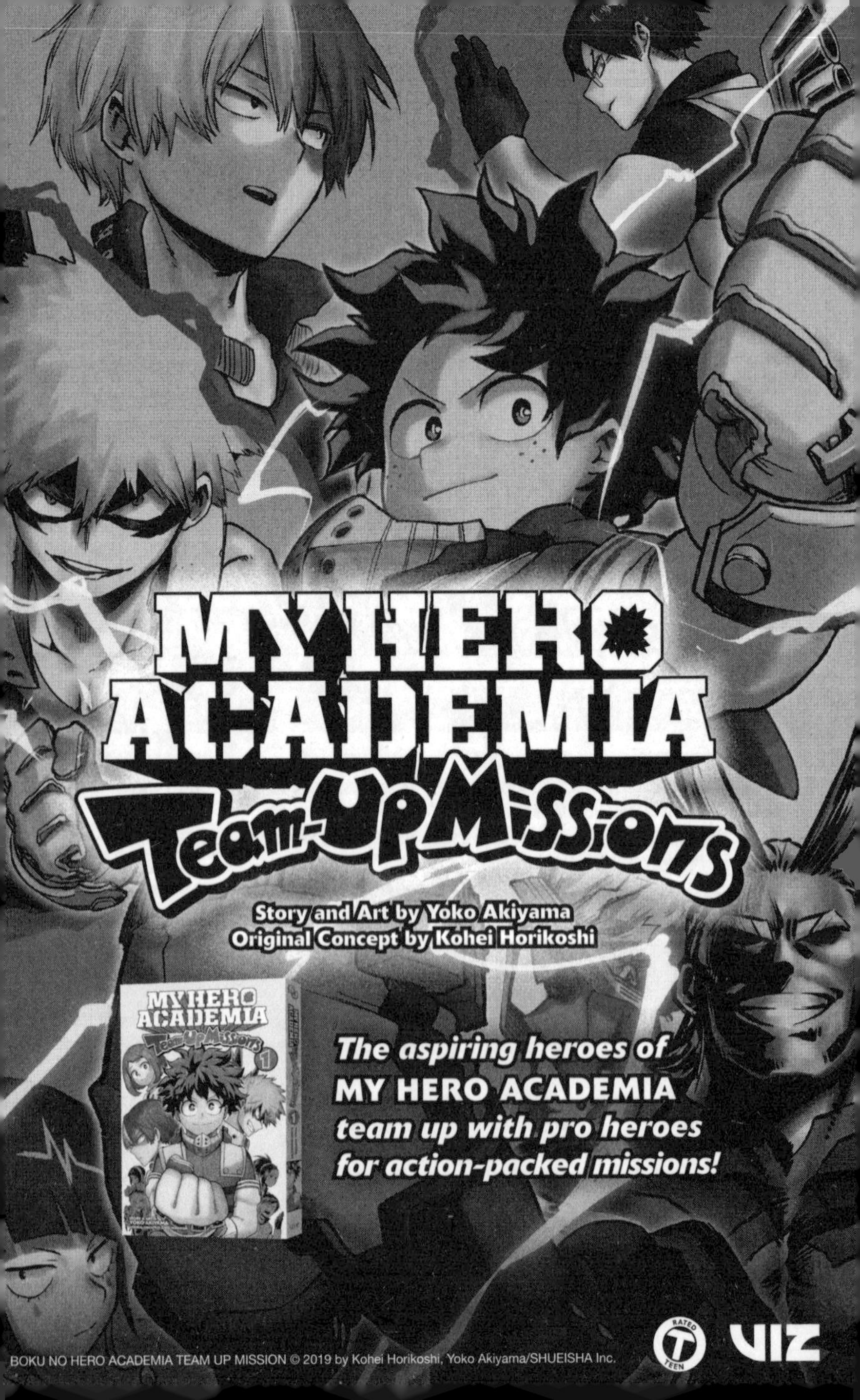
MY HERO ACADEMIA
Team-Up Missions
Story and Art by Yoko Akiyama
Original Concept by Kohei Horikoshi
MY HERO ACADEMIA
Team-Up Missions
1
The aspiring heroes of
MY HERO ACADEMIA
team up with pro heroes
for action-packed missions!
RATED T TEEN
VIZ
BOKU NO HERO ACADEMIA TEAM UP MISSION © 2019 by Kohei Horikoshi, Yoko Akiyama/SHUEISHA Inc.

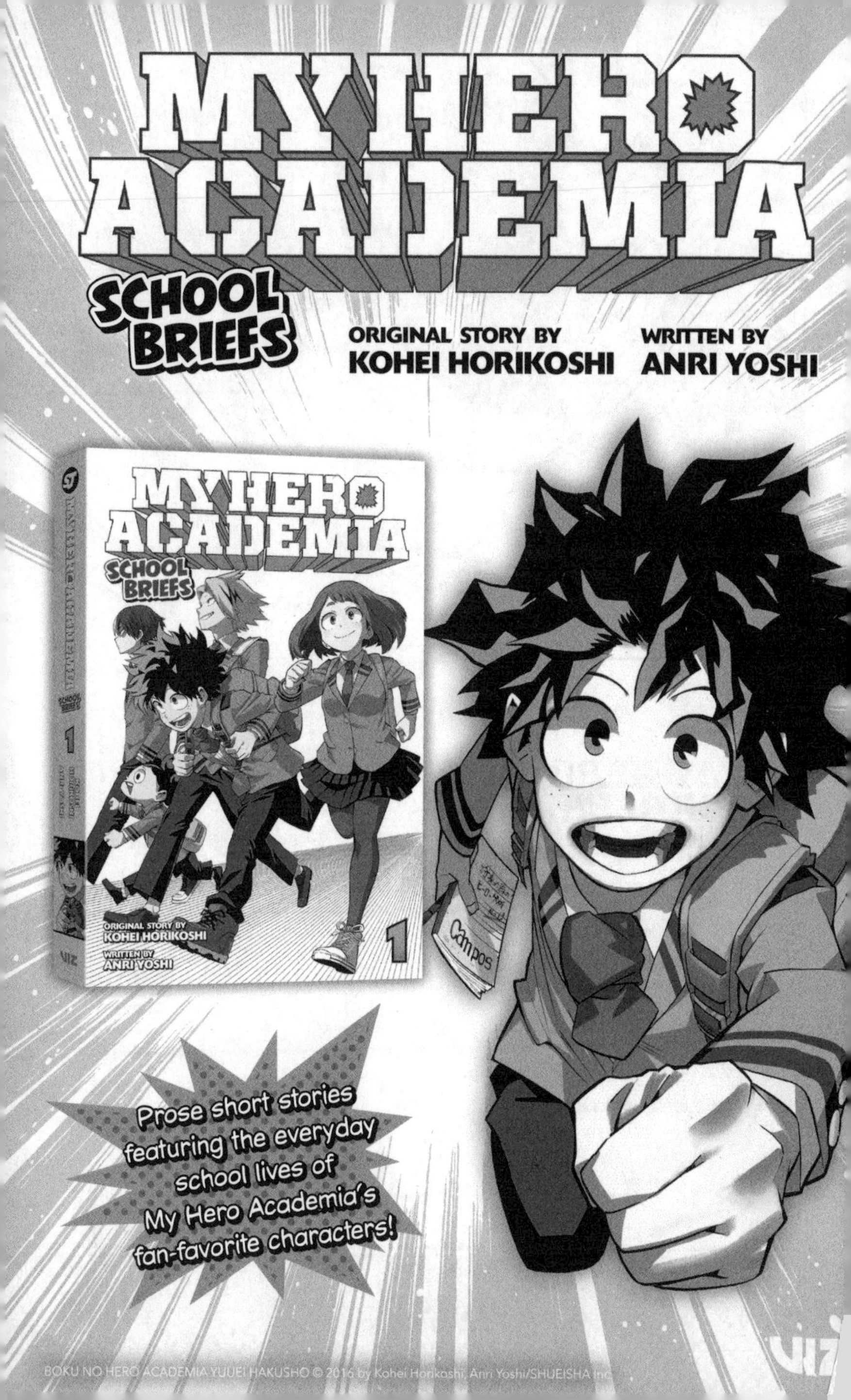
MY HERO ACADEMIA
SCHOOL BRIEFS
ORIGINAL STORY BY
KOHEI HORIKOSHI
WRITTEN BY
ANRI YOSHI
MY HERO ACADEMIA
SCHOOL BRIEFS
ORIGINAL STORY BY
KOHEI HORIKOSHI
WRITTEN BY
ANRI YOSHI
1
Prose short stories featuring the everyday school lives of My Hero Academia's fan-favorite characters!
VIZ
BOKU NO HERO ACADEMIA YUUEI HAKUSHO © 2016 by Kohei Horikoshi, Anri Yoshi/SHUEISHA Inc.

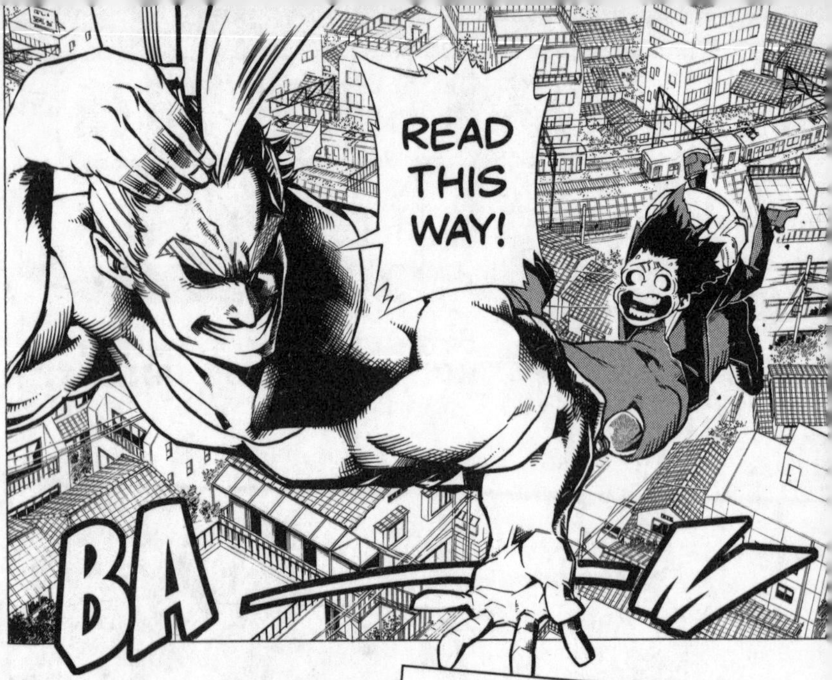
READ THIS WAY!
BA—M

MY HERO ACADEMIA

reads from right to left, starting in the upper-right corner. Japanese is read from right to left, meaning that action, sound effects, and word-balloon order are completely reversed from English order.

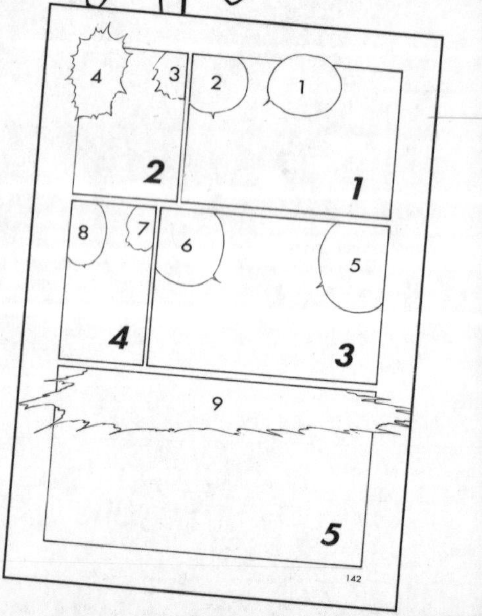
1
2
3
4
1
2
5
6
7
8
3
4
9
5
142